THE COMPLETE
FAMILY COOKBOOK

EDITORIAL
Food Editor: Rachel Blackmore
Assistant Editor: Ella Martin
Editorial Assistant: Sheridan Packer
Editorial Coordinator: Margaret Kelly

RECIPE DEVELOPMENT
Jane Ash, Susan Bell, Belinda Clayton, Penny
Cox, Sheryle Eastwood, Sue Geraghty, Joanne
Glynn, Michelle Gorry, Donna Hay, Anneka
Mitchell, Voula Mantzouridis, Meg Thorley

PHOTOGRAPHY
Andrew Elton, Ashley Mackevicius, Harm Mol,
Yanto Noriento, Andrew Payne

STYLING
Lucy Andrews, Wendy Berecry, Rosemary De
Santis, Carolyn Feinberg, Michelle Gorry,
Donna Hay, Jacqui Hing, Anneka Mitchell,
Anna Philips, Susie Smith

DESIGN AND PRODUCTION
Manager: Sheridan Carter
Layout: Lulu Dougherty
Finished Art: Lulu Dougherty, Gavin Murrell

CLB 3245
This edition published by Colour Library
Books by arrangement with J.B. Fairfax Press
Pty Limited (A.C.N. 003 738 430)

Formatted by J.B. Fairfax Press Pty Limited
Printed by Toppan Printing Co, Singapore

Some of the contents of this book have been
previously published in other J.B. Fairfax
Press publications.

The Complete Family Cookbook
Includes Index
ISBN 1 85833 022 X

Printed in Singapore

THE COMPLETE
FAMILY COOKBOOK

CONTENTS

———●———

INTRODUCTION

Today's family cook is constantly faced with the challenge of what to cook for dinner – and almost every other meal. With an increased number of meals being eaten out and the wide choice of food available for these meals, there is a greater expectation for interesting and tasty meals at home.

Within the pages of The Complete Family Cookbook *you will find recipes and ideas that will not only inspire you as the cook but will also satisfy the tastes and demands of those you are cooking for.*

The wonderful range of recipes, the step-by-step instructions showing special cooking and preparation techniques, and the numerous hints and tips on cooking and food will have you turning to this book time and again for inspiration, advice and help.

For the new cook there is a special section with a guide to the equipment needed to set up a basic kitchen and an explanation of common cooking methods.

With The Complete Family Cookbook *in your kitchen you will never be stuck for interesting family food.*

MEASURING UP

For consistent results when cooking and especially when baking it is important to weigh and measure ingredients correctly and accurately. For good results a set of kitchen scales, a set of measuring spoons and a transparent graduated measuring jug for measuring liquids are important items for every cook's kitchen. In this book you will find that metric and imperial weights and measures have been given. As it is not practical to give exact conversions it is important that you do not switch from one set of measures to the other within a recipe.

All spoon measures given in this book are level; flour is white, plain or standard; and sugar is white unless otherwise stated.

Can sizes vary between countries and manufacturers. You may find the quantities in this book are slightly different from what is available. Use the can size nearest to the suggested size in the recipe.

Where microwave instructions occur in this book a microwave oven with a 650 watt output has been used. Wattage on domestic microwave ovens varies between 500 and 700, and it may be necessary to vary the cooking times slightly, depending on your oven.

LIQUID MEASURES

Metric	Imperial
30 mL	1 fl oz
60 mL	2 fl oz
90 mL	3 fl oz
125 mL	4 fl oz
155 mL	5 fl oz
170 mL	$5^1/_2$ fl oz
185 mL	6 fl oz
220 mL	7 fl oz
250 mL	8 fl oz
500 mL	16 fl oz
600 mL	20 fl oz/1 pt
750 mL	$1^1/_4$ pt
1 litre	$1^3/_4$ pt
1.2 litres	2 pt
1.5 litres	$2^1/_2$ pt
1.8 litres	3 pt
2 litres	$3^1/_2$ pt
2.5 litres	4 pt

WEIGHT MEASURES

Metric	Imperial
15 g	$^1/_2$ oz
30 g	1 oz
45 g	$1^1/_2$ oz
60 g	2 oz
75 g	$2^1/_2$ oz
90 g	3 oz
125 g	4 oz
155 g	5 oz
185 g	6 oz
220 g	7 oz
250 g	8 oz
280 g	9 oz
315 g	10 oz
350 g	11 oz
375 g	12 oz
410 g	13 oz
440 g	14 oz
500 g	16 oz/1 lb
750 g	$1^1/_2$ lb
1 kg	2 lb
1.5 kg	3 lb
2 kg	4 lb
2.5 kg	5 lb

OVEN TEMPERATURES

It should be noted that this is offered as a guide only and that different makes and models of ovens can vary slightly.

°C	°F	Gas Mark	
120	250	$1/2$	Very cool
140	275	1	
150	300	2	Cool
160	325	3	
180	350	4	Moderate
190	375	5	
200	400	6	Hot
220	425	7	
240	475	8	Very hot
250	500	9	Extremely hot

LINEAR MEASURES

Metric	Imperial
3 mm	$1/8$ in
5 mm	$1/4$ in
1 cm	$1/2$ in
2 cm	$3/4$ in
2.5 cm	1 in
5 cm	2 in
7.5 cm	3 in
10 cm	4 in
15 cm	6 in
18 cm	7 in
20 cm	8 in
23 cm	9 in
25 cm	10 in
30 cm	12 in

THE WELL-STOCKED PANTRY

Setting aside some time each week to plan your family's meals for the week ahead will save you time and money. Drawing up a master grocery list as you go, ensures that you have all the ingredients you need to create delicious meals for family and friends. Use the following checklist as a handy reminder to make your shopping easier and quicker.

TIMESAVING TIPS FOR THE FAMILY COOK

❦ Buy meat prepared for cooking. Ask the butcher to cut, slice or bone-out cuts of meat according to your recipe to help cut down on preparation time.

❦ Buy grated cheese.

❦ Buy bottled minced garlic, ginger and chillies. These save having to crush, chop and mince when time is short.

❦ A food processor is the ultimate timesaver in the kitchen. This appliance allows you to grate, shred, chop, blend, mix and purée ingredients in a fraction of the time it would take you to do it by hand.

❦ Look for new and interesting convenience products such as sauces and dressings, prepared pastries and pastry cases, canned fruits and vegetables and dessert ideas.

❦ Keep a selection of bread in the freezer. It defrosts quickly and is a good accompaniment to a meal.

❦ Store frozen meals in containers that can go straight from the freezer to the microwave, to the table and then into the dishwasher.

❦ Get to know your supermarket, and write your shopping list according to the layout of the shelves.

❦ Make double quantities of your favourite soups, casseroles and sauces and freeze half to have on hand for quick meals.

STAPLE ITEMS
- [ ] baking powder
- [ ] bicarbonate of soda
- [ ] cereal flakes
- [ ] cocoa powder
- [ ] coconut: desiccated, shredded
- [ ] cornflour
- [ ] cream of tartar
- [ ] dried breadcrumbs
- [ ] essence: almond, vanilla
- [ ] flour: plain, self-raising, wholemeal
- [ ] gelatine
- [ ] golden syrup
- [ ] honey
- [ ] instant coffee
- [ ] minced chillies
- [ ] minced garlic
- [ ] minced ginger
- [ ] prepared stock (chicken, beef, vegetable), or stock cubes
- [ ] rolled oats
- [ ] sugar: brown, caster, white, icing, raw (muscovado)
- [ ] tomato purée
- [ ] tea
- [ ] white and red wine

PERISHABLE GOODS
- [ ] butter or margarine
- [ ] cheese: Parmesan, mature Cheddar
- [ ] eggs
- [ ] milk
- [ ] natural yogurt

CANNED FOODS
- [ ] apricot halves
- [ ] asparagus spears
- [ ] sweet corn kernels
- [ ] peach halves and slices
- [ ] peeled tomatoes
- [ ] pineapple pieces
- [ ] salmon
- [ ] tuna

FROZEN FOODS
- [ ] frozen vegetables: peas, beans, sweet corn
- [ ] ice cream
- [ ] pastry: filo, prepared or ready-rolled puff and shortcrust
- [ ] selection of bread rolls, loaves and sliced bread

PASTA AND RICE
- [ ] fettuccine
- [ ] instant lasagne sheets
- [ ] macaroni
- [ ] rice: short and long grain white, quick-cooking brown
- [ ] spaghetti: plain, wholemeal

SAUCES AND MUSTARDS
- [ ] mayonnaise
- [ ] mustard: Dijon, French, wholegrain
- [ ] prepared pasta sauce
- [ ] salad dressing
- [ ] sauces: chilli, cranberry, plum, soy, Worcestershire

HERBS AND SPICES
- [ ] cayenne pepper
- [ ] chilli powder
- [ ] cinnamon: ground, sticks
- [ ] curry powder
- [ ] dried herbs: basil, mixed herbs, oregano, sage, tarragon, thyme
- [ ] ground herbs: such as coriander, cumin, paprika, turmeric
- [ ] ground spices: allspice, ginger, mixed spice, nutmeg
- [ ] rosemary: dried leaves, ground
- [ ] whole black peppercorns
- [ ] whole cloves

OILS AND VINEGARS
- [ ] oils: olive, vegetable
- [ ] vinegars: white, brown, cider

DRIED FRUITS, NUTS AND SEEDS
- [ ] dried fruits: apricots, currants, raisins, sultanas
- [ ] ground almonds
- [ ] nuts: such as cashews, pecans, walnuts, chopped mixed nuts
- [ ] poppy seeds
- [ ] sunflower kernels

JAMS AND RELISHES
- [ ] jams: apricot, raspberry, strawberry
- [ ] orange marmalade
- [ ] peanut butter
- [ ] relish
- [ ] sweet fruit chutney

CAKES AND BISCUITS
- [ ] plain sweet biscuits
- [ ] variety packet cake mixes
- [ ] water crackers

chapter one

•

GETTING
STARTED

*This section has been put
together especially to help the new
cook. It details the preparation needed
to cook a recipe successfully. There is also
advice on the equipment required to set
up a basic kitchen, and an explanation
of some of the most common
cooking methods.*

RECIPES AND PREPARATION

The first step in preparing a meal, baking a cake or even making a simple snack is to read the recipe and prepare your ingredients. The following simple steps will ensure that cooking is a pleasure rather than a chore.

1 Before you start cooking, look at the recipe and read through the ingredients list and method. This will alert you to any problems, such as not having an ingredient or finding that the recipe is going to take 2 hours to prepare and you need to have it ready in 30 minutes.

2 Following the ingredients list, collect all the foods you will require. This helps to make sure that you have everything you need for the recipe. The ingredients are always listed in their order of use.

3 Next prepare the food in the state it will be required in the recipe. The secret of many recipes is to add the next ingredient at just the right time. If that ingredient is not ready it can mean that a dish is ruined or at least not as good as it should be.

4 The next step is to go through the method and get out the equipment that you will need.

5 As you read through the method, check to see if the oven will be used and, if so, turn it on to preheat.

6 You are now ready to start making your recipe. Remember, being organised and assembling all your ingredients and equipment before you start will save you time in cooking and cleaning up.

Remember to collect and measure your ingredients and to get out the equipment you will need before you start cooking.

COOKING METHODS

The cooking method you choose will depend on what you are cooking and the effect you wish to achieve. The following will help you better understand the different types of cooking methods most often used.

STEAMING

Using this cooking method the food is set over boiling water and cooked in the steam given off. Place the food in a metal basket, on a wire rack, or in a steamer in a saucepan, set 1-2.5 cm/ $^{1}/_{2}$-1 in above the water. Tightly cover the pan and cook for the required time. Steaming is a popular way of cooking vegetables and fish for the diet-conscious. It is one of the best ways to cook food and retain the maximum number of vitamins and minerals.

SIMMERING

This is when liquids are just hot enough for a few bubbles to form slowly and the bubbles burst below the surface. Simmering takes place at a lower temperature than boiling and should not be confused with boiling.

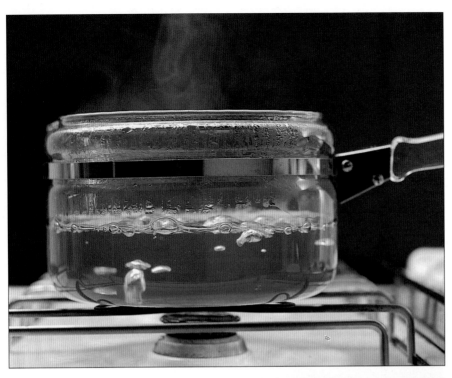

BOILING

This is when liquids are hot enough to form bubbles that rise in a steady pattern and break on the surface. The whole mass of liquid starts to move as the bubbling begins.

Left: Boiling
Below: Pan Cooking

PAN COOKING

The food is cooked in a little fat in a frying pan. The most commonly used fats are butter, margarine or oil. When pan cooking you need to make sure that the fat is hot enough so that the food cooks without absorbing too much fat, but the fat should not be too hot or the food will burn.

DEEP-FRYING

This method of cooking is popular in the cooking of takeaway foods. It is an efficient and quick method if done correctly. To deep-fry, it is important that you have a saucepan large enough to hold the food comfortably. For the safest cooking and the best results, the saucepan used should be wide-topped, deep and heavy-based. A wire basket that fits in the saucepan will make it easier and safer to place the food in the oil and to remove it. When deep-frying, the oil must be at the correct temperature before you add the food – too hot and the food will cook on the outside but

remain undercooked or raw in the centre, not hot enough and the food will absorb oil and be soggy and greasy. When the oil is at the correct temperature, it should be still, with a slight haze coming from the surface and when a cube of bread is dropped in it will brown in 50 seconds.

You could also use a thermometer to check the temperature of the oil. The correct temperature for most food is 190°C/375°F.

GRILLING

Cooking food by direct dry heat. When grilling meat you should place it on a rack in the grill pan, to allow the fat to drip through. Grilling can be used to cook foods such as steaks, chops and sausages, as well as for browning or toasting the top of denser foods. The grill should always be preheated before you start cooking.

Right: Grilling
Below: Baking

BAKING

Cooking food by indirect dry heat. The food can be cooked covered or uncovered, usually in an oven. Cooking meat in this way is called 'roasting'.

When baking cakes, biscuits and breads it is important that the oven is preheated before placing the food in it.

STIR-FRYING

This quick method of cooking is usually done in a wok, but a large frying pan will also give good results. The secret to successful stir-frying is to have all the ingredients prepared before you start cooking. When stir-frying use a large spatula and lift and turn the food quickly so that it comes in frequent contact with the hot cooking surface. Always heat the wok or frying pan first, then add the oil and finally the food. One of the great advantages of stir-frying is that only small quantities of oil need be used.

17

GETTING EQUIPPED

*Having the right equipment makes food
preparation and cooking easy. Use this as a guide for
equipping your kitchen.*

Stockpot

Measuring jug

Sifter

Grate

Soufflé dishes

Casserole dishes

Rolling pin

Potato masher

Mixing bow

Paring knife

Boning knife

Bread knife

Carving knife

Metal
spatula

Meat mallet

Saucepans

Frying pans

Colander

Wooden spoon

Baking tray

Tongs

Cake tins

suring spoons

Rubber spatula

uring cups

Hand-held electric beater

Roasting dish

BLACK&DECKER POWER*Plus*

Wire whisk

BAKING TRAY

A baking tray or baking sheet has a very slightly raised edge and is mainly used for cooking biscuits and unmoulded pastries.

CAKE TINS

These come in many shapes and sizes and it will depend on how much cake baking you intend to do as to how many different types of cake tins you will require. As a start a 20 cm/8 in square tin, a 20 cm/8 in round and a loaf tin will satisfy most basic needs. Other useful cake tins to have are a pair of 20 cm/8 in sandwich tins, a springform tin, a Swiss roll tin and a set of patty tins. Sandwich tins are shallow-sided tins used for making layer cakes.

CASSEROLE DISHES (IN VARIOUS SIZES)

These can be ceramic, pottery, ovenproof glass or metal and are available in a range of sizes and prices. The size and type of casserole dish you decide on will depend on your budget and on how many you are cooking for. It is useful to have several different-sized casserole dishes and to have at least one which is flameproof. A flameproof casserole dish can be used on an element as well as in the oven – useful for pot roasting or when browning meat for a casserole.

ELECTRIC MIXERS

There are two main types of electric mixers available – hand-held and bench top. Hand-held mixers are useful for mixing small quantities of food. The larger bench top models have heavy-duty motors and are needed for mixing heavier doughs and batters.

FOOD PROCESSORS

There are two types of food processors – the one that stands on the bench and the hand-held blender.

The hand-held blender is ideal for chopping, mincing and grinding small quantities of food. It comes with its own chopping bowl and beaker and can be used with these accessories or in an ordinary mixing bowl. The hand-held blender is a light, easily managed appliance, particularly suited to disabled and arthritic cooks, as those difficult and fiddly jobs of cutting and chopping are quickly and safely achieved.

The food processor is ideal for larger quantities of food. Cakes, biscuits and slices are mixed in seconds and pastry is made in minutes. The food processor will chop, grind, mince and purée. For many recipes, the food processor can take the place of an electric mixer; for example, creaming butter and sugar, mixing cake batter and making one-bowl biscuits and slices. Other uses of the food processor include mincing meat, puréeing fruit and vegetables and making pâtés.

FREEZERS

The type of freezer you choose will depend on the size of your family, what you intend to freeze and where you are going to position it. Freezing food preserves its nutritional value and allows you to have a range of cooked and raw foods on hand.

FRYING PANS

The best frying pans are those with heavy bases, as this ensures that the heat spreads evenly and so the food cooks evenly. Nonstick frying pans mean that you can cook with very little or no fat.

KNIVES

A selection of sharp knives is essential for safe, efficient food preparation. A good set of knives is a cook's best investment and will last you many years. At the very least you will need three knives. A paring knife, which is a small knife with a straight blade, is needed for trimming and peeling vegetables. A chopping or chef's knife, which has a heavy, wide blade is used for chopping and cutting vegetables, herbs, meat, poultry and fish. The blade length ranges from 15-30 cm/6-12 in, but for home use a knife with a 20 cm/8 in blade is probably the most useful. A serrated-edged knife is useful for cutting bread, cakes and pastries. The serrated edge cuts through them without tearing. Smaller, serrated-edged knives are used for slicing tomatoes and fruits such as oranges, grapefruit and lemons. The edge on a serrated knife lasts almost indefinitely, but should it need sharpening it must be done professionally.

MEASURING CUPS

These are popular in America and Australia where they are used to measure both dry and liquid ingredients. They are available in nests containing four cups of varying sizes – 1 cup/250 mL/8 fl oz, 1/2 cup/125 mL/4 fl oz, 1/3 cup/90 mL/3 fl oz and 1/4 cup/60 mL/2 fl oz.

MEASURING JUG

This graduated jug is used for measuring liquids. To measure liquids, place the jug on a flat surface, fill to the measuring mark then check the quantity at eye level.

MEASURING SPOONS

These are available in sets containing a tablespoon, teaspoon, $1/2$ teaspoon and $1/4$ teaspoon. They are a quick and accurate way of measuring small quantities of ingredients.

MIXING BOWLS

These come in many shapes and sizes and can be made from a variety of materials. If you have a microwave oven it is useful to have mixing bowls that are microwave-safe.

PASTRY BRUSH

Use a pastry brush to apply glazes, melted butter and the like to surfaces of food and for brushing dishes with oil or butter.

ROASTING DISH

This rectangular metal dish has low sides and is used for cooking roast meats and vegetables. Once the meat is cooked and removed from the dish, the dish is then placed on an element for making the gravy.

ROLLING PIN

This smooth cylinder is 20-50 cm/ 8-12 in long with a 5-6 cm/ $2-2^1/_2$ in diameter. With or without handles a rolling pin can be made from a variety of materials, however the most common is hardwood. A hollow glass rolling pin that can be filled with iced water is useful for pastry making.

SAUCEPANS

One of the most important requirements of a saucepan is that it is the right size for the job. It is therefore necessary to have a range of saucepans in different sizes to suit different jobs. When buying saucepans, don't be tempted by beautiful matching sets, but rather buy a selection of pans to suit your various needs.

When choosing your pans they should be heavy-duty with solid bases, insulated handles and tight-fitting lids.

SCALES

Kitchen scales are a useful tool for any cook and essential if you plan to make cakes, biscuits and the like. Accurate measuring is important for this type of cooking.

SIFTER

Used for sifting dry ingredients to remove lumps and aerate the ingredients. If you do not have a sifter with a spring mechanism, a simple wire sieve does the job just as well.

SOUFFLE DISHES (LARGE AND SMALL)

A soufflé dish is round with high straight sides, that allows the soufflé to rise vertically as it expands. While obviously used for cooking soufflés, soufflé dishes have many other uses. A large soufflé dish is useful for cooking baked vegetable dishes and can also team as a serving dish. Small soufflé dishes or ramekins are good for individual baked dishes and individual desserts, such as chocolate mousse.

SPATULAS (METAL AND RUBBER)

Spatulas with flexible metal blades come in a variety of sizes and are used for spreading icings, fillings and creams. Rubber spatulas are useful for scraping out bowls.

STOCKPOT

This large saucepan should be taller than it is wide and have a handle on either side. The French call this type of saucepan a *fait-tout* which literally means 'do-all'. This pan has a multitude of uses, including stock and soup making and pot roasting. For a domestic kitchen a pan of about 12 litres/21 pt is a good size as it will easily accommodate bulky bones, but can still be safely lifted when full.

WOODEN SPOONS

As wood does not conduct heat, wooden spoons do not get hot and are therefore ideal for use when cooking foods such as sauces and jams, as the spoon can be left in the mixture during cooking.

chapter two

●

SEASON TO TASTE

When used correctly, herbs and spices are a cook's best friend. In this chapter you will find information on the various herbs and spices along with a guide as to which foods they best combine with. However, be adventurous when using these exciting seasonings – you never know what new combination you may discover.

A–Z OF SPICES

Don't be discouraged by their exotic names or by the (false) idea that spices are expensive or complicated to use; they are the greatest asset of a good cook.

ALLSPICE

The seeds of allspice are just slightly larger than peppercorns and dark brown in colour. All-spice is a delicately spicy min-gling of cloves, cinnamon and nutmeg, with cloves predominat-ing. Allspice berries are the dried fruit of a tall, aromatic evergreen of the myrtle and clove family, which can grow to over 12 m/ 40 ft. Picked when green and unripe, the seeds are dried in the sun to a rich, deep brown colour.

ANISEED

The small, oval grey-green ribbed seeds of anise have a warm, sweet, pungent flavour and can be used in sweet and savoury dishes. The aromatic anise annual grows to about 60 cm/2 ft high and is similar to other small members of the parsley family. Anise will grow well in a good summer in light, dry loamy soil in a sunny position. Sow the seeds in mid-spring. The plants pro-duce small white flowers and fern-like leaves.

CARAWAY

A handsome biennial to 60 cm/ 2 ft high with finely cut leaves and clusters of white flowers which produce aromatic seeds with their characteristic flavour. Sow seeds direct in spring or autumn. Needs a sunny, well-drained position protected from wind. Young leaves are used as a garnish for cooked vegetables. The seeds are used in dishes of cabbage, potatoes and parsnips. Also used in some cakes, biscuits and apple pies. Leaves and softer stems can be eaten in salads or cooked with other vegetables.

CARDAMOM

The cardamom bush is a herb-aceous perennial plant of the ginger family and grows nearly 3 m/10 ft high. Cardamom will only grow in a hot climate. It produces slightly pungent, highly aromatic pods holding seeds which are sweet with a camphor-like flavour.

CASSIA

The bark, unripe seeds and the dried leaves of this plant are all used in cooking. Related to cinnamon, the bark can be used in the same way and has a similar taste but is not as strong. The seeds, also known as Chinese cassia buds, are used in drinks and confectionery and are often added to potpourris.

CAYENNE PEPPER

Cayenne pepper, paprika and Tabasco sauce are all made from varieties of peppers. Cayenne is derived from a hot, red variety of pepper called 'bird chilli'. Although cayenne is not as hot as some chilli powders it is very pungent and should be used sparingly. Store in an airtight container in small quantities and in a dark place.

CELERY SEEDS

These seeds, with a bitter celery flavour, are the tiny light brown seeds of the celery plant. They should be used sparingly in casseroles and soups. They are a great addition to pickled vegetables and homemade bread, and will add life to any salad dressing.

CHILLI

Chillies belong to the pepper family and have an especially hot flavour. All varieties of peppers bear certain common character-istics. The bushy chilli shrub prefers tropical or subtropical climates and grows to between 30 to 180 cm/1-6 ft high, depend-ing on the variety. As a general rule, the smaller, narrower and darker the chilli, the greater its pungency; unripe fresh chillies are usually less pungent than ripe fresh ones, and these in turn are milder than dried chillies.

CINNAMON

Cinnamon is the bark of a tree which belongs to the laurel family. The cinnamon tree is a tall, thick evergreen tree which prefers tropical climates. The bark is the most important part of the tree – when ground it pro-vides a sweet spice highly valued for both culinary and medical usage. The leaves are pointed, smooth and tough and the small creamy-white flowers are fol-lowed by dark blue berries. The dried bark is sold in small quills (usually 7.5-15 cm/3-6 in long) or as powder.

CLOVES

The clove tree is an evergreen which grows abundantly near tropical seashores. Cloves are the highly aromatic flower buds of this tree or shrub which is native to the Moluccas or Spice Islands. Nowadays cloves are mostly imported from Zanzibar and Madagascar.

CORIANDER
Coriander is a member of the parsley family. The plant gives off a strong odour which is replaced by a sweet orange-like aroma when the seeds are dried. The round, light brown seeds are milder than many other spices and can be used in large quantities. The taste is fresh with a hint of bitterness and can be improved by gently roasting before grinding.

CUMIN SEEDS
Like coriander and caraway, cumin seed comes from a plant of the parsley family. Cumin is a small and delicate annual which usually grows to 25 cm/10 in in height. Native to the Middle East, cumin now grows in most hot climates. The small, dark brown, elongated seeds have a rich sweet aroma; their flavour is similarly pungent and they should be used sparingly. Cumin seed is often confused with fennel or anise (both sometimes called 'sweet cumin').

DILL SEEDS
The dill plant is another member of the parsley family and the leaves, stalks and the dried seeds can all be used in cooking. The oval, flattened seeds have a fresh, sweet aroma with a slightly bitter taste similar to that of caraway seeds. Dill seeds are dried and used whole or slightly crushed. Add them to dishes towards the end of cooking or when cooking is over to fully enhance their flavour.

FENNEL SEEDS
Another member of the wonderful parsley family, fennel seeds are like plumper, larger versions of anise seeds with a warm and slightly bitter anise flavour. They are curved, ridged and dullish yellow-green in appearance. Fennel seeds have strong digestive qualities and so are often used with rich meats and oily fish.

FENUGREEK
The fenugreek plant which grows from 30 to 60 cm/1 to 2 ft high, is a member of the bean and pea family. Its flowers and pods resemble those of the pea. Each long, narrow pod contains ten to twenty small, hard yellow-brown seeds. The seeds have a slightly bitter-sweet taste and should be used in moderation. Only when roasted do the seeds give off their pungent aroma. Whole or ground fenugreek is most often used in Indian curries.

GINGER
Ginger is an important spice in both East and West. Like other tropical plants of the same family, such as turmeric, it is the knobbly root of the ginger plant which is used as a spice. Fresh ginger does not keep well, so buy only in small quantities. Dried ginger root can be bruised and ground to a powder (its fibres removed) and used as ground ginger, or bruised and infused in the cooking liquid of savoury dishes.

JUNIPER BERRIES
The juniper tree is a small coniferous and prickly evergreen. The round, purple-brown berries are about twice the size of peppercorns with smooth skins. The spicy pine aroma and sweet, resinous flavour varies according to where they are grown. The berries are bought whole and are easy to grind because they are soft. Juniper is commonly used in spice mixtures for meat and are excellent with pork and game.

LAOS POWDER
Laos powder, also known as galangal or galingale, has a peppery ginger taste and is used in the hot and spicy dishes of South-East Asia. Closely related to ginger it is similar in that it is the root of the plant that is powdered. In Europe it is used to flavour liqueurs and bitters.

MACE
Mace and nutmeg are both parts of the fruit of a tropical evergreen tree. Mace blades form the outer casing of the nutmeg and are bright red when harvested, drying to a deep orange.The flavour of mace is similar to nutmeg but more delicate.

MUSTARD SEEDS
Mustard is internationally famous as a condiment and flavouring. The whole seeds are the basis for prepared mustards, and the pungent oil extracted from the seeds and the seeds themselves are also popularly used as culinary spices. There are three main varieties of mustard: black, brown and white. The three plants are very similar in appearance and all bear tiny, spherical, hard seeds. Brown mustard seeds are most commonly used as an Indian cooking spice.

NUTMEG
The small, oval shiny nut, about 4 cm/1½ in long, is dried in its seed coat which is then removed. Nutmeg is slightly milder than mace but has a more nutty flavour – warm and sweetish with a light bitter undertone. Nutmegs can be bought whole or ready-ground. It is best to buy them whole and store in an airtight container. Finely grate as needed.

PAPRIKA

Like cayenne pepper, paprika is a finely ground powder made from the fruit of several different chilli plants. The ripe flesh is used for mild, sweet paprika, the seeds are included for more pungent versions. Mild paprika has a light, sweet smell and almost no pungency; the strongest paprika is similar to cayenne pepper.

PEPPER

Pepper comes from the tropical trailing vine of the *Piperaceae* family. The vines grow to heights of 3.6 m/11 ft and bear long strings of 20-30 small berries which ripen from green to reddish-yellow. Black pepper berries are picked when green and dried whole; for white pepper they are allowed to ripen and turn red and the skin is removed before drying. Green peppercorns are picked when still green and usually pickled.

POPPY SEEDS

Poppy seeds, sometimes called maw seeds, come from the opium poppy. The plant is related to both the common field poppy and garden varieties. It grows to anything from 30 to 120 cm/1 to 4 ft and bears white, pink or lilac flowers and erect oval seed pods. The tiny, hard seeds are very mild and sweetish and acquire a bitter-sweet nutty flavour when cooked.

SAFFRON

Saffron is the most expensive spice in the world. It is the dried stigmas of the flowers of the saffron crocus. The flowers are extracted from the freshly harvested flowers and dried to become irregular, orange-red threads about 4 cm/1$\frac{1}{2}$ in long. It takes about 50 000 stigmas to make up 100 g/3 $\frac{1}{2}$ oz of saffron! Saffron imparts a distinctive aroma, a bitter honey-like taste and a strong yellow colour to food. It's better to buy the threads and store them in an airtight container in a dark place. Ground saffron can vary enormously in quality.

SESAME SEEDS

Sesame is a tropical annual with a pungent smell. The plant grows to anything between 60 and 180 cm/2 and 6 ft. The seed pods contain a large number of small, flat oval seeds in a variety of colours. They may be red, light brown or black and have a rich nutty flavour. Dry roast before use or fry lightly until they just colour and give off a roasted aroma.

STAR ANISE

Star anise is the star-shaped fruit of an oriental evergreen of the magnolia family which can reach a height of 7.3 m/24 ft. When dried it is a brown colour and the flavour is one of pungent aniseed. Whole stars store well in an airtight container, and are preferable to the powdered form.

TAMARIND

Tamarind with its sour flavour is a large pod that grows on the Indian tamarind tree. It is picked, seeded and peeled before being pressed into a dark brown pulp. Tamarind is usually mixed with warm water to give tamarind juice which is then used in chutneys, sauces and curries.

TURMERIC

Turmeric is a typical member of the ginger family and, like ginger, it is the knobbly roots or rhizomes which form the cooking spice. The tropical turmeric has spiky yellow flowers and long, shiny pointed leaves, and can grow to a height of 1 m/3 ft. Turmeric has a strong woody aroma and distinctive, pungent flavour. Because of this it should not be used as a cheap substitute for saffron.

VANILLA

The dark brown pod of vanilla comes from a type of orchid native to South America. It was discovered by the Spaniards in Mexico. When first picked the pod is a yellow green and it is only after curing and drying that it becomes the dark brown we associate with vanilla. Essentially a flavouring used in sweet dishes such as ice cream, custards and rice, it is also popular as a flavouring for wine cups, hot chocolate and coffee drinks. The vanilla pod can be used several times and if kept in a jar of sugar will flavour it to make vanilla sugar.

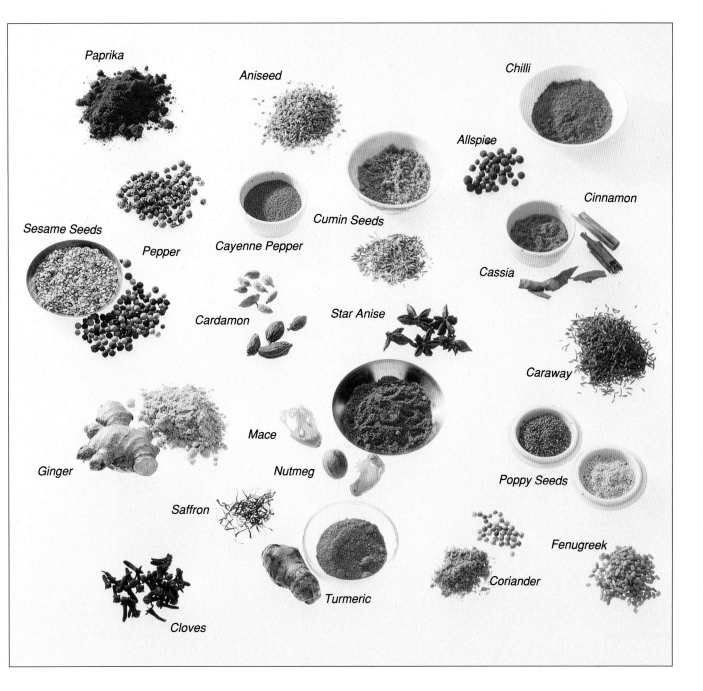

Paprika

Aniseed

Chilli

Allspice

Cumin Seeds

Cinnamon

Sesame Seeds

Pepper

Cayenne Pepper

Cassia

Cardamon

Star Anise

Caraway

Ginger

Mace

Nutmeg

Poppy Seeds

Saffron

Fenugreek

Coriander

Cloves

Turmeric

AT-A-GLANCE SPICE GUIDE

SPICE	SOUPS	MAIN DISHES
Allspice	Beef and minestrone soups	Baked ham, meat loaf, spiced meats
Aniseed	Cream soups	Seafood, pork and poultry dishes
Cardamom	Spiced and curried soups	Curries and spicy dishes of Indian and Middle Eastern origin
Cassia		Chinese dishes and curries
Cayenne Pepper	Soups, especially fish and tomato	Curries and spicy dishes, egg dishes
Chilli – fresh	Spicy soups	All curries and spicy meat, poultry, fish and egg dishes
Chilli – powder	Spicy soups	As for fresh chillies
Coriander – seed	Spicy soups	Curries and spicy meat, poultry, fish dishes
Cumin – seed	Spicy soups	Meat, poultry and fish dishes
Curry Plant	Fish and spicy soups	Casseroles and curries
Dill – seed	Vegetable soups	Lamb, pork and fish dishes
Fennel – seed		Chicken and fish dishes
Fenugreek		Indian and Middle Eastern dishes
Ginger – fresh		Curries
Ginger – ground		Curries, baked ham and fish dishes
Mace		Fish, chicken, beef and veal dishes
Mustard – powder	Leek and celery soups	Grilled meats, ham casseroles
Mustard – seed		Curries, pork, rabbit, veal, some fish dishes
Nutmeg	Cream soups	Fish, chicken, egg and cheese dishes, pasta
Paprika	Most soups	Curries, goulashes, pork, beef, veal and fish dishes
Saffron	Especially fish soups	Chicken, fish, turkey and some egg dishes, paella
Turmeric	Curried and spicy soups	Curries, egg and fish dishes
Vanilla		

VEGETABLE DISHES	DESSERTS AND BAKED PRODUCTS	OTHER USES
Carrot, pea and potato salads	Apple desserts such as pies and crumbles, milk puddings	Pickles, confectionery, stewed fruit
Salads, carrots and courgettes (zucchini)	Biscuits, cakes, fresh fruit, especially good with figs	Cheese dips
Vegetable curries	Breads and yeast cakes, custards, fruit salads	Pickles, stewed fruit, savoury and sweet rice dishes
Ground sprinkle over vegetables		Poached and stewed fruit
		Salad dressings
Spicy vegetable dishes		Salad dressings
Spicy vegetable dishes		Salad dressings, dips, pickles, sauces
Spicy vegetable dishes	Biscuits, cakes, fruit salad	Yogurt dips, salad dressings, stewed fruit
Cabbage, carrots and legume dishes		Pickles, chutneys, marinades, rice dishes
		Stuffings for veal and game
Cucumber, marrow, cabbage and carrots	Biscuits, cakes, fruit salad	Pickles
Potatoes	Biscuits, sprinkle over breads and buns	Salad dressings, sauces for fish
Sprouts used in salads		
	Biscuits, cakes and cooked apple dishes	Marinades
Vegetable curries and spicy legume dishes	Cakes, biscuits, puddings, fruit pies	Pickles, spiced drinks such as mulled wine, stewed fruit
	Biscuits, cakes	Flavour whipped cream, stuffings, pâtés
Braised celery and leeks		Salad dressings, stuffings
Cabbage and celery		Stuffings
Cabbage, carrots and root vegetables	Biscuits, cakes, milk puddings, pastries, fruit salads, junket, sweet breads	Stewed fruits, flavour whipped cream, pâtés
Legume dishes		Rice dishes
	Biscuits, cakes, breads	Savoury rice dishes
	Colouring for cakes and breads	Rice dishes
	Custards, ice cream, milk puddings	Flavour cream, drinks, sugar and cups

A–Z OF HERBS

Few ingredients are as tasty as fresh herbs plucked from a window box or from a special section of your garden. Many grow with just the slightest encouragement, while others need attention, but either way you'll be amply repaid in flavoursome meals.

ANGELICA

This is a stout biennial or perennial herb which grows to 2 m/ 6$\frac{1}{2}$ ft or more. Leaves are soft green and divided into large leaflets. The stems are round, ribbed and hollow with yellow-green flowers which grow in a ball-like cluster. Best suited to cool-climate areas where it can be planted in sun or semi-shade. Shelter from strong wind is desirable because the stems are brittle. Angelica is completely permeated by a unique essence, giving it a delicately sweet and refreshing aroma. Angelica stems can be candied, and can also be used instead of sugar when stewing sour fruits like rhubarb. The roots are edible and can be served as a vegetable. The seeds are used in flavouring gin and some liqueurs.

BASIL

An annual to 60 cm/2 ft high with peppery, clove-scented leaves. There are different types of basil plants but the old favourites sweet basil and bush basil are still the best varieties to grow for the kitchen. Grow from seed in a sunny, moist but well-drained position sheltered from wind. For the best results, sow the seed at the end of spring or at the beginning of summer. Remove the small, white, lipped flower buds to encourage longer life. For a stronger flavour in cooking, use fresh basil leaves as basil loses a lot of its flavour when dried. Excellent with all tomato dishes and torn up in salads. It goes well with carrots, courgettes (zucchini), pasta sauces and chicken.

BAY

A slow-growing evergreen tree with aromatic leaves, also known as bay laurel or sweet bay. Bay trees make excellent tub specimens and should be grown in a sunny sheltered position. Young plants need protection from frosts. The leaves are large, flat, oval and glossy and can be harvested at any time of the year. Bay leaves have a strong flavour and taste rather bitter when fresh so are most often used dried. A bay leaf is one of the three herbs that make up the classic bouquet garni. Use with tomatoes and beetroot and to flavour soups, sauces and stews. Add bay leaves to stores of flour, pulses and similar foods to keep weevils away.

BORAGE

This herb is an annual with thick, soft stems, large leaves and branching hairy stems. Height varies from 30 to 90 cm/1 to 3 ft. Leaves are greyish-green, about 10-15 cm/4-6 in long. Star-like summer flowers in white or blue are most attractive. Flowering can continue through winter in mild areas. Flowers and young leaves can be eaten. The leaves have a delicate, cucumber-like flavour. Finely chop and use as a garnish in salads. The flowers can be candied. Both flowers and leaves can be dipped in a light batter and deep-fried.

CHERVIL

A small spreading annual to 50 cm/20 in. Fern-like leaves have a delicate aniseed flavour. The white flowers, which appear in early summer, grow in small, flat umbels. The seeds which follow resemble caraway seeds but are longer and thinner. The seeds should be sown in shallow drills 30 cm/1 ft apart in spring and autumn. Grow in a partially shaded, sheltered position in rich, moist soil. Keep chervil watered at all times. Chervil leaves are delicious with salad greens and spinach. Use in dressings, garnish for soups, and with fish dishes.

CHIVES

A perennial member of the onion family, chives have hollow onion-flavoured leaves and attractive edible mauve flowers. Chives like a rich, moist soil in full sun; they also grow well indoors in pots on a sunny window sill. They respond to picking in moderation, but a proportion of fresh leaves must be left. In cold climates, chives die back in winter. Chives should be lifted and divided every two or three years in spring or autumn, or immediately after flowering. Use in fresh salads and to flavour potatoes or any of the marrow family. Good in most savoury dishes and excellent with eggs and cream.

CORIANDER

Sometimes called Chinese parsley or cilantro, coriander is an attractive annual to 60 cm/2 ft. The lacy foliage has a distinctive, strong aroma quite different from other similar herbs such as anise, caraway, dill and fennel, all of whose leaves have a warm spicy anise-scent. A mixture of lemon peel and sage is one description of the flavour of fresh coriander leaves. Coriander can be grown either in a sunny spot in the garden or indoors in pots on a sunny window sill, by planting the whole coriander seeds. Sow seeds direct in spring and water generously. Harvest seeds in autumn and dry in a light, airy position. When the small oval coriander seeds have hardened and ripened to a pale fawn colour, they are one of the most deliciously fragrant of all spices used in cooking. Coriander is used in almost every Thai dish. Leaves are tasty in salads and as a garnish for pea soup. The seeds complement mushrooms, cauliflower, beetroot and celery and are commonly used in curries, sausage-making and as a flavouring in cakes.

CURRY PLANT

The curry plant is a shrubby perennial plant that grows into a low spreading bush with silvery-grey, green spiky leaves. Although it is not used in authentic curries, the leaves do have a strong curry-like flavour.

CURRY LEAVES

Not to be confused with the silvery-grey leaves of the curry plant. Curry leaves are small, shiny and evergreen and slightly like small bay leaves. The tree is easily grown and decorative, with an exotic spicy fragrance. Curry leaves are usually chopped and fried in oil at the start of making curry. They quickly turn brown and become crisp when the other ingredients are added. The leaves may also be ground to a powder and used in making curry powder and paste.

DILL

A fast-growing, upright annual to 90 cm/3 ft, dill resembles fennel in that both have hollow stems, feathery leaves and clusters of yellow flowers. The flavour of dill is clean and delicate. Sow seeds in a sunny, well-drained soil in spring and autumn. The seeds can be harvested. Dill grows best in a light, medium-rich soil with plenty of moisture. Dill seeds and leaves can both be eaten. Dill seed flavours and helps the digestion of steamed cabbage, coleslaw, sauerkraut, cucumbers, various chutneys and pickles, pastries, breads, sauces and cooked root vegetables. Both the seeds and leaves with their spicy flavour are used, although the foliage does not have the same concentration of oil as the seeds.

FENNEL

Fast-growing tall annual to 1.5 m/ 5 ft. It has bright green, feathery leaves and clusters of yellow flowers followed by aniseed-flavoured seeds. Grow in a well-drained, sunny position and provide plenty of water. Both leaves and seeds are traditionally used with fish. If baking a whole fish, branches of the foliage make a fragrant bed for the fish to rest on during cooking. Fennel seeds are used in soups, sauces and with lentils, rice and potatoes. Also used in breads and cakes. The leaves are used in salads, relishes and as garnishes.

GARLIC

A bulbous perennial plant with strap-like leaves measuring approximately 2.5 cm/1 in across and 30 cm/1 ft long. A willowy, round flower-stalk thrusts upwards above the leaves, and the flower that appears is a compact collection of mauve-tinted white petals. Plant separated cloves in

early spring in a rich and well-drained soil, preferably in full sun. When the foliage has died down at the end of summer, the bulbs can be carefully lifted. Dig the bulbs, shake them free of dirt and plait several together. Hang the plaited garlic in a dry, well-ventilated place. The whole garlic plant has a pungent, lingering odour – it cannot be called scent or aroma due to the essential oil it contains. The oil is antibiotic and contains vitamins A and B, sulphur and iodine.

GINGER

A tall perennial plant to 1.5 m/ 5 ft high with spikes of white and purple flowers and aromatic rhizomes, ginger prefers a hot, humid climate in a rich, well-drained soil in partial shade. Ginger root has a sweet, hot flavour which goes with meat, fish, vegetables, cakes and sweets. Fresh grated ginger is particularly good with steamed or stir-fried vegetables, especially Chinese cabbage. Ginger is an essential part of many curries, pickles and chutneys.

HORSERADISH

A hardy perennial with long, elliptical dark green leaves. It grows to a height of about 60 cm/2 ft with erect stems and has small, scented, four-petalled white flowers. Often grown for its thick, fleshy, aromatic roots – hot, pungent and full of flavour. Plant in an open sunny position, with a deeply dug, fertile soil. Horseradish sauce uses grated root mixed with cream or some similar viscous liquid. It must be used raw as the cooked roots lose their flavour. Roots can be grated and dried and stored in airtight containers for later use. The leaves are also pungent and tasty and can be chopped and used as a salad ingredient.

LEMON BALM

A perennial to 90 cm/3 ft, lemon balm has dark green, heart-shaped leaves that have a strong lemon scent and flavour. Grow in a rich, well-drained soil in full sun. Pinch back in early summer to encourage new growth. Use only fresh leaves sprinkled over vegetable or fruit salads. Use leaves in fish and poultry dishes, sauces, marinades and stuffings. Lemon balm is sometimes planted in orchards to attract bees to pollinate the fruit blossom.

LEMON GRASS

A grass-like perennial to 3 m/ 10 ft high, lemon grass has pointed aromatic leaves with a delicious lemon scent. It forms a large clump in a sunny, warm position with plenty of water, but needs good drainage. The fleshy white lower part of the leaves is used in South-East Asian dishes. It adds a tangy taste to salads and is a must for curries.

MARJORAM

A fragrant perennial plant to 75 cm/2^1/$_2$ ft high with small oval leaves and clusters of white or mauve flowers. Grow in full sun in a well-drained soil and keep trimmed to encourage fresh, compact growth. Fresh leaves are used in tomato dishes, with any of the cabbage family and green beans. Marjoram is an excellent addition to spicy meat dishes. It can be included in meat sauces for pasta, meat loaves and rice stuffings for vegetables.

MINT

There are many varieties of mint, but spearmint (*Mentha spicata*) and applemint (*Mentha suaveolens*) are the two most commonly used in cooking. They are fast-growing perennials which prefer a rich, moist soil and light shade. Freshly chopped mint can be used with peas, new potatoes, courgettes (zucchini) and mixed green salad. Also good in fruit salads, cooling drinks, jellies, vinegar and lamb sauce.

OREGANO

A small spreading perennial to around 50 cm/20 in. Small, pungent leaves and tiny white or mauve flowers. Grow in a well-drained soil in a sunny position. The common confusion between marjoram and oregano can be resolved by realising that the cultivated marjoram comes from the wild oregano and that the first has a sweet flavour and the second a strong, peppery one. Fresh marjoram leaves are used to season salads and many tomato dishes, especially tomato sauces used with pasta. It is also used with aubergines (eggplant), beans, courgettes (zucchini) and cheese.

PARSLEY

A biennial plant to 60 cm/2 ft high with flat or curly leaves. Parsley is grown from seed which should be sown direct in spring and summer. Parsley likes a rich, well-drained soil in partial or full sun, and responds to frequent feeding. It is one of the best herbs of all and can be added to soups, stews, casseroles, sauces and stuffings. Always include the chopped stems as they are full of flavour and nutriment.

ROSEMARY

A Mediterranean evergreen shrub to around 1.5 m/5 ft high. It has thin, dark-green leaves, silver on the underside, highly aromatic; the pale blue flowers grow along the stems as well as at the tips. Choose a sheltered, sunny spot for planting, preferably against a wall, or in a corner, as rosemary needs all the protection it can get. The leaves, used either fresh or dried, are good with meat dishes, particularly lamb. The flavour is strong so they should be used sparingly.

SAGE

A small perennial shrub with soft, grey-green leaves and blue flowers during summer. Grow in a sunny, well-drained position and trim regularly. Give it plenty of water during summer. The leaves, used either fresh or dried, have a strong, clean flavour which cuts the grease of fatty foods. Use chopped fresh leaves sparingly in salads, potato dishes and with cheese. Use with pork and veal and in seasoning.

SAVORY, SUMMER

An annual to 60 cm/2 ft high with tender, narrow leaves of brownish-green and tiny flowers from pink to lavender. Grow in a sunny, well-drained position with plenty of organic matter added. Summer savory grows easily from seed in both warm and temperate climates. It is traditionally served with broad beans, cooked green beans and green bean salad. Also good in stuffings, rice, soups, sauces and stews.

SAVORY, WINTER

A semi-prostrate perennial with narrow green leaves and pale blue flowers. Likes full sun and a well-drained soil with plenty of organic matter added. Particularly good used in stuffings, rice, soups, sauces and stews.

SORREL

A perennial to 90 cm/3 ft tall with large bright green, arrow-shaped leaves that have a sharp lemony, bitter taste. Sorrel prefers a well-drained, rich soil in sun or semi-shade. Young fresh leaves are excellent in a mixed green salad. A few leaves can be added when cooking spinach. Used in the classic French sorrel soup. Use also in sauces and vegetable purées.

TARRAGON

French tarragon is a bushy perennial to around 1 m/3 ft high. It has dark slender leaves with a slight anise flavour. Grow in a moderately rich, well-drained soil in a sunny spot. French tarragon can only be propagated by division. Use with fish, shellfish, poultry, game, veal, liver, kidneys and in egg dishes. Tarragon vinegar is an essential ingredient in Béarnaise sauce.

THYME

A strongly aromatic shrubby perennial to around 45 cm/18 in high. It has tiny, oval leaves and bears pretty pastel-coloured flowers. There are many varieties including lemon thyme, caraway thyme and a pretty variegated type. All thymes like a sunny position with a light, well-drained soil. Trim to keep compact. Thyme is one of the most successful herbs for drying. Use fresh leaves sparingly with most vegetables including beetroot, tomatoes and courgettes (zucchini). Use in casseroles, meat dishes, pâtés and stuffings.

Basil

Sage

Chives

Parsley

Dill

Rosemary

Coriander

Mint

Oregano

Thyme

AT-A-GLANCE HERB GUIDE

HERB	SOUPS	MAIN DISHES
Angelica		
Basil	Tomato and fish soups	Fish dishes, meat loaves, casseroles
Bay	All soups and stocks	Meat, fish and poultry dishes
Caraway	Vegetable soups	Veal and pork dishes
Chervil	Fish and vegetable soups	Chicken, egg, cheese dishes, casseroles
Chives	Chilled soups, vichysoisse	Egg dishes, meat and chicken dishes
Coriander – fresh	Chilled soups	Oriental and Middle Eastern cooking, seafood, poultry, meat dishes
Curry plant	Fish and spiced soups	Seafood, all curries, casseroles and stews
Dill – fresh	Fish and vegetable soups	Fish, lamb and pork dishes
Fennel – fresh	Fish and vegetable soups	Chicken, fish, pork and egg dishes
Marjoram	Vegetable and meat soups	Casseroles, meat, marinades, meat loaf
Mint	Summer soups	Lamb dishes, trout
Oregano	Minestrone and tomato soups	Italian dishes, pasta and egg dishes, quiches, pizza
Parsley	All soups	All fish, poultry, meat and egg dishes, pasta
Rosemary	Meat stocks, chicken and tomato soups	Lamb and chicken dishes
Sage	Minestrone, chicken, tomato, celery and lentil soups	Meat loaf, pork, cheese and egg dishes
Savory	Vegetable soups	Beef, pork, egg and cheese dishes, pork pies, sausages, dishes made using pulses
Sorrel	Sorrel and vegetable soups	Omelettes, chicken and veal dishes
Tarragon	Fish and tomato soups	Fish, chicken and some egg dishes
Thyme	Vegetable and meat soups and stocks	Meat, chicken and pasta dishes

VEGETABLE DISHES	DESSERTS AND BAKED PRODUCTS	OTHER USES
	Stems are candied and used for decoration, cook with fruit	
Tomato and green salads, baked vegetables dishes		Dips, savouries, herb sandwiches, pasta sauces, stuffings
Vegetable casseroles	Place a leaf on a baked rice pudding or a baked custard	Flavour pâtés and terrines
Vegetable dishes, especially good with cabbage dishes, coleslaw and salads	Biscuits, breads, cakes, pastries	Stewed fruit
Salads, root vegetable dishes	Savoury breads and biscuits	Herb butters, meat sauces
Salads, potato dishes		Dips, herb butters, garnish
Green salads, oriental dishes		Dips, pickles
		Stuffings for veal and game
Especially good with cucumber and cauliflower		Fish sauces, cheese dips
Salads		Stuffings, salad dressings
Tomato dishes, potato and vegetable casseroles	Herb scones	Sauces, herb butters, stuffings
New potatoes, peas, carrots, salads	Fruit salads, ice cream	Summer drinks, mint sauce, stuffings
Onions, potatoes, peppers	Herb bread	Pâtés, stuffings
All vegetables and salads	Herb and savoury breads	Dressings, stuffings, garnish for most savoury dishes
Aubergines (eggplant), tomatoes, cabbage	Herb and savoury breads and scones	Dressings, stuffings, dumplings, pâtés
Salads, vegetarian casseroles	Savoury breads and scones	Herbal teas
Broad and green beans		Stuffings for pork and veal
Spinach		Stuffings for veal, chicken and lamb
Mushrooms, carrots, salads		Sauces, stuffings and dressings
Most vegetable dishes		Sauces, stuffings, herbal teas

chapter three

SATISFYING SOUPS

Filling and nutritious
soups, broths and potages
have always been the mainstay
of the family diet. The basis of a
really tasty soup is a good stock
so it is well worth making your own.
In this chapter you will find recipes
for soups that make great first
courses and some that are
meals in themselves.

Hearty Vegetable Soup,
Creamy Beef and Mushroom Soup,
Red Onion Soup

MUSHROOM AND BURGUNDY SOUP

This robust mushroom soup is quick and easy to make. It is ideal as a first course or light meal.

Serves 6

- [ ] **60 g/2 oz butter**
- [ ] **2 onions, chopped**
- [ ] **500 g/1 lb flat mushrooms, sliced**
- [ ] **2 large potatoes, diced**
- [ ] **125 mL/4 fl oz burgundy or red wine**
- [ ] **375 mL/12 fl oz beef stock**
- [ ] **1 teaspoon ground nutmeg**
- [ ] **500 mL/16 fl oz milk**
- [ ] **freshly ground black pepper**

1   Melt 30 g/1 oz butter in a heavy-based saucepan, add onions and three-quarters of the mushrooms and cook over a medium heat, stirring frequently, for 5 minutes.
2   Add potatoes, wine, stock and nutmeg and bring to the boil. Reduce heat and simmer for 15 minutes or until potatoes are tender. Remove pan from heat and set aside to cool slightly.
3   Transfer vegetable mixture to a food processor or blender and process until smooth. Return to a clean pan, stir in milk and season to taste with black pepper. Cook over a low heat, stirring occasionally, until soup is hot.
4   Melt remaining butter in a large frying pan, add remaining mushrooms and cook for 4-5 minutes. Stir mushrooms into hot soup and serve immediately.

HEARTY VEGETABLE SOUP

Serves 6

- [ ] **100 g/3$\frac{1}{2}$ oz pearl barley**
- [ ] **1.5 litres/2$\frac{1}{2}$ pt water**
- [ ] **45 g/1$\frac{1}{2}$ oz butter**
- [ ] **1 large onion, chopped**
- [ ] **2 cloves garlic, crushed**
- [ ] **1 large carrot, sliced**
- [ ] **1 large potato, cubed**
- [ ] **3 stalks celery, sliced**
- [ ] **1 turnip, diced**
- [ ] **1 large parsnip, diced**
- [ ] **5 tomatoes, peeled, seeded and chopped**
- [ ] **185 mL/6 fl oz tomato purée**
- [ ] **3 tablespoons finely chopped fresh coriander**

1   Place barley and water in a large bowl and set aside to soak overnight.
2   Melt butter in a large heavy-based saucepan and cook onion and garlic over a low heat for 5 minutes or until onion is soft.
3   Add carrot, potato, celery, turnip, parsnip, tomatoes, tomato purée, barley and soaking water to pan. Bring to the boil, then reduce heat and simmer, stirring occasionally, for 20 minutes or until vegetables are tender.
4   Ladle soup into bowls, sprinkle with coriander and serve immediately.

RED ONION SOUP

The secret to this wonderful soup is in the slow cooking of the onions and garlic at the beginning.

Serves 6

- [ ] **60 g/2 oz butter**
- [ ] **1 tablespoon olive oil**
- [ ] **4 large red onions, sliced**
- [ ] **12 whole cloves garlic, peeled**
- [ ] **2 tablespoons flour**
- [ ] **1 teaspoon sugar**
- [ ] **2 x 440 g/14 oz canned beef consommé**
- [ ] **750 mL/1$\frac{1}{4}$ pt water**
- [ ] **4 tablespoons red wine**
- [ ] **1 tablespoon brandy**
- [ ] **1 long bread stick, cut into 12 slices**
- [ ] **3 tablespoons melted butter**
- [ ] **250 g/8 oz grated mature Cheddar**
- [ ] **1 tablespoon chopped fresh parsley**

1   Heat butter and oil in a large, heavy-based saucepan and cook onions and garlic over a low heat for 15-20 minutes or until onions are golden.
2   Add flour and cook over a medium heat, stirring constantly until flour turns a light straw colour. Stir in sugar, consommé, water, wine and brandy. Bring to the boil, then reduce heat and simmer, stirring occasionally, for 30 minutes.
3   Brush bread slices on both sides with melted butter. Place under a preheated grill and toast one side. Sprinkle untoasted side of bread slices with cheese and return to grill until cheese melts.
4   Place 2 slices of bread into each serving bowl. Ladle soup over bread and sprinkle with parsley. Serve immediately.

POTATO AND BRUSSELS SPROUTS SOUP

Serves 4

- [ ] **250 g/8 oz Brussels sprouts, trimmed**
- [ ] **2 large potatoes, diced**
- [ ] **1 litre/1$\frac{3}{4}$ pt chicken or vegetable stock**
- [ ] **125 mL/4 fl oz milk**
- [ ] **freshly ground black pepper**
- [ ] **2 tablespoons chopped walnuts**

1   Place Brussels sprouts, potatoes and stock in a large saucepan and bring to the boil. Reduce heat, cover and simmer for 20-25 minutes or until potatoes are tender. Remove pan from heat and set aside to cool slightly.
2   Place vegetable mixture in a food processor or blender and process until smooth. Return to a clean pan, stir in milk and season to taste with black pepper. Cook over a low heat, stirring occasionally, until soup is hot. To serve, ladle soup into bowls and sprinkle with walnuts.

Nutrition tip: The best vegetables for vitamin C are peppers, chillies, parsley, watercress, broccoli, Brussels sprouts, cauliflower and kohlrabi. These have a higher concentration of vitamin C than citrus fruit but are often overlooked as sources of vitamin C.

CREAMY BEEF AND MUSHROOM SOUP

Serves 6

- [ ] **2 tablespoons vegetable oil**
- [ ] **750 g/1$\frac{1}{2}$ lb lean topside steak, cut into 1 cm/$\frac{1}{2}$ in cubes**
- [ ] **60 g/2 oz butter**
- [ ] **4 carrots, sliced**
- [ ] **2 leeks, sliced**
- [ ] **350 g/11 oz button mushrooms, sliced**
- [ ] **2 cloves garlic, crushed**
- [ ] **3 tablespoons flour**
- [ ] **2 litres/3$\frac{1}{2}$ pt beef stock**
- [ ] **2 tablespoons sherry**
- [ ] **4 potatoes, diced**
- [ ] **sour cream**
- [ ] **2 tablespoons snipped fresh chives**

1   Heat oil in a large, heavy-based saucepan and cook meat in batches

over a medium heat until browned on all sides. Remove meat from pan and set aside.

2   Melt butter in pan and cook carrots and leeks over a low heat for 5 minutes or until leeks are soft. Add mushrooms and garlic and cook for 4-5 minutes longer.

3   Stir in flour and cook for 1 minute. Remove pan from heat and gradually blend in stock and sherry. Bring to the boil, then reduce heat. Return meat to pan with potatoes and simmer for 30 minutes or until meat is tender.

4   Ladle soup into serving bowls, top with a spoonful of sour cream and sprinkle with chives.

Potato and Brussels Sprouts Soup, Minestrone Soup

MINESTRONE SOUP

Minestrone is a substantial main meal soup, both tasty and filling. You can vary the vegetables depending on what is available.

Serves 8

- ☐ **2 tablespoons olive oil**
- ☐ **3 cloves garlic, crushed**
- ☐ **1 onion, chopped**
- ☐ **1 large potato, diced**
- ☐ **1 carrot, diced**
- ☐ **2 large courgettes (zucchini), diced**
- ☐ **125 g/4 oz green beans, trimmed and sliced**
- ☐ **2 tablespoons finely chopped fresh parsley**
- ☐ **1 tablespoon finely chopped fresh basil**
- ☐ **1 teaspoon finely chopped fresh oregano**
- ☐ **3 tablespoons tomato purée**

- ☐ **1.5 litres/2¹/₂ pt chicken stock**
- ☐ **freshly ground black pepper**
- ☐ **440 g/14 oz canned red kidney beans, drained**
- ☐ **100 g/3¹/₂ oz macaroni noodles**
- ☐ **¹/₂ cabbage, finely shredded**

1   Heat oil in a large heavy-based saucepan. Cook garlic and onion for 2-3 minutes. Stir in potato, carrot, courgettes (zucchini) and beans. Cook for 3-4 minutes, stirring frequently.

2   Combine parsley, basil, oregano, tomato purée and stock. Pour over vegetables in pan. Season to taste with black pepper. Cover and simmer for 30 minutes or until vegetables are tender.

3   Add kidney beans. Bring to the boil, drop in macaroni and cook for a further 20 minutes. Add cabbage during last minute of cooking.

CHICKEN AND AVOCADO SOUP

Serves 4

- ☐ **15 g/¹/₂ oz butter**
- ☐ **1 onion, finely chopped**
- ☐ **1 large potato, diced**
- ☐ **1 litre/1³/₄ pt chicken stock**
- ☐ **315 g/10 oz canned sweet corn kernels, drained**
- ☐ **1 cooked chicken, flesh removed and chopped**
- ☐ **freshly ground black pepper**
- ☐ **4 tablespoons sour cream**
- ☐ **1 avocado, stoned, peeled and diced**

1   Melt butter in a large saucepan, add onion and cook, stirring frequently, for 4-5 minutes or until onion is soft. Stir in potato and stock, cover and bring to the boil, then reduce heat and simmer for 15-20 minutes or until potato is tender.
2   Add sweet corn, chicken and black pepper to taste and cook for 5-6 minutes longer or until soup is heated through. To serve, spoon soup into bowls and top with sour cream and avocado.

QUICK SEAFOOD SOUP

Serves 4

- ☐ **4 firm white fish fillets, skinned and bones removed**
- ☐ **30 g/1 oz butter**
- ☐ **2 leeks, sliced**
- ☐ **440 g/14 oz canned tomatoes, undrained and mashed**
- ☐ **1 litre/1³/₄ pt chicken or fish stock**
- ☐ **2 tablespoons tomato purée**
- ☐ **12 oysters**
- ☐ **8 cooked mussels in shells**
- ☐ **1 tablespoon chopped fresh basil**
- ☐ **¹/₂ teaspoon brown sugar**

1   Cut fish fillets into pieces. Melt butter in a large saucepan, add leeks and cook, stirring, for 4-5 minutes or until leeks are soft.
2   Add tomatoes, stock and tomato purée and bring to the boil. Stir in fish, oysters, mussels, basil and sugar and simmer for 5 minutes or until fish is cooked. Serve immediately.

CREAMY ASPARAGUS SOUP

A swirl of unflavoured natural yogurt and freshly chopped chives make a wonderful garnish for this flavoursome soup.

Serves 4

- ☐ **440 g/14 oz canned asparagus cuts**
- ☐ **375 mL/12 fl oz chicken stock**
- ☐ **2 tablespoons snipped fresh chives**
- ☐ **1 clove garlic, crushed**
- ☐ **pinch ground nutmeg**
- ☐ **250 mL/8 fl oz milk**
- ☐ **freshly ground black pepper**

1   Drain asparagus, reserving 125 mL/ 4 fl oz of liquid. Place asparagus cuts, reserved liquid, stock, chives, garlic and nutmeg in a food processor or blender. Process until smooth.
2   Transfer mixture to a saucepan. Bring to the boil, reduce heat and stir in milk. Heat gently, without boiling. Season to taste with pepper.

Creamy Asparagus Soup

BEEF AND HERB DUMPLING SOUP

A hearty soup that is a meal in itself.

Serves 6

- ☐ **60 g/2 oz butter**
- ☐ **2 onions, chopped**
- ☐ **4 rashers bacon, trimmed of fat and chopped**
- ☐ **750 g/1¹/₂ lb lean beef, cut into thin strips**
- ☐ **60 g/2 oz flour, sifted**
- ☐ **1 tablespoon paprika**
- ☐ **2 litres/3¹/₂ pt beef stock**
- ☐ **2 red peppers, halved and roasted**
- ☐ **4 tablespoons tomato purée**
- ☐ **1 tablespoon caraway seeds**
- ☐ **freshly ground black pepper**
- ☐ **2 tablespoons finely chopped fresh coriander**

HERB DUMPLINGS
- ☐ **250 g/8 oz self-raising flour, sifted**
- ☐ **60 g/2 oz butter, cut into small pieces**
- ☐ **2 eggs, lightly beaten**
- ☐ **4 tablespoons milk**
- ☐ **2 tablespoons chopped fresh herbs, such as parsley, coriander, rosemary or thyme**

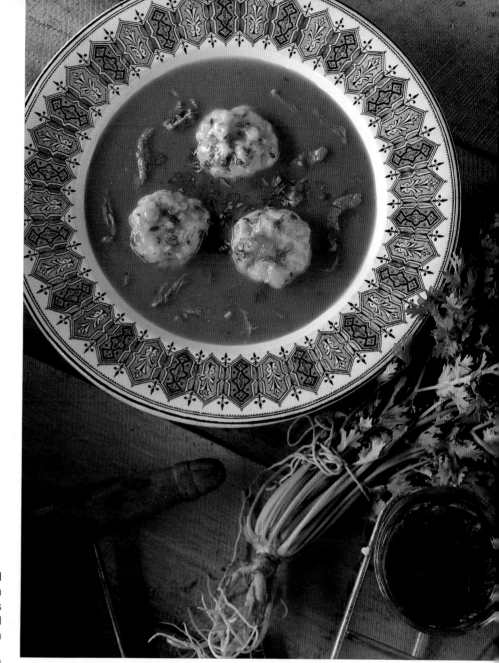

1 Melt butter in a large, heavy-based saucepan and cook onions and bacon over a medium-high heat for 4-5 minutes or until bacon is crisp. Using a slotted spoon remove onions and bacon from pan and set aside.

2 Add beef to pan in small batches and cook over a medium heat to brown all sides. Remove from pan and drain on absorbent kitchen paper.

3 Combine flour and paprika. Add to pan and cook over a medium heat for 1 minute. Remove pan from heat and gradually blend in stock. Return onion mixture and meat to pan. Bring to the boil, then reduce heat and simmer for 1¹/₂ hours or until meat is tender.

4 Remove skin from red peppers and chop. Add red peppers, tomato purée and caraway seeds to pan and simmer for 15 minutes longer. Season to taste with black pepper.

5 To make dumplings, place self-raising flour in a large mixing bowl. Rub in butter with fingertips until mixture resembles coarse breadcrumbs. Combine eggs, milk and herbs. Pour into flour mixture and mix to a smooth dough. Shape tablespoons of mixture into small balls. Cook dumplings in boiling water in a large saucepan for 10-12 minutes or until they rise to the surface. Remove dumplings using a slotted spoon. To serve, place a few dumplings in each bowl, ladle soup over and sprinkle with parsley. Serve immediately.

Cook's tip: To roast peppers, place them under a hot grill and cook until the skin blisters and chars. Place in a paper or freezer bag and leave for 10 minutes or until cool enough to handle. The skins will then slip off.

Beef and Herb Dumpling Soup

SPICY PUMPKIN SOUP

A less spicy soup can be made by omitting the coriander, cumin and chilli powder. Instead, stir in 2 teaspoons chopped fresh parsley with the cream.

Serves 4

- ☐ 1 tablespoon vegetable oil
- ☐ 1 onion, chopped
- ☐ 1 clove garlic, crushed
- ☐ ½ teaspoon ground coriander
- ☐ ½ teaspoon ground cumin
- ☐ ½ teaspoon chilli powder
- ☐ 1 kg/2 lb pumpkin, chopped
- ☐ 1 litre/1³/₄ pt chicken stock
- ☐ 90 mL/3 fl oz cream (double)
- ☐ freshly ground black pepper

1   Heat oil in a saucepan and cook onion over a medium heat for 3-4 minutes or until soft. Add garlic, coriander, cumin and chilli powder and cook for 1 minute longer.
2   Add pumpkin and stock to pan, bring to the boil, then reduce heat and simmer for 15-20 minutes or until pumpkin is tender. Remove pan from heat and set aside to cool slightly. Place pumpkin and cooking liquid in batches in a food processor or blender and process until smooth.
3   Return soup to a clean saucepan, stir in cream, season to taste with black pepper and cook over a medium heat, without boiling, until heated.

Serving suggestion: Accompany soup with crusty bread and follow with a crisp garden salad.

Cook's tip: Instead of using a food processor to purée the soup, you can remove the cooked pumpkin from the stock and mash it, using a potato masher or fork, then mix in cooking liquid and complete as in recipe.

Spicy Pumpkin Soup, Creamy Broccoli Soup

CHILLED TOMATO SOUP

Serve this delightfully refreshing, low-calorie soup, with Tomato Minted Ice Cubes if desired.

Serves 4

- ☐ 1 tablespoon olive oil
- ☐ 1 onion, chopped
- ☐ 1 clove garlic, crushed
- ☐ 1 litre/1³/₄ pt vegetable stock
- ☐ 2 tablespoons finely chopped fresh mint
- ☐ 440 g/14 oz canned tomatoes, drained
- ☐ 2 courgettes (zucchini), grated
- ☐ freshly ground black pepper

1   Heat oil in a saucepan and cook onion and garlic over a medium heat for 3-4 minutes or until onion is soft. Add stock and mint, bring to the boil, then reduce heat and simmer for 5 minutes.
2   Place tomatoes and stock mixture in a food processor or blender and process until smooth. Stir in courgettes (zucchini) and season to taste with black pepper. Chill well before serving.

Serving suggestion: Place three Tomato Minted Ice Cubes (see recipe) in a serving bowl and pour chilled soup over.

Freeze it: Half the soup can be frozen in an airtight freezerproof container. Defrost at room temperature for 2-3 hours and then rechill, or defrost in the refrigerator overnight.

TOMATO MINTED ICE CUBES

- ☐ fresh mint leaves
- ☐ 185 mL/6 fl oz tomato juice
- ☐ 185 mL/6 fl oz water

Place a mint leaf in each space of an ice cube tray. Mix together tomato juice and water and pour into ice cube tray. Freeze.

Cook's tip: To store ice cubes, remove from tray and store in a sealed freezer bag.

CREAMY BROCCOLI SOUP

Serves 4

- [ ] **1 tablespoon vegetable oil**
- [ ] **1 onion, chopped**
- [ ] **1 litre/1³/₄ pt chicken stock**
- [ ] **1 potato, chopped**
- [ ] **375 g/12 oz broccoli florets**
- [ ] **1 tablespoon chopped fresh parsley**
- [ ] **freshly ground black pepper**

1 Heat oil in a saucepan and cook onion over a medium heat for 3-4 minutes or until soft. Add stock, potato and broccoli, bring to the boil, then reduce heat and simmer for 10-15 minutes or until potato is tender.
2 Transfer mixture to a food processor or blender and process until smooth.
3 Return soup to a clean saucepan, stir in parsley and season to taste with black pepper. Cook over a medium heat until heated.

Serving suggestion: Serve with a swirl of cream and accompany with grilled cheese-topped bagels.

CHICKEN AND CORN SOUP

Serves 4

- [ ] **1 tablespoon vegetable oil**
- [ ] **1 onion, sliced**
- [ ] **pinch ground cumin**
- [ ] **1 potato, diced**
- [ ] **1 litre/1³/₄ pt chicken stock**
- [ ] **185 g/6 oz cooked chicken, chopped**
- [ ] **220 g/7 oz canned sweet corn kernels**
- [ ] **freshly ground black pepper**
- [ ] **1 tablespoon finely chopped fresh parsley**

1 Heat oil in a saucepan and cook onion and cumin over a medium heat for 3-4 minutes or until soft. Add potato and stock, bring to the boil, then reduce heat and simmer for 10-15 minutes or until potato is tender.
2 Remove onion and potato, using a slotted spoon, and place in a food processor or blender and process until smooth. Return potato purée to stock mixture and whisk to combine. Stir in chicken and sweet corn and cook over a low heat until heated. Season to taste with black pepper.

Serving suggestion: Sprinkle with parsley and serve with a slice of crusty bread.

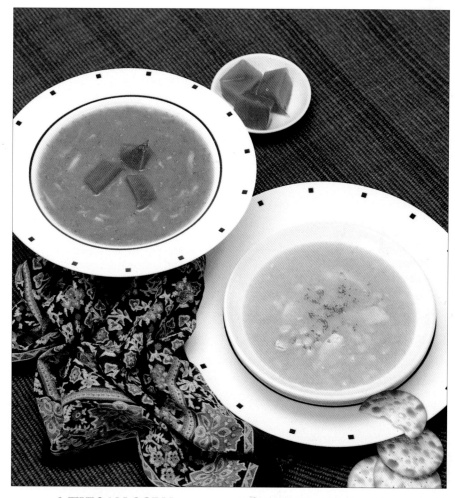

MEXICAN CORN CHOWDER

For a less spicy but just as delicious soup you can omit the chilli.

Serves 6

- [ ] **15 g/¹/₂ oz butter**
- [ ] **2 rashers bacon, chopped**
- [ ] **1 onion, finely chopped**
- [ ] **2 stalks celery, chopped**
- [ ] **1 small fresh red chilli, finely chopped**
- [ ] **500 mL/16 fl oz chicken stock**
- [ ] **1 teaspoon ground cumin**
- [ ] **1 teaspoon dried thyme**
- [ ] **2 tablespoons flour blended with 60 mL/2 fl oz milk**
- [ ] **440 mL/14 fl oz milk**
- [ ] **440 g/14 oz canned sweet corn kernels, drained**
- [ ] **freshly ground black pepper**

1 Melt butter in a large saucepan, add bacon, onion, celery and chilli and cook, stirring, for 4-5 minutes or until onion is soft.
2 Add stock, cumin and thyme and bring to the boil, reduce heat and simmer for 10 minutes.
3 Stir flour mixture into stock mixture, then stir in milk and sweet corn kernels. Cook, stirring constantly, until soup comes to the boil, then reduce heat and simmer for 5 minutes. Season to taste with black pepper.

Freeze it: Soups freeze well and can be frozen for up to 3 months. Remember when freezing any liquid to leave a 5 cm/2 in space between the liquid and the lid of the container as liquid expands during freezing.

*Chilled Tomato Soup,
Chicken and Corn Soup*

FRESH TOMATO SOUP

Bursting with flavour, this satisfying soup makes a great winter luncheon served with crusty bread, or try it chilled on hot summer days. If you find the soup is too tart, a teaspoon of sugar stirred into it will sweeten the flavour.

Serves 6

- [ ] 1 tablespoon olive oil
- [ ] 1 carrot, chopped
- [ ] 1 onion, chopped
- [ ] 2 stalks celery, chopped
- [ ] 1 clove garlic, crushed
- [ ] 6 tomatoes, peeled, seeded and chopped
- [ ] 440 g/14 oz canned tomatoes, drained and chopped
- [ ] 1 litre/1³/₄ pt chicken stock
- [ ] 1 teaspoon chopped fresh thyme, or ¹/₄ teaspoon dried thyme
- [ ] ¹/₂ teaspoon Tabasco sauce
- [ ] 250 mL/8 fl oz cream (double)
- [ ] 2 tablespoons finely chopped fresh basil
- [ ] freshly ground black pepper

1   Heat oil in a large saucepan, add carrot, onion, celery and garlic and cook for 3-4 minutes or until onion softens.
2   Stir in fresh and canned tomatoes, chicken stock, thyme and Tabasco sauce. Bring to the boil and simmer, uncovered, for 30 minutes. Remove from heat.
3   Place in a food processor or blender and process until smooth. Return soup to a clean pan and bring just to a simmer. Remove from heat and stir in cream and basil. Season to taste with black pepper.

Cook's tip: When serving soup as a starter, allow approximately 250 mL/8 fl oz of soup per person. For soup as a main course, serves may be a little larger.

CONSOMME

Consommé is the French word for a soup based on meat stock that has been enriched, concentrated and then clarified. It is the simplest, yet most sophisticated, soup and you may serve it hot or cold. The perfect garnish for consommé is thin strips of blanched carrot and leek.

Serves 6

- [ ] 1 litre/1³/₄ pt cold beef stock
- [ ] 250 g/8 oz minced beef
- [ ] 1 small onion, chopped
- [ ] 1 small carrot, chopped
- [ ] 1 small leek, chopped
- [ ] 4 whole black peppercorns
- [ ] bouquet garni
- [ ] 2 egg whites, lightly beaten
- [ ] 1 tablespoon dry sherry

1   Place stock, beef, onion, carrot, leek, peppercorns, bouquet garni and egg whites in a large saucepan, bring slowly to the boil, whisking continuously. Reduce heat, stir in sherry and simmer gently for 1¹/₂ hours, without stirring.
2   Remove from heat and set aside to stand for 20 minutes. A thick brown scum will have formed on the surface of the stock, skim off scum and strain stock carefully through muslin. Remove fat from surface using absorbent kitchen paper.

Cook's tip: Consommé should be clear. If your consommé is cloudy it may be because the stock was greasy, unstrained or of poor quality. Whisking the stock after it reaches boiling point or not allowing it to stand before straining will also cause the consommé to become cloudy. Remember that the pan and muslin cloth must be very clean when you are making consommé.

CREAM OF MUSHROOM AND HAZELNUT SOUP

A delightfully creamy soup that makes a great starter for a special occasion or is a delicious meal in itself served with crusty French bread and a crispy salad.

Serves 4

- ☐ **60 g/2 oz butter**
- ☐ **3 tablespoons flour**
- ☐ **1 litre/1³/₄ pt milk**
- ☐ **2 teaspoons oil**
- ☐ **6 spring onions, chopped**
- ☐ **125 g/4 oz button mushrooms, sliced**
- ☐ **60 g/2 oz hazelnuts, toasted, skins removed, and finely chopped**
- ☐ **1 teaspoon paprika**
- ☐ **125 mL/4 fl oz cream (double)**
- ☐ **freshly ground black pepper**

1 Melt butter in a medium saucepan. Stir in flour and cook for 1 minute. Remove from heat and gradually stir in milk. Return pan to heat and bring slowly to the boil, stirring constantly. Simmer for 3 minutes, remove from heat and set aside.

2 Heat oil in a medium saucepan and cook spring onions for 2 minutes. Add mushrooms, hazelnuts and paprika and cook for 2-3 minutes longer. Stir in milk mixture, bring to the boil, then reduce heat and simmer gently for 10 minutes.

3 Remove from heat, place in a food processor or blender and process until smooth. Return soup to a clean pan and reheat gently. Stir in cream and season to taste with black pepper.

Cook's tip: For a taste variation, replace hazelnuts with toasted, finely chopped almonds.

Consommé, Fresh Tomato Soup, Cream of Mushroom and Hazelnut Soup

CURRIED CHICKEN SOUP

Serves 6

- ☐ 60 g/2 oz butter
- ☐ 2 onions, chopped
- ☐ 2 cloves garlic, crushed
- ☐ 2 large parsnips, chopped
- ☐ 4 stalks celery, chopped
- ☐ 3 tablespoons flour
- ☐ 1 tablespoon curry powder
- ☐ 1.5 litres/2^1/$_2$ pt chicken stock
- ☐ 185 g/6 oz fresh or frozen green peas
- ☐ 500 g/1 lb chopped, cooked chicken
- ☐ 250 g/8 oz sour cream
- ☐ 3 tablespoons finely chopped fresh flat leaf parsley
- ☐ 2 tablespoons chopped fresh dill

1 Melt butter in a large saucepan, cook onions, garlic, parsnips and celery over a low heat for 5-6 minutes or until vegetables are soft. Stir in flour and curry powder and cook for 1 minute longer.

2 Remove pan from heat and gradually blend in stock. Cook over a medium heat, stirring constantly until mixture boils and thickens. Reduce heat, and stir in peas and chicken and cook for 10 minutes.

3 Remove pan from heat and whisk in sour cream, then stir in parsley and dill. Cook over a low heat, stirring frequently, for 3-4 minutes or until warmed through. Serve immediately.

PEA AND HAM SOUP

Variations of this soup have been around since the Middle Ages. This one with ham is perfect for a fireside supper.

Serves 6

- ☐ 750 g/1^1/$_2$ lb dried split peas, rinsed
- ☐ 4 litres/7 pt water
- ☐ 500 g/1 lb bacon bones
- ☐ 4 onions, finely chopped
- ☐ 4 tablespoons chopped celery leaves
- ☐ 4 stalks celery, chopped
- ☐ 250 g/8 oz ham, cut into 1 cm/^{1}/$_2$ in cubes
- ☐ freshly ground black pepper

1   Place split peas and water in a large, heavy-based saucepan and set aside to stand overnight.

2   Add bacon bones to pan with peas. Bring to the boil, then reduce heat and simmer for 2 hours or until soup thickens.

3   Stir in onion, celery leaves and celery and cook over a low heat for 20 minutes longer.

4   Remove bacon bones from soup and discard. Add ham and cook until heated through. Season to taste with black pepper.

5   Ladle soup into serving bowls.

POTATO BACON CHOWDER

Serves 6

- [ ] **250 g/8 oz bacon, chopped**
- [ ] **30 g/1 oz butter**
- [ ] **2 large onions, chopped**
- [ ] **4 stalks celery, chopped**
- [ ] **2 teaspoons dried thyme**
- [ ] **2 tablespoons flour**
- [ ] **1.5 litres/2¹/₂ pt chicken stock**
- [ ] **2 large potatoes, cubed**
- [ ] **300 g/9¹/₂ oz sour cream**
- [ ] **3 tablespoons chopped fresh parsley**
- [ ] **2 tablespoons snipped fresh chives**

1   Place bacon in a large, heavy-based saucepan and cook over a medium heat for 5 minutes or until golden and crisp. Remove from pan and drain on absorbent kitchen paper.

2   Melt butter in pan and cook onions, celery and thyme over a low heat for 4-5 minutes or until onion is soft.

3   Return bacon to pan, then stir in flour and cook for 1 minute. Remove pan from heat and gradually blend in stock. Bring to the boil, then reduce heat. Add potatoes and cook for 10 minutes or until potatoes are tender.

4   Remove pan from heat and stir in sour cream and parsley. Return to heat and cook without boiling, stirring constantly, for 1-2 minutes. Ladle soup into bowls, sprinkle with chives and serve immediately.

Left: Pea and Ham Soup,
Curried Chicken Soup
Right: Potato Bacon Chowder

chapter four

●

SENSATIONAL STARTERS

Designed to stimulate the
taste buds, these recipes are the
perfect start to any meal. For a
barbecue you might like to serve
the Bite-sized Kebabs, while the
Smoked Salmon and Watercress
Roulade makes a great first
course for an elegant
dinner party.

Sesame Prawn Balls,
Beef and Vegetable Lettuce Cups

SESAME PRAWN BALLS

These delicious morsels make a perfect light meal that would be ideal for a luncheon.

Serves 6

- [ ] 1 kg/2 lb medium uncooked prawns, shelled and deveined
- [ ] 1 onion, chopped finely
- [ ] ¹/₂ teaspoon garam masala
- [ ] ¹/₄ teaspoon ground turmeric
- [ ] 185 g/6 oz rice flour
- [ ] 1 teaspoon sesame oil
- [ ] 15 g/¹/₂ oz finely chopped fresh coriander
- [ ] 3 tablespoons sesame seeds
- [ ] oil for deep-frying
- [ ] shredded lettuce

SAUCE
- [ ] 1 tablespoon cornflour
- [ ] 250 mL/8 fl oz chicken stock
- [ ] 125 mL/4 fl oz prepared tamarind sauce
- [ ] 2 tablespoons soy sauce
- [ ] 1 tablespoon lime juice
- [ ] 1 tablespoon finely chopped coriander

1   Place prawns, onion and spices in a food processor or blender and process until smooth. Stir in rice flour, oil and coriander. Cover and refrigerate mixture for 1 hour. Using wet hands, roll mixture into small balls, then roll in seeds. Refrigerate for 1 hour.
2   To make sauce, blend cornflour with stock in saucepan. Stir in tamarind sauce, soy sauce, lime juice and coriander. Bring to the boil, stirring constantly, reduce heat and simmer, uncovered, for 5 minutes.
3   Heat oil in a large saucepan. Cook balls until golden and cooked through. Serve balls on a bed of shredded lettuce with sauce spooned over.

GARLIC SESAME PRAWNS

Serves 6

- [ ] 1 teaspoon sesame oil
- [ ] 1 kg/2 lb uncooked prawns, shelled and deveined, tails left intact
- [ ] 2 cloves garlic, crushed
- [ ] 1 teaspoon grated fresh ginger
- [ ] 2 tablespoons dry sherry
- [ ] 185 mL/6 fl oz fish or chicken stock

- [ ] 2 teaspoons soy sauce
- [ ] 60 g/2 oz canned pimento, finely chopped
- [ ] 2 tablespoons snipped fresh chives
- [ ] 1 tablespoon barbecue sauce
- [ ] 3 teaspoons cornflour blended with 3 tablespoons water
- [ ] freshly ground black pepper
- [ ] 2 tablespoons toasted sesame seeds

1   Heat oil in a nonstick frying pan, add prawns, garlic and ginger and stir-fry for 3-4 minutes or until prawns change colour.
2   Add sherry, stock, soy sauce, pimento, chives and barbecue sauce and cook for 2-3 minutes longer. Stir in cornflour mixture and cook, stirring constantly, until sauce boils and thickens. Season to taste with black pepper and serve sprinkled with sesame seeds.

MOZZARELLA PARCELS

This antipasto-style starter also makes a delicious lunch or supper dish, served with crusty bread.

Serves 4

- [ ] 4 spring onions
- [ ] 200 g/6¹/₂ oz mozzarella cheese
- [ ] 4 slices ham
- [ ] 12 sun-dried tomatoes or 4 tomatoes, sliced
- [ ] 24 green olives

LEMON DRESSING
- [ ] 1 clove garlic, crushed
- [ ] 2 tablespoons olive oil
- [ ] 1 tablespoon lemon juice
- [ ] 1 tablespoon chopped fresh basil
- [ ] freshly ground black pepper

1   Cut green tops from spring onions and place tops in a bowl. Reserve spring onion bulbs for another use. Pour boiling water over tops, then drain and cut into strips. Set aside.
2   Cut mozzarella cheese into four slices. Wrap each slice of mozzarella in a slice of ham and tie with a spring onion strip.
3   To make dressing, place garlic, oil, lemon juice, basil and black pepper to taste in a screwtop jar and shake well to combine. Arrange a Mozzarella Parcel, tomatoes and olives on individual serving plates or on a large platter. Drizzle with dressing and serve immediately.

BEEF AND VEGETABLE LETTUCE CUPS

These tasty lettuce cups make an attractive entertaining dish. The filling can be made up in advance then reheated just before placing in the lettuce cups.

Serves 8

- [ ] 1 tablespoon olive oil
- [ ] 500 g/1 lb minced beef
- [ ] 1 teaspoon ground cinnamon
- [ ] 1 teaspoon ground turmeric
- [ ] 1 teaspoon ground sweet paprika
- [ ] 2 tablespoons chopped fresh mint
- [ ] 2 tablespoons chopped fresh parsley
- [ ] 3 tablespoons tomato purée
- [ ] 125 mL/4 fl oz red wine
- [ ] 125 mL/4 fl oz beef stock
- [ ] 410 g/13 oz canned red kidney beans, drained and rinsed
- [ ] 2 tablespoons chopped pimento
- [ ] 2 red onions, sliced
- [ ] 250 g/8 oz baby yellow squash, chopped
- [ ] 250 g/8 oz mangetout (snow peas), sliced diagonally
- [ ] 8 large lettuce cups, washed, drained

1   Heat oil in a large frying pan or wok. Add beef and cook over a high heat for 10 minutes or until meat is well browned and all the liquid has evaporated. Stir in cinnamon, turmeric, paprika, mint, parsley, tomato purée, wine, stock, beans and pimento, and cook over a medium heat for 5 minutes.
2   Stir in onions, squash and mangetout (snow peas). Cook until vegetables are crisp but tender, and almost all liquid has evaporated. Spoon beef and vegetables into lettuce cups. Serve immediately.

MUSHROOM AND COURGETTES BREAD BASKETS

These delicious bread baskets make wonderful containers for all sorts of different foods. Try filling them with creamy curried vegetables or with salad.

Serves 6
Oven temperature 200°C, 400°F, Gas 6

☐ **1 loaf unsliced wholemeal bread**
☐ **vegetable oil**

MUSHROOM FILLING
☐ **30 g/1 oz butter**
☐ **1 clove garlic, crushed**
☐ **1 teaspoon ground cumin**
☐ **2 small courgettes (zucchini), cut into 5 cm/2 in lengths**
☐ **200 g/6¹/₂ oz button mushrooms**
☐ **100 g/3¹/₂ oz flat mushrooms, sliced**
☐ **100 g/3¹/₂ oz oyster mushrooms**
☐ **2 tablespoons lemon juice**
☐ **6 spring onions, cut into 5 cm/2 in pieces**
☐ **2 tablespoons finely chopped fresh mint**
☐ **freshly ground black pepper**
☐ **fresh mint sprigs**

1   Remove crusts from bread and cut into six thick slices. Remove centre from each slice. Leave base intact to form baskets. Brush all surfaces with oil and bake for 10-15 minutes or until baskets are golden in colour.

2   To make filling, melt butter in a frypan. Add garlic and cumin and cook for 1-2 minutes. Toss courgettes (zucchini) and cook for 3-4 minutes. Remove from pan and set aside.

3   Combine mushrooms with lemon juice and add to pan. Cook for 3-4 minutes. Return courgettes (zucchini) with spring onions to the pan and cook for 2-3 minutes longer. Stir in chopped mint and season to taste with pepper.

4   Spoon filling into baskets and garnish with mint sprigs.

Mushroom and Courgettes Bread Baskets

TABBOULEH-FILLED TOMATOES

Serves 4
Oven temperature 200°C, 400°F, Gas 6

☐ **4 large tomatoes**

TABBOULEH FILLING
☐ **3 tablespoons burghul (cracked wheat)**
☐ **8 spring onions, chopped**
☐ **3 cloves garlic, crushed**
☐ **3 tablespoons finely chopped fresh parsley**
☐ **2 tablespoons finely chopped fresh mint**
☐ **1 tablespoon olive oil**
☐ **freshly ground black pepper**

1   Cut tops from tomatoes with a sharp knife. Scoop out pulp using a teaspoon, chop and reserve. Place tomato shells upside down on absorbent kitchen paper to drain.

2   To make filling, place burghul (cracked wheat) in a bowl, cover with boiling water and set aside to soak for 10 minutes. Drain and place in a bowl, add reserved tomato pulp, spring onions, garlic, parsley, mint and oil and mix to combine. Season to taste with black pepper.

3   Spoon filling into tomato shells and place on a lightly greased baking tray and bake for 10 minutes or until heated through.

CHEESE CIGARS WITH CORIANDER PESTO

A pesto made of coriander is the perfect accompaniment to these tasty Cheese Cigars – serve as an indulgent snack or as a pre-dinner treat.

Makes 12

☐ **12 slices white sandwich bread, crusts removed**
☐ **2 teaspoons prepared hot English mustard**
☐ **4 tablespoons finely grated fresh Parmesan cheese**
☐ **60 g/2 oz grated mozzarella cheese**
☐ **1 tablespoon snipped fresh chives**
☐ **cayenne pepper**
☐ **1 egg, lightly beaten**
☐ **vegetable oil for cooking**

CORIANDER PESTO
☐ **3 large bunches/300 g/9½ oz fresh coriander**
☐ **2 cloves garlic, crushed**
☐ **60 g/2 oz pine nuts**
☐ **125 mL/4 fl oz olive oil**
☐ **60 g/2 oz grated fresh Parmesan cheese**

1   Roll each slice of bread with a rolling pin, to flatten as much as possible.

2   Combine mustard, Parmesan cheese, mozzarella cheese, chives, and cayenne pepper to taste in a bowl. Divide mixture between bread slices and spread over half of each bread slice. Brush unspread halves of bread slices with egg. Roll each slice up tightly using the egg to seal rolls. Arrange side by side on a tray. Cover and refrigerate until ready to cook.

3   Heat 2 cm/¾ in of oil in a frypan. When hot, cook cigars a few at a time until evenly golden all over. Drain on absorbent kitchen paper.

4   To make pesto, place coriander leaves, garlic and pine nuts in a food processor or blender and process until finely chopped. With machine running, slowly pour in oil and process mixture until smooth. Add cheese and process to blend. Serve with hot cigars.

Cheese Cigars with Coriander Pesto

CRUDITES WITH HERB MAYONNAISE

Serves 10

- ☐ **a selection of vegetables such as broccoli and cauliflower florets, carrot sticks and new baby potatoes**

HERB MAYONNAISE
- ☐ **30 g/1 oz fresh parsley sprigs**
- ☐ **30 g/1 oz fresh basil leaves**
- ☐ **125 g/4 oz mayonnaise**
- ☐ **90 g/ 3 oz sour cream**
- ☐ **2 teaspoons French mustard**
- ☐ **freshly ground black pepper**

1 Steam or microwave vegetables separately until just tender. Drain, refresh under cold running water, drain again and set aside.

2 To make mayonnaise, place parsley and basil in a food processor or blender and process to finely chop. Add mayonnaise, sour cream, mustard and black pepper to taste and process to combine.

To serve: Arrange vegetables on a large platter and accompany with Herb Mayonnaise.

Cook's tip: This mayonnaise is delicious served with any lightly cooked or steamed vegetables. You might like to try serving mangetout (snow peas), courgettes (zucchini), asparagus or cucumber on this platter instead of, or as well as, the vegetables that are suggested in the recipe.

CHEESY WALNUT FLANS

Serves 6
Oven temperature 180°C, 350°F, Gas 4

CHEESE PASTRY
- ☐ **155 g/5 oz butter, softened**
- ☐ **1 tablespoon vegetable oil**
- ☐ **185 g/6 oz Gorgonzola or blue cheese, crumbled**
- ☐ **2 egg yolks**
- ☐ **2 tablespoons water**
- ☐ **250 g/8 oz flour, sifted**

WALNUT AND CHEESE FILLING
- ☐ **125 g/4 oz chopped walnuts, lightly toasted**
- ☐ **375 g/12 oz ricotta cheese**
- ☐ **30 g/1 oz grated Parmesan cheese**
- ☐ **3 eggs, lightly beaten**
- ☐ **185 mL/6 fl oz milk**
- ☐ **¹/₂ teaspoon ground nutmeg**
- ☐ **¹/₂ teaspoon freshly ground black pepper**
- ☐ **1 tablespoon snipped fresh chives**

1 To make pastry, place butter and oil in bowl and beat until soft and creamy. Stir in cheese, egg yolks and water and mix to combine. Add flour and mix to form a soft dough. Roll dough into a ball, wrap in plastic food wrap and refrigerate for 30 minutes.

2 Roll out pastry between two layers of greaseproof paper and cut to fit six well-greased 12 cm/5 in flan tins. Line pastry flans with baking paper, fill with uncooked rice and bake for 8 minutes. Remove rice and paper and bake for 5 minutes longer.

3 To make filling, place walnuts, ricotta cheese, Parmesan cheese, eggs, milk, nutmeg, black pepper and chives in a bowl and mix to combine. Spoon filling into pastry cases and bake for 15 minutes or until filling is firm.

Crudités with Herb Mayonnaise

CHEESE AND BACON NACHOS

Serves 6
Oven temperature 180°C, 350°F, Gas 4

- [ ] **6 rashers bacon, chopped**
- [ ] **6 spring onions, chopped**
- [ ] **4 jalapeño chillies, finely chopped**
- [ ] **200 g/6¹⁄₂ oz packet corn chips**
- [ ] **125 g/4 oz grated mature Cheddar**
- [ ] **250 g/8 oz sour cream**

1   Place bacon, spring onions and chillies in a nonstick frying pan and cook over a medium heat for 4-5 minutes or until bacon is crisp. Remove bacon mixture from pan and drain on absorbent kitchen paper.
2   Place corn chips in a shallow ovenproof dish and sprinkle with bacon mixture and cheese. Bake for 5-8 minutes or until heated through and cheese is melted. Serve immediately, accompanied by sour cream for dipping.

Jalapeño chillies: These are the medium-to-dark green chillies that taper to a blunt end and are 5-7.5 cm/2-3 in long and 2-2.5 cm/³⁄₄-1 in wide. They are medium-to-hot in taste and are also available canned or bottled.

SMOKED SALMON AND WATERCRESS ROULADE

Serves 10
Oven temperature 180°C, 350°F, Gas 4

- [ ] **1 bunch/90 g/3 oz watercress**
- [ ] **1 teaspoon finely chopped fresh parsley**
- [ ] **2 eggs, separated**
- [ ] **2 tablespoons flour**
- [ ] **freshly ground black pepper**

SMOKED SALMON FILLING
- [ ] **60 g/2 oz cream cheese**
- [ ] **2 tablespoons sour cream**
- [ ] **90 g/3 oz smoked salmon**
- [ ] **1 teaspoon lemon juice**
- [ ] **1¹⁄₂ teaspoons gelatine dissolved in 1¹⁄₂ tablespoons hot water, cooled**

1   Place watercress leaves, parsley, egg yolks, flour and black pepper to taste in a food processor and process until mixture is smooth. Transfer watercress mixture to a bowl. Place egg whites in a bowl and beat until stiff peaks form. Fold egg white mixture into watercress mixture.
2   Spoon roulade mixture into a greased and lined 26 x 32 cm/10¹⁄₂ x 12³⁄₄ in Swiss roll tin and bake for 5 minutes or until just cooked. Turn roulade onto a damp teatowel and roll up from short side. Set aside to cool.
3   To make filling, place cream cheese, sour cream, smoked salmon and lemon juice in a food processor and process until mixture is smooth. Stir gelatine mixture into smoked salmon mixture.
4   Unroll cold roulade, spread with filling and reroll. Cover and chill. Cut into slices to serve.

BRUSCHETTA WITH TOMATO AND OLIVES

Bruschetta is the garlic bread of Italy. Delicious cooked on the barbecue, it can be eaten plain or topped with fresh tomatoes or roasted red pepper.

Serves 4

- ☐ **60 mL/2 fl oz olive oil**
- ☐ **2 cloves garlic, crushed**
- ☐ **8 thick slices crusty bread**

TOMATO OLIVE TOPPING
- ☐ **3 large ripe tomatoes, peeled and diced**
- ☐ **2 tablespoons finely chopped red pepper**
- ☐ **6 black olives, finely chopped**
- ☐ **1/2 red onion, finely chopped**
- ☐ **2 tablespoons finely chopped fresh basil**
- ☐ **1 tablespoon olive oil**
- ☐ **1 tablespoon balsamic or red wine vinegar**
- ☐ **freshly ground black pepper**

1   To make topping, place tomatoes, red pepper, olives, onion, basil, oil, vinegar and black pepper to taste in a bowl and toss to combine.

2   Preheat barbecue or grill to a medium heat. Combine oil and garlic and brush both sides of each slice of bread. Cook bread on lightly oiled barbecue or under grill for 2-3 minutes each side or until toasted. Serve immediately, topped with Tomato Olive Topping.

CHICKEN LIVER PATE

Makes 4 x 185 mL/6 fl oz pâté pots

- ☐ **500 g/1 lb chicken livers, chopped**
- ☐ **4 tablespoons dry sherry**
- ☐ **90 g/30 g butter**
- ☐ **2 spring onions, chopped**
- ☐ **1 clove garlic, crushed**
- ☐ **4 tablespoons cream**
- ☐ **1/4 teaspoon mixed spice**
- ☐ **1/2 teaspoon ground thyme**
- ☐ **freshly ground black pepper**
- ☐ **100 g/3 1/2 oz butter, melted**

1   Place livers in a bowl. Cover with sherry and stand for 2 hours. Drain and reserve liquid.

2   Melt half the butter in a frying pan. Stir in spring onions, garlic and livers. Cook over a medium heat for 3 minutes, then pour in reserved liquid and cook for 1 minute more. Remove pan from heat.

3   Place liver mixture in a food processor or blender. Melt remaining butter and combine with cream, mixed spice and thyme, then blend into liver mixture. Season to taste with black pepper. Pour pâté into individual pâté pots, top with melted butter and refrigerate overnight.

SALMON PATE

Makes 4 x 185 mL/6 fl oz pâté pots

- ☐ **220 g/7 oz canned red salmon, drained**
- ☐ **125 g/4 oz ricotta cheese**
- ☐ **125 g/4 oz mayonnaise**
- ☐ **2 teaspoons grated lemon rind**
- ☐ **2 tablespoons lemon juice**
- ☐ **3 spring onions**
- ☐ **125 g/4 oz butter, melted**

1   Combine salmon, ricotta, mayonnaise, lemon rind, lemon juice and spring onions in a food processor. Add butter and process until smooth.

2   Spoon salmon pâté into individual pâté pots, top with melted butter and refrigerate overnight.

Left: Smoked Salmon and Watercress Roulade
Above: Chicken Liver Pâté, Salmon Pâté

ASPARAGUS GINGER AND CASHEW STIR-FRY

The combination of asparagus and ginger is wonderful, as it allows the true taste of asparagus to come through.

Serves 6

- ☐ 1 tablespoon vegetable oil
- ☐ 2 teaspoons sesame oil
- ☐ 1 tablespoon finely chopped fresh ginger
- ☐ 750 g/1½ lb prepared asparagus spears, cut into 4 cm/1½ in pieces
- ☐ 60 g/2 oz roughly chopped roasted cashew nuts
- ☐ 1 tablespoon soy sauce

1 Heat vegetable and sesame oils together in a wok or frying pan. Stir in ginger and cook for 1 minute.
2 Add asparagus and cook for 4-5 minutes or until tender, crisp and bright green. Stir in cashews and soy sauce. Cook for 1-2 minutes until heated through. Serve immediately.

BAKED ASPARAGUS ROLL-UPS

These roll-ups are delicious as a snack before dinner. To reduce fat content, use light cream cheese.

Makes 28
Oven temperature 200°C, 400°C, Gas 6

- ☐ 28 prepared asparagus spears
- ☐ 14 slices thin wholemeal bread, crusts removed
- ☐ 250 g/8 oz cream cheese
- ☐ ½ teaspoon prepared hot mustard
- ☐ 100 g/3½ oz sliced ham, finely chopped
- ☐ 125 g/4 oz butter, melted

1 Boil, steam or microwave asparagus until just tender. Refresh under cold running water. Drain well and set aside.
2 Flatten bread slices using a rolling pin. Combine cream cheese, mustard and ham and spread over each slice of bread.
3 Arrange 2 asparagus spears on each bread slice with tips toward outside edges. Roll up, cut each roll in half and secure with a toothpick. Place seam side down on a baking tray lined with baking paper.
4 Brush with butter and bake for 15-20 minutes or until lightly browned.

TUNA PATE

Serves 4

- ☐ 220 g/7 oz canned tuna, drained and flaked
- ☐ 1 small cucumber, peeled, seeded and chopped
- ☐ 250 mL/8 fl oz tomato juice
- ☐ 5 teaspoons gelatine dissolved in 125 mL/4 fl oz hot water
- ☐ 1 tablespoon chopped fresh dill
- ☐ 1 teaspoon grated lemon rind
- ☐ 1 teaspoon lemon juice
- ☐ 2 teaspoons finely chopped capers
- ☐ 1 teaspoon horseradish relish
- ☐ 3 tablespoons natural yogurt
- ☐ freshly ground black pepper

1 Place tuna, cucumber, tomato juice, gelatine mixture, dill, lemon rind, lemon juice, capers, horseradish relish and yogurt in a food processor or blender and process until smooth.
2 Season to taste with black pepper. Spoon tuna mixture into four individual dishes or moulds and refrigerate until firm. To serve, turn out and accompany with crackers or Melba toast.

Cook's tip: To make Melba toast, cut bread into slices of a medium thickness and lightly toast. Cut crusts from toast and split each slice of toast horizontally. Cut each slice in half diagonally and bake at 180°C/350°F/Gas 4 for 5-7 minutes or until the edges curl and the toast is golden.

Asparagus Orange Hollandaise Pastry Sandwich, Asparagus Ginger and Cashew Stir-Fry, Baked Asparagus Roll-Ups

TIME SAVER
To save time, prepare the Baked Asparagus Roll-ups to final stage earlier, then bake when required.

ASPARAGUS ORANGE HOLLANDAISE PASTRY SANDWICH

These tasty pastry sandwiches make an ideal entrée.

Serves 6
Oven temperature 220°C, 425°F, Gas 7

- ☐ **1 sheet prepared puff pastry**
- ☐ **1 egg yolk, lightly beaten**
- ☐ **18 prepared asparagus spears**
- ☐ **1 orange, thinly sliced**

ORANGE HOLLANDAISE SAUCE
- ☐ **3 egg yolks**
- ☐ **1 tablespoon lemon juice**
- ☐ **2 tablespoons orange juice**
- ☐ **125 g/4 oz butter, melted**

1   Cut pastry sheet in half, then each half into six even pieces. Place on a baking tray lined with baking paper. Brush each pastry piece with egg yolk. Bake for 10-15 minutes or until pastry is puffed and golden.
2   Boil, steam or microwave asparagus until tender. Drain and keep warm.
3   To make sauce, place egg yolks, lemon juice and orange juice in a food processor or blender and process until light and frothy. With food processor running, slowly pour in melted butter.
4   Place sauce in the top of a double boiler. Cook gently over a low heat until sauce thickens. Arrange 3 asparagus spears on half the pastry pieces and spoon over sauce. Top with remaining pastry and garnish with orange slices.

Microwave it: Hollandaise sauce can be quickly and easily made in a microwave oven. In a small jug, whisk together egg yolks, lemon and orange juices. Whisk into the melted butter. Cook on MEDIUM (50%) power for 1¹/₂ minutes or until sauce thickens, stirring every 30 seconds.

CHAMPAGNE TEMPURA

Serves 4

- [ ] 8 small cauliflower florets
- [ ] 8 button mushrooms
- [ ] 12 green beans, trimmed
- [ ] 1 red pepper, sliced
- [ ] 1 green apple, cored and sliced
- [ ] 2 slices pineapple, quartered
- [ ] vegetable oil for deep-frying

CHAMPAGNE BATTER
- [ ] 90 g/3 oz self-raising flour, sifted
- [ ] 75 g/2$\frac{1}{2}$ oz cornflour, sifted
- [ ] 1 egg, lightly beaten
- [ ] 125 mL/4 fl oz iced water
- [ ] 125 mL/4 fl oz chilled champagne
- [ ] 2 ice cubes

DIPPING SAUCE
- [ ] 3 tablespoons sour cream
- [ ] 3 tablespoons mayonnaise
- [ ] 1 tablespoon chopped fresh herbs

1   To make batter, place flour and cornflour in a bowl. Mix together egg, water and champagne, pour into flour mixture and stir until smooth. Do not overbeat. Place ice cubes in batter.

2   Heat oil in a large deep saucepan until a cube of bread dropped in browns in 50 seconds. Dip cauliflower, mushrooms, beans, red pepper, apple and pineapple pieces into batter and cook a few pieces at a time in oil until golden brown. Using a slotted spoon remove cooked vegetable pieces and drain on absorbent kitchen paper.

3   To make sauce, place sour cream, mayonnaise and herbs in a bowl and mix to combine. Serve as a dipping sauce with hot vegetables.

SALMON SOUFFLES

Serves 4
Oven temperature 200°C, 400°F, Gas 6

- [ ] 220 g/7 oz canned red salmon, drained and flaked
- [ ] 100 g/3$\frac{1}{2}$ oz bottled oysters, drained, rinsed and chopped
- [ ] 2 teaspoons finely chopped capers
- [ ] 1 teaspoon finely chopped fresh dill
- [ ] 2-3 dashes Tabasco sauce
- [ ] 250 g/8 oz cottage cheese
- [ ] freshly ground black pepper
- [ ] 4 egg whites

1   Combine salmon, oysters, capers, dill, Tabasco sauce and cottage cheese in a bowl. Season to taste with black pepper.

2   Beat egg whites until stiff peaks form and fold lightly through salmon mixture. Spoon into four lightly greased individual soufflé dishes and bake for 30-35 minutes.

Cook's tip: When incorporating egg whites into a mixture, firstly mix in 1 tablespoon of the beaten egg whites, this loosens the mixture and makes it easier to fold in the remaining egg whites.

MUSHROOMS WITH CHILLI BUTTER

Makes 20

- [ ] 20 button mushrooms, stalks removed

CHILLI BUTTER
- [ ] 60 g/2 oz butter
- [ ] $\frac{1}{2}$ fresh red chilli, finely chopped
- [ ] $\frac{1}{2}$ teaspoon ground cumin
- [ ] 1 tablespoon finely chopped fresh parsley

1   To make Chilli Butter, place butter, chilli, cumin and parsley in a food processor or blender and process until smooth. Shape butter into a log, wrap in plastic food wrap and chill until required.

2   Cut butter log into twenty pieces, place a piece of butter on each mushroom and cook under a preheated grill for 4-5 minutes

or until butter melts and mushrooms are cooked. Serve immediately with toothpicks so that your guests can spear a mushroom then eat it.

Cook's tip: When handling fresh chillies do not put your hands near your eyes or allow them to touch your lips. To avoid discomfort and burning, wear rubber gloves. Freshly minced chilli is also available in jars from supermarkets.

CAMEMBERT SURPRISE WITH BANANA SAUCE

Serves 4

- ☐ **4 x 125 g/4 oz Camembert cheese**
- ☐ **2 ripe bananas, sliced**
- ☐ **lemon juice**

- ☐ **2 teaspoons desiccated coconut**
- ☐ **1 egg, beaten**
- ☐ **3 tablespoons milk**
- ☐ **flour**
- ☐ **375 g/12 oz dried breadcrumbs**
- ☐ **vegetable oil for cooking**

BANANA SAUCE
- ☐ **2 ripe bananas**
- ☐ **125 mL/4 fl oz coconut milk**
- ☐ **2 tablespoons cream (double)**
- ☐ **¼ teaspoon ground mixed spice**
- ☐ **1 teaspoon lemon juice**

1 Halve Camemberts horizontally. Sprinkle banana slices with lemon juice and arrange on 4 of the Camembert halves. Sprinkle with coconut and top with remaining cheese halves. Press together firmly.

2 Combine egg and milk. Dip each

Camembert in flour, egg mixture and breadcrumbs. Repeat crumbing process. Chill until firm.

3 Heat oil in a frying pan and cook Camemberts until golden. Drain on absorbent paper and serve with sauce.

4 To prepare sauce, peel and roughly chop bananas. Place into the bowl of a food processor, add coconut milk, cream, spice and lemon juice. Process until smooth. Serve sauce separately or spooned over Camembert.

Cook's tip: Use a toothpick to hold each Camembert together while preparing and cooking. Remove toothpick before serving.

Left: Salmon Soufflés
Above: Camembert Surprise with Banana Sauce

CARROTS WRAPPED IN SPINACH

A colourful and interesting dish which can be prepared in advance and baked when required. To serve, turn out and top with a fresh herb sauce.

Serves 6
Oven temperature 200°C, 400°F, Gas 6

- ☐ **6 carrots, sliced**
- ☐ **30 g/1 oz butter**
- ☐ **2 egg yolks**
- ☐ **freshly ground black pepper**
- ☐ **spinach leaves**

1 Boil, steam or microwave carrots until tender. Allow to cool. Place in a food processor or blender with butter and egg yolks and process until smooth. Season to taste with black pepper.
2 Lightly grease six individual soufflé dishes or ramekins. Blanch spinach leaves and use to line ramekins, leaving some of the leaves to hang over the side. Spoon carrot mixture into the ramekins and fold over spinach leaves to cover. Bake for 25-30 minutes or until set.

SALMON AND CRAB AVOCADO

Serves 4

- ☐ **1 large avocado**
- ☐ **2 tablespoons lemon juice**

CRAB AND SALMON FILLING
- ☐ **1 avocado, stoned, peeled and chopped**
- ☐ **100 g/3¹/₂ oz crab pieces, flaked**
- ☐ **4 slices smoked salmon, chopped**
- ☐ **3 tablespoons cream (double)**
- ☐ **2 teaspoons mayonnaise**
- ☐ **1 tablespoon tomato sauce**
- ☐ **2-3 dashes Tabasco sauce**
- ☐ **2 teaspoons lemon juice**

1 To make filling, place avocado, crab, salmon, cream, mayonnaise, tomato sauce, Tabasco sauce and lemon juice in a bowl and mix to combine
2 Cut avocado into quarters, remove the stone and brush avocado with lemon juice. Spoon filling into cavity of each quarter and serve immediately.

SAVOURY CARROT AND CHEESE PARCELS

To prevent the parcel tops from becoming too brown, cover with foil if necessary, and remove for the last few minutes of cooking.

Serves 6
Oven temperature 200°C, 400°F, Gas 6

- ☐ **12 sheets filo pastry**
- ☐ **125 mL/4 fl oz olive oil**

FILLING
- ☐ **30 g/1 oz butter**
- ☐ **1 onion, chopped**
- ☐ **2 carrots, coarsely grated**
- ☐ **1 tablespoon finely chopped fresh dill**
- ☐ **1 tablespoon finely snipped fresh chives**
- ☐ **4 tablespoons finely chopped fresh parsley**
- ☐ **250 g/8 oz mozzarella cheese, grated**
- ☐ **freshly ground black pepper**

HERB SAUCE
- ☐ **30 g/1 oz butter**
- ☐ **2 tablespoons flour**
- ☐ **375 mL/12 fl oz milk**
- ☐ **1 tablespoon finely chopped fresh dill**
- ☐ **1 tablespoon finely snipped fresh chives**
- ☐ **2 tablespoons finely chopped fresh parsley**

1 For each parcel, cut 2 sheets of filo in half. Brush each sheet with olive oil and stack the 4 sheets together.
2 To make filling, melt butter in a small frying pan. Add onion and cook for 2-3 minutes or until soft. Mix with carrots, dill, chives and parsley. Place spoonfuls of mixture in the centre of each pastry stack. Top with cheese and season to taste with black pepper.
3 Gather up the corners of the pastry over the filling to make a bag. Press together firmly and gently twist just above the filling to seal. Carefully fan out pastry tops attractively and brush each parcel with remaining olive oil. Place on an oiled baking tray. Bake for 20 minutes or until crisp and golden.
4 To make sauce, melt butter in a saucepan, stir in flour and cook for 1 minute. Slowly mix in milk, dill, chives and parsley, stirring constantly until sauce boils and thickens. Serve immediately.

Microwave it: The sauce can be made quickly and easily in the microwave using a 1 litre/1³/₄ pt microwave-safe jug. Melt butter on HIGH (100%) for 30 seconds, mix in flour, milk, dill, chives and parsley. Cook on HIGH (100%) for 3-4 minutes or until sauce thickens.

SPICY CARROTS WITH CASHEW NUTS

Try this adaptation of an Indian recipe – it is a wonderful way of cooking and serving carrots.

Serves 4

- ☐ **2 tablespoons vegetable oil**
- ☐ **500 g/1 lb carrots, cut lengthwise into thick strips**
- ☐ **1 large onion, sliced**
- ☐ **1 teaspoon grated fresh ginger**
- ☐ **1 teaspoon garam masala**
- ☐ **¹/₂ teaspoon chilli powder**
- ☐ **1 tablespoon flour**
- ☐ **185 g/6 oz cashew nuts**
- ☐ **250 mL/8 fl oz chicken stock**

1 Heat oil in a heavy-based saucepan. Add carrots and onion and cook for 5 minutes. Stir in ginger, garam masala, chilli powder, flour, cashews and stock. Cook over a medium heat, stirring, until mixture thickens. Reduce heat.
2 Simmer over a low heat, stirring frequently, for 15-20 minutes or until carrots are tender.

Spicy Carrots with Cashew Nuts, Carrots Wrapped in Spinach, Savoury Carrot and Cheese Parcels

MANDARIN AND SMOKED CHICKEN SALAD

Serves 4

- [ ] **250 g/8 oz mangetout (snow peas), trimmed**
- [ ] **375 g/12 oz chopped smoked chicken**
- [ ] **300 g/9¹/₂ oz canned mandarin segments, drained**
- [ ] **60 g/2 oz bean sprouts**
- [ ] **125 g/4 oz canned water chestnuts, drained and thinly sliced**

MUSTARD DRESSING
- [ ] **4 tablespoons vegetable oil**
- [ ] **1 tablespoon white wine vinegar**
- [ ] **¹/₂ teaspoon Dijon mustard**
- [ ] **freshly ground black pepper**

1 Boil, steam or microwave mangetout (snow peas) until they just change colour. Drain, refresh under cold running water and pat dry with absorbent kitchen paper.
2 Place mangetout (snow peas), chicken, mandarins, bean sprouts and water chestnuts in a large salad bowl.
3 To make dressing, place oil, vinegar, mustard and black pepper to taste in a screwtop jar and shake well to combine. Spoon dressing over salad and toss. Serve immediately.

PEPPER AND SPINACH SALAD

The sweetness of the peppers mixed with a tangy vinaigrette makes a wonderful starter or part of an anti-pasto platter. Make at least an hour before serving to allow the flavour to develop.

Serves 6

- [ ] **2 red peppers, halved and seeded**
- [ ] **1 yellow pepper, halved and seeded**
- [ ] **1 green pepper, halved and seeded**
- [ ] **500 g/1 lb spinach, stalks removed and leaves shredded**
- [ ] **125 g/4 oz button mushrooms**
- [ ] **155 g/5 oz pitted black olives**

BALSAMIC DRESSING
- [ ] **125 mL/4 fl oz olive oil**
- [ ] **60 mL/2 fl oz balsamic vinegar**
- [ ] **2 teaspoons chopped fresh basil**
- [ ] **1 teaspoon chopped fresh marjoram**
- [ ] **freshly ground black pepper**

1 Place red, yellow and green peppers skin side up under a preheated grill and cook until skins are black and charred. Place peppers in a plastic food bag, seal and set aside for 5 minutes or until cool enough to handle. Remove peppers from bag, peel away skins and wash under cold water. Pat dry with absorbent kitchen paper and cut into strips. Set aside to cool completely.
2 Arrange spinach on a serving platter, top with peppers, mushrooms and olives.
3 To make dressing, place oil, vinegar, basil, marjoram and black pepper to taste in a screwtop jar and shake well to combine. Spoon dressing over salad.

Balsamic vinegar: This is a dark Italian vinegar. Made by the special processing of wines and musts from the Modena province, it is an interesting addition to any salad dressing and can also be used in sauces for meats or vegetables. Balsamic vinegar is available from supermarkets and delicatessens but if you cannot find it use red wine vinegar in its place.

BITE-SIZED KEBABS

These kebabs make a delicious starter for a barbecue meal, but are just as good when cooked under a grill. If cooking on a barbecue, make sure that the skewers are long enough so that you do not burn your fingers.

Each recipe is enough for 10 skewers

- [ ] **10 lightly oiled bamboo skewers**

CUCUMBER AND SCALLOPS
- [ ] **1 clove garlic, crushed**
- [ ] **1 spring onion, finely chopped**
- [ ] **1 tablespoon finely chopped fresh basil**
- [ ] **1 tablespoon olive oil**
- [ ] **2 tablespoons white wine vinegar**
- [ ] **freshly ground black pepper**
- [ ] **10 scallops, cleaned or 1 firm white fish fillet cut in 2.5 cm/ 1 in cubes**
- [ ] **10 thin slices cucumber, skin left on**

1 Place garlic, spring onion, basil, oil, vinegar and black pepper to taste in a bowl and whisk to combine. Add scallops or fish pieces, and cucumber slices and toss to coat, then set aside to marinate for 30 minutes.
2 Preheat a barbecue or grill to a high heat. Drain scallops or fish pieces, and cucumber, reserving marinade. Top each cucumber slice with a scallop or fish piece so that the cucumber folds halfway around the scallop or fish. Brush with reserved marinade and cook on lightly oiled barbecue or under grill, turning several times, for 2-3 minutes or until scallops or fish pieces are cooked.

CHICKEN AND MUSHROOMS
- [ ] **1 tablespoon lime or lemon juice**
- [ ] **1 tablespoon vegetable oil**
- [ ] **pinch chilli powder**
- [ ] **1 chicken breast fillet, skin removed, cut into 10 cubes**
- [ ] **5 button mushrooms, halved**

1 Place lime or lemon juice, oil and chilli powder in a bowl and mix to combine. Add chicken and mushrooms and toss to combine. Set aside to marinate for 30 minutes.
2 Preheat a barbecue or grill to a high heat. Drain chicken and mushrooms, reserving marinade. Thread a chicken cube and a mushroom half onto each bamboo skewer. Brush with reserved marinade and cook on lightly oiled barbecue or under grill, turning several times, for 4-5 minutes or until chicken is cooked.

BACON AND PRAWNS
- [ ] **1 tablespoon Dijon mustard**
- [ ] **1 clove garlic, crushed**
- [ ] **¹/₄ red pepper, finely chopped**
- [ ] **1 tablespoon finely chopped fresh dill**
- [ ] **2 tablespoons olive oil**
- [ ] **2 tablespoons lemon juice**
- [ ] **freshly ground black pepper**
- [ ] **10 large cooked prawns, shelled and deveined, tails left intact**
- [ ] **5 rashers bacon, cut into ten 7.5 cm/3 in strips**

1 Place mustard, garlic, red pepper, dill, oil, lemon juice and black pepper to taste in a bowl and mix to combine. Add prawns and toss to coat. Set aside to marinate for 30 minutes.
2 Preheat a barbecue or grill to a high

heat. Drain prawns and reserve marinade. Wrap a strip of bacon around each prawn and thread onto bamboo skewers. Brush with reserved marinade and cook on lightly oiled barbecue or under grill, turning several times, for 2-3 minutes or until bacon is cooked and crisp.

LETTUCE ROLL-UPS

These roll-ups make an interesting light starter that can be prepared several hours in advance.

Serves 6

- ☐ **6 large lettuce leaves**
- ☐ **60 g/2 oz bean sprouts**
- ☐ **2 mangoes, peeled and chopped**
- ☐ **250 g/8 oz canned water chestnuts, drained and sliced**
- ☐ **2 teaspoons finely chopped preserved ginger**
- ☐ **2 teaspoons finely chopped fresh mint**
- ☐ **3 tablespoons mayonnaise**
- ☐ **1 tablespoon natural yogurt**

1   Tear lettuce leaves in half lengthwise. Place sprouts, mangoes, water chestnuts, ginger and mint in a bowl and toss. Add mayonnaise and yogurt and mix to combine.
2   Place a spoonful of mixture on each lettuce leaf half. Roll up tightly and secure with a toothpick. Chill until ready to serve.

Cook's tip: Canned mangoes can be used in place of the fresh mangoes if you wish.

HOT CHILLI PRAWNS

Serves 6

- ☐ **1.5 kg/3 lb uncooked large prawns, shelled, deveined, tails left intact**

CHILLI MARINADE
- ☐ **2 teaspoons cracked black peppercorns**
- ☐ **2 tablespoons sweet chilli sauce**
- ☐ **1 tablespoon soy sauce**
- ☐ **1 clove garlic, crushed**
- ☐ **60 mL/2 fl oz lemon juice**

MANGO CREAM
- ☐ **1 mango, peeled, stoned and roughly chopped**
- ☐ **3 tablespoons coconut milk**

1   To make marinade, place black peppercorns, chilli sauce, soy sauce, garlic and lemon juice in a bowl and mix to combine. Add prawns, toss to coat, cover and set aside to marinate for 1 hour. Toss several times during marinating.
2   To make Mango Cream, place mango flesh and coconut milk in a food processor or blender and process until smooth.
3   Preheat a barbecue to a medium heat. Drain prawns and cook on lightly oiled barbecue for 3-4 minutes or until prawns change colour. Serve immediately with Mango Cream.

Coconut milk: This can be purchased in a number of forms: canned, as a long-life product in cartons, or as a powder to which you add water. Once opened it has a short life and should be used within a day or so. It is available from Asian food stores and some supermarkets, however if you have trouble finding it you can easily make your own. To make coconut milk, place 500 g/1 lb desiccated coconut in a bowl and add 750 mL/1¼ pt boiling water. Set aside to stand for 30 minutes, then strain, squeezing the coconut to extract as much liquid as possible. This will make a thick coconut milk. The coconut can be used again to make a weaker coconut milk.

Hot Chilli Prawns

chapter five

MAIN MEALS WITH FLAIR

In this chapter you will find
dishes to suit all occasions. Recipes
such as Family Chicken Casserole
and Red Currant Lamb Roast make the
perfect family meal, while Honey-glazed
Pork is just the right dish for last-minute
entertaining. Look out for the Masterclass
step-by-step recipes that show you
special techniques and the
secrets to ensure perfect
results everytime.

Paprika Beef, Tomato and Thyme
Shanks, Lamb Pot Roast

TOMATO AND THYME SHANKS

Serves 4
Oven temperature 150°C, 300°F, Gas 2

- [ ] **4 lamb shanks**
- [ ] **2 spring onions, chopped**
- [ ] **1 red pepper, chopped**
- [ ] **250 mL/8 fl oz tomato sauce**
- [ ] **125 mL/4 fl oz cider vinegar**
- [ ] **250 mL/8 fl oz water**
- [ ] **1 clove garlic, crushed**
- [ ] **1 teaspoon finely chopped fresh thyme**
- [ ] **freshly ground black pepper**

1   Place shanks, spring onions and red pepper in a large casserole dish. Combine tomato sauce, vinegar, water, garlic and thyme and pour over shanks.
2   Cover and bake for 2¹/₂ hours or until meat is very tender. Season to taste with black pepper. Serve immediately or allow to cool and serve at room temperature.

PAPRIKA BEEF

Serves 8

- [ ] **1 kg/2 lb chuck steak, cut into 2.5 cm/1 in squares**
- [ ] **4 tablespoons oil**
- [ ] **2 onions, sliced**
- [ ] **125 mL/4 fl oz dry white wine**
- [ ] **250 mL/8 fl oz water**
- [ ] **185 g/6 oz stuffed green olives**
- [ ] **4 tablespoons chopped fresh flat leaf parsley**

YOGURT MARINADE
- [ ] **1 teaspoon ground turmeric**
- [ ] **1¹/₂ tablespoons mild paprika**
- [ ] **¹/₂ teaspoon chilli powder**
- [ ] **220 g/7 oz natural yogurt**
- [ ] **2 teaspoons grated lemon rind**

1   To make marinade, combine turmeric, paprika, chilli powder, yogurt and rind in a bowl. Add steak and toss to coat. Cover and refrigerate for 2-4 hours or overnight.
2   Heat oil in a large saucepan. Add onions and cook over a medium heat for about 5 minutes or until onions soften. Add steak and marinade and cook over a high heat for about 10 minutes.
3   Stir in wine and water. Bring to the boil, cover and simmer for about 1¹/₂ hours or until steak is tender. Stir in olives and parsley and cook over a medium heat for 3 minutes longer. Season to taste.

LAMB POT ROAST

Serves 6
Oven temperature 180°C, 350°F, Gas 4

- [ ] **2 kg/4 lb leg of lamb**
- [ ] **2 cloves garlic, cut into slivers**
- [ ] **6 small sprigs fresh rosemary**
- [ ] **freshly ground black pepper**
- [ ] **6 potatoes, halved lengthwise**
- [ ] **2 tablespoons lemon juice**
- [ ] **4 tomatoes, peeled and chopped**
- [ ] **2 onions, chopped**
- [ ] **125 mL/4 fl oz chicken stock**
- [ ] **3 tablespoons dry vermouth**
- [ ] **1 cm/¹/₂ in piece lemon peel**
- [ ] **small piece cinnamon stick**
- [ ] **30 g/1 oz butter**

1   Cut slits in the surface of the lamb with a sharp knife. Insert garlic slivers and rosemary sprigs. Dust with black pepper, place in a baking dish and bake for 1 hour. Remove dish from oven and drain off juices.
2   Cut potato halves part way down through rounded side. Brush with lemon juice and arrange around lamb. Top with tomatoes and onions. Combine stock and vermouth and pour over lamb and vegetables. Add the lemon peel and cinnamon stick. Dot with butter and bake for 1¹/₂ hours longer.
3   Remove lamb from baking dish. Wrap in aluminium foil and stand for 15 minutes before carving. Skim any excess fat from baking dish contents. To serve, slice meat and accompany with potatoes, and tomato and onion sauce.

CRUSTY INDIVIDUAL LAMB AND KIDNEY PIES

Serves 4
Oven temperature 180°C, 350°F, Gas 4

LAMB AND KIDNEY FILLING
- [ ] **750 g/1¹/₂ lb best neck chops**
- [ ] **3 lamb kidneys**
- [ ] **60 g/2 oz butter**
- [ ] **1 onion, chopped**
- [ ] **3 rashers bacon, chopped**
- [ ] **2 tablespoons flour**
- [ ] **3 tablespoons red wine**
- [ ] **185 mL/6 fl oz chicken stock**
- [ ] **1 tablespoon tomato purée**
- [ ] **¹/₂ teaspoon sugar**
- [ ] **1 tablespoon finely chopped fresh thyme**
- [ ] **freshly ground black pepper**

SOUR CREAM CRUST
- [ ] **125 g/4 oz butter, softened**
- [ ] **300 g/9¹/₂ oz sour cream**
- [ ] **1 egg**
- [ ] **185 g/6 oz self-raising flour**
- [ ] **1 tablespoon finely chopped fresh parsley**

1   To make filling, remove meat from bones and trim of all visible fat. Cut into 2.5 cm/1 in cubes. Trim kidneys of all visible fat and soak in salted water for 10 minutes. Wipe kidneys dry with absorbent kitchen paper, skin and cut into slices.
2   Melt 30 g/1 oz butter in a large saucepan and cook meat in batches until browned on all sides. Remove from pan and set aside. Add kidneys to pan and cook for 1-2 minutes or until kidneys just change colour. Remove from pan and set aside. Add onion and bacon to pan and cook, stirring, for 2-3 minutes or until onion is golden. Remove from pan and set aside.
3   Melt remaining butter in pan, add flour and cook, stirring, for 3-4 minutes or until a light straw colour. Stir in wine, stock, tomato purée and sugar and cook over a medium heat, stirring constantly, until sauce boils and thickens. Add thyme and season to taste with black pepper. Return meat, kidneys and onion mixture to pan, cover, bring to simmering and simmer for 1¹/₂ hours or until meat is tender. Remove pan from heat and set aside to cool slightly.
4   To make crust, place butter, sour cream and egg in a bowl and mix to combine. Stir in 125 g/4 oz self-raising flour and parsley and mix well. Divide two-thirds of the crust mixture into four equal portions. Press each portion over the base and sides of four individual dishes, and spoon in filling. Lightly knead remaining self-raising flour into remaining dough. Press out on a lightly floured surface, using palm of hand, to 1 cm/¹/₂ in thick and cut into rounds using a 3 cm/1¹/₄ in biscuit cutter. Top filling with dough rounds, overlapping them slightly and bake for 30 minutes or until crust is golden and cooked.

Cook's tip: To skin kidneys, nick skin on the rounded skin of each kidney and draw it back on each side until it is attached by the core only. Draw out as much core as possible and cut, with skin, close to the kidney.

STEAK WITH FRENCH MUSTARD SAUCE

Serves 4

- ☐ **4 lean rib eye steaks (Scotch fillet)**
- ☐ **30 g/1 oz butter**

FRENCH MUSTARD SAUCE

- ☐ **2 spring onions, finely chopped**
- ☐ **1 tablespoon wholegrain mustard**
- ☐ **2 teaspoons French mustard**
- ☐ **125 mL/4 fl oz dry white wine**
- ☐ **3 tablespoons water**
- ☐ **1 teaspoon honey**
- ☐ **¹/₄ teaspoon dried thyme**
- ☐ **2 tablespoons cream or evaporated skim milk**
- ☐ **1¹/₂ tablespoons grated mature Cheddar**

1 Trim meat of all visible fat. Melt butter in a frying pan, cook steaks for 4-5 minutes each side. Remove from pan and keep warm.

2 To make sauce, add spring onion to pan and sauté for 1 minute. Stir in combined mustards, wine, water, honey and thyme. Cook over a medium heat for 3-4 minutes until sauce has reduced slightly.

3 Remove pan from heat and stir in cream or skim milk, and cheese. Spoon sauce over steaks and serve.

MARINATED SATAY CHICKEN WINGS

Satay sauce is available in supermarkets. To make your own, combine 1 tablespoon peanut butter, 1 tablespoon soy sauce, ¹/₂ teaspoon crushed garlic, 1 teaspoon lemon juice and a pinch of chilli powder.

Serves 4

- ☐ **750 g/1¹/₂ lb chicken wings**

MARINADE

- ☐ **¹/₄ teaspoon five spice powder**
- ☐ **¹/₄ teaspoon chilli powder**
- ☐ **2 tablespoons satay sauce**
- ☐ **¹/₂ teaspoon curry powder**
- ☐ **1 teaspoon cornflour**
- ☐ **¹/₂ teaspoon sugar**
- ☐ **1 teaspoon oyster sauce**
- ☐ **2 tablespoons dry white wine**
- ☐ **3 tablespoons oil**
- ☐ **3 onions, cut into eighths**
- ☐ **2 teaspoons grated fresh ginger**

1 Combine chicken wings with five spice powder, chilli powder, satay sauce, curry powder, cornflour, sugar, oyster sauce and white wine. Allow to stand for at least 10-15 minutes to absorb flavour. Drain chicken wings, reserving marinade.

2 Heat 1 tablespoon oil in a frying pan or wok. Add onions and ginger and sauté 2-3 minutes until onion is transparent. Remove from pan and set aside.

3 Heat remaining oil. Add chicken wings and cook over a high heat until well browned on both sides. Reduce heat and cook a further 10-15 minutes until tender. Return onions and ginger to pan and pour over reserved marinade. Toss over a high heat for 2-3 minutes or until sauce boils.

Cook's tip: Marinating chicken or meat in a mixture containing wine, soy sauce, fruit juice and herbs or spices will tenderise the meat and add flavour. Marinate the meat or chicken in a glass or plastic bowl for at least 1 hour. But, for really tasty, succulent results, marinate covered overnight in the refrigerator.

Steak with French Mustard Sauce, Marinated Satay Chicken Wings

BEEF WRAPPED IN PASTRY WITH RED WINE SAUCE

Succulent beef surrounded by mush-rooms and wrapped in puff pastry, this dish is sure to impress – this Master Class shows you how easy it is.

Serves 6
Oven temperature 220°C, 425°F, Gas 7

☐ **60 g/2 oz butter**
☐ **1 kg/2 lb fillet steak, in one piece, trimmed**
☐ **1 onion, chopped**
☐ **375 g/12 oz button mushrooms, finely chopped**
☐ **freshly ground black pepper**
☐ **pinch ground nutmeg**
☐ **1 tablespoon finely chopped fresh parsley**
☐ **500 g/1 lb prepared or ready-rolled puff pastry**
☐ **1 egg, lightly beaten**

RED WINE SAUCE
☐ **250 mL/8 fl oz dry red wine**
☐ **1 teaspoon finely chopped fresh thyme, or ¹/₄ teaspoon dried thyme**
☐ **1 teaspoon finely chopped fresh parsley**
☐ **freshly ground black pepper**
☐ **100 g/3 oz butter, cut into eight pieces**
☐ **2 teaspoons cornflour, blended with 1 tablespoon water**

1   Melt half the butter in a heavy-based frying pan. When sizzling, add fillet and cook over a medium heat for 10 minutes, turning to brown and seal on all sides. Remove pan from heat and set aside to cool completely.

2   Melt remaining butter in pan and cook onion for 5 minutes, or until soft. Add mushrooms and cook over a medium heat for 15 minutes, or until mushrooms give up all their juices, and these evaporate. Stir during cooking to prevent them sticking. Season to taste with black pepper and nutmeg, stir in parsley and set aside to cool completely.

3   Roll out pastry to a length 7.5 cm/3 in longer than meat and wide enough to wrap around fillet. Spread half mushroom mixture down centre of pastry and place fillet on top. Spread remaining mushroom mixture on top of fillet. Cut corners out of pastry. Brush pastry edges with egg. Wrap pastry around fillet like a parcel, tucking ends in. Turn pastry-wrapped fillet over, place on a lightly greased baking tray and freeze for 10 minutes.

4   Roll out remaining pastry to a 10 x 30 cm/4 x 12 in length and cut into strips 1 cm/¹/₂ in wide. Remove fillet from freezer and brush pastry all over with egg. Arrange 5 pastry strips diagonally over pastry parcel, then arrange remaining strips diagonally in opposite direction. Brush top of strips only with egg. Bake for 30 minutes for medium-rare beef. Place on a warmed serving platter and set aside to rest in a warm place for 10 minutes.

5   To make sauce, place wine in a small saucepan and cook over a medium heat until reduced by half. Add thyme and parsley and season to taste with black pepper. Remove pan from heat and quickly whisk in 1 piece of butter at a time, ensuring that each piece of butter is completely whisked in and melted before adding next. Pour in cornflour mixture and stir over a medium heat until sauce thickens. Serve with beef.

Roll out pastry to a length 7.5 cm/ 3 in longer than meat and wide enough to wrap around fillet. Spread half mushroom mixture down centre of pastry, and remaining mixture on top of fillet.

Wrap pastry around fillet like a parcel, tucking ends in.

Roll out remaining pastry and cut into strips 1 cm/¹/₂ in wide. Brush pastry parcel with egg. Arrange 5 pastry strips diagonally over parcel, and remaining strips diagonally in opposite direction.

LAMB WITH TANGY APRICOT SAUCE

Serves 4

- ☐ **8 lamb noisettes**

TANGY APRICOT SAUCE
- ☐ **125 g/4 oz apricot jam**
- ☐ **1 tablespoon soy sauce**
- ☐ **1 clove garlic, crushed**
- ☐ **1/2 teaspoon ground cinnamon**
- ☐ **1 tablespoon white wine vinegar**

1   Grill, pan cook or barbecue noisettes for 4-5 minutes each side or until cooked to your liking. Set aside and keep warm.
2   To make sauce, place jam, soy sauce, garlic, cinnamon and vinegar in a small saucepan and cook, stirring, over a low heat until jam melts and all ingredients are blended. Spoon sauce over noisettes.

Cook's tip: Noisettes are rolled, boneless loin chops. The meat is rolled up tightly and tied. Most butchers are happy to prepare noisettes for you if you order them in advance.

CHICKEN STIR-FRY

Serves 4

- ☐ **500 g/1 lb chicken breast fillets, thinly sliced**
- ☐ **1 red pepper, sliced**
- ☐ **350 g/11 oz broccoli, broken into florets**
- ☐ **2 small courgettes (zucchini), chopped**
- ☐ **1 carrot, chopped**
- ☐ **2 teaspoons cornflour blended with 1 tablespoon water**
- ☐ **2 teaspoons grated fresh ginger**
- ☐ **1 tablespoon honey**
- ☐ **2 tablespoons soy sauce**
- ☐ **1 tablespoon sweet chilli sauce**
- ☐ **1 tablespoon hoisin sauce**

1   Heat a nonstick frying pan and cook chicken for 3-4 minutes or until tender. Remove from pan and set aside.
2   Add red pepper, broccoli, courgettes (zucchini) and carrot to pan and stir-fry for 2-3 minutes.
3   Stir in cornflour mixture, ginger, honey, soy sauce, chilli sauce and hoisin sauce and cook over a medium heat for 2-3 minutes or until sauce boils and thickens.
4   Return chicken to pan and stir-fry for 2-3 minutes longer or until heated through.

QUICK CUTLET CRUMBLE

Serves 4

- ☐ **4 x 200 g/6 1/2 oz white fish cutlets**
- ☐ **2 tablespoons lime juice**

HERB TOPPING
- ☐ **125 g/4 oz wholemeal breadcrumbs, made from stale bread**
- ☐ **45 g/1 1/2 oz instant rolled oats**
- ☐ **2 tablespoons finely chopped fresh coriander**
- ☐ **2 tablespoons finely snipped fresh chives**
- ☐ **2 teaspoons olive oil**
- ☐ **1 tablespoon vinegar**
- ☐ **freshly ground black pepper**

1 Brush fish cutlets with lime juice and grill for 5 minutes on one side.

2 To make topping, place breadcrumbs, oats, coriander, chives, oil, vinegar and black pepper to taste in a bowl and mix to combine.

3 Turn fish and top each cutlet with topping and grill for 5 minutes, or until cooked through and topping is golden.

Serving suggestion: Garnish with lemon and accompany with baby new potatoes and a green salad.

TAGLIATELLE WITH TUNA

Serves 4

☐ **375 g/12 oz dried wholemeal tagliatelle or spaghetti**

TUNA SAUCE
☐ **1 onion, finely chopped**

☐ **1 clove garlic, crushed**
☐ **440 g/14 oz canned tomatoes, undrained and mashed**
☐ **1 tablespoon tomato purée**
☐ **1 tablespoon dry red wine**
☐ **2 courgettes (zucchini), sliced**
☐ **440 g/14 oz canned tuna in water, drained and flaked**
☐ **1 tablespoon finely shredded fresh basil**

1 Cook pasta in a large saucepan of boiling water following packet directions. Drain, set aside and keep warm.

2 To make sauce, heat a nonstick frypan and cook onion, garlic and 1 tablespoon of juice from tomatoes for 4-5 minutes, or until onion is soft. Stir in tomatoes, tomato purée, wine and courgettes (zucchini) and cook over a low heat for 5 minutes.

3 Add tuna and basil to pan and cook gently until heated through.

Serving suggestion: Place pasta on serving plates, spoon sauce over and garnish with basil. Serve with a mixed lettuce and herb salad and crusty bread.

Microwave it: To make Tuna Sauce in a microwave oven, place onion and garlic in a microwave-safe dish and cook on HIGH (100%) for 2 minutes. Stir in tomatoes, tomato purée, wine and courgettes (zucchini) and cook on HIGH (100%) for 3-4 minutes longer. Add tuna and basil and cook on HIGH (100%) for 3-4 minutes, longer.

Left: Chicken Stir-Fry
Above: Quick Cutlet Crumble,
Tagliatelle with Tuna

PORK WITH SAUERKRAUT

Serves 6

- ☐ **30 g/1 oz butter**
- ☐ **750 g/1½ lb pork fillets, sliced**
- ☐ **2 onions, sliced**
- ☐ **2 green apples, cored, peeled and sliced**
- ☐ **2 teaspoons ground paprika**
- ☐ **1 teaspoon caraway seeds**
- ☐ **freshly ground black pepper**
- ☐ **185 mL/6 fl oz chicken stock**
- ☐ **3 tablespoons dry white wine**
- ☐ **2 tablespoons tomato purée**
- ☐ **440 g/14 oz canned or bottled sauerkraut, drained**
- ☐ **125 g/4 oz sour cream**

1   Melt butter in a large saucepan and cook pork slices over a medium heat for 3-4 minutes each side, or until meat just changes colour. Remove from pan and set aside.

2   Add onions and apples to pan and cook for 4-5 minutes or until onions are soft. Stir in paprika and caraway seeds and cook over a medium heat for 1 minute. Season to taste with black pepper.

3   Combine stock, wine and tomato purée. Pour into pan and cook over a medium heat, stirring constantly to lift sediment from base of pan. Bring to the boil, then reduce heat and simmer for 10 minutes.

4   Return meat to pan, stir in sauerkraut and cook for 2-3 minutes. Remove pan from heat, stir in sour cream and serve immediately.

Sauerkraut: To make sauerkraut, you will require about 3 kg/6 lb cabbage. Trim cabbage, cut into quarters, remove core, and finely shred. Place in a large bowl, sprinkle with 60 g/2 oz salt, mix to combine. Set aside until cabbage wilts. Pack firmly into a sterilised wide-mouthed 4 litre/ 7 pt crock or glass jar. Cover surface of cabbage with a clean muslin cloth. Choose a china or glass saucer or plate that fits snugly into the top of the container, place on top of muslin and weight heavily. Place in a warm place – around 21°C/70°F is ideal. The cabbage must be covered by liquid.

As the cabbage ferments, bubbles and scum rise to the surface. Each day rinse weight, plate and muslin in warm water. Remove any scum and replace muslin, plate and weight. Fermentation takes 2-4 weeks. Store in glass jars, covered with the brine.

BOILED BEEF DINNER

Simple and satisfying,
this Boiled Beef Dinner is served
with creamy mashed potatoes and
horseradish cream. There are sure to
be requests for second helpings.

Serves 6

- ☐ **1.5 kg/3 lb corned silverside**
- ☐ **2 tablespoons brown sugar**
- ☐ **1 tablespoon cider vinegar**
- ☐ **2 sprigs fresh mint**
- ☐ **1 onion, studded with 4 whole cloves**
- ☐ **6 peppercorns**
- ☐ **6 small carrots**
- ☐ **6 small onions**
- ☐ **3 parsnips, halved**

REDCURRANT GLAZE
- ☐ **155 g/5 oz redcurrant jelly**
- ☐ **2 tablespoons orange juice**
- ☐ **1 tablespoon Grand Marnier**

1 Place meat in a large heavy-based saucepan. Add brown sugar, vinegar, mint, onion, peppercorns and enough water to cover meat. Bring to the boil, then reduce heat and simmer for 1¹/₄-1¹/₂ hours.

2 Add carrots, onions and parsnips to pan and cook over a low heat for 40 minutes longer or until vegetables are tender.

3 To make glaze, place redcurrant jelly, orange juice and Grand Marnier in a small saucepan and cook over a low heat, stirring occasionally, until well blended. Transfer meat to a serving plate and brush with redcurrant mixture. Slice meat and serve with vegetables and any remaining redcurrant mixture.

Cook's tip: To make horseradish cream, whip 125 mL/4 fl oz cream (double) until soft peaks form then fold through 3 tablespoons horseradish relish.

Pork with Sauerkraut, Boiled Beef Dinner

ROAST CHICKEN WITH CURRIED RICE STUFFING

Serves 4
Oven temperature 180°C, 350°F, Gas 4

- ☐ **1.5 kg/3 lb chicken**
- ☐ **4 rashers bacon, chopped**
- ☐ **4 spring onions, chopped**
- ☐ **2 teaspoons curry powder**
- ☐ **155 g/5 oz rice, cooked**
- ☐ **60 g/2 oz soft breadcrumbs, made from stale bread**
- ☐ **1 tablespoon olive oil**

TOMATO SAUCE
- ☐ **30 g/1 oz butter**
- ☐ **1 onion, chopped**
- ☐ **1 green pepper, chopped**
- ☐ **125 g/4 oz mushrooms, sliced**
- ☐ **440 g/14 oz canned tomatoes**
- ☐ **2 tablespoons tomato purée**
- ☐ **3 tablespoons red wine**
- ☐ **1 tablespoon sugar**
- ☐ **125 mL/4 fl oz water**

1 Wash chicken and pat dry on absorbent paper. Cook bacon, spring onions and curry powder in a frying pan until bacon is crisp. Remove from heat and stir in rice and breadcrumbs.

2 Fill chicken with rice mixture, securing opening with a skewer. Place in a baking dish, brush with oil and bake for 1½ hours, basting frequently with juices from baking dish.

3 To make sauce, melt butter in a saucepan and cook onion, green pepper and mushrooms for 2-3 minutes. Stir in undrained tomatoes, tomato purée, wine, sugar and water and season to taste.

4 Cook over a medium heat, stirring occasionally, for 8-10 minutes until sauce has reduced by a quarter. Break chicken into serving portions, spoon sauce over and serve.

Time saver: Precious time can be saved by keeping cooked rice or pasta in the refrigerator or freezer, it is then ready to use in dishes calling for cooked rice or pasta or can easily be reheated in the microwave oven to accompany a meal.

Below: Roast Chicken with Curried Rice Stuffing
Right: Redcurrant Lamb Roast, Brandied Beef with Horseradish Sauce

REDCURRANT LAMB ROAST

Serves 6
Oven temperature 180°C, 350°F, Gas 4

- ☐ **1.5 kg/3 lb lean leg of lamb**

GINGER BASTE
- ☐ **30 g/1 oz butter**
- ☐ **1 teaspoon grated fresh ginger**
- ☐ **1 clove garlic, crushed**
- ☐ **1 teaspoon soy sauce**
- ☐ **1 tablespoon redcurrant jelly**

REDCURRANT SAUCE
- ☐ **2 tablespoons redcurrant jelly**

□ 1 teaspoon salt

PINEAPPLE SAUCE
□ 2¹/₂ tablespoons brown sugar
□ 1¹/₂ tablespoons light soy sauce
□ 250 g/8 oz canned crushed pineapple
□ 2 teaspoons grated fresh ginger
□ 2 teaspoons cornflour blended with 2 tablespoons water

1   Place pork in a lightly oiled baking dish and rub salt well into rind. Bake for 20 minutes, then reduce heat to 180°C/350°F/ Gas 4 and cook a further 1¹/₂ hours until well browned and tender.
2   To make sauce, combine brown sugar, soy sauce, pineapple and ginger and pour over pork during the last 20 minutes of cooking, basting with sauce occasionally.
3   Remove pork from dish and keep warm in a low oven. Skim excess fat from meat juices. Whisk in blended cornflour and water, stir over heat until sauce boils and thickens. Slice pork and serve with sauce.

BRANDIED BEEF WITH HORSERADISH SAUCE

Serves 6
Oven temperature 180°C, 350°F, Gas 4

□ 1.5 kg/3 lb beef fillet
□ freshly ground black pepper
□ 30 g/1 oz butter
□ 3 tablespoons brandy

HORSERADISH SAUCE
□ 125 mL/4 fl oz mayonnaise
□ 125 mL/4 fl oz natural yogurt
□ 1 teaspoon lemon juice
□ 1 teaspoon horseradish relish
□ 1 avocado, stoned, peeled and chopped

1   Trim all visible fat from meat and sprinkle with black pepper. Tie with string at even intervals so it will keep its shape during cooking. Heat butter over a high heat in a baking dish and sear meat on all sides until golden brown. Spoon brandy over meat and bake 25-35 minutes until cooked as desired, basting frequently with juices from baking dish.
2   To make sauce, combine mayonnaise, yogurt, lemon juice, horseradish and avocado in a food processor or blender. Process until thoroughly combined. Slice beef and serve with sauce.

Cook's tip: To sear a rolled roast, heat butter or oil in pan, add meat and roll back and forth to brown on all sides.

□ 250 mL/8 fl oz chicken stock
□ 2 tablespoons chopped fresh mint
□ 1 tablespoon cornflour blended with 3 tablespoons port

1   Trim meat of excess fat and place in a baking dish. To make baste, combine butter, ginger, garlic, soy sauce and 1 tablespoon redcurrant jelly in a saucepan. Stir over a medium heat until butter melts.
2   Pour over lamb and bake for 1¹/₄-1¹/₂ hours until cooked as desired, basting frequently with liquid from baking dish. Remove meat and keep warm.

3   To make sauce, place baking dish on top of stove. Combine redcurrant jelly, stock and mint. Bring to the boil, whisk in blended cornflour, stirring until sauce thickens. Slice meat and serve with sauce.

PORK LOIN WITH PINEAPPLE SAUCE

Serves 6
Oven temperature 250°C, 500°F, Gas 9

□ 1.5 kg/3 lb boned rolled loin pork, rind scored

CRUSTY CHICKEN GOULASH

Serves 4
Temperature 180°C, 350°F, Gas 4

CHICKEN FILLING

- [ ] **2 tablespoons vegetable oil**
- [ ] **2 large onions, chopped**
- [ ] **500 g/1 lb chicken fillets, cut into thin strips**
- [ ] **$^1/_2$ tablespoon paprika**
- [ ] **2 tablespoons seasoned flour**
- [ ] **1 tablespoon tomato purée**
- [ ] **125 mL/4 fl oz red wine**
- [ ] **125 mL/4 fl oz chicken stock**
- [ ] **3 tablespoons natural yogurt**

SOUR CREAM CRUST

- [ ] **125 g/4 oz butter, softened**
- [ ] **300 g/9$^1/_2$ oz sour cream**
- [ ] **1 egg**
- [ ] **125 g/4 oz self-raising flour**
- [ ] **1 tablespoon chopped fresh parsley**

Combine butter, sour cream and egg in a bowl. Stir in sifted flour.

Press crust into a 2 litre/3$^1/_2$ pt greased casserole, working mixture up to cover sides and base of dish.

1   To make filling, heat half the oil in a frying pan. Cook onions for 2-3 minutes until golden, remove from pan and set aside. Coat chicken in combined paprika and seasoned flour.

2   Heat remaining oil in pan. Cook chicken for 2-3 minutes. Return onions to pan, stir in combined tomato purée, wine and stock. Bring to the boil, stirring constantly, then reduce heat and simmer covered for 6-7 minutes. Remove from heat and stir in yogurt.

3   To make crust, combine butter, sour cream and egg in a bowl. Stir in sifted flour and parsley, mixing until well combined. To assemble, place mixture in a 2 litre/ 3$^1/_2$ pt greased casserole, working mixture up to cover sides and base of dish. Spoon in filling, cover and bake for 35 minutes. Uncover and bake a further 10 minutes.

Spoon filling into crust, cover and bake.

BASIC MEATLOAF

Serve this meatloaf hot with vegetables as a main meal, or cold cut into slices for sandwiches. Try one of the tasty toppings below to change the flavour completely.

Serves 4
Oven temperature 180°C, 350°F, Gas 4

- ☐ **500 g/1 lb lean beef mince**
- ☐ **60 g/2 oz breadcrumbs, made from stale bread**
- ☐ **3 tablespoons beef stock**
- ☐ **1 onion, grated**
- ☐ **1 carrot, grated**
- ☐ **2 eggs, lightly beaten**
- ☐ **1 teaspoon dried mixed herbs**
- ☐ **1 teaspoon Worcestershire sauce**
- ☐ **freshly ground black pepper**

1   Place meat, breadcrumbs, stock, onion, carrot, eggs, mixed herbs and sauce in a bowl. Season to taste with pepper and mix well to combine.
2   Press mixture into a lightly greased 11 x 21 cm/4$^1/_2$ x 8$^1/_2$ in ovenproof loaf tin and bake for 40-45 minutes. Drain off any liquid, cover and allow to stand for 10 minutes before turning out and serving.

HONEY-GLAZED MEATLOAF

Serves 4
Oven temperature 180°C, 350°F, Gas 4

- ☐ **1 quantity Basic Meatloaf mixture**

HONEY-GLAZED TOPPING
- ☐ **30 g/1 oz pepitas (Mexican pumpkin seeds)**
- ☐ **30 g/1 oz sunflower seeds**
- ☐ **2 tablespoons pine nuts**
- ☐ **2 tablespoons honey**
- ☐ **1 tablespoon brown sugar**
- ☐ **2 tablespoons lemon juice**
- ☐ **$^1/_2$ teaspoon dry mustard**

1   Prepare and cook Basic Meatloaf as directed in recipe.
2   To make topping, combine pepitas, sunflower seeds and pine nuts. Turn meatloaf onto an ovenproof plate and spread top with seed mixture.
3   Place honey, brown sugar, lemon juice and mustard in a saucepan and heat until honey melts and all ingredients are blended. Pour mixture over meatloaf and bake at 200°C/400°F/Gas 6 for 10 minutes.

INDIVIDUAL PASTRY-WRAPPED MEATLOAVES

Serves 4
Oven temperature 180°C, 350°F, Gas 4

- ☐ **1 quantity Basic Meatloaf mixture**
- ☐ **4 sheets prepared puff pastry, thawed**
- ☐ **1 egg, lightly beaten**

1   Make up Basic Meatloaf mixture and divide into four equal portions. Press one portion of meat mixture down the centre of each pastry sheet to form a rectangle.
2   Brush edges of pastry with egg and wrap up like a parcel. Decorate top with leaves cut from pastry scraps. Place rolls on a greased roasting rack in a baking dish. Brush pastry with egg and bake for 25-30 minutes, or until pastry is golden and crisp.

TEX-MEX MEATLOAF

Serves 4
Oven temperature 180°C, 350°F, Gas 4

- ☐ **1 quantity Basic Meatloaf mixture**

TEX-MEX TOPPING
- ☐ **125 mL/4 fl oz tomato sauce**
- ☐ **1 tablespoon barbecue sauce**
- ☐ **1 teaspoon brown sugar**
- ☐ **1 teaspoon chilli sauce**
- ☐ **2 tablespoons finely chopped green pepper**
- ☐ **30 g/1 oz packet corn chips, crushed**
- ☐ **60 g/2 oz grated mature Cheddar**

1   Prepare and cook Basic Meatloaf as directed in recipe.
2   To make topping, combine tomato sauce, barbecue sauce, brown sugar, chilli sauce and pepper. Turn meatloaf onto an ovenproof plate. Spread Tex-Mex Topping over surface of meatloaf. Top with corn chips and cheese and bake at 200°C/400°F/Gas 6 for 10 minutes or until cheese melts.

Tex-Mex Meatloaf, Individual Pastry-wrapped Meatloaves, Chilli Con Carne, Melting Meatballs

SHAPING MINCE
When shaping minced meat, dampen your hands and work on a lightly floured or dampened surface – this will prevent the mince from sticking to your hands and the surface. You will usually need to add an egg to the mince mixture to bind it and make it easier to shape.

MELTING MEATBALLS

Serves 4

- ☐ 1 quantity Basic Meatloaf mixture
- ☐ 90 g/3 oz mature Cheddar, cut into 12 x 2 cm/³/₄ in cubes
- ☐ 45 g/1¹/₂ oz unprocessed bran
- ☐ 3 tablespoons finely chopped pistachio nuts
- ☐ flour
- ☐ 1 egg, lightly beaten
- ☐ oil for cooking

1   Make up meatloaf mixture as directed in recipe and divide into twelve equal portions. Wrap one portion of meat around each cheese cube, to make a ball. Repeat with remaining meat and cheese.

2   Combine bran and pistachio nuts. Coat meatballs in flour, dip in egg and roll in bran mixture.

3   Heat oil in a frying pan and cook meatballs for 6-8 minutes or until golden brown and cooked through.

CHILLI CON CARNE

Serves 4

- ☐ 1 tablespoon vegetable oil
- ☐ 1 onion, chopped
- ☐ 2 cloves garlic, crushed
- ☐ 3 small red chillies, finely chopped
- ☐ 500 g/1 lb lean beef mince
- ☐ ¹/₄ teaspoon ground cloves
- ☐ ¹/₂ teaspoon ground cumin
- ☐ 1 teaspoon dried oregano leaves
- ☐ 2 teaspoons paprika
- ☐ 440 g/14 oz canned tomatoes, undrained and mashed
- ☐ 1 tablespoon tomato purée
- ☐ 125 mL/4 fl oz beef stock
- ☐ 315 g/10 oz canned red kidney beans, drained and rinsed
- ☐ freshly ground black pepper

1   Heat oil in a frying pan, cook onion, garlic and chillies for 2-3 minutes or until onion is soft.

2   Stir in minced beef, cloves, cumin, oregano and paprika. Cook for 5-6 minutes or until meat browns. Combine tomatoes, tomato purée and stock and pour into pan. Reduce heat and simmer for 20 minutes or until liquid reduces by half.

3   Add kidney beans and cook for 10 minutes longer, or until heated through. Season to taste with black pepper.

SPICY SEAFOOD CAKES

Serves 4

- ☐ **500 g/1 lb potatoes, chopped**
- ☐ **250 mL/8 fl oz water**
- ☐ **2 lime leaves**
- ☐ **155 g/5 oz uncooked prawns, shelled and deveined**
- ☐ **100 g/3½ oz scallops**
- ☐ **250 g/8 oz white fish fillets**
- ☐ **60 g/2 oz grated mature Cheddar**
- ☐ **2 tablespoons flour**
- ☐ **2 eggs, lightly beaten**
- ☐ **1 tablespoon lemon juice**
- ☐ **2 tablespoons lime juice**
- ☐ **2 teaspoons grated lemon rind**
- ☐ **1 small fresh red chilli, seeded and finely chopped**
- ☐ **1 tablespoon finely chopped fresh coriander**
- ☐ **freshly ground black pepper**
- ☐ **125 g/4 oz dried breadcrumbs**
- ☐ **oil for shallow-frying**

PLUM SAUCE
- ☐ **4 tablespoons fruit chutney, large pieces chopped**
- ☐ **125 g/4 oz plum jam**
- ☐ **1 tablespoon red wine vinegar**
- ☐ **1 teaspoon Chinese five spice**

1   Boil, steam or microwave potatoes until tender. Drain well and mash.

2   Place water and lime leaves into a frying pan and heat over a medium heat until simmering. Reduce heat, add prawns and scallops and cook for 2-3 minutes or until prawns just change colour. Remove seafood from liquid and drain on absorbent kitchen paper. Place in a food processor or blender and process until smooth.

3   Bring liquid back to the simmer and cook fish for 10-15 minutes, or until it flakes when tested with a fork. Remove pan from heat and allow fish to cool in the liquid. When cool, remove from pan and flake with a fork.

4   Combine potatoes, prawn mixture, fish, cheese, flour, eggs, lemon and lime juices, lemon rind, chilli and coriander in a large bowl and mix well. Season to taste with black pepper. Shape mixture into eight patties, coat with breadcrumbs and refrigerate for 30 minutes.

5   Heat oil in a frying pan, cook patties until golden brown on each side. Drain on absorbent kitchen paper.

6   To make sauce, place chutney, jam, vinegar and five spice in saucepan. Bring to the boil, stirring constantly, and simmer for 5 minutes. Serve with seafood cakes.

BAKED STUFFED FISH

Bream has been used for this recipe, however any whole fish, such as snapper or emperor, is suitable to use.

Serves 4

Oven temperature 180°C, 350°F, Gas 4

- ☐ **1 tablespoon olive oil**
- ☐ **1 small onion, finely chopped**
- ☐ **1 clove garlic, crushed**
- ☐ **3 spinach leaves, stalks removed and leaves finely shredded**
- ☐ **2 rashers bacon, finely chopped**
- ☐ **2 tablespoons currants**
- ☐ **2 tablespoons pine nuts, toasted**
- ☐ **60 g/2 oz breadcrumbs, made from stale bread**
- ☐ **1 egg, lightly beaten**
- ☐ **2 teaspoons lemon juice**
- ☐ **1 tablespoon chopped fresh parsley**
- ☐ **1 tablespoon chopped fresh rosemary**
- ☐ **freshly ground black pepper**
- ☐ **2 whole fish, about 600 g/20 oz each, cleaned and scaled**
- ☐ **250 mL/8 fl oz dry white wine**
- ☐ **60 g/2 oz butter, melted**

1   Heat oil in a nonstick frying pan and cook onion and garlic for 3-4 minutes or until onion is soft. Add spinach and bacon and cook for 5 minutes longer, or until spinach wilts. Remove from heat.

2   Combine spinach mixture, currants, pine nuts, breadcrumbs, egg, lemon juice, parsley and rosemary in a large bowl. Season to taste with black pepper and mix well.

3   Divide mixture into two portions and fill the cavities of each fish. Close securely, using skewers or toothpicks. Place in a greased shallow baking dish, pour wine over and brush fish with butter.

4   Bake for 35-40 minutes, or until fish flakes when tested with a fork. Baste frequently during cooking.

Cook's tip: Fish is cooked when it flakes easily when tested with a fork; if it is overcooked it will be dry and tough.

THAI FISH

These grilled fish with their spicy flavour are sure to become a favourite.

Serves 4

- ☐ **4 small whole fish**

CHILLI MARINADE
- ☐ **2 small fresh red chillies, seeded and finely chopped**
- ☐ **1 clove garlic, crushed**
- ☐ **2 teaspoons grated fresh ginger**
- ☐ **1½ tablespoons chopped fresh coriander**
- ☐ **2 tablespoons lime juice**
- ☐ **2 tablespoons peanut oil**
- ☐ **1 teaspoon ground cumin**
- ☐ **freshly ground black pepper**

1   Rinse fish under cold running water and pat dry with absorbent kitchen paper. Score flesh with a sharp knife to make 2-3 diagonal cuts along the body. Place in a shallow dish.

2   To make marinade, combine chillies, garlic, ginger, coriander, lime juice, oil and cumin in a small bowl. Season to taste with black pepper. Pour over fish and rub well into the flesh. Cover and marinate for 2 hours, or preferably overnight in the refrigerator.

3   Remove fish from marinade and grill under a medium heat for 8-10 minutes, or until fish flakes when tested with a fork. Baste frequently with marinade and turn halfway through cooking.

Cook's tip: These tasty fish are also great barbecued or pan cooked.

Spicy Seafood Cakes, Thai Fish, Baked Stuffed Fish

SEAFOOD WITH MANGOES

Squid is also known as cuttlefish or calamari.

Serves 4

- [ ] **250 g/8 oz calamari (squid)**
- [ ] **250 g/8 oz large uncooked prawns, shelled and deveined**
- [ ] **250 g/8 oz scallops, cleaned**
- [ ] **$^1/_4$ teaspoon sugar**
- [ ] **1 teaspoon cornflour**
- [ ] **2 tablespoons vegetable oil**
- [ ] **2 teaspoons grated fresh ginger**
- [ ] **440 g/14 oz canned sliced mangoes or apricots, drained and cut into 1 cm/$^3/_4$ in strips**
- [ ] **6 spring onions, cut into 1 cm/$^3/_4$ in diagonal slices**

SAUCE

- [ ] **2 teaspoons cornflour blended with 185 mL/6 fl oz chicken stock**
- [ ] **2 tablespoons dry white wine**
- [ ] **1 tablespoon soy sauce**
- [ ] **1 teaspoon sesame oil**
- [ ] **2 tablespoons white vinegar**
- [ ] **2 teaspoons sugar**

1 Clean squid, cut into halves and spread out flat with inside facing up. Mark in a diamond pattern with a sharp knife, then cut into diagonal pieces. Combine squid, prawns and scallops with sugar and cornflour.

2 Heat vegetable oil in frying pan or wok. Stir-fry seafood for 2-3 minutes until just tender. Remove and set aside. Add ginger to pan and stir-fry for 1 minute.

3 To make sauce, combine blended cornflour with wine, soy sauce, sesame oil, vinegar and sugar. Pour into pan and stir until sauce is boiling. Reduce heat and simmer for 3 minutes. Return seafood to pan with mangoes or apricots and spring onions. Toss for 2-3 minutes until heated through.

Cook's tip: To prepare squid, pull away tentacles and intestines from body. Pull feather out of the body and discard. Cut the tentacles from intestines and discard intestines. Rinse the body and tentacles under cold, running water and peel skin away from the body. Drain well and pat dry on absorbent paper. Halve the bodies lengthwise and score the surface with a sharp knife in a diamond pattern.

Like all seafood, squid only requires minimal cooking. Overcooking will cause toughness.

Clean squid, cut in halves and spread out flat with inside facing up. Mark in a diamond pattern, then cut into diagonal pieces.

Shell and devein prawns.

Return seafood to pan with mangoes or apricots and spring onions.

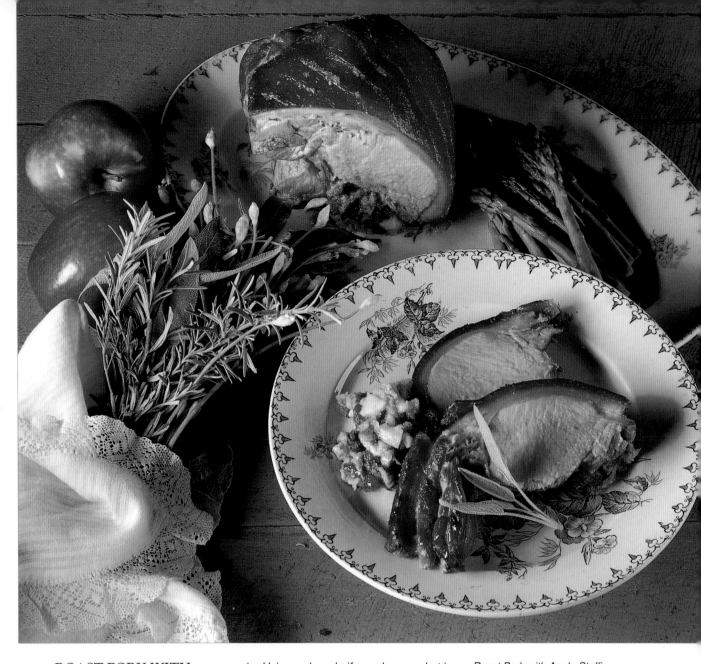

ROAST PORK WITH APPLE STUFFING

Serves 6
Oven temperature 250°C, 500°F, Gas 9

- ☐ **1.5 kg/3 lb loin of pork, with bone in and rind scored**
- ☐ **1 tablespoon salt**

APPLE STUFFING
- ☐ **30 g/1 oz butter**
- ☐ **1 green apple, cored, peeled and finely chopped**
- ☐ **60 g/2 oz breadcrumbs, made from stale bread**
- ☐ **1 teaspoon finely grated lemon rind**
- ☐ **1 teaspoon ground allspice**
- ☐ **1 tablespoon apple jelly**
- ☐ **3 tablespoons sultanas**

1   Using a sharp knife, make a pocket in the pork by separating bones from meat, leaving both ends intact.

2   To make stuffing, melt butter in a frying pan and cook apple for 2-3 minutes or until soft. Remove pan from heat and stir in breadcrumbs, lemon rind, allspice, apple jelly and sultanas.

3   Pack mixture into pocket in pork and place on a roasting rack in a baking dish. Rub rind of pork with salt and bake for 20 minutes. Reduce heat to 190°C/375°F/ Gas 5 and bake for 1 hour longer or until meat is cooked through. Stand for 10 minutes before carving.

Roast Pork with Apple Stuffing

TARRAGON PORK WITH VEGETABLES

Serves 6

- ☐ 30 g/1 oz butter
- ☐ 1 kg/2 lb boned and rolled shoulder of pork
- ☐ 2 onions, chopped
- ☐ 1 leek, chopped
- ☐ 750 mL/1¼ pt chicken stock
- ☐ 3 tablespoons lemon juice
- ☐ 1 teaspoon cracked black pepper
- ☐ 2 bay leaves
- ☐ 1 turnip, chopped
- ☐ 12 new baby potatoes
- ☐ 2 carrots, chopped
- ☐ 2 stalks celery, chopped
- ☐ 3 tablespoons redcurrant jelly
- ☐ 2 tablespoons chopped fresh tarragon

1 Heat butter in a large saucepan, add pork and cook over a high heat until browned on all sides. Reduce heat to low, add onions and leek and cook for 5 minutes or until onions are soft.

2 Stir in stock, lemon juice, black pepper and bay leaves and bring to the boil. Reduce heat, cover and simmer, turning meat occasionally, for 30 minutes. Add turnip, potatoes, carrots and celery and simmer for 15 minutes longer or until vegetables are tender and meat is cooked.

3 Remove meat and vegetables from pan, set aside and keep warm. Bring juices in pan to the boil and boil, uncovered, for 2 minutes. Stir in redcurrant jelly and tarragon and simmer for 5 minutes. To serve, slice pork and spoon over sauce. Accompany with vegetables.

Cook's tip: There are two types of tarragon – French and Russian. While they look very similar, the Russian tarragon has a coarser leaf and is virtually tasteless.

Tarragon is a herb which is best used fresh, as its essential oils are volatile and are lost in drying. When a recipe calls for tarragon it usually refers to French tarragon.

HOT CHICKEN AND POTATO CURRY

Serves 4

- ☐ 10 new baby potatoes, halved
- ☐ 2 onions, cut into eighths
- ☐ 1 clove garlic, crushed
- ☐ ½ teaspoon curry paste (Vindaloo)
- ☐ 440 g/14 oz canned tomatoes, undrained and mashed
- ☐ 250 mL/8 fl oz chicken stock
- ☐ 2 tablespoons dry white wine
- ☐ 2 tablespoons mango chutney
- ☐ 3 teaspoons curry powder
- ☐ 2 teaspoons ground cumin
- ☐ 4 tablespoons tomato purée
- ☐ 2 chicken breast fillets, cut into 2 cm/¾ in cubes
- ☐ 1 tablespoon finely chopped fresh coriander

1 Boil, steam or microwave potatoes until just tender. Set aside to cool.

2 Place onions, garlic, curry paste (Vindaloo) and 1 tablespoon of juice from tomatoes in a saucepan and cook for 2-3 minutes, or until onion is soft.

3 Combine tomatoes, stock, wine, chutney, curry powder, cumin and tomato purée. Stir into onion mixture and cook over a medium heat for 2-3 minutes. Add chicken and potatoes and cook over a low heat for 5 minutes, or until chicken is tender. Just prior to serving, sprinkle with coriander.

Hot Chicken and Potato Curry

FARMHOUSE CHICKEN CASSEROLE

Serves 4
Oven temperature 200°C, 400°F, Gas 6

- ☐ **1.5 kg/3 lb chicken pieces**
- ☐ **3 tablespoons seasoned flour**
- ☐ **60 g/2 oz butter**
- ☐ **2 cloves garlic, crushed**
- ☐ **600 mL/1 pt chicken stock**
- ☐ **2 tablespoons tomato purée**
- ☐ **1 tablespoon vegetable oil**
- ☐ **1 turnip, diced**
- ☐ **2 small carrots, diced**
- ☐ **1 parsnip, diced**
- ☐ **8 small onions**
- ☐ **3 rashers bacon, trimmed and chopped**
- ☐ **8 new baby potatoes, quartered**
- ☐ **freshly ground black pepper**
- ☐ **3 tablespoons finely chopped fresh parsley**

1   Toss chicken in flour to coat. Shake off excess flour and reserve 1 tablespoon.
2   Melt butter in a large frying pan and cook chicken over a medium heat until brown on all sides. Transfer to a large casserole dish.
3   Add garlic and reserved flour to pan and cook over a low heat for 1 minute. Combine stock and tomato purée. Remove pan from heat and gradually blend in stock mixture. Cook over a medium heat, stirring constantly, until mixture boils and thickens. Pour over chicken in dish. Cover and bake chicken for 30 minutes.
4   Heat oil in a large frying pan and cook turnip, carrots and parsnip over a medium heat for 3-4 minutes. Remove from pan and set aside. Add onions and bacon to pan and cook for 4-5 minutes or until bacon is crisp.
5   Stir turnip, carrots, parsnip, onion mixture, potatoes, black pepper to taste and parsley into chicken mixture and bake for 40 minutes longer or until vegetables are tender.

LAMB POT ROAST

Pot roasting dates back to prehistoric times when clay pots were filled with game, whole cuts of meat or poultry, and vegetables, then hung over a fire to simmer. Lean meats that need long slow cooking, are ideal for pot roasting.

Serves 6

- ☐ **90 g/3 oz butter**
- ☐ **1.5-2 kg/3-4 lb leg of lamb**
- ☐ **440 g/14 oz canned tomatoes, mashed and undrained**
- ☐ **125 mL/4 fl oz red wine**
- ☐ **2 tablespoons tomato purée**
- ☐ **1 tablespoon Worcestershire sauce**
- ☐ **¼ teaspoon mixed dried herbs**
- ☐ **1 teaspoon sugar**
- ☐ **freshly ground black pepper**
- ☐ **vegetable oil**
- ☐ **3 carrots, halved lengthwise**
- ☐ **3 turnips, halved lengthwise**
- ☐ **6 small onions**
- ☐ **3 large potatoes, halved**

1   Melt 30 g/1 oz butter in a large heavy-based saucepan and cook meat on all sides until well browned.
2   Combine tomatoes, red wine, tomato purée, Worcestershire sauce, herbs, sugar and black pepper to taste. Pour over meat, bring to the boil, then reduce heat, cover, and simmer for 1½ hours or until meat is tender.
3   About 30 minutes before meat finishes cooking, heat oil and remaining butter in a large heavy-based frying pan. Add carrots, turnips, onions and potatoes and cook until vegetables are lightly browned. Reduce heat to low and cook gently for 15-20 minutes or until vegetables are tender.
4   Remove meat from pan, place on a serving platter, set aside and keep warm. Bring sauce that remains in pan to the boil and cook for 10 minutes or until sauce reduces and thickens slightly. Serve sauce with meat and vegetables.

Cook's tip: A nut of veal, a whole chicken or a piece of topside beef are also delicious cooked in this way.

*Crusty Steak and Kidney Pie,
Farmhouse Chicken Casserole,
Lamb Pot Roast*

CRUSTY STEAK AND KIDNEY PIE

This modern version of steak and kidney pudding, is just as tasty as the original, but easier to make and lighter to eat.

Serves 4
Oven temperature 180°C, 350°F, Gas 4

- ☐ **500 g/1 lb flank skirt steak**
- ☐ **3 lamb kidneys**
- ☐ **60 g/2 oz butter**
- ☐ **1 onion, chopped**
- ☐ **3 rashers bacon, chopped**
- ☐ **2 tablespoons flour**
- ☐ **185 mL/6 fl oz beef stock**
- ☐ **3 tablespoons red wine**
- ☐ **1 tablespoon tomato purée**
- ☐ **¹/₂ teaspoon sugar**
- ☐ **1 tablespoon finely chopped fresh parsley**
- ☐ **freshly ground black pepper**

SOUR CREAM CRUST
- ☐ **125 g/4 oz butter, softened**
- ☐ **300 g/9¹/₂ oz sour cream**
- ☐ **1 egg**
- ☐ **185 g/6 oz self-raising flour**
- ☐ **1 tablespoon finely chopped fresh thyme**

1 Trim meat of all visible fat and cut into 2.5 cm/1 in pieces. Trim kidneys of all visible fat and soak in salted water for 10 minutes. Wipe dry with absorbent kitchen paper. Nick skin on rounded side of each kidney and draw it back on each side until it is attached by the core only. Draw out as much core as possible and cut, with skin, close to kidney. Cut each kidney into slices.
2 Melt 30 g/1 oz butter in a large saucepan and cook meat in batches until browned on all sides. Remove from pan and set aside. Add kidney to pan and cook for 1-2 minutes to seal. Remove from pan and set aside. Stir in onion and bacon and cook for 2-3 minutes or until onion is golden. Remove from pan and set aside.
3 Melt remaining butter in pan, add flour and cook for 3-4 minutes or until a light straw colour. Combine stock, wine, tomato purée and sugar. Remove pan from heat and gradually blend in stock mixture. Cook over a medium heat, stirring constantly, until sauce boils and thickens. Stir in parsley and season to taste with black pepper. Return meat mixture to pan, cover and simmer gently for 1¹/₂-2 hours or until meat is tender. Set aside to cool slightly.
4 To make crust, combine butter, sour cream and egg in a bowl. Sift in 125 g/4 oz

flour and add thyme. Mix until well combined. Spread two-thirds of mixture over base and sides of a shallow ovenproof dish, then spoon in meat mixture. Lightly knead remaining flour into the remaining dough. Press out on a lightly floured surface, using palm of hand, to 1 cm/¹/₂ in thick and cut into rounds using a 3 cm/1¹/₄ in metal pastry cutter. Top filling with dough rounds, overlapping them slightly. Bake for 30 minutes, or until crust is golden.

MEDITERRANEAN FISH STEW

Serves 6

- ☐ **10 green-lipped mussels, scrubbed and beards removed**
- ☐ **250 g/8 oz uncooked prawns**
- ☐ **750 g/1¹/₂ lb firm white fish fillets, cut into large pieces**
- ☐ **250 g/8 oz calamari (squid) rings**

TOMATO SAUCE
- ☐ **1 tablespoon olive oil**
- ☐ **2 leeks, sliced**
- ☐ **2 cloves garlic, crushed**
- ☐ **125 mL/4 fl oz dry white wine**
- ☐ **1 large red pepper, chopped**
- ☐ **440 g/14 oz canned tomatoes, undrained and mashed**
- ☐ **125 mL/4 fl oz chicken stock**
- ☐ **1 teaspoon grated lemon rind**
- ☐ **1 bay leaf**
- ☐ **pinch cayenne pepper**
- ☐ **3 tablespoons chopped fresh parsley**
- ☐ **freshly ground black pepper**

1 To make sauce, heat oil in a large saucepan, add leeks and garlic and cook for 3-4 minutes or until leeks are tender. Stir in wine and cook over a high heat until wine is nearly evaporated. Mix in red pepper, tomatoes, stock, lemon rind, bay leaf and cayenne pepper and bring to the boil.
2 Add mussels to sauce and cook until shells open. Discard any mussels that do not open after 5 minutes. Remove mussels from pan and set aside. Stir in prawns, fish and calamari (squid) and cook for 2-3 minutes. Return mussels to pan, stir in parsley and season to taste with black pepper and serve immediately.

MIDDLE EASTERN LAMB WITH BEANS

Serves 6

- ☐ **1 tablespoon vegetable oil**
- ☐ **1 large onion, sliced**
- ☐ **750 g/1¹/₂ lb lean lamb, cubed**
- ☐ **750 g/1¹/₂ lb green beans, trimmed**
- ☐ **3 tablespoons tomato purée**
- ☐ **¹/₄ teaspoon ground nutmeg**
- ☐ **¹/₂ teaspoon ground cinnamon**
- ☐ **water**

1 Heat oil in a large frying pan, add onion and cook, stirring occasionally, for 5 minutes or until onion is soft. Transfer onion to a casserole dish.
2 Brown lamb in frying pan, then add to casserole. Add beans, tomato purée, nutmeg, cinnamon and just enough water to cover the meat.
3 Cover and bake for 1¹/₂ hours or until lamb is tender and sauce has thickened.

Serving suggestion: This casserole is delicious served with rice or noodles.

GOLDEN-COATED CHICKEN DRUMSTICK

Serves 4
Oven temperature 180°C, 350°F, Gas 4

- ☐ **4 chicken drumsticks, skin removed**
- ☐ **flour**
- ☐ **1 egg, lightly beaten**
- ☐ **1 tablespoon vegetable oil**

RICE BRAN COATING
- ☐ **45 g/1¹/₂ oz rice bran**
- ☐ **45 g/1¹/₂ oz wholemeal breadcrumbs, made from stale bread**
- ☐ **¹/₄ teaspoon dried ground rosemary**
- ☐ **3 tablespoons grated Parmesan cheese**

1 To make coating, combine rice bran, breadcrumbs, rosemary and Parmesan cheese. Coat drumsticks with flour, dip in egg and coat well with crumb mixture.
2 Brush a baking dish with oil, add drumsticks and bake, turning and basting frequently for 1 hour or until chicken is cooked.

LEBANESE PIZZA

Serves 6
Oven temperature 180°C, 350°F, Gas 4

- [ ] **185 g/6 oz cracked wheat, soaked in 500 mL/16 fl oz hot water for 10-15 minutes**
- [ ] **1 onion, chopped**
- [ ] **1 clove garlic, crushed**
- [ ] **500 g/1 lb lean lamb mince**
- [ ] **1/2 teaspoon mixed herbs**
- [ ] **1 tablespoon lemon juice**
- [ ] **1 tablespoon chopped fresh mint**
- [ ] **1/2 teaspoon chilli powder**

TOMATO AND HUMMUS TOPPING
- [ ] **250 g/8 oz hummus**
- [ ] **2 tomatoes, sliced**
- [ ] **8 spinach leaves, blanched and chopped**
- [ ] **3 tablespoons pine nuts**
- [ ] **4 tablespoons grated mature Cheddar**

1   Drain cracked wheat and set aside. Cook onion and garlic in a nonstick frying pan for 3 minutes or until onion is soft. Transfer cracked wheat and onion mixture to a bowl and combine with lamb, mixed herbs, lemon juice, mint and chilli powder.

2   Press meat mixture into a 30 cm/12 in pizza tray and cook for 20 minutes or until base is firm. Drain off any juices.

3   To make topping, spread meat pizza base with hummus then top with tomato slices and spinach. Sprinkle with pine nuts and cheese. Cook under a preheated grill for 3-4 minutes or until cheese melts.

Serving suggestion: Cut pizza into wedges and serve with crusty bread and a salad.

Lebanese Pizza

BEEF AND MUSHROOM PIE

*Homemade puff pastry takes a
little time to make but the result
is well worth it.*

Serves 4
Oven temperature 220°C, 425°F, Gas 7

PUFF PASTRY
- ☐ **90 g/3 oz butter, softened**
- ☐ **90 g/3 oz lard, softened**
- ☐ **250 g/8 oz flour**
- ☐ **125 mL/4 fl oz cold water**

BEEF AND MUSHROOM FILLING
- ☐ **1 kg/2 lb lean topside beef, cut
  into 2.5 cm/1 in cubes**
- ☐ **60 g/2 oz seasoned flour**
- ☐ **60 g/2 oz butter**
- ☐ **3 tablespoons olive oil**
- ☐ **2 onions, chopped**
- ☐ **2 cloves garlic, crushed**
- ☐ **250 g/8 oz button mushrooms,
  sliced**
- ☐ **125 mL/4 fl oz red wine**
- ☐ **125 mL/4 fl oz beef stock**
- ☐ **1 bay leaf**
- ☐ **2 tablespoons finely chopped
  fresh parsley**
- ☐ **1 tablespoon Worcestershire
  sauce**
- ☐ **freshly ground black pepper**
- ☐ **1 tablespoon cornflour blended
  with 2 tablespoons water**
- ☐ **1 egg, lightly beaten**

1   To make filling, toss meat in flour to
coat. Shake off excess flour. Melt butter
and oil in a large heavy-based saucepan
and cook meat in batches for 3-4 minutes
or until browned on all sides. Remove
meat from pan and set aside.

2   Add onions and garlic to pan and cook
over a medium heat for 3-4 minutes or until
onion is soft. Stir in mushrooms and cook
for 2 minutes longer. Combine wine and
stock, pour into pan and cook for 4-5
minutes, stirring constantly to lift sediment
from base of pan. Bring to the boil, then
reduce heat. Return meat to pan with bay
leaf, parsley, Worcestershire sauce and
black pepper to taste. Cover and simmer
for 1¹/₂ hours or until meat is tender. Stir in
cornflour mixture and cook, stirring, until
mixture thickens. Remove pan from heat
and set aside to cool.

3   To make pastry, place butter and lard
in a bowl and mix until well combined.
Cover and refrigerate until firm. Place flour
in a large mixing bowl. Cut one-quarter of
butter mixture into small pieces and rub
into flour using fingertips until mixture
resembles coarse breadcrumbs. Mix in
enough water to form a firm dough.

4   Turn pastry onto a floured surface and
knead lightly. Roll pastry out to a 15 x 25
cm/6 x 10 in rectangle. Cut another one-
quarter of butter mixture into small pieces
and place over top two-thirds of pastry.
Fold the bottom third of pastry up and top
third of pastry down to give three even

layers. Half turn pastry to have open end
facing you and roll out to a rectangle as
before. Repeat folding and rolling twice.
Cover pastry and refrigerate for 1 hour.

5   Place cooled filling in a 1 litre/³/₄ pt oval
pie dish. On a lightly floured surface, roll
out pastry 4 cm/1¹/₂ in larger than pie dish.
Cut off a 1 cm/¹/₂ in strip from pastry edge.
Brush rim of dish with water and press
pastry strip onto rim. Brush pastry strip
with water. Lift pastry top over filling and
press gently to seal edges. Trim and knock
back edges to make a decorative edge.
Brush with egg and bake for 30 minutes or
until pastry is golden and crisp.

*Cut one-
quarter of
butter mixture
into small
pieces and
place over top
two-thirds of
pastry.*

*Fold the bottom
third of pastry up
and the top third
of pastry down to
give three even
layers.*

GLAZED MINTED
LAMB RACKS

Serves 4
Oven temperature 180°C, 350°F, Gas 4

- [ ] **2 lean lamb racks, each containing 6 cutlets**

CRACKED WHEAT SEASONING
- [ ] **4 tablespoons cracked wheat (burghul)**
- [ ] **30 g/1 oz breadcrumbs, made from stale bread**
- [ ] **3 tablespoons finely chopped fresh parsley**
- [ ] **1 tablespoon finely chopped fresh mint**
- [ ] **1 teaspoon grated lemon rind**
- [ ] **1 tablespoon pine nuts, toasted**
- [ ] **2 teaspoons mint jelly**
- [ ] **1 apple, cored, peeled and grated**
- [ ] **15 g/1¹/₂ oz butter, melted**
- [ ] **freshly ground black pepper**

MINT GLAZE
- [ ] **3 tablespoons mint jelly**
- [ ] **2 tablespoons orange juice**
- [ ] **2 tablespoons honey**

1   Using a sharp knife, separate bones from meat, leaving both ends intact, this makes a pocket for the seasoning. Trim excess fat from outside of racks.
2   To make seasoning, cover cracked wheat with boiling water and set aside to soak for 15 minutes. Drain and rinse under cold running water. Dry on absorbent kitchen paper and place in a mixing bowl with breadcrumbs, parsley, mint, lemon rind, pine nuts, mint jelly, apple, butter, and black pepper to taste. Pack mixture firmly into pockets. Place racks in a baking dish.
3   To make glaze, place mint jelly in a saucepan and cook over a medium heat until melted. Stir in orange juice and honey. Brush racks with glaze and bake for 30-35 minutes or until cooked to individual taste. Baste frequently with glaze during cooking.

ROAST VEGETABLES

Serves 4
Oven temperature 180°C, 350°F, Gas 4

- [ ] **4 potatoes, halved**
- [ ] **4 pieces pumpkin**
- [ ] **4 brown onions**
- [ ] **1 tablespoon vegetable oil**

1   Boil or steam potatoes for 5 minutes,
drain and dry on absorbent kitchen paper. Set aside until cool enough to handle. Score the upper rounded side of potatoes with a fork. This helps to crisp potatoes during cooking.
2   Brush potatoes, pumpkin and onions with oil, place in a baking dish and bake for 1 hour or until golden and crisp. Remove from baking dish and keep warm.

BEEF WITH SWEET AND
SOUR SAUCE

Serves 4

- [ ] **2 tablespoons vegetable oil**
- [ ] **500 g/1 lb lean rump steak, cut into thin strips**
- [ ] **1 onion, cut into eighths**
- [ ] **2 cloves garlic, crushed**
- [ ] **1 teaspoon grated fresh ginger**
- [ ] **100 g/3¹/₂ oz oyster mushrooms, sliced**
- [ ] **2 stalks celery, sliced diagonally**
- [ ] **2 carrots, sliced diagonally**
- [ ] **¹/₂ red pepper, chopped**
- [ ] **¹/₂ green pepper, chopped**
- [ ] **440 g/14 oz canned baby sweet corn, drained**
- [ ] **100 g/3¹/₂ oz mangetout (snow peas), trimmed**

SWEET AND SOUR SAUCE
- [ ] **2 teaspoons chilli sauce**
- [ ] **2 tablespoons white vinegar**
- [ ] **2 tablespoons tomato sauce**
- [ ] **2 tablespoons brown sugar**
- [ ] **2 tablespoons dry sherry**
- [ ] **1 tablespoon cornflour blended with 125 mL/4 fl oz pineapple juice**

1   Heat oil in a large frying pan or wok, add meat and stir-fry for 2-3 minutes or until it just changes colour. Remove meat from pan and set aside.
2   Add onion, garlic and ginger to pan and stir-fry for 1 minute. Stir in mushrooms, celery, carrots, red and green pepper, sweet corn and mangetout (snow peas) and stir-fry for 2-3 minutes. Remove from pan and set aside.
3   To make sauce, place chilli sauce, vinegar, tomato sauce, brown sugar, sherry and cornflour mixture in a small bowl and whisk to combine. Pour into pan and cook for 1 minute or until mixture boils and thickens. Return meat and vegetables to pan and stir-fry for 1-2 minutes or until heated through.

GARLICKY LAMB POT ROAST

Serves 8

- [ ] **1.5 kg/3 lb leg of lamb, tunnel boned**
- [ ] **¹/₂ teaspoon ground nutmeg**
- [ ] **¹/₂ teaspoon ground cinnamon**
- [ ] **¹/₂ teaspoon ground black pepper**
- [ ] **2 tablespoons olive oil**
- [ ] **500 mL/16 fl oz chicken stock**
- [ ] **2 tablespoons lemon juice**
- [ ] **250 g/8 oz sweet potato, cut into matchsticks**
- [ ] **250 g/8 oz green beans, trimmed**

GARLICKY STUFFING
- [ ] **3 cloves garlic, crushed**
- [ ] **1 teaspoon garam masala**
- [ ] **125 g/4 oz breadcrumbs, made from stale bread**
- [ ] **2 tablespoons pine nuts**
- [ ] **1 tablespoon currants**
- [ ] **1 teaspoon finely grated lemon rind**

1   To make stuffing, place garlic, garam masala, breadcrumbs, pine nuts, currants and lemon rind in a bowl and mix to combine. Spoon stuffing into lamb cavity and secure with string.

2   Place nutmeg, cinnamon and black pepper in a cup and mix to combine. Rub spice mixture over all surfaces of lamb.

3   Heat oil in a large saucepan, add meat and cook over a high heat until browned on all sides. Add stock, cover and simmer, turning occasionally, for 25 minutes. Stir in lemon juice and simmer for 25 minutes longer.

4   Remove lamb from pan, set aside and keep warm. Add sweet potato to stock in pan and cook for 5 minutes, then add beans and cook for 10 minutes longer or until sweet potato and beans are tender. To serve, slice lamb and accompany with vegetables and pan juices.

Glazed Minted Lamb Racks with Roast Vegetables

VEAL GOULASH

Makes 4 servings

- ☐ 4 x 125 g/4 oz lean veal steaks, cut 1 cm/¹/₂ in thick
- ☐ 1¹/₂ tablespoons paprika
- ☐ 2 tablespoons flour
- ☐ freshly ground black pepper
- ☐ 1 tablespoon vegetable oil
- ☐ 2 onions, chopped
- ☐ 1 clove garlic, crushed
- ☐ 1 tablespoon tomato purée
- ☐ 3 tablespoons red wine
- ☐ 125 mL/4 fl oz beef stock
- ☐ 60 g/2 oz sour cream or natural yogurt

1   Trim meat of all visible fat and cut into 2 cm/³/₄ in cubes. Place paprika, flour and black pepper to taste in a plastic food bag, add meat and shake to coat meat evenly. Shake off excess flour.

2   Heat oil in a large saucepan and cook onion and garlic over a medium heat for 3-4 minutes or until onion is soft. Combine tomato purée, wine and stock. Stir stock mixture and meat into onion mixture. Bring to the boil, then reduce heat and simmer, covered, for 25-30 minutes or until meat is tender.

3   Remove from heat and stir in the sour cream or yogurt. Serve immediately.

Serving suggestion: Serve with fettuccine and boiled, steamed or microwaved vegetables of your choice.

LAMB WITH REDCURRANT SAUCE

Serves 4

- ☐ 4 large, lean, lamb chump chops

REDCURRANT SAUCE
- ☐ 1 tablespoon lime or lemon juice
- ☐ 125 g/4 oz redcurrant jelly
- ☐ 2 tablespoons Dijon mustard

1   Grill, pan cook or barbecue chops for 4-5 minutes each side or until cooked to your liking. Set aside and keep warm.

2   To make sauce, place lime or lemon juice, redcurrant jelly and mustard in small saucepan and cook over a low heat, stirring, for 4-5 minutes or until jelly melts and all ingredients are combined. Spoon sauce over chops and serve.

WHOLE FISH WITH LEEK AND RICE STUFFING

Serves 4
Oven temperature 180°C, 350°F, Gas 4

- ☐ 1 x 1.5 kg/3 lb whole fish, such as snapper or bream, cleaned and skin scored
- ☐ 125 mL/4 fl oz dry white wine
- ☐ 60 g/2 oz butter, melted

LEEK AND RICE STUFFING
- ☐ 185 g/6 oz rice
- ☐ 2 tablespoons olive oil
- ☐ 2 leeks, sliced
- ☐ 2 cloves garlic, crushed
- ☐ 3 tablespoons pine nuts
- ☐ 4 tablespoons sultanas
- ☐ 1 stalk celery, chopped
- ☐ 3 tablespoons chopped fresh parsley
- ☐ 1 teaspoon lemon juice
- ☐ 1 teaspoon finely grated lemon rind
- ☐ freshly ground black pepper

1   To make stuffing, cook rice following packet directions, then drain and set aside. Heat oil in a large frying pan and cook leeks and garlic for 3-4 minutes or until leeks are soft. Remove pan from heat and stir in rice, pine nuts, sultanas, celery, parsley, lemon juice, lemon rind and black pepper to taste.

2   Fill cavity of fish with stuffing, close cavity and secure with wooden skewers or toothpicks. Place fish in a lightly greased, shallow baking dish. Pour wine over fish and bake for 35-40 minutes or until fish is cooked. Baste 3-4 times during cooking.

3   Place fish on a serving platter, cover, set aside and keep warm. Pour juices from baking dish into a small saucepan, bring to the boil and boil for 4-5 minutes or until juices are reduced by half. Spoon over fish and serve immediately.

Microwave it: Whole fish cooks well in the microwave oven – but remember the eyes should be removed before cooking as they can explode.

To cook this dish in the microwave oven, prepare the fish and stuffing as described in the recipe, then place in a shallow microwave-safe dish, pour over wine, cover and cook on MEDIUM-HIGH (70%), allowing 5-6 minutes per 500 g/1 lb fish.

STEAK WITH A DEVILLED MARINADE

Serves 4

- ☐ 4 boneless rib eye steaks (Scotch fillet), trimmed of all visible fat

DEVILLED MARINADE
- ☐ 1 teaspoon curry powder
- ☐ 2 tablespoons brown sugar
- ☐ 2 tablespoons tomato sauce
- ☐ 2 teaspoons Worcestershire sauce
- ☐ 1 teaspoon soy sauce
- ☐ 2 teaspoons lime juice

1   To make marinade, place curry powder, sugar, tomato sauce, Worcestershire sauce, soy sauce and lime juice in a small bowl and whisk to combine.

2   Place steak in a shallow glass or ceramic dish, pour over marinade, cover and set aside to marinate for 2-4 hours.

3   Remove meat from marinade and cook under a preheated medium-high grill for 3-4 minutes each side or until cooked to your liking. Baste frequently with any remaining marinade during cooking.

The perfect steak: Everyone has their own preference on how they like their steak cooked; steak can be cooked to rare, medium-rare and well-done. Rare meat is springy to touch, medium meat less springy and well-done has very little give in it. When testing for doneness do not pierce or cut the meat with a knife as this causes loss of juices and dryness.

BAKED AUBERGINE WITH LAMB

Serves 8
Oven temperature 180°C, 350°F, Gas 4

- [ ] 8 long aubergines (eggplant), each about 125 g/4 oz
- [ ] salt
- [ ] 125 mL/4 fl oz tomato purée
- [ ] 125 mL/4 fl oz chicken stock
- [ ] 4 tablespoons grated Parmesan cheese
- [ ] 30 g/1 oz butter

LAMB STUFFING
- [ ] 500 g/1 lb lean lamb mince
- [ ] 1 onion, finely chopped
- [ ] 1 clove garlic, crushed
- [ ] 1 small red pepper, chopped
- [ ] 2 tablespoons finely chopped fresh basil
- [ ] ½ teaspoon dried oregano
- [ ] ¼ teaspoon chilli powder
- [ ] freshly ground black pepper

1   Remove stems from aubergines (eggplants). Cut almost through each aubergine (eggplant) crosswise at 2 cm/³⁄₄ in intervals, taking care not to cut right through. Sprinkle cut surfaces liberally with salt and set aside to stand for 30 minutes. Rinse under cold running water and pat dry with absorbent kitchen paper.
2   To make stuffing, place lamb, onion, garlic, red pepper, basil, oregano, chilli powder and black pepper to taste in a bowl and mix well to combine. Spoon a generous amount of the meat mixture into each cut of each aubergine (eggplant) and place aubergines (eggplant) in a baking dish.
3   Place tomato purée and stock in a bowl, whisk to combine and pour over aubergines (eggplant). Sprinkle aubergines (eggplant) with Parmesan cheese, dot with butter and bake, basting frequently with pan juices, for 45 minutes or until aubergines (eggplant) are tender.

Veal Goulash

PORK WITH CABBAGE AND CARAWAY SEEDS

Serves 4
Oven temperature 180°C, 350°F, Gas 4

- ☐ 4 large, lean, pork butterfly steaks
- ☐ 15 g/¹/₂ oz butter

RICE FILLING
- ☐ ¹/₄ savoy cabbage, finely shredded
- ☐ 1 stalk celery, finely sliced
- ☐ 90 g/3 oz white rice, cooked
- ☐ 1 teaspoon caraway seeds
- ☐ 2 tablespoons sour cream or natural yogurt
- ☐ freshly ground black pepper

WINE SAUCE
- ☐ 2 tablespoons brown sugar
- ☐ 30 g/1 oz butter
- ☐ 3 tablespoons dry white wine
- ☐ 125 mL/4 fl oz chicken stock
- ☐ 3 tablespoons cider vinegar
- ☐ ¹/₂ teaspoon cornflour blended with 1 teaspoon of water

1   Place each steak between two sheets of plastic food wrap and pound lightly with a rolling pin.
2   To make filling, boil, steam or microwave cabbage and celery, separately, until just tender. Drain and refresh under cold running water. Dry between sheets of absorbent kitchen paper.
3   Combine cabbage, celery, rice, caraway seeds, sour cream or yogurt and black pepper to taste. Divide mixture between steaks and spread over one half of each steak. Fold steaks over and secure with toothpicks. Melt butter in a frying pan, cook steaks on both sides until golden brown. Place in a baking dish. Set aside.
4   To make sauce, place sugar and butter in pan and cook until sugar dissolves. Blend in wine, stock and vinegar and simmer for 3 minutes. Pour over steaks in baking dish. Bake, uncovered, for 20-30 minutes or until tender. Baste with sauce frequently during cooking. Remove steaks from dish, set aside and keep warm.
5   Strain sauce from dish and place in a small saucepan. Stir in cornflour mixture and heat until sauce thickens slightly. Spoon over steaks and serve.

Cook's tip: Butterfly pork steaks are cut from the mid loin area, boned, cut almost in half and opened out flat. Try placing a fruit or savoury filling on one side of the steak, then folding it over and securing with toothpicks. You can then pan cook or bake these steaks.

ROASTED PORK LOIN

Serves 8
Oven temperature 250°C, 500°F, Gas 9

- ☐ 1.5 kg/3 lb boneless pork loin
- ☐ 1 tablespoon coarse cooking salt

SEASONING
- ☐ 30 g/1 oz butter
- ☐ 4 spinach leaves, stalks removed and leaves shredded
- ☐ 3 tablespoons pine nuts
- ☐ 30 g/1 oz breadcrumbs, made from stale bread
- ☐ ¹/₄ teaspoon ground nutmeg
- ☐ freshly ground black pepper

CHUNKY APPLE AND PEAR SAUCE
- ☐ 1 small green apple, cored, peeled and sliced
- ☐ 1 small pear, cored, peeled and sliced
- ☐ 2 teaspoons chopped dried dates
- ☐ 4 tablespoons apple juice
- ☐ 2 teaspoons honey
- ☐ 1 teaspoon grated lemon rind
- ☐ pinch ground cloves

1   Unroll loin and make a cut in the middle of the fleshy part of the meat, making a space for the seasoning. Score the rind with a sharp knife, cutting down into the fat under the rind.
2   To make seasoning, melt butter in a frying pan. Cook spinach and pine nuts for 2-3 minutes or until spinach wilts. Remove pan from heat and stir in breadcrumbs, nutmeg, and black pepper to taste. Spread spinach mixture over cut flap.
3   Roll up loin firmly and secure with string. Place in a baking dish. Rub all over rind with salt and bake for 20 minutes. Reduce temperature to 180°C/350°F/Gas 4 and bake for 1 hour longer or until juices run clear when tested with a skewer in the meatiest part.
4   To make sauce, place apple, pear, dates, apple juice, honey, lemon rind and cloves in a small saucepan. Cover and bring to the boil. Reduce heat and simmer for 5 minutes, or until apple is tender.

Cook's tip: When you buy pork it should be pale-fleshed with a sweet smell, not slimy or bloody. With improved technology and butchering you can now buy smaller, leaner cuts of pork – meat that is ideal for today's lifestyle.

MUSTARD SAUCE

Serves 4

- ☐ 30 g/1 oz butter
- ☐ 1¹/₂ tablespoons flour
- ☐ 2 teaspoons Dijon-style mustard
- ☐ 185 mL/6 fl oz chicken stock
- ☐ 1 teaspoon lime juice
- ☐ freshly ground black pepper
- ☐ 3 tablespoons mayonnaise

1   Melt butter in a saucepan, stir in flour and mustard and cook for 1 minute. Remove pan from heat and blend in stock and lime juice. Season to taste with black pepper.
2   Cook over a medium heat, stirring frequently, until sauce boils and thickens. Remove from heat and stir in mayonnaise.

TOMATO AND PASSION FRUIT SAUCE

Serves 4

- ☐ 1 tomato, peeled, seeded and chopped
- ☐ 1 small apple, cored, peeled and grated
- ☐ 2 tablespoons orange juice
- ☐ 1 tablespoon tomato purée
- ☐ 1¹/₂ tablespoons apricot jam
- ☐ ¹/₄ teaspoon yellow mustard seeds
- ☐ pulp 2 passion fruit

Place tomato, apple, orange juice, tomato purée, jam, mustard seeds and passion fruit pulp in a saucepan. Cook over a medium heat, stirring frequently, until sauce boils and all ingredients are well blended.

HONEY-GLAZED PORK

Serves 4
Oven temperature 180°C, 350°F, Gas 4

☐ **500 g/1 lb pork fillets**

GLAZE
☐ **1 tablespoon honey**
☐ **1 tablespoon orange juice**
☐ **1 teaspoon light soy sauce**

Trim meat of all visible fat and connective tissue. Place in a baking dish. Combine honey, orange juice and soy sauce and brush over fillets. Bake for 30 minutes. Halfway through cooking turn and brush with any leftover glaze. Slice fillets, spoon over sauce of your choice, and serve.

Cook's tip: Pork fillets are lean pieces of meat taken from the loin ribs. Fillets are quick and easy to cook and they have no waste. You can roast or pan cook pork fillets, then serve, sliced, with a sauce.

BANANA AND APRICOT SAUCE

Serves 4

☐ **1 banana, chopped**
☐ **1 teaspoon lemon juice**
☐ **440 g/14 oz canned apricot halves**
☐ **¼ teaspoon ground cinnamon**
☐ **2 tablespoons coconut milk**

1   Place banana, lemon juice, undrained apricots, cinnamon and coconut milk in a food processor or blender and process until smooth.
2   Transfer to a small saucepan and cook gently without boiling, until heated through.

Top: Roasted Pork Loin
Centre: Honey-glazed Pork with Banana and Apricot Sauce, Mustard Sauce, Tomato and Passion Fruit Sauce
Bottom: Pork with Cabbage and Caraway Seeds

CHICKEN WITH SPINACH RICOTTA AND LEMON FILLING

If chicken marylands are unavailable, you can substitute drumsticks or thighs. If you prefer, substitute cottage cheese for ricotta and fresh spinach in place of frozen.

Serves 4
Oven temperature 180°C, 350°F, Gas 4

- [ ] **4 chicken marylands (leg and thigh joints)**

SPINACH FILLING
- [ ] **125 g/4 oz frozen spinach, thawed**
- [ ] **1 clove garlic, crushed**
- [ ] **125 g/4 oz ricotta cheese**
- [ ] **2 teaspoons grated Parmesan cheese**
- [ ] **1 teaspoon grated lemon rind**
- [ ] **ground nutmeg**
- [ ] **30 g/1 oz butter, melted**

TOMATO SAUCE
- [ ] **315 g/10 oz canned tomato purée**
- [ ] **2 teaspoons Worcestershire sauce**

1   To make filling, squeeze spinach to remove excess liquid and combine with garlic, ricotta cheese, Parmesan cheese, lemon rind and pinch nutmeg.

2   Loosen skin on chicken with fingers. Push spinach filling gently under skin down to the drumstick. Arrange marylands in an ovenproof dish, brush with melted butter and bake for 35-40 minutes.

3   To make sauce, combine tomato purée and Worcestershire sauce in a saucepan and simmer gently for 3-4 minutes. Spoon sauce over chicken and serve.

Squeeze excess liquid from spinach. Combine with other filling ingredients.

Loosen skin on chicken using fingers.

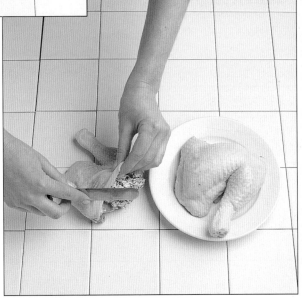

Push spinach filling gently under skin down to the drumstick.

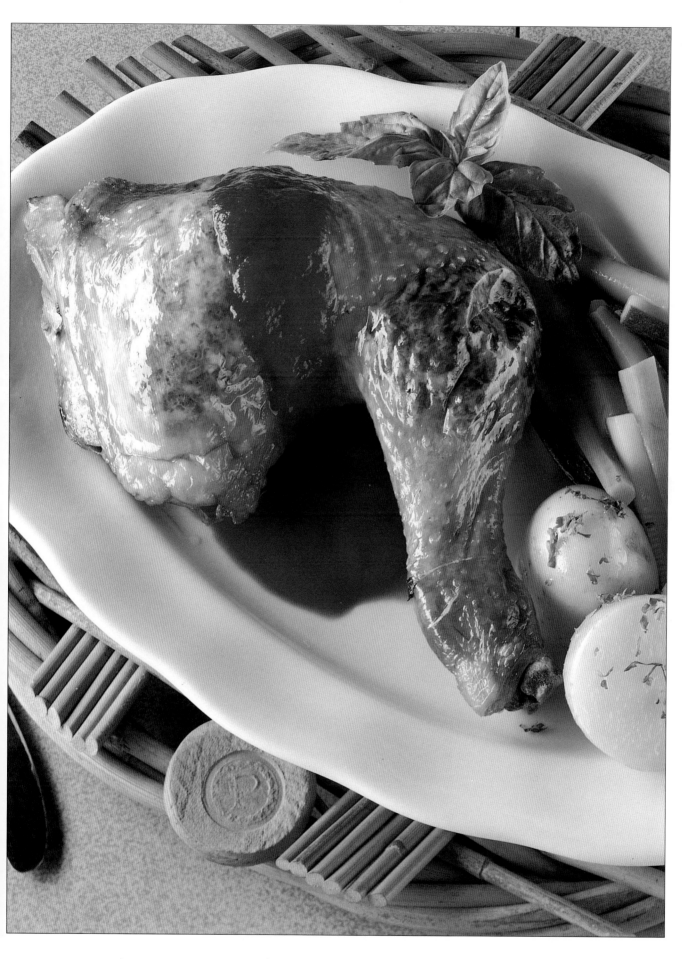

THAI-FLAVOURED WHOLE CHILLI FISH

For this delicious fish dish baby bream was used, but you might like to use small snapper or similar small fish.

Serves 4

- [ ] **4 small whole fish, such as snapper or bream**
- [ ] **1 fresh red chilli, seeded and finely sliced**

SPICY MARINADE
- [ ] **1 tablespoon chopped fresh coriander (including root and stem)**
- [ ] **1 teaspoon grated fresh ginger**
- [ ] **1 clove garlic, crushed**
- [ ] **¹/₂ teaspoon chilli paste (sambal oelek)**
- [ ] **1 teaspoon sugar**
- [ ] **2 teaspoons ground turmeric**
- [ ] **1 tablespoon peanut oil**
- [ ] **1 tablespoon vinegar**
- [ ] **1 tablespoon water**

1   Clean fish and rinse under cold running water. Pat dry with absorbent kitchen paper and arrange in a deep tray.

2   To make marinade, combine coriander, ginger, garlic, chilli paste, sugar, turmeric, oil, vinegar and water. Pour over fish and rub well into the skin and flesh. Cover and refrigerate for 2 hours.

3   Barbecue or grill fish for 3-4 minutes each side or until flesh flakes when tested with a fork. Serve fish with any remaining marinade. Top with chilli slices.

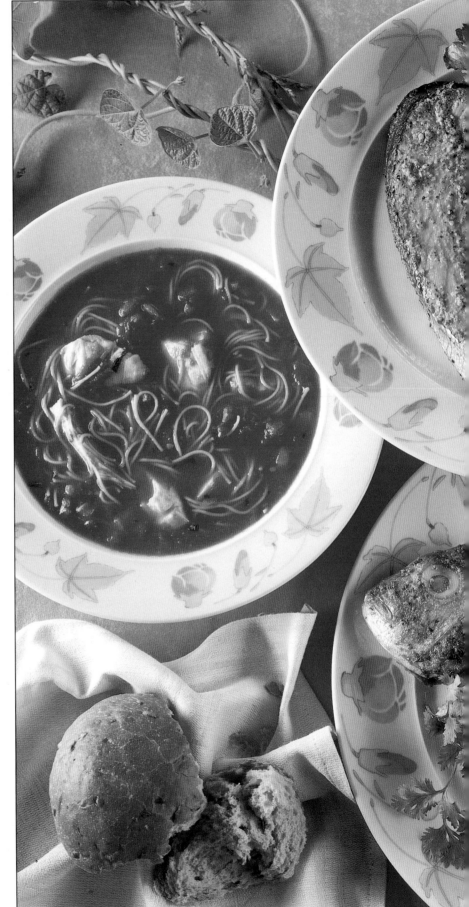

Salmon Cutlets with Basil Sauce, Thai-flavoured Whole Chilli Fish, Fish and Basil Vermicelli Soup

SALMON CUTLETS WITH BASIL SAUCE

Serves 4

- ☐ **4 x 125 g/4 oz salmon cutlets**
- ☐ **freshly ground black pepper**

BASIL SAUCE
- ☐ **1 bunch fresh basil, leaves removed**
- ☐ **2 tablespoons lemon juice**
- ☐ **1 tablespoon olive oil**
- ☐ **1 clove garlic, crushed**
- ☐ **4 tablespoons grated Parmesan cheese**
- ☐ **3 tablespoons pine nuts, toasted**

1 Place fish cutlets in a glass dish and season to taste with black pepper.
2 To make sauce, place basil leaves, lemon juice, olive oil, garlic, Parmesan and pine nuts in a food processor or blender and process until smooth.
3 Spoon half the sauce over fish. Cover and refrigerate for 30 minutes. Grill or barbecue fish for 4-5 minutes each side or until flesh flakes when tested with a fork. Serve fish with remaining sauce.

FISH AND BASIL VERMICELLI SOUP

Serves 6

- ☐ **1 tablespoon olive oil**
- ☐ **1 onion, finely chopped**
- ☐ **2 cloves garlic, crushed**
- ☐ **2 x 440 g/14 oz canned tomatoes, undrained and mashed**
- ☐ **3 tablespoons tomato purée**
- ☐ **¹/₂ teaspoon sugar**
- ☐ **750 mL/1¹/₄ pt water**
- ☐ **1 kg/2 lb fish cutlets, such as mackerel or groper**
- ☐ **2 teaspoons grated lemon rind**
- ☐ **2 tablespoons finely chopped fresh basil**
- ☐ **100 g/3¹/₂ oz vermicelli**
- ☐ **freshly ground black pepper**

1 Heat oil in a large saucepan. Cook onion and garlic for 2-3 minutes or until onion is soft. Stir in tomatoes, tomato purée, sugar and 250 mL/8 fl oz water. Bring to the boil, reduce heat and simmer, covered, for 10 minutes.
2 Poach fish cutlets in remaining 500 mL/16 fl oz of water, drain and reserve cooking liquid. Remove skin from fish and flake fish into large pieces.
3 Add lemon rind, basil, vermicelli and reserved liquid. Cover and simmer for 5-6 minutes or until vermicelli is cooked. Season to taste with black pepper. Stir in fish and cook 23 minutes to heat through.

GARLIC AND ROSEMARY MACKEREL CUTLETS

Serves 4

- ☐ **1 tablespoon olive oil**
- ☐ **30 g/1 oz butter**
- ☐ **2 cloves garlic, crushed**
- ☐ **4 large mackerel cutlets or thick fillets**
- ☐ **3 tablespoons lemon juice**
- ☐ **2 teaspoons fresh rosemary leaves or ¹/₂ teaspoon dried rosemary**
- ☐ **freshly ground black pepper**

1 Heat oil and butter in a large frying pan, add garlic and cook for 1 minute. Add fish and cook for 3-4 minutes each side or until browned.
2 Pour over lemon juice, sprinkle with rosemary and season to taste with black pepper. Cover and simmer for 5-8 minutes or until fish flakes when tested with a fork. Serve immediately.

Nutrition tip: Omega-3 fats found in fish reduce the tendency for the blood to clot and so lessen its 'stickness'. They can lower blood pressure and reduce the fatty build-up on blood vessel walls. They occur in all fish, but are particularly rich in oily fish such as herring, salmon, tuna, mackerel, sardines and ocean trout. Try to aim to eat fish at least three times a week.

ORIENTAL LAMB AND SPINACH

Serves 4

- [ ] **500 g/1 lb lean lamb leg steaks, cut into thin slices**
- [ ] **2 tablespoons oyster sauce**
- [ ] **2 tablespoons dry white wine**
- [ ] **1 teaspoon sugar**
- [ ] **$^1/_2$ teaspoon sesame oil**
- [ ] **1 bunch/500 g/1 lb spinach, washed**
- [ ] **2 teaspoons grated fresh ginger**
- [ ] **2 tablespoons vegetable oil**
- [ ] **$^1/_2$ teaspoon cornflour blended with 3 tablespoons chicken stock**

1 Combine meat with oyster sauce, wine, sugar and sesame oil. Wash spinach, remove thick white stalks and cut into 2.5 cm slices, then cut leaves into large pieces.
2 Heat oil in frying pan or wok. Stir-fry meat in two batches for 2-3 minutes each batch until meat browns. Remove and set aside. Add spinach stalks and ginger to pan and cook gently for 3 minutes. Return meat to pan and stir in spinach leaves.
3 Pour in blended cornflour and toss over high heat for 3-4 minutes until spinach has softened.

Cook's tip: Substituting chicken fillets or pork fillets for the lamb makes a change.

RED PEPPERED BEEF

This recipe is delicious served with rice or noodles.

Serves 4

- [ ] **500 g/1 lb rump steak, cut into thin strips**
- [ ] **2 teaspoons cornflour**
- [ ] **4 tablespoons soy sauce**
- [ ] **3 tablespoons vegetable oil**
- [ ] **2 red peppers, cut into thin strips**
- [ ] **1 small fresh red chilli, finely chopped**
- [ ] **3 spring onions, cut into 5 cm/2 in lengths**
- [ ] **1 clove garlic, crushed**
- [ ] **2 teaspoons grated fresh ginger**
- [ ] **1 teaspoon sugar**
- [ ] **2 tablespoons dry sherry**

Red Peppered Beef, Tangy Lemon Chicken, Oriental Lamb and Spinach

1   Sprinkle meat strips with cornflour and 2 tablespoons soy sauce. Toss to coat and leave for 5 minutes.

2   Heat 1 tablespoon oil in a frying pan or wok, add peppers, chilli, spring onions, garlic and ginger and cook for 2-3 minutes. Remove from pan and set aside.

3   Heat remaining oil and stir-fry meat for 2-3 minutes. Return pepper mixture to the pan. Combine remaining soy sauce, sugar and sherry. Pour into pan and stir-fry pepper mixture a further minute to heat through.

Cook's tip: Never scour your wok when washing as this will cause the food to stick the next time you use it.

The best way to clean your wok is to wash it in warm soapy water using a soft cloth. Then rinse thoroughly in plenty of hot running water. Wipe dry with absorbent paper towel. It is a good idea to oil your wok lightly before you put it away. This will keep it well seasoned.

TANGY LEMON CHICKEN

Serves 4

- [ ] **1 medium cooked chicken**
- [ ] **2 tablespoons vegetable oil**
- [ ] **2 teaspoons grated fresh ginger**
- [ ] **3 tablespoons lemon juice**
- [ ] **250 mL/8 fl oz chicken stock**
- [ ] **1¹/₂ tablespoons honey**
- [ ] **2 tablespoons sugar**
- [ ] **1 tablespoon cornflour blended with 1 tablespoon water**
- [ ] **2 spring onions, chopped**

1   Cut chicken into serving pieces. Heat oil in frying pan or wok and stir-fry chicken for 2-3 minutes. Remove, set aside and keep warm.

2   Stir in ginger and cook for 1 minute. Pour in combined lemon juice, stock, honey and sugar. Add blended cornflour to pan and cook for 1-2 minutes until the sauce thickens.

3   Return chicken to pan and heat through gently. Serve sprinkled with spring onions.

TANGY BROCCOLI AND LAMB

Serves 6

- [ ] **2 tablespoons vegetable oil**
- [ ] **500 g/1 lb lean lamb, cut into strips**
- [ ] **2 teaspoons grated fresh ginger**
- [ ] **1 clove garlic, crushed**
- [ ] **500 g/1 lb broccoli, cut into small florets**
- [ ] **4 stalks celery, sliced diagonally**
- [ ] **125 g/4 oz bean sprouts**
- [ ] **2 tablespoons sesame seeds, toasted**

ORIENTAL SAUCE
- [ ] **1 tablespoon sesame oil**
- [ ] **1 tablespoon soy sauce**
- [ ] **3 tablespoons oyster sauce**
- [ ] **2 tablespoons dry sherry**

1   Heat 1 tablespoon oil in a wok or large frying pan. Add lamb, ginger and garlic and stir-fry for 3-4 minutes or until lamb changes colour. Remove meat mixture from pan, set aside and keep warm.

2   Heat remaining oil in pan, add broccoli and celery and stir-fry until broccoli is bright green. Return meat mixture to pan, add sprouts and stir-fry for 1-2 minutes longer.

3   To make sauce, place sesame oil, soy sauce, oyster sauce and sherry in a small bowl and whisk to combine. Add sauce to meat mixture and cook for 1-2 minutes or until heated. Sprinkle with sesame seeds and serve immediately.

Serving suggestion: For a complete meal accompany with rice or noodles.

BEEF WITH SATAY SAUCE

Serves 6

- [ ] **750 g/1¹/₂ lb lean topside or boneless blade steak**

SOY AND GINGER MARINADE
- [ ] **2 tablespoons soy sauce**
- [ ] **2 teaspoons cornflour**
- [ ] **2 tablespoons honey**
- [ ] **1 teaspoon grated fresh ginger**
- [ ] **1 clove garlic, crushed**
- [ ] **1 teaspoon finely grated lemon rind**
- [ ] **1 tablespoon dry sherry**

SATAY SAUCE
- [ ] **125 g/4 oz peanut butter**
- [ ] **3 tablespoons finely chopped unsalted peanuts**
- [ ] **185 mL/6 fl oz chicken stock**
- [ ] **4 tablespoons dry white wine**
- [ ] **1 tablespoon soy sauce**
- [ ] **1 teaspoon finely grated lemon rind**
- [ ] **1 teaspoon grated fresh ginger**
- [ ] **1 clove garlic, crushed**
- [ ] **1 teaspoon chilli sauce**
- [ ] **¹/₂ teaspoon curry paste**

1   Cut meat into 2.5 cm/1 in cubes and thread onto twelve lightly oiled skewers. Place skewers in a shallow glass or ceramic dish.

2   To make marinade, place soy sauce, cornflour, honey, ginger, garlic, lemon rind and sherry in small bowl and whisk to combine. Pour marinade over meat, cover and set aside to marinate for 2-3 hours or overnight.

3   Remove skewers from marinade and cook under preheated medium-high grill, turning and basting frequently with any remaining marinade for 5-6 minutes or until cooked to your liking.

4   To make sauce, place peanut butter, peanuts, stock, wine, soy sauce, lemon rind, ginger, garlic, chilli sauce and curry paste in a saucepan and cook, stirring, over a low heat for 2-3 minutes or until heated through and all ingredients are blended. Spoon sauce over skewers and serve.

Marinating: This is a clever way of tenderising and adding flavour to less tender cuts of meat. To make a basic marinade you require oil; flavourings such as herbs and spices; and an acid ingredient such as wine, soy sauce, lemon or wine vinegar to break down tough meat fibres. Place the meat and marinade in a bowl, cover and store in the refrigerator until required. The quantity of marinade should be just sufficient to form a pool to coat the meat. Turn the meat occasionally during marinating to ensure all sides come into contact with the marinade.

MARINATED RABBIT IN RED WINE SAUCE

Serves 6
Oven temperature 180°C, 350°F, Gas 4

- ☐ 3 x 1 kg/2 lb rabbits, cleaned and each sectioned into 4 portions
- ☐ 60 g/2 oz butter
- ☐ 2 tablespoons olive oil
- ☐ 6 rashers bacon, chopped
- ☐ 12 baby onions
- ☐ 3 tablespoons flour
- ☐ 750 mL/1¼ pt chicken stock
- ☐ 3 tablespoons port
- ☐ 2 tablespoons French mustard
- ☐ 3 tablespoons tomato purée
- ☐ 250 g/8 oz button mushrooms
- ☐ 440 g/14 oz canned butter beans
- ☐ 2 bay leaves
- ☐ 1 tablespoon chopped fresh oregano
- ☐ freshly ground black pepper

RED WINE MARINADE
- ☐ 1 large carrot, diced
- ☐ 2 stalks celery, sliced
- ☐ 1 large onion, sliced
- ☐ 3 bay leaves
- ☐ 2 cloves garlic, crushed
- ☐ 4 whole cloves
- ☐ 1 tablespoon finely chopped fresh tarragon
- ☐ 1 tablespoon finely chopped fresh parsley
- ☐ 125 mL/4 fl oz olive oil
- ☐ red wine

1   To make marinade, place carrot, celery, sliced onion, bay leaves, garlic, cloves, tarragon, parsley and oil in a large glass or ceramic bowl. Add rabbit and enough red wine to cover mixture. Cover and set aside to marinate overnight. Strain marinade into a clean bowl and reserve. Discard vegetables.

2   Melt 30 g/1 oz butter with oil in a large deep baking dish. Add rabbit and bake for 20-25 minutes or until lightly browned. Remove rabbit from pan, set aside and keep warm. Place baking dish with meat juices over a high heat. Stir in bacon and baby onions and cook for 4-5 minutes or until onions are golden. Remove from pan and set aside.

3   Melt remaining butter in pan, stir in flour and cook over a medium heat until dark brown, taking care not to burn. Combine 750 mL/1¼ pt reserved marinade, chicken stock and port. Remove pan from heat and gradually blend in marinade mixture. Cook over a medium heat, stirring constantly, until sauce boils and thickens.

4   Reduce heat and whisk in mustard and tomato purée. Return rabbit, bacon and onions to pan and bake for 30 minutes. Stir in mushrooms, beans, bay leaves and oregano. Season to taste with black pepper and bake for 30 minutes longer, or until rabbit is tender.

RABBIT-FILLED PEPPERS

Serves 4
Oven temperature 180°C, 350°F, Gas 4

- ☐ 4 red or green peppers
- ☐ 60 g/2 oz butter
- ☐ 750 g/1½ lb rabbit, boned and flesh finely chopped
- ☐ 2 onions, chopped
- ☐ 125 g/4 oz mushrooms, chopped
- ☐ 3 spinach leaves, stalks removed and leaves chopped
- ☐ 125 mL/4 fl oz dry white wine
- ☐ 125 mL/4 fl oz chicken stock
- ☐ 1 tablespoon tomato purée
- ☐ freshly ground black pepper
- ☐ 2 tablespoons chopped fresh parsley
- ☐ 3 teaspoons chopped fresh rosemary

1   Cut a 2.5 cm/1 in slice from the top of each pepper and set aside. Scrape seeds from peppers. Place pepper shells on a baking tray and bake for 20 minutes or until shells are tender but still holding their shape.

2   Melt butter in a frying pan, add rabbit and onions and cook, stirring, for 5 minutes or until lightly browned. Add mushrooms and spinach and cook, stirring, for 1 minute longer. Stir in wine, bring to the boil and boil until liquid is reduced by half. Stir in stock, tomato purée and black pepper to taste, bring back to the boil, then reduce heat and simmer for 15 minutes. Stir in parsley and rosemary.

3   Fill pepper shells with rabbit mixture, top with reserved pepper tops and bake for 15 minutes.

LAMB AND VEGETABLE HOTPOT

Serves 6

- ☐ 750 g/1½ lb leg of lamb, cut into 2 cm/¾ in cubes
- ☐ 2 tablespoons seasoned flour
- ☐ 15 g/½ oz butter
- ☐ 2 tablespoons oil
- ☐ 6 baby onions, peeled and bases left intact
- ☐ 6 baby new potatoes
- ☐ 2 cloves garlic, crushed
- ☐ 3 stalks celery, sliced
- ☐ 1 red pepper, sliced
- ☐ 2 rashers bacon, chopped
- ☐ 1 carrot, sliced
- ☐ 375 mL/12 fl oz beef stock
- ☐ 125 mL/4 fl oz red wine
- ☐ 1 tablespoon tomato purée
- ☐ 2 tablespoons finely chopped fresh rosemary
- ☐ 250 g/8 oz green beans, trimmed and cut into 2.5 cm/1 in lengths
- ☐ 1 tablespoon cornflour blended with 2 tablespoons water
- ☐ freshly ground black pepper

1   Toss meat in flour. Heat butter and 1 tablespoon oil in a large heavy-based saucepan and cook meat in batches until brown on all sides. Remove from pan and set aside.

2   Heat remaining oil in pan and cook onions and potatoes until brown on all sides. Remove from pan and set aside. Add garlic, celery, red pepper and bacon and cook for 4-5 minutes. Return meat, onions and potatoes to pan. Mix in carrot, stock, wine, tomato purée and rosemary, bring to the boil, then reduce heat and simmer, covered, for 1 hour or until meat is tender. Stir in beans and cornflour mixture, season to taste with black pepper and cook for 10 minutes longer.

Lamb and Vegetable Hotpot,
Marinated Rabbit in Red Wine Sauce

ROAST CHICKEN WITH BREAD STUFFING

A stuffing transforms succulent roast chicken into something extra special. For a change, instead of placing the stuffing in the cavity of the bird try placing it between the skin and the flesh.

Serves 4
Oven temperature 180°C, 350°F, Gas 4

- ☐ 1 x 1.5 kg/3 lb chicken
- ☐ 30 g/1 oz butter, melted
- ☐ 2 cloves garlic, crushed

BASIC BREAD STUFFING
- ☐ 125 g/4 oz breadcrumbs, made from stale bread
- ☐ 1 onion, finely chopped
- ☐ 60 g/2 oz butter, melted
- ☐ 1 egg, lightly beaten
- ☐ 90 g/3 oz pine nuts, toasted
- ☐ 2 teaspoons chopped fresh parsley
- ☐ 1 tablespoon chopped fresh rosemary
- ☐ freshly ground black pepper

1 To make stuffing, combine breadcrumbs, onion, butter, egg, pine nuts, parsley and rosemary in a bowl and mix well. Season to taste with black pepper and fill cavity of chicken with stuffing. Secure opening with metal or bamboo skewers.
2 Tuck wings under body of chicken and tie legs together. Place bird breast side up in a baking dish. Combine butter and garlic, brush over chicken and bake, turning several times, for 1-1½ hours or until bird is cooked.

STUFFING VARIATIONS
Fruity Stuffing: Soak 125 g/4 oz chopped mixed fruit in 125 mL/4 fl oz of dry white wine for 30 minutes. Mix into the basic stuffing. Fruits such as apricots, prunes and currants are popular choices. Replace the rosemary with 1 teaspoon mixed spice.
Ham and Mushroom Stuffing: Add to the basic stuffing 125 g/4 oz finely chopped ham, 90 g/3 oz sliced button mushrooms that have been cooked in 1 teaspoon olive oil, and 1 tablespoon Dijon mustard.
Hot 'n' Spicy Stuffing: Add ½ teaspoon chilli powder to the basic stuffing. Replace pine nuts with the same quantity of sunflower seeds and replace parsley and rosemary with 1 teaspoon ground cumin and 1 teaspoon garam masala.

Cook's tip: To test when a bird is cooked, place a skewer into the thickest part of the bird and when the skewer is removed the juices should run clear. If the juices are tinged pink return the bird to the oven and continue cooking.

On completion of cooking allow whole birds to stand for 10-20 minutes. This tenderises the meat by allowing the juices to settle into the flesh.

FETA DRUMSTICKS

Serves 6
Oven temperature 180°C, 350°F, Gas 4

- ☐ 30 g/1 oz butter
- ☐ 1 clove garlic, crushed
- ☐ 1 bunch/500 g/1 lb English spinach, finely shredded
- ☐ 2 slices ham, finely chopped
- ☐ 125 g/4 oz feta cheese, broken into small pieces
- ☐ 1 teaspoon ground coriander
- ☐ 3 teaspoons ground nutmeg
- ☐ freshly ground black pepper
- ☐ 12 chicken drumsticks
- ☐ 2 tablespoons olive oil

1 Melt butter in a frying pan, add garlic and cook for 1 minute. Stir in half the spinach and cook for 3-4 minutes, or until spinach is tender. Remove from pan and set aside. Repeat with remaining spinach.
2 Combine spinach mixture, ham, cheese, coriander and 1 teaspoon nutmeg. Season to taste with black pepper. Ease skin carefully away from drumstick to form a pocket. Place a spoonful of mixture into the pocket and pull skin over. Repeat with remaining mixture and drumsticks.
3 Brush drumsticks with oil, sprinkle with remaining nutmeg and place in a baking dish. Bake for 30 minutes, or until drumsticks are cooked through.

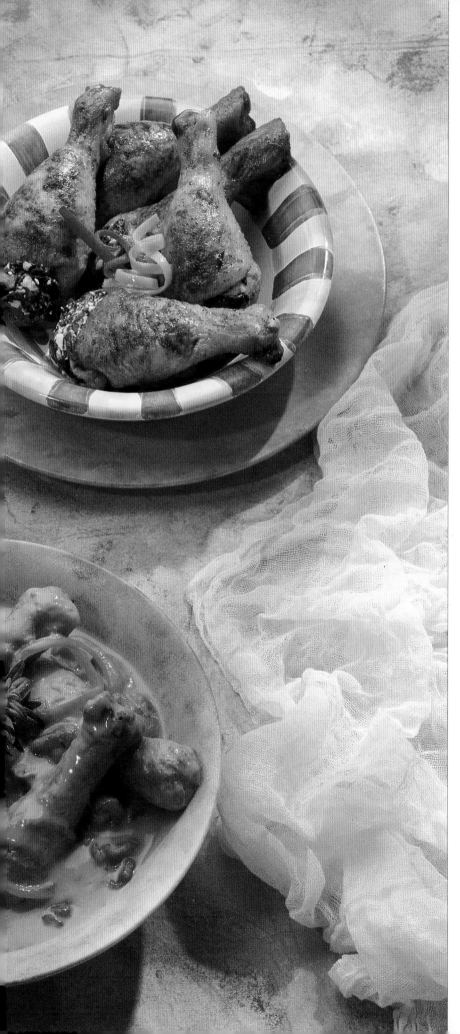

CHICKEN DRUMSTICK CASSEROLE

Serves 4

- ☐ **8 chicken drumsticks**
- ☐ **60 g/2 oz flour**
- ☐ **3 tablespoons olive oil**
- ☐ **1 onion, sliced**
- ☐ **1 clove garlic, crushed**
- ☐ **30 g/1 oz butter**
- ☐ **250 mL/8 fl oz dry red wine**
- ☐ **125 mL/4 fl oz chicken stock**
- ☐ **440 g/14 oz canned tomatoes, undrained and mashed**
- ☐ **2 teaspoons finely chopped fresh rosemary**
- ☐ **250 g/8 oz button mushrooms, halved**
- ☐ **3 tablespoons cream**
- ☐ **freshly ground black pepper**

1 Coat drumsticks with 4 tablespoons of flour. Heat 2 tablespoons oil in a large frying pan, add drumsticks and brown. Remove from pan and set aside.
2 Add onion and garlic to pan and cook for 3-4 minutes or until onion is soft. Add butter and melt. Stir in remaining flour and cook for 1 minute. Return chicken to pan.
3 Combine wine, stock, tomatoes and rosemary and add to pan. Bring to the boil and simmer for 30 minutes, or until drumsticks are cooked through.
4 Heat remaining oil in a small frying pan and cook mushrooms for 3-4 minutes. Stir mushrooms and cream into chicken mixture. Season to taste with black pepper.

Cook's tip: You may wish to use a variety of chicken pieces, such as wings or thighs, with the drumsticks. If you are watching your weight, remove the skin from the chicken before cooking. Most of the fat in the chicken is found in the skin.

Feta Drumsticks, Chicken Drumstick Casserole

WHOLE FISH WITH ORANGE AND TOMATO BUTTER

Serves 2

- ☐ **1 kg/2 lb whole snapper**
- ☐ **30 g/1 oz butter**
- ☐ **3 spring onions, finely chopped**
- ☐ **1 clove garlic, crushed**
- ☐ **1 large orange, segmented**
- ☐ **1 tablespoon chopped fresh parsley**
- ☐ **30 g/1 oz breadcrumbs, made from stale bread**

ORANGE AND TOMATO BUTTER
- ☐ **125 g/4 oz butter, softened**
- ☐ **3 teaspoons grated orange rind**
- ☐ **1 tablespoon orange juice**
- ☐ **2 teaspoons tomato sauce**
- ☐ **freshly ground black pepper**

Run a knife inside fish across bones, starting from head and working down to the tail to remove bones. Take care not to cut through back.

Segment orange for stuffing.

1   Run a knife inside fish across bones, starting from head and working down to the tail to remove bones, taking care not to cut through back. Turn fish and repeat with other side. Cut centre bone at both ends and gently lift out bone.

2   Melt butter in a frying pan. Cook spring onions and garlic for 1-2 minutes. Remove from heat and stir in orange, parsley and breadcrumbs, then spread inside fish. Place on a greased sheet of aluminium foil, fold aluminium foil over at top and completely seal ends. Barbecue until fish is tender and flesh flakes when tested.

3   To make Orange and Tomato Butter, combine butter, rind, juice and sauce and mix well. Season to taste with black pepper. Form into a sausage shape on a piece of aluminium foil, wrap and refrigerate until firm. Cut into slices and serve with fish.

Cook's tip: Snapper is a warm water sea fish with a delicate white flesh – if unavailable, substitute sea bream or any other white-fleshed fish.

Form Orange and Tomato Butter into a sausage shape on a piece of aluminium foil, wrap and refrigerate until firm.

LAMB CASSEROLE WITH A CHEESY COBBLER TOPPING

Serves 4
Oven temperature 180°C, 350°F, Gas 4

- [ ] **750 g/1¹/₂ lb lean diced lamb**
- [ ] **flour**
- [ ] **2 tablespoons olive oil**

MUSHROOM SAUCE
- [ ] **125 g/4 oz mushrooms, sliced**
- [ ] **1 clove garlic, crushed**
- [ ] **3 spring onions, chopped**
- [ ] **1 teaspoon Dijon mustard**
- [ ] **315 mL/10 fl oz chicken stock**
- [ ] **2 teaspoons cornflour blended with 125 mL/4 fl oz cream (double) or evaporated milk**
- [ ] **freshly ground black pepper**

CHEESY COBBLER TOPPING
- [ ] **250 g/8 oz self-raising flour**
- [ ] **pinch cayenne pepper**
- [ ] **pinch chilli powder**
- [ ] **125 g/4 oz butter**
- [ ] **1 egg, lightly beaten**
- [ ] **125 mL/4 fl oz milk**
- [ ] **90 g/3 oz grated mature Cheddar**
- [ ] **¹/₂ teaspoon dry mustard**

1 Toss meat in flour. Heat oil in a large frying pan, add meat and cook in batches until browned on all sides. Transfer meat to a shallow ovenproof casserole dish.
2 To make sauce, add mushrooms, garlic and spring onions to pan and cook, stirring frequently, until mushrooms are soft. Place mushroom mixture on top of meat. Combine Dijon mustard and stock, pour into pan and bring to the boil. Whisk cornflour mixture into stock mixture and cook over a medium heat, stirring constantly, until sauce boils and thickens. Spoon sauce over meat and mushrooms, cover and bake for 40 minutes or until meat is tender.
3 To make topping, sift flour, cayenne and chilli powder together into a large bowl. Rub in 90 g/3 oz butter until mixture resembles fine breadcrumbs. Combine egg and milk and pour into flour mixture all at once. Stir ingredients together to give a soft, sticky dough. Turn dough onto a lightly floured surface and knead briefly. Roll out dough to 1 cm/¹/₂ in thick and cut into 5 cm/ 2 in rounds.
4 Remove casserole dish from oven, uncover and quickly top with dough rounds. Melt remaining butter and combine with cheese and mustard. Spread cheese mixture over topping and bake at 220°C/ 425°F/Gas 7 for 12-15 minutes or until topping is golden and cooked through.

HAM STEAKS WITH CRANBERRY SAUCE

If you prefer, substitute cream cheese or ricotta cheese for the cottage cheese.

Serves 4

- [ ] **15 g/¹/₂ oz butter**
- [ ] **4 ham steaks**

CRANBERRY SAUCE
- [ ] **125 mL/4 fl oz cranberry sauce**
- [ ] **3 tablespoons redcurrant jelly**
- [ ] **1 tablespoon port (optional)**

TOPPING
- [ ] **250 g/8 oz cottage cheese**
- [ ] **2 spring onions, finely chopped**
- [ ] **60 g/2 oz alfalfa sprouts**

1 Melt butter in a frying pan and cook ham steaks over medium heat for 1-2 minutes each side. Remove from pan and keep warm.
2 To make sauce, combine cranberry sauce, redcurrant jelly and port, if used, in the pan. Stir over low heat until well mixed.
3 Combine cottage cheese and spring onions. Top each steak with sprouts and cottage cheese mixture and spoon sauce over to serve.

BEEF IN COCONUT MILK

A thick, spicy sauce coats the meat and makes for a satisfying meal.

Serves 4

- [ ] **2 onions, chopped**
- [ ] **1 tablespoon chilli paste (sambal oelek)**
- [ ] **3 tablespoons chopped almonds**
- [ ] **¹/₂ teaspoon dried shrimp paste**
- [ ] **250 mL/8 fl oz water**
- [ ] **2 tablespoons groundnut (peanut) oil**
- [ ] **500 g/1 lb lean topside steak, cut into 2.5 cm/1 in cubes**
- [ ] **250 mL/8 fl oz coconut milk**
- [ ] **1 tablespoon mango chutney**
- [ ] **2 tablespoons lime or lemon juice**

1 Place onions, chilli paste (sambal oelek), almonds, shrimp paste and 1 tablespoon water in a food processor or blender and process until smooth.
2 Heat oil in a large saucepan, add onion

mixture and cook over a low heat, stirring, for 5 minutes. Add meat and cook, stirring, for 2-3 minutes or until meat just changes colour.
3 Stir in remaining water, cover, bring to simmering and simmer for 1 hour or until meat is tender.
4 Place coconut milk, chutney and lime or lemon juice in a bowl and mix to combine. Stir into meat mixture, bring back to simmering and simmer, stirring occasionally, for 10-15 minutes longer or until heated through.

Coconut milk: You can make coconut milk using desiccated coconut and water. To make, place 500 g/1 lb desiccated coconut in a bowl, pour over 750 mL/1¹/₄ pt boiling water and allow to stand for 30 minutes. Strain, squeezing the coconut to extract as much liquid as possible. This will make a thick coconut milk. The coconut can be used again to make a weaker coconut milk.

BRUSSELS SPROUTS AND HAM PIE

This impressive deep dish pie is a meal in itself. You can serve it with a mixed green salad and some crusty bread, and finish the meal with fresh fruit. What could be easier or more delicious for a family meal or for casual entertaining?

Serves 6
Oven temperature 200°C, 400°F, Gas 6

- [ ] **155 g/5 oz prepared puff pastry**
- [ ] **1 egg, lightly beaten with 1 tablespoon water**

BRUSSELS SPROUTS AND HAM FILLING
- [ ] **500 g/1 lb Brussels sprouts, trimmed**
- [ ] **30 g/1 oz butter**
- [ ] **3 tablespoons flour**
- [ ] **375 mL/12 fl oz milk**
- [ ] **125 g/4 oz grated mature Cheddar**
- [ ] **250 g/8 oz piece ham, diced**
- [ ] **freshly ground black pepper**

1 To make filling, boil, steam or microwave Brussels sprouts until just tender. Refresh under cold running water, cut into quarters and set aside.
2 Melt butter in saucepan, stir in flour and cook for 1 minute. Gradually stir in milk and cook, stirring constantly, for 4-5 minutes or

until sauce boils and thickens. Remove pan from heat, add Brussels sprouts, cheese, ham and black pepper to taste and mix to combine. Set aside to cool completely.

3   Spoon cooled filling into a 1 litre/1³/₄ pt capacity pie dish. Roll out pastry to 5 cm/ 2 in larger than pie dish, Cut off a 1 cm/ ¹/₂ in strip from pastry edge. Brush rim of dish with water and press pastry strip onto rim. Brush pastry strip with water. Lift pastry top over filling and press gently to seal edges. Trim and knock back edges to make a decorative edge. Cut slits in top of pie and decorate with pastry leaves made from trimming. Brush pastry with egg mixture and bake for 30 minutes or until pastry is golden and crisp.

STEAKS WITH GARLIC TOMATO CONCASSE

For a change try the concasse with lamb chops or chicken fillets.

Serves 6

☐ **6 x 125 g/4 oz boneless rib eye steaks (Scotch fillet)**

GARLIC TOMATO CONCASSE
☐ **4 large tomatoes, peeled and chopped**
☐ **2 cloves garlic, crushed**
☐ **2 tablespoons finely chopped chives**
☐ **freshly ground black pepper**

1   To make concasse, place tomatoes, garlic and chives in a saucepan. Cook over a medium heat for 8-10 minutes or until tomatoes are just soft. Season to taste with black pepper.

2   Trim all visible fat from meat. Heat a nonstick frying pan and cook steaks over medium-high heat for 4-5 minutes each side. Spoon sauce over steaks and serve immediately.

ATHENIAN LAMB KEBABS

These Mediterranean-flavoured kebabs will quickly become a family favourite.

Serves 6

☐ **750 g/1¹/₂ lb lean lamb, cubed and trimmed of fat**
☐ **12 bay leaves**
☐ **1 large onion, cut into eighths**
☐ **12 cherry tomatoes**

Athenian Lamb Kebabs

☐ **1 green pepper, cubed**

LEMON MARINADE
☐ **1 tablespoon olive oil**
☐ **3 tablespoons lemon juice**
☐ **1 teaspoon finely chopped fresh rosemary**
☐ **3 tablespoons finely chopped fresh parsley**
☐ **freshly ground black pepper**
☐ **dash Tabasco sauce**

1   To make marinade, combine oil, lemon juice, rosemary, parsley, black pepper to taste and Tabasco sauce in a glass bowl. Add meat, toss to coat and marinate for 30 minutes.

2   Remove meat from marinade and thread on to twelve oiled wooden skewers, alternating with bay leaves, onion, tomatoes and pepper.

3   Barbecue or grill kebabs slowly, turning and basting frequently with remaining marinade, until well browned and cooked.

CHEESE, SALAMI AND SPINACH STRUDEL

Serves 6
Oven temperature 180°C, 350°F, Gas 4

- [ ] **8 sheets filo pastry**
- [ ] **3 tablespoons olive oil**

FILLING
- [ ] **4 slices mozzarella cheese**
- [ ] **15 slices soft salami**
- [ ] **125 mL/4 fl oz tomato sauce**
- [ ] **1/2 teaspoon dried sweet basil leaves**
- [ ] **6 spinach leaves, shredded**
- [ ] **1 egg, beaten**
- [ ] **315 g/10 oz canned or bottled red peppers, drained and sliced**
- [ ] **125 g/4 oz pepperoni salami, skin removed and cut into thin slices**
- [ ] **20 stuffed olives, cut in half lengthwise**
- [ ] **2 tablespoons grated Parmesan cheese**

1   Lay pastry sheets on top of each other, brushing between each layer with oil.
2   Place a layer of mozzarella evenly down the long edge of pastry, leaving about 5 cm/2 in at each end, and top with rolled up soft salami. Pour over combined tomato sauce and basil. Arrange spinach over tomato sauce, top evenly with beaten egg. Place peppers over spinach then top with a row each of pepperoni slices and olives.
3   Roll up tightly to enclose filling and tuck ends under. Transfer to an oven tray, brush with oil, sprinkle with Parmesan cheese and bake for 30 minutes or until lightly browned. Serve sliced.

Cook's tip: When working with filo pastry, cover any sheets that are not immediately in use with a dampened tea towel, to prevent them from drying out.

PEPPERED ROAST WITH BRANDY CREAM SAUCE

Serves 4
Oven temperature 200°C, 400°F, Gas 6

- [ ] **1 piece rump steak, 4 cm/1¹/₂ in thick and about 750 g/1¹/₂ lb in weight**
- [ ] **4 tablespoons cracked black peppercorns**
- [ ] **2 teaspoons vegetable oil**

SAUCE
- [ ] **125 mL/4 fl oz beef stock**
- [ ] **3 tablespoons dry white wine**
- [ ] **2 teaspoons brandy**
- [ ] **2 tablespoons cream**

1   Trim all visible fat from meat. Press both sides of steak into peppercorns.
2   Heat oil in a baking dish. Add meat and brown well on each side. Transfer to oven. Bake for 30-35 minutes or until cooked as desired. Remove meat from dish and cover with aluminium foil. Stand 5 minutes before serving.
3   To make sauce, combine stock, wine and brandy and pour into baking dish. Stir over medium heat for 2-3 minutes lifting sediment from base of dish. Remove from heat and whisk in cream. Slice steak, spoon over sauce and serve.

Microwave it: Prepare ingredients. Preheat browning dish on 100% (HIGH) for 7 minutes. Add oil and steak and cook on MEDIUM/HIGH (70%) 10 minutes, turning after 5 minutes. Remove from dish and stand covered for 10 minutes. Combine stock, wine and brandy. Pour into browning dish. Cook on HIGH (100%) for 2-3 minutes, stirring during cooking.

Ham Steaks with Cranberry Sauce,
Cheese, Salami and Spinach Strudel,
Peppered Roast with Brandy Cream Sauce

BEEF AND PICKLED VEGETABLE OMELETTE

The Chinese mixed vegetables used as the filling for this omelette are available from most Oriental supermarkets.

Serves 4

- ☐ **2 tablespoons groundnut (peanut) oil**
- ☐ **250 g/8 oz lean beef mince**
- ☐ **2 tablespoons bottled Chinese mixed vegetables (tung chai), drained and chopped**
- ☐ **1 teaspoon honey**
- ☐ **2 tablespoons soy sauce**
- ☐ **6 spring onions, finely chopped**
- ☐ **6 eggs, lightly beaten**

1 Heat half the oil in a frying pan, add mince, vegetables, honey, soy and spring onions, and stir-fry for 3-4 minutes. Remove from pan, set aside and keep warm.

2 Heat remaining oil in a clean frying pan. Pour in a quarter of the beaten eggs. Swirl pan over heat to make a thin omelette.

3 Spoon a quarter of the meat mixture into the centre of the omelette and fold over the edges.

4 Remove from pan and keep warm. Repeat with remaining eggs and meat mixture. Cut omelettes into slices and serve immediately.

Beef and Pickled Vegetable Omelette

CHICKEN WITH AROMATIC SPICES AND CASHEWS

The addition of coconut milk to aromatic spices gives this quick curry a special touch.

Serves 4

- ☐ **1 onion, finely chopped**
- ☐ **2 cloves garlic, crushed**
- ☐ **¹/₂ teaspoon sugar**
- ☐ **¹/₂ teaspoon black mustard seeds**
- ☐ **¹/₂ teaspoon curry paste**
- ☐ **pinch chilli powder**
- ☐ **1 teaspoon fish sauce**
- ☐ **1 tablespoon lime or lemon juice**
- ☐ **500 g/1 lb chicken pieces**
- ☐ **1 tablespoon groundnut (peanut) oil**
- ☐ **1 stalk lemon grass, finely chopped**
- ☐ **250 mL/8 fl oz coconut milk**
- ☐ **125 mL/4 fl oz water**
- ☐ **3 tablespoons chopped roasted cashews**

1 Combine onion, garlic, sugar, mustard seeds, curry paste, chilli powder, fish sauce and lime or lemon juice in a glass bowl. Add chicken, toss well and set aside to marinate for 30 minutes.

2 Heat oil in a large frying pan and stir-fry lemon grass for a few seconds. Add the chicken mixture to the pan and cook for 4-5 minutes each side.

3 Stir in the coconut milk and water. Simmer for 15-20 minutes or until chicken is tender and sauce thickens. To serve, top with cashews.

Cook's tip: Lemon grass is used extensively in Sri Lankan and Southeast Asian cookery. It is used to flavour curry, meat and fish dishes as well as sweet desserts. Lemon grass is available from Asian supermarkets in both the fresh and dried forms. There is also a powdered form available which is called 'sereh'; this is strong in flavour and should be used with discretion. If lemon grass is unavailable lemon balm, lemon verbena and lemon rind are possible substitutes.

LAMB WITH GINGER AND HONEY

Lamb, ginger and honey are a wonderful combination in this timesaving treat.

Serves 4

- ☐ **2 tablespoons groundnut (peanut) oil**
- ☐ **3 cloves garlic, crushed**
- ☐ **1 tablespoon grated fresh ginger**
- ☐ **500 g/1 lb lean lamb steaks, cut into thin strips**
- ☐ **1 onion, cut into eighths**
- ☐ **200 g/6¹/₂ oz oyster mushrooms, sliced**
- ☐ **155 g/5 oz mangetout (snow peas)**
- ☐ **2 tablespoons soy sauce**
- ☐ **1 tablespoon honey**
- ☐ **2 teaspoons lime juice**

1 Heat half the oil in a frying pan or wok and stir-fry garlic and ginger for a few seconds. Add meat in batches and stir-fry for 2-3 minutes each batch. Remove from pan and set aside.

2 Heat remaining oil and cook onion, mushrooms and mangetout (snow peas) for 2-3 minutes. Return meat to the pan with vegetables and stir-fry for 1 minute.

3 Combine soy sauce, honey and lime juice and add to the pan. Stir-fry for 1-2 minutes more or until heated through. Serve immediately.

Chicken with Aromatic Spices and Cashews, Lamb with Ginger and Honey

CHICKEN AND SPINACH PARCELS

If you are having a dinner party, these chicken parcels make a great main course. Prepare them earlier in the day and cook when required.

Serves 4
Oven temperature 200°C, 400°F, Gas 6

- ☐ **4 x 125 g/4 oz boneless chicken breast fillets**
- ☐ **4 tablespoons chicken stock**
- ☐ **4 tablespoons dry sherry**
- ☐ **freshly ground black pepper**

SPINACH FILLING
- ☐ **8 spinach leaves, stalks removed and leaves shredded**
- ☐ **1 large carrot, cut into thin strips**
- ☐ **1 stalk celery, cut into thin strips**
- ☐ **1 leek, cut into thin strips**
- ☐ **pinch ground nutmeg**

1 Place chicken breasts between two sheets of plastic food wrap and pound lightly to flatten.
2 Steam or microwave spinach, carrot, celery and leek until tender. Refresh under cold running water. Pat dry on absorbent paper. Season to taste with nutmeg and black pepper.
3 Cut four large squares of baking paper and top each with a chicken breast. Place spinach, carrot, celery and leek over half of each breast. Fold to enclose filling. Sprinkle with stock, sherry and black pepper to taste. Seal the edges of the paper carefully and place parcels on an oven tray. Bake for 15-20 minutes or until tender. Chill for 1 hour before serving.

ORIENTAL CHICKEN SALAD

Our light chicken salad is easy to prepare and makes a tasty alternative to heavier, more traditional chicken salads.

Serves 4

- ☐ **4 x 125 g/4 oz boneless chicken breast fillets**
- ☐ **1 large carrot**
- ☐ **¹/₂ bunch/125 g/4 oz watercress**
- ☐ **¹/₄ red cabbage, shredded**
- ☐ **100 g/3¹/₂ oz bean sprouts**
- ☐ **4 tablespoons lime juice**

ORIENTAL MARINADE
- ☐ **2 tablespoons dry sherry**
- ☐ **1 tablespoon soy sauce**
- ☐ **2 teaspoons hoisin sauce**
- ☐ **2 teaspoons groundnut (peanut) oil**
- ☐ **2 cloves garlic, crushed**

1 Place chicken fillets between two sheets of plastic food wrap and pound lightly to flatten.
2 To make marinade, combine sherry, soy sauce, hoisin sauce, oil and garlic in a glass bowl. Add chicken fillets and marinate for 1-2 hours.
3 Remove chicken from marinade and barbecue or grill slowly, turning and basting frequently with remaining marinade. Cool and slice thinly.
4 Using a vegetable peeler, slice carrot thinly, lengthwise. Stand slices in iced water for 5-10 minutes. Drain and arrange attractively on individual serving plates with watercress, cabbage and bean sprouts. Sprinkle with lime juice and top with chicken slices. Serve chilled.

Oriental Chicken Salad,
Chicken and Spinach Parcels

CREAMY CHICKEN PIE

Serves 6
Oven temperature 200°C, 400°F, Gas 6

CHEESE PASTRY
- [ ] **250 g/8 oz flour, sifted**
- [ ] **60 g/2 oz mature Cheddar, grated**
- [ ] **1 teaspoon mustard powder**
- [ ] **¹/₂ teaspoon cayenne pepper**
- [ ] **185 g/6 oz butter, chilled and cut into small cubes**
- [ ] **1 egg yolk, lightly beaten**
- [ ] **3-4 tablespoons water, chilled**

CHICKEN FILLING
- [ ] **1 tablespoon olive oil**
- [ ] **750 g/1¹/₂ lb boneless chicken breast fillets, chopped**
- [ ] **60 g/2 oz butter**
- [ ] **1 clove garlic, crushed**
- [ ] **1 stalk celery, chopped**
- [ ] **1 onion, chopped**
- [ ] **3 tablespoons flour**
- [ ] **250 mL/8 fl oz chicken stock**
- [ ] **250 mL/8 fl oz milk**
- [ ] **1 tablespoon chopped fresh parsley**
- [ ] **1 tablespoon chopped fresh rosemary or 1 teaspoon dried rosemary**
- [ ] **freshly ground black pepper**

1 To prepare pastry, place flour, cheese, mustard and cayenne pepper in a bowl and mix to combine. Rub in butter cubes with fingertips until the mixture resembles coarse breadcrumbs.

2 Mix in egg yolk and enough water to form a soft dough with metal spatula or round-ended knife. Turn onto a lightly floured surface and knead gently until smooth. Wrap pastry in plastic food wrap and refrigerate for 30 minutes.

3 To make filling, heat oil in a large frying pan and cook chicken in batches over a high heat for 3 minutes or until browned. Remove chicken from pan and set aside.

4 Melt butter in a frying pan, add garlic, celery and onion and cook, stirring, for 3-4 minutes or until onion is soft. Stir in flour and cook for 1 minute longer. Remove pan from heat and whisk in stock and milk. Return pan to heat and cook, stirring constantly, for 4-5 minutes or until sauce boils and thickens. Add chicken, parsley, rosemary and black pepper to taste to sauce and mix well to combine. Remove pan from heat and set aside to cool completely.

5 Place cooled filling in a 1 litre/1³/₄ pt capacity pie dish. Roll out pastry to 5 mm/¹/₄ in thick. Brush rim of pie dish with a little water and place pastry over the filling. Trim edges with a knife and decorate as desired. Brush with a little milk and bake for 30-35 minutes or until pastry is golden.

Pastry-making tips: Place your utensils in the refrigerator to chill for 15-20 minutes before making pastry.

The best pastry is made using chilled butter and water.

Always rest the pastry in the refrigerator for 30 minutes before baking; this will minimise shrinkage during cooking.

VEAL ESCALOPES

Serve this easy veal dish with a fresh green salad.

Serves 4

- [ ] **8 veal escalopes (schnitzels)**
- [ ] **seasoned flour**
- [ ] **1 egg, lightly beaten**
- [ ] **185 g/6 oz breadcrumbs, made from stale bread**
- [ ] **60 g/2 oz butter**
- [ ] **8 slices prosciutto**
- [ ] **125 g/4 oz grated mozzarella cheese**
- [ ] **3 tablespoons grated Parmesan cheese**
- [ ] **125 mL/4 fl oz cream (double)**

1 Coat veal in flour, then dip in egg and coat in breadcrumbs.

2 Melt butter in a large frying pan until foaming. Add veal and cook for 2 minutes each side or until golden. Wrap each escalope (schnitzel) in a slice of prosciutto, place in a shallow baking dish, sprinkle with mozzarella and Parmesan cheese and spoon over cream. Cook under a preheated high grill for 3-4 minutes or until cheese melts and is golden. Serve immediately.

Creamy Chicken Pie

FIERY CHICKEN NOODLE SOUP

Serves 6

- ☐ 100 g/3¹/₂ oz fresh egg noodles
- ☐ 2 tablespoons peanut oil
- ☐ 2 onions, chopped
- ☐ 2 cloves garlic, crushed
- ☐ 1 fresh red chilli, finely sliced
- ☐ 1 teaspoon curry paste (Vindaloo)
- ☐ ¹/₂ teaspoon powdered saffron
- ☐ 1 tablespoon finely chopped fresh lemon grass
- ☐ 1 litre/1³/₄ pt coconut milk
- ☐ 350 mL/11 fl oz chicken stock
- ☐ 375 g/12 oz cooked chicken, finely chopped
- ☐ 3 spinach leaves, finely shredded

1   Cook noodles in a large saucepan of boiling water for 3-4 minutes or until tender. Drain and rinse noodles under cold running water. Drain and place in individual bowls.
2   Heat oil in a large saucepan, cook onions for 2-3 minutes or until golden. Stir in garlic, chilli, curry paste (Vindaloo), saffron and lemon grass. Cook for 1 minute over medium heat.
4   Combine coconut milk and chicken stock, add to pan with chicken and spinach. Simmer for 3-4 minutes. Pour over noodles in bowls to serve.

TANDOORI BEEF RIBS

Serves 4

- ☐ 8 beef spareribs
- ☐ 2 tablespoons groundnut (peanut) oil

YOGURT MARINADE
- ☐ 250 g/8 oz natural yogurt
- ☐ 1¹/₂ teaspoons grated fresh ginger
- ☐ 2 cloves garlic, crushed
- ☐ 3 teaspoons hot chilli sauce
- ☐ 1 teaspoon ground cumin
- ☐ 1 teaspoon ground cardamom
- ☐ 1 tablespoon finely chopped fresh coriander
- ☐ few drops red food colouring
- ☐ 1 tablespoon tamarind paste
- ☐ 125 mL/4 fl oz water

1   Trim meat of all visible fat and set aside.
2   To make marinade, combine yogurt, ginger, garlic, chilli, cumin, cardamom, coriander and food colouring. Blend tamarind paste with water and fold into yogurt mixture.
3   Rub marinade into meat and set aside, covered, for at least 3 hours or overnight.
4   Remove meat from marinade and brush with oil. Grill or barbecue over a medium heat for 8-10 minutes, turning and basting frequently with marinade.

DRY BEEF CURRY

Serve this hot curry with plenty of yogurt or our Cucumber Pickle to soothe and cool the palate.

Serves 4

- ☐ **4 tablespoons melted ghee or clarified butter**
- ☐ **500 g/1 lb chuck steak, cubed**
- ☐ **1 large onion, chopped**
- ☐ **2 fresh red chillies, finely sliced**
- ☐ **2 cloves garlic, crushed**
- ☐ **1 teaspoon ground coriander**
- ☐ **1 teaspoon ground saffron**
- ☐ **1 teaspoon ground cumin**
- ☐ **1 teaspoon black mustard seeds**
- ☐ **1 tablespoon ground garam masala**
- ☐ **125 mL/4 fl oz water**
- ☐ **2 large tomatoes, peeled and chopped**
- ☐ **2 curry leaves**
- ☐ **1 small cinnamon stick**
- ☐ **3 tablespoons natural yogurt**

1   Heat 3 tablespoons ghee in a large saucepan, cook meat in batches until brown on all sides. Remove from pan and set aside.

2   Heat remaining ghee in pan, add onion and chilli, and cook for 2-3 minutes or until onion is soft and golden brown. Stir in garlic, coriander, saffron, cumin, mustard seeds and half the garam masala. Cook for 1 minute longer.

3   Combine water, tomatoes, curry leaves and cinnamon stick. Stir into pan with onion mixture. Bring to the boil, then reduce heat to simmer. Return meat to the pan and simmer for 1¹/₂ hours or until meat is tender.

4   Remove pan from heat and stir in remaining garam masala and yogurt. Simmer gently for 5 minutes.

Cook's tip: The secret of a good curry depends on how well the onions are browned in the first stage of cooking. Heat the oil or ghee first, add the onions and cook until golden brown. Stir gently throughout cooking, being careful not to burn. Once cooked, add the spices and meat, and stir to coat meat well.

Left: Dry Beef Curry, Tandoori Beef Ribs
Far left: Fiery Chicken Noodle Soup

ROAST TURKEY

The Spaniards brought turkeys to Europe from North America in the 1520s. Cooks soon developed wonderful dishes for special occasions with delicious stuffings and accompaniments. Try this Roast Turkey for a Christmas or Thanksgiving dinner.

Serves 10
Oven temperature 180°C, 350°F, Gas 4

- ☐ **4 kg/8 lb turkey**
- ☐ **60 g/2 oz butter, melted**
- ☐ **250 mL/8 fl oz chicken stock**

VEAL FORCEMEAT
- ☐ **30 g/1 oz butter**
- ☐ **1 onion, finely chopped**
- ☐ **1 rasher bacon, finely chopped**
- ☐ **250 g/8 oz lean veal mince**
- ☐ **185 g/6 oz breadcrumbs, made from stale bread**
- ☐ **¹/₂ teaspoon finely grated lemon rind**
- ☐ **1 tablespoon finely chopped fresh parsley**
- ☐ **¹/₂ teaspoon dried sage**
- ☐ **pinch ground nutmeg**
- ☐ **freshly ground black pepper**
- ☐ **1 egg, lightly beaten**

APPLE AND CHESTNUT STUFFING
- ☐ **440 g/14 oz canned chestnut purée, sieved**
- ☐ **2 cooking apples, cored, peeled and grated**
- ☐ **185 g/6 oz breadcrumbs, made from stale bread**
- ☐ **1 onion, finely chopped**
- ☐ **1 stalk celery, finely chopped**
- ☐ **4 tablespoons finely chopped walnuts**
- ☐ **45 g/1¹/₂ oz butter, melted**
- ☐ **1 tablespoon finely chopped fresh parsley**
- ☐ **pinch ground nutmeg**
- ☐ **1 egg, lightly beaten**

1   To make forcemeat, melt butter in a frying pan and cook onion and bacon for 4-5 minutes or until bacon is crisp. Add veal, breadcrumbs, lemon rind, parsley, sage, nutmeg, black pepper to taste and egg. Mix well to combine.

2   To make stuffing, combine chestnut purée, apples, breadcrumbs, onion, celery, walnuts, parsley, butter, black pepper to taste, nutmeg and egg.

3   Remove giblets and neck from turkey. Wipe turkey inside and out and dry well. Place stuffing in body cavity and lightly fill neck end of turkey with forcemeat. Secure openings with metal skewers and truss legs and wings.

4   Place turkey on a roasting rack in a baking dish. Brush turkey with butter, then pour chicken stock into dish. Bake for 3-3¹/₂ hours or until tender. Baste frequently with pan juices during cooking. Set aside to stand for 20 minutes before carving.

To make forcemeat, melt butter in a frying pan and cook onion and bacon for 4-5 minutes.

Place stuffing in body cavity and lightly fill neck end of turkey with forcemeat.

Secure openings of turkey with metal skewers and truss legs and wings.

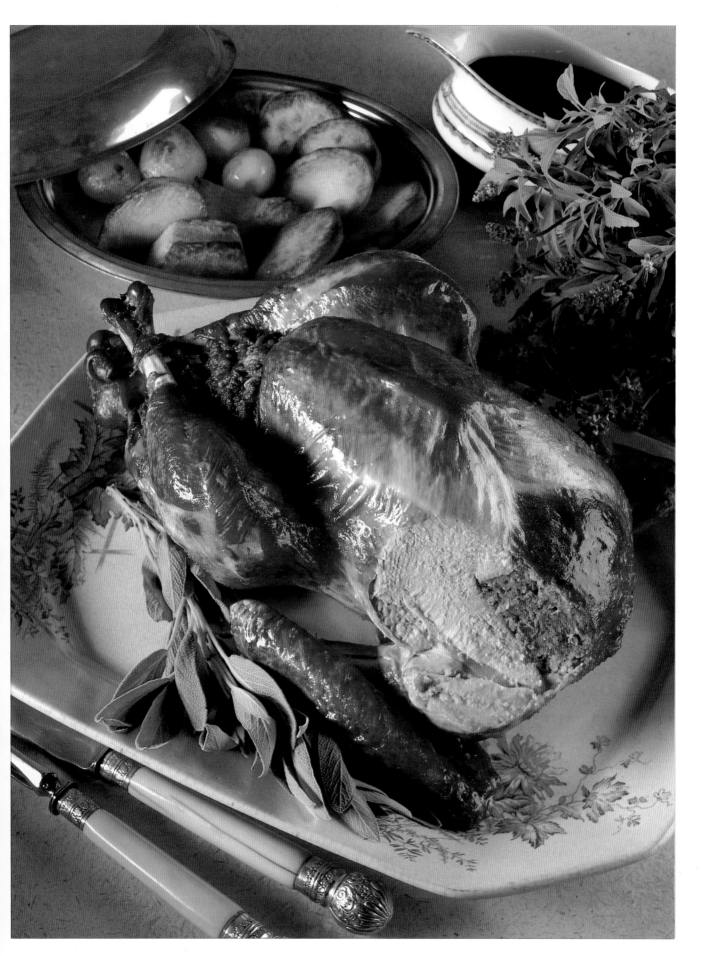

LAMB WITH EGG SAUCE

It is important when making this recipe that you do not allow the lamb to boil after adding the egg yolks. This dish is wonderful served with fried aubergine (eggplant) and roasted red peppers.

Serves 8

- [ ] 1 kg/2 lb cubed lamb
- [ ] 3 tablespoons lemon juice
- [ ] 2 tablespoons olive oil
- [ ] 30 g/1 oz butter
- [ ] 1 onion, sliced
- [ ] 4 slices ham, chopped
- [ ] 1 tablespoon flour
- [ ] 250 mL/8 fl oz dry white wine
- [ ] 60 mL/2 fl oz beef stock
- [ ] 1 tablespoon finely grated lemon rind
- [ ] 3 egg yolks, beaten
- [ ] 2 tablespoons chopped fresh parsley
- [ ] 1 tablespoon chopped fresh marjoram or 1 teaspoon dried marjoram

1 Place lamb and 1 tablespoon lemon juice in a bowl and toss to combine. Cover and set aside to marinate for 30 minutes. Drain lamb and pat dry with absorbent kitchen paper.
2 Heat oil and butter in a large frying pan, add onion and cook for 4-5 minutes or until soft. Add ham and lamb to pan and cook for 4-5 minutes longer.
3 Stir in flour and cook, stirring, for 3-4 minutes, then stir in wine and stock and bring to the boil. Reduce heat, cover and simmer for 30 minutes or until lamb is tender.
4 Stir in lemon rind and remaining lemon juice and cook for 3 minutes longer. Stir in egg yolks and cook, without boiling, for 3-4 minutes or until heated through. Remove pan from heat, stir in parsley and marjoram and serve immediately.

TOMATO AND BEEF CASSEROLE WITH SESAME SEED TOPPING

Serves 4
Oven temperature 180°C, 350°F, Gas 4

BEEF BURGERS
- [ ] 500 g/1 lb lean beef mince
- [ ] 1 clove garlic, crushed
- [ ] 1 onion, chopped
- [ ] 1 egg, beaten
- [ ] 4 tablespoons instant rolled oats
- [ ] 1 tablespoon oyster sauce
- [ ] 1 tablespoon tomato sauce
- [ ] 2 tablespoons olive oil

TOMATO SAUCE
- [ ] 1 onion, chopped
- [ ] 440 g/14 oz canned tomatoes, undrained and mashed
- [ ] 2 tablespoons tomato purée
- [ ] ½ teaspoon sugar
- [ ] 2 teaspoons cornflour blended with 2 tablespoons water

SESAME SEED TOPPING
- [ ] 5 slices bread, buttered, crusts removed
- [ ] 2 tablespoons sesame seeds

1 To make burgers, place mince, garlic, onion, egg, oats, oyster sauce and tomato sauce in a bowl and mix to combine. Shape meat mixture into eight patties. Heat oil in a large frying pan and cook burgers for 2-3 minutes each side or until browned. Transfer burgers to a casserole dish. Drain juices from pan.
2 To make sauce, add onion to pan and cook for 2-3 minutes or until soft. Add tomatoes, tomato purée and sugar and bring to the boil. Whisk in cornflour mixture and cook, stirring constantly, for 4-5 minutes or until sauce thickens. Pour sauce over burgers.
3 To make topping, cut buttered bread into cubes and arrange over sauce, sprinkle with sesame seeds and bake for 35-40 minutes or until topping is golden.

COTTAGE PIE

It's always a problem knowing what to do with leftover roast meat. This version of the traditional cottage pie solves all those worries in next to no time.

Serves 4
Oven temperature 200°C, 400°F, Gas 6

- [ ] 375 g/12 oz cooked cold meat, such as lamb or beef, finely chopped
- [ ] 1 onion, grated
- [ ] 1 tablespoon tomato sauce
- [ ] 1 tablespoon chopped fresh parsley
- [ ] 1 teaspoon dried thyme
- [ ] ½ teaspoon dried sage
- [ ] ½ teaspoon dried oregano
- [ ] freshly ground black pepper
- [ ] 1 tomato, sliced

INSTANT POTATO TOPPING
- [ ] 125 g/4 oz instant dried potato flakes
- [ ] 250 mL/8 fl oz boiling water
- [ ] 125 mL/4 fl oz milk
- [ ] 30 g/1 oz butter, melted
- [ ] 30 g/1 oz crushed potato crisps

1 Place meat, onion, tomato sauce, parsley, thyme, sage, oregano and black pepper to taste in a bowl and mix to combine. Spoon meat mixture into a 20 cm/8 in ovenproof dish and top with tomato slices.
2 To make topping, place instant potato flakes, water, milk and butter in a bowl, mix to combine and spread over top of meat mixture. Sprinkle with potato crisps and bake for 20-25 minutes or until top is golden and pie is heated through. Allow pie to stand for 5 minutes before serving.

Microwave it: For an even faster meal you can easily make the Cottage Pie in the microwave oven. Use a 20 cm/8 in microwave-safe dish and cook on HIGH (100%) for 4-5 minutes. Stand for 5 minutes before serving.

PORK WITH ORANGE AND CRANBERRY SAUCE

Serves 4

- [ ] 4 x 125 g/4 oz butterfly pork steaks
- [ ] cracked black peppercorns
- [ ] 1 tablespoon olive oil

CRANBERRY MARINADE
- [ ] 250 mL/8 fl oz orange juice
- [ ] 2 teaspoons finely grated orange rind
- [ ] ¼ teaspoon ground cloves
- [ ] 3 tablespoons cranberry sauce

1 To make marinade, place orange juice, orange rind, cloves and cranberry sauce in a bowl and mix to combine. Place steaks in a shallow glass or ceramic dish, pour over marinade, cover and set aside to marinate for 1-2 hours.
2 Remove steaks from marinade and reserve marinade. Coat steaks with peppercorns. Heat oil in a large frying pan, add steaks and cook for 4-5 minutes each side or until cooked. Set aside and keep warm.
3 Strain reserved marinade and pour into a saucepan. Bring to the boil and boil until reduced slightly. Spoon sauce over steaks and serve immediately.

MEXICAN CHILLI PASTA

Serves 4

- ☐ **750 g/1¹/₂ lb tomato fettuccine**

MEXICAN CHILLI SAUCE
- ☐ **2 onions, chopped**
- ☐ **1 clove garlic, crushed**
- ☐ **2 fresh red chillies, finely chopped**
- ☐ **1 tablespoon water**
- ☐ **440 mL/14 fl oz canned tomato purée**
- ☐ **440 g/14 oz canned red kidney beans, drained**

1 Cook fettuccine in boiling water in a large saucepan following packet directions. Drain, set aside and keep warm.
2 To make sauce, cook onions, garlic, chillies and water in large saucepan for 3-4 minutes, or until onions are soft. Stir in tomato purée and red kidney beans, bring to the boil, then reduce heat and simmer for 4-5 minutes, or until sauce thickens. Spoon sauce over pasta.

HONEY BEEF

Serves 4

- ☐ **1 tablespoon vegetable oil**
- ☐ **500 g/1 lb lean rump steak, cut into thin strips**
- ☐ **1 red pepper, cut into thin strips**
- ☐ **4 spinach leaves, shredded**
- ☐ **3 spring onions, cut into 3 cm/1¹/₄ in diagonal lengths**
- ☐ **1 parsnip, cut into thin strips**
- ☐ **1 clove garlic, crushed**
- ☐ **2 teaspoons grated fresh ginger**
- ☐ **4 tablespoons soy sauce**
- ☐ **2 teaspoons honey**
- ☐ **2 teaspoons cornflour blended with 2 tablespoons dry sherry**

1 Heat 2 teaspoons oil in a frying pan or wok. Add meat, red pepper, spinach, spring onions and parsnip, and stir-fry for 2-3 minutes, or until meat changes colour. Remove mixture from pan and set aside.
2 Heat remaining oil and stir-fry garlic and ginger for 1-2 minutes. Return beef mixture to the pan. Combine soy sauce, honey and cornflour mixture, pour into pan and cook for 1-2 minutes longer or until heated through. Serve immediately.

Mexican Chilli Pasta, Honey Beef

123

GOLDEN OAT FISH FILLETS

This recipe can be made with any white-fleshed fish, such as perch, sole, halibut or hake. Lemon pepper seasoning is a mixture of pepper, salt, sugar, lemon peel and lemon extract.

Serves 4

- ☐ **3 tablespoons fine oatmeal**
- ☐ **60 g/2 oz rolled oats**
- ☐ **60 g/2 oz breadcrumbs, made from stale bread**
- ☐ **¹/₂ teaspoon lemon pepper seasoning**
- ☐ **4 x 125 g/4 oz fish fillets**
- ☐ **flour**
- ☐ **1 egg, beaten**
- ☐ **30 g/1 oz butter**
- ☐ **1 tablespoon vegetable oil**

1   Place oatmeal, oats, breadcrumbs and lemon pepper in a bowl and mix to combine. Coat fish with flour, then dip in egg and coat with oatmeal mixture.
2   Heat butter and oil in a large frying pan, add fish and cook for 2-3 minutes each side or until golden and cooked through.

BLUE VEIN BEEF CASSEROLE

Serves 4
Oven temperature 180°C, 350°F, Gas 4

- ☐ **2 tablespoons olive oil**
- ☐ **750 g/1¹/₂ lb blade steak, cut into 5 cm/2 in cubes**
- ☐ **250 mL/8 fl oz beef stock**
- ☐ **125 mL/4 fl oz tomato purée**
- ☐ **2 tablespoons port**
- ☐ **¹/₄ teaspoon ground cumin**
- ☐ **1 cinnamon stick**
- ☐ **12 small white onions**
- ☐ **90 g/3 oz blue vein cheese, cut into 1 cm/¹/₂ in cubes**

1   Heat oil in a large frying pan, add meat and cook, stirring, for 5 minutes or until browned. Transfer to a casserole dish.
2   Add stock, tomato purée, port, cumin and cinnamon stick to pan and bring to the boil. Pour stock mixture over beef, cover and bake for 1 hour.
3   Boil or microwave onions until just tender. Drain, add to casserole dish with meat and cook for 30 minutes longer. Sprinkle blue vein cheese over top of casserole, cover and stand for 10 minutes before serving.

CHILLI AND CHICKEN PEPPERS

If you can find different-coloured peppers, this dish will look spectacular, but using only one variety makes no difference to the delicious flavour. Leftover Christmas turkey is ideal to use in place of the chicken.

Serves 4
Oven temperature 200°C, 400°F, Gas 6

- ☐ **3 red peppers**
- ☐ **2 green peppers**

CHILLI AND CHICKEN FILLING
- ☐ **1 tablespoon vegetable oil**
- ☐ **2 spring onions, chopped**
- ☐ **1 clove garlic, crushed**
- ☐ **1 cooked chicken, skin removed, flesh removed and chopped**
- ☐ **250 g/8 oz cream cheese, softened**
- ☐ **1 teaspoon chilli sauce**
- ☐ **2 eggs, lightly beaten**
- ☐ **60 g/2 oz grated mature Cheddar**
- ☐ **freshly ground black pepper**
- ☐ **60 g/2 oz grated mozzarella cheese**
- ☐ **paprika**

1   Cut tops from peppers and reserve. Remove seeds and core from peppers. Dice 1 red pepper and reserved tops and reserve. Blanch remaining 4 pepper shells in boiling water or in the microwave until just soft. Place upside down on absorbent kitchen paper to drain.
2   To make filling, heat oil in a large frying pan, add reserved diced red and green peppers, spring onions and garlic and cook, stirring, for 5 minutes or until peppers are soft. Place chicken, cream cheese, chilli sauce, eggs, mature Cheddar and black pepper to taste in a bowl, add peppers mixture and mix to combine. Spoon filling into pepper shells, top with mozzarella cheese and sprinkle with paprika.
3   Place filled peppers close together in a lightly greased shallow baking dish and bake for 30-40 minutes or until filling is bubbling hot and cheese is golden.

BEEF POT ROAST

Polenta makes a great accompaniment to this traditional Italian dish.

Serves 4

- ☐ **1.5 kg/3 lb piece topside beef**
- ☐ **60 g/2 oz butter**
- ☐ **1 onion, chopped**
- ☐ **250 mL/8 fl oz dry white wine**

ROSEMARY MARINADE
- ☐ **2 cloves garlic, crushed**
- ☐ **2 whole cloves**
- ☐ **pinch ground cinnamon**
- ☐ **600 mL/1 pt white wine vinegar**
- ☐ **2 stalks celery, chopped**
- ☐ **sprig fresh rosemary**
- ☐ **5 whole black peppercorns**

1   To make marinade, place garlic, cloves, cinnamon, vinegar, celery, rosemary and black peppercorns in a large bowl and mix to combine. Add beef and turn to coat. Cover and refrigerate for 12 hours or overnight. Remove beef from marinade. Strain marinade, reserve solids and discard liquid.
2   Melt butter in a large heavy-based saucepan, add meat and brown on all sides. Remove meat from pan and set aside.
3   Add onion and reserved solids to pan and cook over a low heat, stirring, for 5 minutes or until onion is soft. Return meat to pan, pour in wine and bring to the boil. Reduce heat, cover and simmer for 2¹/₂ hours or until meat is very tender. To serve, cut meat into slices and serve with any sauce that has formed during cooking.

Polenta: Simply, this is cooked yellow maize flour. To cook polenta, bring a large saucepan of water to the boil and gradually whisk in polenta. Reduce heat and cook, stirring frequently, for 20 minutes.

BEEF WITH PUMPKIN AND LEMON GRASS

Serve this unusual and flavoursome dish accompanied by bowls of natural yogurt and topped with freshly chopped coriander.

Serves 4

- ☐ **2 tablespoons vegetable oil**
- ☐ **2 onions, chopped**
- ☐ **1 teaspoon whole allspice**
- ☐ **1 cinnamon stick**
- ☐ **1 teaspoon grated fresh ginger**
- ☐ **2 green peppers, sliced**
- ☐ **750 g/1½ lb chuck steak, cut into 4 cm/1½ in cubes**
- ☐ **2 tablespoons chopped fresh lemon grass**
- ☐ **500 mL/16 fl oz chicken stock**
- ☐ **500 g/1 lb pumpkin, cut into 4 cm/1½ in cubes**
- ☐ **2 cloves garlic, crushed**

1 Heat oil in large heavy-based saucepan. Cook onions over a medium heat until golden. Stir in allspice, cinnamon, ginger and peppers.
2 Add meat to pan and cook over a high heat until browned. Stir in lemon grass and chicken stock. Bring to the boil, reduce heat and simmer, covered, for 45 minutes.
3 Stir in pumpkin, cover and simmer for 45 minutes or until beef is tender. Remove from heat and stir in garlic. Season to taste.

SEASONED SAUSAGE RAGOUT

For a complete meal, serve this tasty ragout with a chilled tomato salad and crusty French bread.

Serves 6

- ☐ **500 g/1 lb lean beef mince**
- ☐ **60 g/2 oz finely chopped fresh parsley**
- ☐ **60 g/2 oz finely chopped fresh basil**
- ☐ **3 tablespoons pine nuts**
- ☐ **1 tablespoon olive oil**
- ☐ **2 cloves garlic, crushed**
- ☐ **1 teaspoon cracked black peppercorns**
- ☐ **185 g/6 oz breadcrumbs, made from stale bread**
- ☐ **60 g/2 oz grated fresh Parmesan cheese**
- ☐ **seasoned flour**
- ☐ **oil for deep-frying**
- ☐ **12 whole baby potatoes**
- ☐ **12 whole baby onions**
- ☐ **3 tablespoons soy sauce**
- ☐ **125 mL/4 fl oz lemon juice**
- ☐ **250 mL/8 fl oz chicken stock**
- ☐ **250 mL/8 fl oz dry white wine**
- ☐ **3 tablespoons chopped fresh basil**

1 Combine mince, parsley, basil, nuts, olive oil, garlic, black peppercorns, breadcrumbs and cheese in large bowl and mix until well combined. Shape into 12 sausages, 10 cm/4 in long. Roll in seasoned flour.
2 Heat oil in a deep frying pan. Cook sausages a few at a time until browned but not cooked through. Remove sausages and drain on absorbent kitchen paper. Repeat with remaining sausages.
3 Arrange sausages, potatoes and onions in a deep saucepan. Combine soy sauce, lemon juice, stock, wine and basil in a bowl and pour into pan. Bring to the boil, reduce heat and simmer, covered, for 20 minutes or until potatoes are tender. Thicken sauce in pan, if desired.

Beef with Pumpkin and Lemon Grass, Seasoned Sausage Ragout

chapter six

———•———

THE VEGETARIAN ALTERNATIVE

In today's health-aware
society many people are choosing
to include vegetarian meals in
their general eating plan: in many
families one or more members
choose vegetarian meals all the
time. In this chapter you will
find a host of exciting vegetarian
meals to suit any occasion.

Mushroom Gougère,
Wholemeal Spinach Quiche,
Spinach and Basil Risotto

MUSHROOM GOUGERE

Serves 4
Oven temperature 200°C, 400°F, Gas 6

CHOUX PASTRY
- [ ] **250 mL/8 fl oz water**
- [ ] **90 g/3 oz polyunsaturated margarine**
- [ ] **125 g/4 oz flour, sifted**
- [ ] **4 eggs**

MUSHROOM FILLING
- [ ] **155 g/5 oz button mushrooms, sliced**
- [ ] **3 eggs, lightly beaten**
- [ ] **155 g/5 oz sour cream**
- [ ] **125 mL/4 fl oz cream (double)**
- [ ] **1 tablespoon flour**
- [ ] **125 g/4 oz grated mature Cheddar**
- [ ] **1 tablespoon chopped fresh parsley**
- [ ] **freshly ground black pepper**
- [ ] **pinch ground nutmeg**

1 To make pastry, place water and margarine in a saucepan. Cover and cook over a medium heat until margarine melts and mixture just boils. Remove pan from heat and add flour all at once. Stir vigorously with a wooden spoon, over a low heat, until mixture forms a ball and pulls away from sides of pan. Set aside to cool slightly.
2 Add eggs one at a time, beating well after each addition until mixture is smooth and glossy. Spread mixture around sides of a greased shallow ovenproof dish.
3 To make filling, combine mushrooms, eggs, sour cream, cream, flour, cheese and parsley. Season to taste with black pepper and nutmeg. Spoon filling into centre of pastry and bake for 35-40 minutes or until filling is firm and pastry is puffed and golden.

VEGETABLE CHILLI

Serves 6
Oven temperature 180°C, 350°F, Gas 4

- [ ] **1 large aubergine (eggplant) cut into 1 cm/^{1}/$_2$ in cubes**
- [ ] **salt**
- [ ] **4 tablespoons olive oil**
- [ ] **1 large onion, chopped**
- [ ] **1 clove garlic, crushed**
- [ ] **1 green pepper, sliced**
- [ ] **440 g/14 oz canned tomatoes, undrained and mashed**
- [ ] **2 courgettes (zucchini), sliced**

- [ ] **1 teaspoon chilli powder**
- [ ] **^{1}/$_2$ teaspoon ground cumin**
- [ ] **4 tablespoons finely chopped fresh parsley**
- [ ] **500 g/1 lb canned three bean mix**
- [ ] **freshly ground black pepper**

1 Sprinkle aubergine (eggplant) with salt and set aside to stand for 15-20 minutes. Rinse under cold running water and pat dry with absorbent kitchen paper.
2 Heat oil in a large frying pan, add aubergine (eggplant) and cook, stirring frequently, until aubergine (eggplant) is tender. Add more oil during cooking if necessary. Transfer aubergine (eggplant) to a large casserole dish.
3 Add onion, garlic and green pepper to pan and cook, stirring, for 5 minutes or until onion is soft. Stir in tomatoes, courgettes (zucchini), chilli powder, cumin, parsley, beans and black pepper to taste and cook for 10 minutes. Transfer to casserole dish, cover and bake for 1^1/$_2$ hours or until skin of aubergine (eggplant) is tender and casserole is bubbling hot.

SPINACH AND BASIL RISOTTO

Risotto is an Italian favourite. Wonderful as a first course, main course or an accompaniment to meat, fish or poultry, it is nutritious and easy to make.

Serves 4

- [ ] **1 bunch/500 g/1 lb spinach, stalks removed and leaves chopped**
- [ ] **250 mL/8 fl oz water**
- [ ] **60 g/2 oz polyunsaturated margarine**
- [ ] **1 large onion, finely chopped**
- [ ] **2 cloves garlic, crushed**
- [ ] **440 g/14 oz brown rice**
- [ ] **125 mL/4 fl oz white wine**
- [ ] **1.2 litres/2 pt hot chicken stock**
- [ ] **4 tablespoons pine nuts, toasted**
- [ ] **30 g/1 oz fresh basil leaves**
- [ ] **2 tablespoons olive oil**

1 Place spinach and water in a saucepan and cook over a medium heat for 1-2 minutes. Bring to the boil and cook for 1 minute or until spinach is tender. Remove from heat and set aside to cool.
2 Place spinach mixture in a food processor or blender and process until smooth. Set aside.
3 Melt margarine in a saucepan and cook onion and garlic for 4-5 minutes or until onion is soft. Add rice to pan and stir to coat with butter mixture. Pour in wine and half the chicken stock. Cook over a medium heat, stirring occasionally, until almost all the liquid is absorbed. Stir in remaining stock with reserved spinach mixture and cook until almost all the liquid is absorbed.
4 Place 3 tablespoons pine nuts, basil and oil in a food processor or blender and process until smooth. Stir into rice mixture. Sprinkle with remaining pine nuts and serve immediately.

VEGETARIAN PIE

Serves 6
Oven temperature 190°C, 375°F, Gas 5

- [ ] **170 g/5^1/$_2$ oz brown rice, cooked**
- [ ] **250 g/8 oz grated mature Cheddar**
- [ ] **4 tablespoons grated Parmesan cheese**
- [ ] **2 spring onions, chopped**
- [ ] **2 courgettes (zucchini), grated**
- [ ] **1 red pepper, diced**
- [ ] **315 g/10 oz canned asparagus cuts, drained**
- [ ] **3 tablespoons pine nuts, toasted**
- [ ] **3 eggs, lightly beaten**
- [ ] **200 g/6^1/$_2$ oz natural yogurt**
- [ ] **freshly ground black pepper**

1 Place rice, Cheddar, Parmesan cheese, spring onions, courgettes (zucchini), red pepper, asparagus, pine nuts, eggs, yogurt and black pepper to taste in a bowl and mix to combine.
2 Spoon rice mixture into a greased, deep-sided 23 cm/9 in springform tin and bake for 40 minutes or until firm. Allow to stand for 5 minutes in tin before serving. Serve cut into wedges.

Microwave it: While you do not really save time cooking rice in the microwave, you are assured of a perfect result and no messy pot. It is also a great way to cook rice that is to be used in a recipe such as this one.

To cook brown rice in the microwave, place 220 g/7 oz rice and 750 mL/1^1/$_4$ pt water or stock in a large microwave-safe dish. Cook, uncovered, on HIGH (100%) for 30 minutes or until all the liquid is absorbed and the rice is tender.

THAI VEGETABLE PUFFS WITH DIPPING SAUCE

Spice-laden, savoury-filled parcels served with a traditional Thai dipping sauce.

Makes 24

- ☐ **375 g/12 oz prepared or ready-rolled puff pastry, thawed**
- ☐ **oil for deep-frying**

SPICY VEGETABLE FILLING
- ☐ **30 g/1 oz polyunsaturated margarine**
- ☐ **1 teaspoon curry powder**
- ☐ **¹/₂ teaspoon ground cumin**
- ☐ **¹/₂ teaspoon garam masala**
- ☐ **1 small onion, finely chopped**
- ☐ **1 large carrot, grated**
- ☐ **1 courgette (zucchini), grated**
- ☐ **1 tablespoon crunchy peanut butter**
- ☐ **2 large potatoes, cooked and mashed**

DIPPING SAUCE
- ☐ **250 mL/8 fl oz white vinegar**
- ☐ **185 g/6 oz white sugar**
- ☐ **1 small fresh red chilli, finely chopped**
- ☐ **1 small cucumber, peeled, seeded and finely chopped**

1 Roll out pastry to 3 mm/¹/₈ in thick and, using a 7.5 cm/3 in round pastry cutter, cut out 24 rounds.
2 To make filling, melt margarine in a saucepan, stir in curry powder, cumin and garam masala and cook for 1 minute. Add onion, carrot and courgette (zucchini) and cook, stirring occasionally, for 5 minutes or until vegetables are tender. Stir in peanut butter. Place potatoes in a bowl, add vegetable mixture and mix to combine.
3 Lay a pastry round in the palm of your hand and place a teaspoon of filling in the centre. Wet edge of pastry with a little water, fold pastry over filling and pinch edges together. Repeat with remaining pastry rounds and filling.
4 To make sauce, place vinegar and sugar in a small saucepan and cook over a low heat, stirring frequently and without boiling, until sugar dissolves. Mix in chilli and cucumber and bring to the boil, then reduce heat and simmer, uncovered, for 5 minutes or until sauce reduces and thickens slightly.
5 Heat oil in a large saucepan until a cube of bread dropped in browns in 50 seconds, then cook a few puffs at a time for 3-4 minutes or until crisp and golden. Drain on absorbent kitchen paper and serve immediately with sauce.

SPINACH PIE

Serve this quick-to-make pie hot or cold. Any leftovers are great to put in school or office lunch boxes.

Serves 8
Oven temperature 200°C, 400°F, Gas 6

- ☐ **8 spinach leaves, stalks removed and leaves shredded**
- ☐ **30 g/1 oz polyunsaturated margarine**
- ☐ **1 onion, finely chopped**
- ☐ **125 g/4 oz ricotta cheese**
- ☐ **125 g/4 oz feta cheese, crumbled**
- ☐ **60 g/2 oz grated mature Cheddar**
- ☐ **3 tablespoons grated Parmesan cheese**
- ☐ **4 eggs, lightly beaten**
- ☐ **¹/₄ teaspoon ground nutmeg**
- ☐ **freshly ground black pepper**
- ☐ **8 sheets filo pastry**
- ☐ **3 tablespoons olive oil**

1 Boil, steam or microwave spinach until just tender. Drain and cool completely, then squeeze to remove excess liquid. Chop spinach finely and place in a bowl.
2 Melt margarine in a frying pan, add onion and cook for 5 minutes or until golden. Add onion, ricotta cheese, feta cheese, Cheddar and Parmesan cheese to spinach and mix to combine. Mix eggs, nutmeg and black pepper to taste into spinach mixture.
3 Layer 4 sheets of pastry together, brushing between each sheet with oil. Repeat with remaining sheets. Line a deep lightly greased ovenproof dish with a pastry layer. Trim edges with scissors about 2.5 cm/1 in from the edge of dish. Spoon in spinach filling, then fold remaining pastry layer in half and place on top of spinach filling. Gently fold edges of pastry together, brush top with oil and bake for 40-45 minutes or until pastry is golden and crisp.

WHOLEMEAL SPINACH QUICHE

Serves 6
Oven temperature 220°C, 425°F, Gas 7

- ☐ **155 g/5 oz wholemeal flour, sifted and husks returned**
- ☐ **2 tablespoons vegetable oil**
- ☐ **1 egg, lightly beaten**
- ☐ **1 tablespoon iced water**

SPINACH FILLING
- ☐ **30 g/1 oz polyunsaturated margarine**
- ☐ **1 onion, finely chopped**
- ☐ **¹/₂ bunch/250 g/8 oz spinach, stalks removed and leaves finely shredded**
- ☐ **3 eggs, lightly beaten**
- ☐ **300 g/9¹/₂ oz sour cream**
- ☐ **pinch ground nutmeg**
- ☐ **freshly ground black pepper**
- ☐ **60 g/2 oz grated mature Cheddar**

1 Place flour in a large mixing bowl. Combine oil, egg and water, add to flour and mix to a firm dough. Turn dough onto a floured surface and knead lightly. Cover and refrigerate for 30 minutes.
2 Roll out pastry and line the base and sides of a lightly greased 23 cm/9 in flan tin. Trim edges and line base with baking paper. Fill with dried beans or rice and blind bake for 15 minutes. Remove beans and paper and bake for 10 minutes longer. Remove from oven and set aside to cool slightly.
3 To make filling, melt margarine in a frying pan and cook onion over a medium heat for 4-5 minutes or until soft. Stir in spinach and cook for 2-3 minutes or until spinach wilts. Remove pan from heat and set aside.
4 Combine eggs, sour cream, nutmeg, black pepper to taste and cheese. Spread spinach mixture over pastry base, then carefully spoon in egg mixture. Reduce temperature to 180°C/350°F/Gas 4 and bake for 30 minutes or until firm.

CORN ROULADE WITH MUSHROOM FILLING

Serves 4
Oven temperature 220°C, 425°F, Gas 7

- ☐ **60 g/2 oz polyunsaturated margarine**
- ☐ **4 tablespoons wholemeal flour**
- ☐ **185 mL/6 fl oz milk**
- ☐ **3 eggs, separated**
- ☐ **125 g/4 oz canned creamed sweet corn**

MUSHROOM FILLING
- ☐ **90 mL/3 fl oz vegetable stock or water**
- ☐ **3 tablespoons thick sour cream or natural yogurt**
- ☐ **2 tablespoons chopped fresh basil**
- ☐ **15 g/^{1}/$_2$ oz polyunsaturated margarine**
- ☐ **185 g/6 oz mushrooms, finely chopped**
- ☐ **1 onion, finely chopped**
- ☐ **1 tablespoon flour**

SAUCE
- ☐ **30 g/1 oz polyunsaturated margarine**
- ☐ **1 onion, chopped**
- ☐ **2 teaspoons flour**
- ☐ **250 mL/8 fl oz vegetable stock or water**
- ☐ **200 g/6^1/$_2$ oz canned sweet red peppers, drained and chopped**

1 Melt margarine in a saucepan, stir in flour and cook for 1 minute. Gradually blend in milk and cook over a medium heat, stirring frequently, until mixture boils and thickens. Whisk in egg yolks and sweet corn. Whisk egg whites until stiff peaks form and gently fold through sweet corn mixture. Spread mixture into a lightly greased and lined 26 x 32 cm/10^1/$_2$ x 12^1/$_2$ in Swiss roll tin. Bake for 15-20 minutes or until puffed and golden.
2 To make filling, whisk together stock, sour cream and basil. Melt margarine in a saucepan, add mushrooms and onion and cook for 5 minutes or until onion is soft. Add flour and cook for 1 minute. Gradually stir in stock mixture and cook over a medium heat, stirring constantly, until mixture boils and thickens.
3 To make sauce, melt margarine in a saucepan and cook onion for 3 minutes, stir in flour and cook for 1 minute longer. Gradually mix in stock and peppers and cook over a medium heat, stirring frequently, until sauce boils and thickens.

4 Turn roulade onto a wire rack covered with a clean teatowel and remove paper. Quickly spread with warm filling and gently roll up from the short side, with the help of the teatowel. Serve roulade sliced with warm sauce.

GINGERED VEGETABLES IN BREAD BASKETS

Serves 4

- ☐ **oil for deep-frying**
- ☐ **2 large pitta breads, split through the centre**

FILLING
- ☐ **8 baby new potatoes, cut into bite-sized pieces**
- ☐ **1 carrot, chopped**
- ☐ **1 courgette (zucchini), chopped**
- ☐ **250 g/8 oz mangetout (snow peas)**
- ☐ **250 g/8 oz green and yellow squash, trimmed and quartered**
- ☐ **1 tablespoon grated root ginger**
- ☐ **2 tablespoons honey**
- ☐ **2 tablespoons orange juice**
- ☐ **2 tablespoons chopped macadamia or brazil nuts, toasted**
- ☐ **2 tablespoons finely snipped fresh chives**

1 Heat oil in a wok or large saucepan and cook pitta breads one at a time. Press with the head of a metal soup ladle to form a basket. Drain on absorbent kitchen paper. Set aside and keep warm.
2 To make filling, boil, steam or microwave potatoes, carrot, courgette (zucchini), mangetout (snow peas) and squash separately until tender. Set aside and keep warm.
3 Combine ginger, honey, orange juice, nuts and chives in a large bowl. Add vegetables and toss to coat. Spoon filling into warm baskets and serve immediately.

WARM BASIL SUMMER SALAD

Any small pasta with a good shape for catching the dressing can be used for this salad. You might like to try small shell pasta or small spiral shapes.

Serves 6

- ☐ **250 g/8 oz small pasta shapes**
- ☐ **2 tablespoons finely chopped sun-dried tomatoes**
- ☐ **^{1}/$_2$ red pepper, finely sliced**
- ☐ **^{1}/$_2$ green pepper, finely sliced**
- ☐ **2 spring onions, chopped**
- ☐ **12 black olives**
- ☐ **2 tablespoons finely chopped basil**
- ☐ **2 tablespoons grated Parmesan cheese**

RED WINE VINEGAR DRESSING
- ☐ **1 clove garlic, crushed**
- ☐ **1 tablespoon olive oil**
- ☐ **3 tablespoons red wine vinegar**
- ☐ **^{1}/$_4$ teaspoon chilli powder**
- ☐ **freshly ground black pepper**

1 Cook pasta in boiling water following packet instructions. Drain, set aside and keep warm.
2 Place tomatoes, red and green pepper, spring onions, olives and basil in a large salad bowl.
3 To make dressing, place garlic, oil, vinegar and chilli powder in a screwtop jar and shake well to combine. Season to taste with black pepper.
4 Add warm pasta and dressing to salad bowl and toss lightly to combine. Sprinkle with Parmesan cheese and serve while pasta is still warm.

Gingered Vegetables in Bread Baskets,
Warm Basil Summer Salad,
Corn Roulade with Mushroom Filling

CHEESY MUSHROOM SLICE

This recipe is an ideal one to cook ahead. Prepare the whole dish, cover and refrigerate overnight. Bake when you are ready the next day. The flavour develops if allowed to stand before cooking.

Serves 6
Oven temperature 180°C, 350°F, Gas 4

- [ ] **60 g/2 oz polyunsaturated margarine**
- [ ] **3 rashers bacon, chopped**
- [ ] **375 g/12 oz mushrooms, sliced**
- [ ] **4 spring onions, chopped**
- [ ] **1 small green pepper, chopped**
- [ ] **1 small red pepper, chopped**
- [ ] **6 thick slices white bread, crusts removed**
- [ ] **125 g/4 oz grated mature Cheddar**
- [ ] **6 eggs**
- [ ] **500 mL/16 fl oz milk**
- [ ] **1 tablespoon mayonnaise**
- [ ] **1 teaspoon French mustard**
- [ ] **1 teaspoon Worcestershire sauce**
- [ ] **2 tablespoons chopped fresh parsley**

1   Melt margarine in a frying pan. Cook bacon until crisp. Stir in mushrooms, spring onions and peppers and cook until mushrooms are soft.

2   Cut bread slices into 2.5 cm/1 in pieces. Place half the bread in a single layer in a greased 18 x 30 cm/7 x 12 in ovenproof dish. Spoon over mushroom mixture and top with remaining bread. Sprinkle over cheese.

3   Whisk together eggs, milk, mayonnaise, mustard and Worcestershire sauce. Pour over bread mixture, sprinkle top with parsley and bake for 50-60 minutes.

Trim crusts from bread and cut into 2.5 cm/1 in pieces.

Place half the bread in a single layer in a greased ovenproof dish and spoon mushroom mixture over.

Pour eggs, milk, mayonnaise, mustard and sauce over bread mixture.

VEGETABLE AND NUT STIR-FRY

Serves 6

- ☐ **2 tablespoons vegetable oil**
- ☐ **2 onions, cut into eighths**
- ☐ **2 carrots, cut into thin strips**
- ☐ **2 stalks celery, cut into thin strips**
- ☐ **2 teaspoons ground turmeric**
- ☐ **2 cloves garlic, crushed**
- ☐ **6 spring onions, chopped**
- ☐ **2 tablespoons white vinegar**
- ☐ **2 tablespoons sugar**
- ☐ **1 mango, stoned, peeled and chopped**
- ☐ **125 g/4 oz mangetout (snow peas), trimmed**
- ☐ **185 mL/6 fl oz vegetable stock**
- ☐ **125 g/4 oz roasted cashew nuts**

1 Heat oil in a wok or frying pan. Add onions, carrots and celery and stir-fry for 5 minutes or until lightly browned. Combine turmeric, garlic, spring onions, vinegar and sugar and stir into wok.

2 Add mango, mangetout (snow peas) and stock and stir-fry for 5 minutes, or until vegetables are just tender. Fold through nuts and serve immediately.

WARM RED CABBAGE SALAD

Make this wonderful warm salad in autumn when apples and red cabbage are plentiful and at their best.

Serves 6

- ☐ **1 tablespoon olive oil**
- ☐ **1 clove garlic, crushed**
- ☐ **1 red onion, thinly sliced**
- ☐ **2 tablespoons balsamic vinegar**
- ☐ **1/2 small red cabbage, shredded**
- ☐ **2 green apples, cored, peeled and thinly sliced**
- ☐ **1 tablespoon finely snipped fresh chives**
- ☐ **1 tablespoon finely chopped fresh dill**
- ☐ **60 g/2 oz slivered almonds, toasted**
- ☐ **60 g/2 oz feta cheese, crumbled**

1 Heat oil in a large frying pan. Add garlic and onion and cook over a medium heat for 2-3 minutes. Stir in vinegar and cook for 1 minute longer.

2 Add cabbage to pan, toss lightly and cook for 4-5 minutes, or until cabbage just starts to wilt and change colour. Transfer all contents of the pan to a salad bowl. Toss through apples, chives and dill. Sprinkle top of the salad with almonds and cheese and serve while salad is still warm.

Balsamic vinegar: Balsamic vinegar is a dark Italian vinegar made by the special processing of wines and musts from the Modena province. It is an interesting addition to any salad dressing, and can also be used in sauces for meats or vegetables. Balsamic vinegar is available from delicatessens and some supermarkets.

BLUE CHEESE AND APPLE OMELETTE

Serves 1

- ☐ **15 g/1/2 oz polyunsaturated margarine**
- ☐ **2 eggs**
- ☐ **2 teaspoons water**
- ☐ **freshly ground black pepper**

APPLE FILLING
- ☐ **15 g/1/2 oz polyunsaturated margarine**
- ☐ **1/2 small green apple, cored and thinly sliced**
- ☐ **30 g/1 oz blue cheese, crumbled**
- ☐ **1 teaspoon finely snipped chives**

1 To make filling, melt margarine in a small frying pan and cook apple over a gentle heat for 2-3 minutes or until just heated through. Remove from pan and set aside to keep warm.

2 To make omelette, melt margarine in another small frying pan. Lightly whisk together eggs and water. Season to taste with black pepper and pour into pan. Cook over a medium heat, continually drawing in the edge of the omelette with a fork during cooking, until no liquid remains and the omelette is lightly set.

3 Top omelette with apple slices, blue cheese and chives and fold in half. Slip onto a plate and serve immediately.

Cook's tip: If peeled apples are soaked in cold water with a tablespoon of lemon juice for 15 minutes they remain pale when cooked.

The easiest way to slice apples neatly is to core them first, then peel, halve and finally cut them into even slices.

INDIAN EGG CURRY

A delicious egg curry that combines all the tastes of India.

Serves 6
Oven temperature 180°C, 350°F, Gas 4

- ☐ **6 hard-boiled eggs, halved lengthwise**

CURRY SAUCE
- ☐ **1 tablespoon vegetable oil**
- ☐ **1 large onion, finely chopped**
- ☐ **1 clove garlic, chopped**
- ☐ **1 tablespoon finely chopped fresh ginger**
- ☐ **1 teaspoon ground cumin**
- ☐ **1 teaspoon ground coriander**
- ☐ **¹/₂ teaspoon chilli powder**
- ☐ **1 teaspoon ground turmeric**
- ☐ **440 g/14 oz canned tomatoes, undrained and mashed**
- ☐ **125 mL/4 fl oz coconut milk**
- ☐ **freshly ground black pepper**

1 To make sauce, heat oil in a frying pan, add onion, garlic and ginger and cook, stirring occasionally, for 5 minutes or until onion is soft. Stir in cumin, coriander, chilli powder and turmeric and cook for 2 minutes longer.

2 Add tomatoes and coconut milk and bring to the boil, then reduce heat and simmer for 15 minutes or until sauce reduces and thickens. Season to taste with black pepper.

3 Place eggs in a shallow baking dish, spoon sauce over, cover and bake for 20 minutes or until heated through.

Cook's tip: When boiling eggs, to prevent a grey-green ring forming around the yolk, take care not to overcook the eggs, and cool cooked eggs immediately under cold running water.

*Warm Red Cabbage Salad,
Blue Cheese and Apple Omelette,
Vegetable and Nut Stir-Fry*

EASY VEGETABLE AND RICE PIE

Serves 4
Oven temperature 220°C, 425°F, Gas 7

- ☐ **375 g/12 oz prepared or ready-rolled puff pastry**
- ☐ **1 egg, lightly beaten with 1 tablespoon water**
- ☐ **1 tablespoon sesame seeds**

VEGETABLE AND RICE FILLING
- ☐ **30 g/1 oz polyunsaturated margarine**
- ☐ **1 onion, chopped**
- ☐ **1 teaspoon ground turmeric**
- ☐ **1 teaspoon ground cumin**
- ☐ **1 teaspoon ground coriander**
- ☐ **$^1/_2$ red pepper, chopped**
- ☐ **1 carrot, chopped**
- ☐ **1 stalk celery, chopped**
- ☐ **1 courgette (zucchini), chopped**
- ☐ **125 g/4 oz rice, cooked**
- ☐ **2 eggs, lightly beaten**

1   To make filling, melt margarine in a large frying pan, add onion, turmeric, cumin and coriander and cook for 5 minutes or until onion is soft. Add red pepper, carrot, celery and courgette (zucchini) and cook, stirring occasionally, for 5 minutes longer. Remove pan from heat, add rice, eggs and black pepper to taste to vegetable mixture and mix to combine.

2   Roll out pastry to 5 mm/$^1/_4$ in thick and cut two 25 cm/10 in circles using a dinner plate or cake tin as a guide. Place one pastry circle on a lightly greased baking tray. Top with filling, spreading out evenly with a fork, leaving a 2.5 cm/1 in border. Moisten border with a little of the egg and water mixture.

3   Top with remaining pastry circle, pressing edges together firmly to seal. Knock back edges with finger and knife to make a decorative scalloped edge.

4   Pierce top of pie several times with a fork. Brush with remaining egg and water mixture, sprinkle with sesame seeds and bake for 15-20 minutes or until pastry is crisp and golden.

Cook's tip: Any leftover cooked vegetables can be used in this pie. For a completely different flavour you might like to use fresh or dried mixed herbs in place of the spices.

Vegetables with Almond Curry,
Spicy Vegetable Loaf

SPICY VEGETABLE LOAF

Serves 6
Oven temperature 180°C, 350°F, Gas 4

- [ ] **1 tablespoon olive oil**
- [ ] **1 clove garlic, crushed**
- [ ] **1 onion, finely chopped**
- [ ] **¹/₂ teaspoon chilli powder**
- [ ] **¹/₂ teaspoon ground cumin**
- [ ] **¹/₂ teaspoon ground coriander**
- [ ] **¹/₂ teaspoon ground turmeric**
- [ ] **250 g/8 oz red lentils**
- [ ] **1 carrot, grated**
- [ ] **1 large potato, grated**
- [ ] **440 g/14 oz canned tomatoes, undrained and mashed**
- [ ] **500 mL/16 fl oz vegetable stock**
- [ ] **3 egg whites**
- [ ] **140 g/4¹/₂ oz rolled oats**
- [ ] **freshly ground black pepper**

1   Heat oil in a large frying pan and cook garlic, onion, chilli powder, cumin, coriander and turmeric for 4-5 minutes or until onion is soft.
2   Add lentils, carrot, potato, tomatoes and stock. Bring to the boil, cover and simmer for 30 minutes or until lentils are tender. Remove from heat and set aside to cool slightly. Beat egg whites until stiff peaks form and fold into lentil mixture.
3   Stir in rolled oats and mix well to combine. Season to taste with black pepper. Spoon into a lightly greased and lined 15 x 25 cm/6 x 10 in loaf tin. Bake for 1 hour or until cooked.

VEGETABLES WITH ALMOND CURRY

Serves 4

- [ ] **1 tablespoon olive oil**
- [ ] **1 onion, sliced**
- [ ] **1 clove garlic, crushed**
- [ ] **1 teaspoon ground cumin**
- [ ] **1 teaspoon ground coriander**
- [ ] **1 teaspoon ground turmeric**
- [ ] **2 carrots, peeled and sliced**
- [ ] **125 g/4 oz red lentils**
- [ ] **440 g/14 oz canned peeled tomatoes, undrained and mashed**
- [ ] **375 mL/12 fl oz vegetable stock**
- [ ] **1 teaspoon chilli sauce, or according to taste**
- [ ] **500 g/1 lb pumpkin, cut into 2 cm/³/₄ in cubes**
- [ ] **¹/₂ cauliflower, cut into florets**
- [ ] **2 tablespoons blanched almonds**
- [ ] **freshly ground black pepper**
- [ ] **4 tablespoons natural yogurt**

1   Heat oil in a large saucepan and cook onion, garlic, cumin, coriander, turmeric and carrots for 5 minutes or until onion is soft.
2   Stir in lentils, tomatoes and stock. Bring to the boil, reduce heat, cover and simmer for 15 minutes.
3   Add chilli sauce, pumpkin and cauliflower. Cook for 15-20 minutes longer or until pumpkin is tender. Mix in almonds and season to taste with black pepper. Ladle curry into bowls and top with a spoonful of yogurt.

CORN AND CHILLI SOUFFLE

Serves 4

- [ ] **60 g/2 oz polyunsaturated margarine**
- [ ] **1 onion, finely chopped**
- [ ] **1 fresh red chilli, seeded and finely chopped**
- [ ] **3 tablespoons flour**
- [ ] **125 mL/4 fl oz milk**
- [ ] **315 g/10 oz canned creamed sweet corn**
- [ ] **4 egg yolks, lightly beaten**
- [ ] **freshly ground black pepper**
- [ ] **5 egg whites**
- [ ] **3 tablespoons breadcrumbs made from stale bread**

1   Melt margarine in a saucepan, add onion and chilli and cook over a medium heat, stirring frequently, for 10 minutes, or until onion is soft and golden. Stir in flour and cook for 1 minute. Remove from heat and gradually stir in milk and sweet corn. Return to heat and cook, stirring constantly, until mixture boils and thickens. Remove from heat and beat in egg yolks. Season to taste with black pepper.
2   Place egg whites in a bowl and beat until stiff peaks form. Fold gently into sweet corn mixture.
3   Grease an 18 cm/7 in soufflé dish and sprinkle with breadcrumbs. Grease a paper collar, sprinkle with breadcrumbs and attach to soufflé dish.
4   Spoon soufflé mixture into prepared dish and bake for 30-35 minutes or until soufflé is puffed and golden. Serve immediately.

CHUNKY HOTPOT

Serves 4

- [ ] **2 tablespoons vegetable oil**
- [ ] **1 clove garlic, crushed**
- [ ] **1 small fresh red chilli, chopped**
- [ ] **1 onion, chopped**
- [ ] **2 teaspoons curry powder**
- [ ] **2 teaspoons ground cumin**
- [ ] **1 teaspoon garam masala**
- [ ] **2 tablespoons chopped fresh coriander**
- [ ] **1 tablespoon chopped fresh ginger**
- [ ] **1 head broccoli, broken into small florets**
- [ ] **3 carrots, chopped**
- [ ] **2 parsnips, chopped**
- [ ] **1 large potato, cubed**
- [ ] **375 g/12 oz baby squash, halved**
- [ ] **1 tablespoon flour**
- [ ] **375 mL/12 fl oz water**
- [ ] **200 mL/6¹/₂ fl oz coconut milk**
- [ ] **125 g/4 oz roasted cashew nuts, chopped**

1   Heat oil in a large saucepan. Cook garlic, chilli, onion, curry powder, cumin, garam masala, coriander and ginger over a low heat for 1 minute. Add broccoli, carrots, parsnips, potato and squash. Cook for 5-8 minutes over a medium heat.

2   Stir in flour and cook for 1 minute. Remove pan from heat and gradually blend in water. Cook over a medium heat, stirring constantly, until mixture boils and thickens. Reduce heat, cover and simmer for 10-15 minutes, or until vegetables are tender.

3   Whisk in coconut milk and cook over a low heat for 2-3 minutes. Spoon into individual bowls and sprinkle with cashew nuts to serve.

STIR-FRIED VEGETABLES WITH EGGS

Often called Egg Foo Yung and traditionally made with prawns, fish or beef, this popular recipe is delicious made just with vegetables.

Serves 2

- [ ] **125 g/4 oz mangetout (snow peas), trimmed**
- [ ] **185 g/6 oz fresh asparagus, cut into 5 cm/2 in pieces**
- [ ] **3 eggs**
- [ ] **1 teaspoon sesame oil**
- [ ] **3 tablespoons water**
- [ ] **1 teaspoon dry sherry**
- [ ] **1 teaspoon soy sauce**
- [ ] **freshly ground black pepper**
- [ ] **1 tablespoon vegetable oil**
- [ ] **3 spring onions, chopped**

1   Boil, steam or microwave mangetout (snow peas) and asparagus separately until just tender. Drain and refresh under cold running water, drain again and set aside.

2   Place eggs, sesame oil, water, sherry and soy sauce in a bowl and whisk to combine. Season to taste with black pepper.

3   Heat oil in a wok or frying pan, add egg mixture and stir-fry for 1 minute, or until egg just begins to set. Add mangetout (snow peas), asparagus and spring onions and stir-fry for 1 minute longer. Serve immediately.

POTATO AND PESTO BAKE

Serves 4
Oven temperature 180°C, 350°F, Gas 4

- [ ] **8 potatoes, thickly sliced**

PESTO
- [ ] **60 g/2 oz basil leaves**
- [ ] **2 cloves garlic, crushed**
- [ ] **2 tablespoons pine nuts**
- [ ] **125 mL/4 fl oz olive oil**
- [ ] **4 tablespoons grated fresh Parmesan cheese**

SOUR CREAM TOPPING
- [ ] **300 mL/9¹/₂ fl oz sour cream**
- [ ] **60 g/2 oz grated mature Cheddar**
- [ ] **freshly ground black pepper**

1   Boil, steam or microwave potato slices until almost tender. Drain and layer potatoes in the bottom of a greased ovenproof dish.

2   To make Pesto, place basil, garlic, pine nuts, oil and Parmesan in a food processor or blender and process until smooth. Spread over potatoes.

3   To make topping, spoon sour cream over Pesto and top with Cheddar and black pepper to taste. Bake for 10 minutes or until potatoes are soft and top is golden brown.

Chunky Hotpot, Potato and Pesto Bake, Singapore Noodle Stir-Fry

SINGAPORE NOODLE STIR-FRY

Serves 4

- ☐ 410 g/13 oz rice noodles
- ☐ 1 tablespoon sesame oil
- ☐ 1 onion, chopped
- ☐ 1 tablespoon sesame seeds
- ☐ 2 fresh red chillies, chopped
- ☐ 185 g/6 oz sliced bamboo shoots
- ☐ 4 tablespoons bean sprouts
- ☐ ¼ cabbage, finely shredded
- ☐ 1 carrot, finely chopped
- ☐ 1 red pepper, diced

SWEET AND SOUR SAUCE
- ☐ 3 tablespoons plum sauce
- ☐ 1 tablespoon sugar
- ☐ 1 tablespoon white wine vinegar
- ☐ 185 mL/6 fl oz vegetable stock
- ☐ 2 teaspoons cornflour blended with 1 tablespoon water

1   Place noodles in a large saucepan of boiling water and cook until tender. Drain and set aside.
2   Heat oil in pan, add onion and cook 3 minutes or until tender. Stir in sesame seeds and chillies, and cook for 2 minutes.
3   Add bamboo shoots, bean sprouts, cabbage, carrot and red pepper. Cook for 5 minutes, stirring frequently.
4   To make sauce, combine plum sauce, sugar, vinegar and stock. Add to pan with vegetables. Bring to the boil, then reduce heat and simmer for 2 minutes. Pour in cornflour mixture, and stir until mixture thickens slightly. Toss through noodles and serve immediately.

INDONESIAN COOKED SALAD

Poppadums are the perfect accompaniment to this unusual salad of lightly cooked vegetables topped with eggs and a spicy peanut sauce.

Serves 4

- ☐ 2 potatoes, cut into chunks
- ☐ 4 carrots, sliced
- ☐ 250 g/8 oz green beans, sliced
- ☐ 250 g/8 oz spinach, stalks removed
- ☐ 2 tablespoons vegetable oil
- ☐ 125 g/4 oz bean sprouts
- ☐ 1 small cucumber, cut into sticks
- ☐ 2 hard-boiled eggs, quartered
- ☐ 1 large onion, sliced

PEANUT SAUCE
- ☐ 1 tablespoon vegetable oil
- ☐ 1 small onion, chopped
- ☐ 1 clove garlic, crushed
- ☐ 250 mL/8 fl oz coconut milk
- ☐ 1 tablespoon lemon juice
- ☐ 5 tablespoons peanut butter
- ☐ ½ teaspoon chilli powder
- ☐ 1 bay leaf

1   Boil, steam or microwave potatoes, carrots, beans and spinach, separately, until just tender. Drain and layer in a deep dish.
2   Heat 1 tablespoon oil in a wok or frying pan and stir-fry bean sprouts and cucumber for 2-3 minutes. Drain and sprinkle over vegetables in dish. Heat remaining oil in pan and cook onion for 4-5 minutes or until golden. Drain and set aside.
3   To make sauce, heat oil in a saucepan and cook onion and garlic for 4-5 minutes, or until onion is soft. Stir in coconut milk, lemon juice, peanut butter, chilli powder and bay leaf. Cook over a medium heat, stirring constantly, until mixture thickens.
4   Arrange eggs over vegetables, pour sauce over and top with sliced onion.

Indonesian Cooked Salad

AUBERGINE LASAGNE

Serves 4
Oven temperature 180°C, 350°F, Gas 4

- [ ] 1 tablespoon olive oil
- [ ] ¹/₂ teaspoon cracked black peppercorns
- [ ] 3 tablespoons lemon juice
- [ ] 1 large aubergine (eggplant), about 500 g/1 lb, halved lengthwise and cut into 5 mm/¹/₄ in thick slices
- [ ] 30 g/1 oz wholemeal breadcrumbs, made from stale bread
- [ ] 3 tablespoons grated Parmesan cheese
- [ ] 1 large onion, chopped
- [ ] 2 cloves garlic, crushed
- [ ] 440 g/14 oz canned peeled tomatoes, drained, chopped and 1 tablespoon juice reserved
- [ ] 185 mL/6 fl oz tomato purée
- [ ] 2 tablespoons white wine
- [ ] 1 teaspoon dried oregano
- [ ] 1 teaspoon dried basil
- [ ] pinch cayenne pepper
- [ ] 6 wholemeal instant lasagne sheets
- [ ] 185 g/6 oz ricotta cheese
- [ ] 3 tablespoons grated mozzarella cheese

1   Combine olive oil, black peppercorns and lemon juice and brush aubergine (eggplant) slices. Cook under a preheated grill for 3-4 minutes each side or until golden. Combine breadcrumbs and Parmesan cheese and set aside.

2   Heat a nonstick frying pan and cook onion, garlic and reserved tomato juice over a medium heat for 2-3 minutes. Add tomatoes, tomato purée, wine, oregano, basil and cayenne pepper and cook for 5 minutes longer.

3   Spread one-third of the tomato mixture over base of a 15 x 25 cm/6 x 10 in ovenproof dish. Top with 3 lasagne sheets, half of the breadcrumb mixture and cover with a layer of aubergine (eggplant). Top with half the ricotta cheese. Repeat layers, ending with a layer of tomato mixture. Top with mozzarella cheese and bake for 45 minutes.

PUMPKIN SEED DIP

This dip is delicious served on a platter of raw vegetables as a snack or as part of a light meal.

Serves 6

- [ ] 100 g/3¹/₂ oz pumpkin seeds, toasted
- [ ] 1 tablespoon lemon juice
- [ ] 2 tablespoons balsamic vinegar
- [ ] 1 clove garlic, crushed
- [ ] ¹/₂ teaspoon Dijon mustard

Place pumpkin seeds, lemon juice, vinegar, garlic and mustard in a food processor or blender and process until smooth. Chill before serving.

Aubergine Lasagne

chapter seven

RICE AND PASTA TO PLEASE

Rice and pasta are important staple foods for much of the world's population. Quick and easy to prepare and inexpensive, they are also the perfect ingredient for the family cook. The recipes in this chapter show you exciting ways in which to use these ever-popular foods.

Hot Pasta and Mushrooms,
Gingered Noodles and Vegetables,
Herby Tomato and Pasta Salad

TUNA-FILLED SHELLS

These shells are fun to eat hot or cold as finger food, or they can be served with a sauce as a first course.

Makes 16 filled shells

- ☐ **16 giant pasta shells**

TUNA FILLING
- ☐ **250 g/8 oz ricotta cheese, drained**
- ☐ **440 g/14 oz canned tuna in brine, drained and flaked**
- ☐ **1/2 red pepper, diced**
- ☐ **1 tablespoon chopped capers**
- ☐ **1 teaspoon snipped fresh chives**
- ☐ **4 tablespoons grated Swiss cheese**
- ☐ **pinch ground nutmeg**
- ☐ **freshly ground black pepper**
- ☐ **2 tablespoons grated Parmesan cheese**

1 Cook 8 pasta shells in a large saucepan of boiling water until al dente. Drain, rinse under cold running water and drain again. Set aside in a single layer. Repeat with remaining shells.
2 To make filling, place ricotta cheese and tuna in a bowl and mix to combine. Mix in red pepper, capers, chives 2 tablespoons grated Swiss cheese, nutmeg and black pepper to taste.
3 Fill each shell with ricotta mixture, and place in a single layer in a lightly greased, shallow ovenproof dish. Sprinkle with Parmesan cheese and remaining Swiss cheese. Place under a preheated grill and cook until cheese melts.

GINGERED NOODLES AND VEGETABLES

The flat Oriental noodles that we have used in this recipe are different from egg noodles; they are made from flour and water and are available from Chinese food stores.

Serves 6

- ☐ **1 tablespoon groundnut (peanut) oil**
- ☐ **2 teaspoons grated fresh ginger**
- ☐ **1 clove garlic, crushed**
- ☐ **1 onion, sliced**
- ☐ **1 carrot, sliced diagonally**
- ☐ **2 stalks celery, sliced diagonally**
- ☐ **100 g/3 1/2 oz bean sprouts**
- ☐ **200 g/6 1/2 oz mangetout (snow peas), trimmed**
- ☐ **500 g/1 lb flat Oriental noodles, cooked**
- ☐ **freshly ground black pepper**

1 Heat oil in a wok or large frying pan. Add ginger and garlic, and stir-fry for 1-2 minutes. Stir in onion and carrot, and stir-fry for 4-5 minutes.
2 Add celery, bean sprouts and mangetout (snow peas), and stir-fry for 2-3 minutes.
3 Stir in noodles, and stir-fry 3-4 minutes or until noodles are heated through. Season to taste with black pepper and serve immediately.

HERBY TOMATO AND PASTA SALAD

As a luncheon, this salad needs only crusty bread to accompany it.

Serves 6

- ☐ **250 g/8 oz spinach tagliatelle**
- ☐ **250 g/8 oz plain tagliatelle**
- ☐ **2 courgettes (zucchini), cut into matchsticks**
- ☐ **1 small red pepper, sliced**
- ☐ **1 small green pepper, sliced**
- ☐ **200 g/6 1/2 oz green beans, cooked**

TOMATO AND BASIL DRESSING
- ☐ **4 ripe tomatoes, peeled and roughly chopped**
- ☐ **1 clove garlic, crushed**
- ☐ **2 teaspoons olive oil**
- ☐ **2 teaspoons red wine vinegar**
- ☐ **2 tablespoons finely chopped fresh basil**
- ☐ **1 tablespoon finely chopped fresh parsley**
- ☐ **1 tablespoon finely chopped fresh chives**
- ☐ **freshly ground black pepper**

1 Cook both tagliatelles together in boiling water in a large saucepan following packet directions. Rinse under cold running water, drain and set aside to cool completely.
2 Place cold tagliatelles, courgettes (zucchini), peppers and beans in a large salad bowl.
3 To make dressing, place tomatoes, garlic, oil and vinegar in a food processor or blender. Process until smooth. Stir in basil, parsley and chives, and season to taste with black pepper. Spoon dressing over pasta and vegetables. Toss lightly to coat all ingredients with dressing.

HOT PASTA AND MUSHROOMS

Creamy mushroom sauce and hot pasta – the food that dreams are made of! A green salad and crusty bread will complete your meal.

Serves 4

- ☐ **300 g/9 1/2 oz macaroni**
- ☐ **3 tablespoons finely chopped fresh parsley**
- ☐ **2 tablespoons grated Parmesan cheese**

MUSHROOM SAUCE
- ☐ **2 teaspoons vegetable oil**
- ☐ **1 onion, sliced**
- ☐ **500 g/1 lb mushrooms, sliced**
- ☐ **1 teaspoon paprika**
- ☐ **2 tablespoons tomato purée**
- ☐ **250 mL/8 fl oz evaporated milk**
- ☐ **freshly ground black pepper**

1 Cook macaroni in boiling water in a large saucepan following packet directions. Drain, set aside and keep warm.
2 To make sauce, heat oil in a nonstick frying pan. Cook onion and mushrooms until they are soft. Blend together paprika, tomato purée and milk. Stir into mushroom mixture and cook gently over a low heat for 5 minutes. Season to taste with black pepper.
3 Place pasta in a heated serving dish and spoon over sauce. Toss gently to combine. Sprinkle with parsley and Parmesan to serve.

Perfect pasta: The secret of cooking perfect pasta is to bring a large pot of water to a rolling boil. Add a splash of oil to prevent the pasta from sticking together (do not add salt, as it toughens the pasta). Immerse your pasta, bring back to the boil, then cook 2-3 minutes for fresh or 5-8 minutes for dried. Pasta should taste 'al dente' – just cooked, but with no hard core in the centre. Drain and place in bowls, ready for the sauce.

FETTUCCINE WITH BLACK BEAN SAUCE

This East meets West type of dish uses Asian ingredients for the sauce and Italian pasta as the base. If you wish, in place of the fettuccine you could use Asian noodles.

Serves 4

- ☐ **2 teaspoons vegetable oil**
- ☐ **1 clove garlic, crushed**
- ☐ **1 red chilli, seeded and finely chopped**
- ☐ **1 tablespoon canned black beans, washed, drained**
- ☐ **1 tablespoon soy sauce**
- ☐ **1 tablespoon vinegar**
- ☐ **1 tablespoon oyster sauce**
- ☐ **500 mL/16 fl oz vegetable stock**
- ☐ **2 teaspoons brown sugar**
- ☐ **2 tablespoons cornflour blended with 4 tablespoons cold water**
- ☐ **500 g/1 lb fettuccine**

1   Heat oil in a large frypan, add garlic and chilli and cook for 1 minute. Combine black beans, soy, vinegar, oyster sauce, stock, sugar and cornflour mixture. Pour black bean mixture into pan, and simmer for 5 minutes, or until sauce thickens.

2   Cook pasta in boiling water in a large saucepan following the packet directions. Drain and place in a serving dish. Toss sauce through and serve.

TORTELLINI WITH SWEET RED PEPPER SAUCE

Serves 4

- ☐ **500 g/1 lb tortellini**

SWEET RED PEPPER SAUCE
- ☐ **1 tablespoon vegetable oil**
- ☐ **1 onion, chopped**
- ☐ **440 g/14 oz canned sweet red peppers, drained and chopped**
- ☐ **125 mL/4 fl oz water**
- ☐ **1 tablespoon honey**
- ☐ **1 tablespoon chopped fresh oregano**

1   Cook tortellini in boiling water in a large saucepan, following packet directions. Drain, set aside and keep warm.

2   To make sauce, heat oil in small pan, add onion and cook for 3 minutes or until tender. Place red peppers, water, honey, oregano and onion in a food processor or blender and process until smooth.

3   Place sweet pepper sauce into a large saucepan and heat until simmering. Pour sauce over hot tortellini and serve.

Fettuccine with Black Bean Sauce, Tortellini with Sweet Red Pepper Sauce

CURRIED TUNA LASAGNE

Serves 6
Oven temperature 190°C, 375°F, Gas 5

- [ ] **9 sheets instant lasagne noodles**
- [ ] **440 g/14 oz canned tuna, drained and flaked**
- [ ] **15 g/¹/₂ oz butter**
- [ ] **2 stalks celery, finely chopped**
- [ ] **1 onion, chopped**

CURRY SAUCE
- [ ] **30 g/1 oz butter**
- [ ] **4 tablespoons flour**
- [ ] **2 teaspoons curry powder**
- [ ] **500 mL/16 fl oz milk**
- [ ] **185 mL/6 fl oz water**
- [ ] **2 eggs, beaten**
- [ ] **2 tablespoons grated mature Cheddar**

CHEESE TOPPING
- [ ] **2 tablespoons grated mature Cheddar**
- [ ] **1 teaspoon curry powder**
- [ ] **¹/₂ teaspoon paprika**

SALMON RICE AND SPINACH LOAF

Serves 4
Oven temperature 200°C, 400°F, Gas 6

- [ ] **10 spinach leaves, stalks removed**
- [ ] **440 g/14 oz canned salmon, drained**
- [ ] **3 eggs**
- [ ] **3 tablespoons sour cream or natural yogurt**
- [ ] **2 tablespoons mayonnaise**
- [ ] **1 tablespoon lemon juice**
- [ ] **90 g/3 oz cooked rice**
- [ ] **2 tablespoons grated Parmesan cheese**
- [ ] **freshly ground black pepper**

1   Wet spinach leaves and boil or steam until soft.

2   Line the base and sides of a greased ovenproof 10 x 23 cm/4 x 9 in loaf tin with half of the spinach leaves, allowing some of the leaves to hang over the sides.

3   Squeeze excess moisture from remaining leaves, then chop and combine with all the remaining ingredients. Season to taste with black pepper. Spoon salmon mixture into spinach-lined tin. Enclose with the overhanging spinach leaves, cover and bake for 45 minutes or until firm. Stand for 10 minutes before serving.

Microwave it: This loaf cooks quickly in the microwave. Preparation of the loaf is the same, but remember to use a microwave-safe dish. Cover, then cook on HIGH (100%) for 13 minutes. Stand 5 minutes before serving.

1 To make sauce, melt butter in a saucepan. Stir in flour and curry powder and cook for 2-3 minutes. Remove from heat, whisk in combined milk and water. Stir over a medium heat until sauce boils and thickens. Blend in eggs and cheese.

2 Spoon a little sauce over the base of a shallow ovenproof dish. Top with 3 lasagne sheets and spread over half the tuna.

3 Melt butter in a frying pan and cook celery and onion until onion is soft. Spread half onion mixture over tuna and top with a layer of sauce. Repeat layers, finishing with noodles then sauce.

4 To make topping, combine cheese, curry powder and paprika. Sprinkle over top and bake for 30-35 minutes or until tender.

WHOLEMEAL SPAGHETTI WITH TOMATOES AND ASPARAGUS

Serves 4

☐ **500 g/1 lb wholemeal spaghetti**

ASPARAGUS SAUCE
☐ **1 tablespoon olive oil**
☐ **1 clove garlic, crushed**
☐ **440 g/14 oz canned tomatoes, drained and chopped**
☐ **300 g/9$\frac{1}{2}$ oz canned asparagus cuts, drained**
☐ **1 tablespoon chopped fresh parsley**
☐ **1 tablespoon brown sugar**
☐ **2 tablespoons red wine**
☐ **freshly ground black pepper**

1 Cook spaghetti in boiling water following the packet instructions. Drain and keep warm.

2 To make sauce, heat oil in a frying pan and cook garlic for 1 minute. Stir in tomatoes, asparagus, parsley, sugar and wine and season to taste with black pepper. Cover and simmer for 15-20 minutes. Spoon sauce over hot spaghetti and serve with Parmesan cheese if desired.

Left: Salmon Rice and Spinach Loaf
Below: Curried Tuna Lasagne, Wholemeal Spaghetti with Tomatoes and Asparagus

COATED CHILLI RICE BALLS

Makes 16

- ☐ 3 teaspoons olive oil
- ☐ 1 onion, finely chopped
- ☐ 315 g/10 oz long grain rice
- ☐ 1/2 teaspoon ground turmeric
- ☐ 750 mL/1 1/4 pt chicken stock
- ☐ 1/2 teaspoon chilli powder
- ☐ freshly ground black pepper
- ☐ 3 spring onions, finely chopped
- ☐ 15 g/1/2 oz butter
- ☐ 3 tablespoons grated mature Cheddar
- ☐ 2 eggs, lightly beaten
- ☐ 125 g/4 oz mozzarella cheese, cut into 1 cm/3/4 in cubes
- ☐ 90 g/3 oz dried breadcrumbs
- ☐ oil for cooking

1   Heat oil in a frying pan and cook onion for 2-3 minutes or until soft. Stir in rice and turmeric and cook for 1-2 minutes or until rice is coated with oil.

2   Pour in 185 mL/6 fl oz stock and bring to the boil. Cook, stirring frequently, until liquid has almost evaporated. Add remaining stock, chilli powder and black pepper to taste. Simmer for 10-15 minutes or until liquid has been absorbed. Remove pan from heat and stir through spring onions, butter and Cheddar.

3   Lightly fold eggs through, taking care not to mash rice grains. Divide rice mixture into sixteen equal portions. Take a cheese cube and, with hands, mould one portion of rice around cheese, to form a ball. Repeat with remaining rice and cheese portions.

4   Coat balls in breadcrumbs and refrigerate for 30 minutes. Heat oil in a deep saucepan and cook four to five balls at a time, until golden. Remove, drain on absorbent kitchen paper and serve.

MUSHROOM AND BACON SAUCE

This sauce is best used with the long varieties of pasta such as fettuccine, taglierini, spaghetti or linguine.

Serves 4

- ☐ 1 small head broccoli, cut into small florets
- ☐ 2 teaspoons olive oil
- ☐ 4 rashers bacon, chopped
- ☐ 125 g/4 oz button mushrooms, sliced
- ☐ 1 clove garlic, crushed
- ☐ 300 mL/9 1/2 fl oz cream (double)
- ☐ freshly ground black pepper
- ☐ 3 tablespoons finely chopped fresh parsley

1   Boil, steam or microwave broccoli until just tender. Drain and refresh under cold running water. Drain and set aside.

2   Heat oil in a frying pan and cook bacon for 3-4 minutes or until crisp. Stir in mushrooms and garlic and cook for 2-3 minutes.

3   Pour in cream, bring to the boil, stirring frequently and simmer for 5 minutes or until sauce thickens. Season to taste with black pepper, add broccoli and heat through. Spoon sauce over hot, cooked pasta. Sprinkle with parsley and serve.

SEAFOOD AND TOMATO SAUCE

Any combination of seafood can be used in this sauce.

Serves 4

- ☐ 1 tablespoon olive oil
- ☐ 4 spring onions, finely chopped
- ☐ 1 clove garlic, crushed
- ☐ 1 small fresh red chilli, finely chopped
- ☐ 500 g/1 lb cooked prawns, shelled, deveined and chopped
- ☐ 125 g/4 oz scallops, halved, with coral removed
- ☐ 440 g/14 oz canned tomatoes, undrained and mashed
- ☐ 3 tablespoons red wine
- ☐ 3 tablespoons chicken stock
- ☐ 2 teaspoons tomato purée
- ☐ 1 teaspoon sugar
- ☐ 2 teaspoons chopped fresh basil
- ☐ 1 tablespoon chopped fresh parsley
- ☐ 8 oysters in the shell

1   Heat oil in a large saucepan and cook spring onions, garlic and chilli for 1 minute. Stir in prawns and scallops and cook for 2 minutes longer.

2   Combine tomatoes, wine, stock, tomato purée and sugar and pour into pan with prawn mixture. Bring to the boil, then reduce heat and simmer, uncovered, for 10 minutes.

3   Add basil and parsley. Cook for 2-3 minutes. Spoon sauce over hot, cooked pasta. Garnish with oysters in their shells.

TUNA AND OLIVE SAUCE

Serves 4

- ☐ **30 g/1 oz butter**
- ☐ **2 tablespoons flour**
- ☐ **125 mL/4 fl oz milk**
- ☐ **3 tablespoons chicken stock**
- ☐ **440 g/14 oz tuna in brine, drained and liquid reserved**
- ☐ **1 tablespoon finely chopped fresh dill**
- ☐ **12 black olives, pitted and sliced**
- ☐ **2 tablespoons capers, finely chopped**
- ☐ **2-3 drops Tabasco sauce**
- ☐ **3 tablespoons cream (double)**
- ☐ **2 tablespoons lemon juice**
- ☐ **freshly ground black pepper**

1   Melt butter in a saucepan, add flour and cook for 1 minute. Remove from heat.
2   Blend in milk, stock and tuna liquid, stirring over a medium heat until sauce boils and thickens.
3   Reduce heat and add dill, olives, capers, Tabasco, cream and lemon juice. Season to taste with black pepper and stir well to combine.
4   Break up tuna into smaller chunks and fold through sauce. Cook for 2-3 minutes. Spoon sauce over hot, pasta and serve.

PASTA PARCELS WITH BLUE CHEESE SAUCE

Serves 8
Oven temperature 180°C, 350°F, Gas 4

- ☐ **8 spinach lasagne sheets, approximately 16 cm/6¹/₂ in square, cooked**

SPINACH FILLING
- ☐ **500 g/1 lb spinach, stalks removed, leaves blanched and squeezed to remove excess water**
- ☐ **4 hard-boiled eggs, chopped**
- ☐ **125 g/4 oz prosciutto or lean ham, finely chopped**
- ☐ **1 tablespoon finely chopped red onion**
- ☐ **1 clove garlic, crushed**
- ☐ **freshly ground black pepper**

BLUE CHEESE SAUCE
- ☐ **100 g/3¹/₂ soft blue cheese**
- ☐ **375 mL/12 fl oz cream (single)**
- ☐ **1¹/₂ tablespoons Dijon mustard**
- ☐ **3-4 tablespoons lemon juice**
- ☐ **2 tablespoons chopped hazelnuts or almonds, toasted**

1   To make filling, shred spinach finely. Place spinach, hard-boiled eggs, prosciutto or ham, onion, garlic and black pepper to taste in a bowl and mix to combine.
2   To make sauce, place blue cheese, cream, mustard and lemon juice in a food processor or blender and process until well blended, then stir in hazelnuts or almonds.
3   To assemble parcels, divide filling between lasagne sheets, forming a mould in centre of each sheet. Fold in corners of pasta like an envelope to form a parcel. Place parcels in a shallow ovenproof dish, spoon sauce over, cover with aluminum foil and bake for 20 minutes or until heated through.

Left: Coated Chilli Rice Balls
Above: Seafood and Tomato Sauce,
Tuna and Olive Sauce,
Pasta with Mushroom and Bacon Sauce

FETTUCCINE WITH VEAL CREAM SAUCE

Serves 4

- ☐ **500 g/1 lb fettuccine**
- ☐ **1 tablespoon olive oil**
- ☐ **500 g/1 lb thin veal steaks, cut into strips**
- ☐ **1 clove garlic, crushed**
- ☐ **1 teaspoon chopped fresh parsley**
- ☐ **2 teaspoons paprika**
- ☐ **1¹/₂ tablespoons brandy**
- ☐ **2 tablespoons tomato purée**
- ☐ **410 g/13 oz sour cream**
- ☐ **freshly ground black pepper**

1 Cook fettuccine in boiling water in a large saucepan until al dente. Drain, set aside and keep warm.
2 Heat oil in a large frying pan and cook veal for 3-4 minutes or until browned. Add garlic, parsley and paprika and cook for 1-2 minutes longer. Stir in brandy and cook until evaporated. Whisk in tomato purée and sour cream. Season to taste with black pepper and bring to the boil. Reduce heat and simmer until sauce reduces and thickens. Stir in pasta and toss to coat.

CHICKEN LIVERS AND MUSHROOMS ON SPAGHETTI

A variation of a sauce created for the great singer Caruso.

Serves 4

- ☐ **500 g/1 lb spaghetti**
- ☐ **1 tablespoon vegetable oil**
- ☐ **90 g/3 oz grated fresh Parmesan cheese**

TOMATO SAUCE
- ☐ **1 tablespoon vegetable oil**
- ☐ **30 g/1 oz butter**
- ☐ **1 onion, finely diced**
- ☐ **2 cloves garlic, crushed**
- ☐ **12 small button mushrooms, halved**
- ☐ **440 g/14 oz canned tomatoes, undrained and mashed**
- ☐ **1 teaspoon sugar**
- ☐ **300 mL/9¹/₂ fl oz chicken stock**
- ☐ **ground black pepper**

CHICKEN LIVER SAUCE
- ☐ **30 g/1 oz butter**
- ☐ **250 g/8 oz chicken livers, trimmed and sliced**
- ☐ **1 teaspoon finely chopped fresh thyme, or ¹/₄ teaspoon dried thyme**

- ☐ **90 mL/3 fl oz Marsala**
- ☐ **1 tablespoon finely chopped fresh parsley**

1 To make Tomato Sauce, heat oil and butter in a frying pan, and cook onion until soft. Add garlic and mushrooms and cook for 2-3 minutes longer. Combine tomatoes and sugar and add to mushrooms. Cook over a low heat for 10 minutes. Stir in stock and simmer for 30 minutes longer or until sauce reduces and thickens. Season to taste with black pepper.
2 To make Chicken Liver Sauce, melt butter in a saucepan and cook chicken livers and thyme over a medium heat until livers change colour. Increase heat, stir in Marsala and cook for 1-2 minutes. Stir in parsley.
3 Cook spaghetti in boiling water in a large saucepan until al dente. Drain and fold through oil.
4 Arrange half spaghetti on a warm serving platter, top with half chicken liver mixture, then half Tomato Sauce. Sprinkle over half Parmesan cheese, then repeat layers. Serve immediately.

Fettuccine with Veal Cream Sauce, Spirelli with Ham and Artichokes

PAPPARDELLE WITH PEAS AND BACON

Pappardelle is a strong pasta which goes with rich sauces. It is ideal to serve with game.

Serves 4

- [ ] **60 g/2 oz butter**
- [ ] **1 onion, sliced**
- [ ] **1 clove garlic, crushed**
- [ ] **pinch chilli flakes, or to taste**
- [ ] **3 rashers bacon, chopped**
- [ ] **90 g/3 oz shelled peas, blanched**
- [ ] **1 teaspoon finely chopped fresh mint**
- [ ] **1 tablespoon finely chopped fresh parsley**
- [ ] **freshly ground black pepper**
- [ ] **500 g/1 lb pappardelle**
- [ ] **2 eggs, lightly beaten**
- [ ] **90 mL/3 fl oz cream (single)**
- [ ] **1½ tablespoons grated fresh pecorino cheese**

1   Melt butter in a large frying pan and cook onion, garlic and chilli for 6-8 minutes. Add bacon and cook for 5 minutes longer. Stir in peas, mint and 2 teaspoons parsley. Season to taste with black pepper. Set aside and keep warm.

2   Cook pappardelle in boiling water in a large saucepan until al dente. Drain, then add to pea mixture, toss lightly to coat and remove from heat. Combine eggs, cream, pecorino and remaining parsley and stir into pasta mixture. Serve as soon as eggs begin to set and cling to pasta – this will take only a few seconds. The sauce should be slightly runny.

SPIRELLI WITH HAM AND ARTICHOKES

Serves 4

- [ ] **500 g/1 lb spirelli**
- [ ] **2 teaspoons olive oil**
- [ ] **315 g/10 oz ham, cut into strips**
- [ ] **6 canned artichoke hearts, sliced lengthwise**
- [ ] **3 eggs, beaten with 1 tablespoon grated fresh Parmesan cheese**
- [ ] **freshly ground black pepper**

1   Cook spirelli in boiling water in a large saucepan following packet directions or until al dente. Drain, set aside and keep warm.

2   Heat oil in a frying pan and cook ham and artichoke hearts for 1-2 minutes.

3   Add pasta and toss to combine. Remove from heat and quickly stir in egg mixture. Season to taste with black pepper. Serve as soon as the eggs start to stick to spirelli – this will take only a few seconds.

Pappardelle with Peas and Bacon, Chicken Livers and Mushrooms on Spaghetti

TORTELLINI WITH CREAMY TOMATO SAUCE

Serves 4

- [ ] **500 g/1 lb tortellini**
- [ ] **4 tablespoons grated Parmesan cheese**
- [ ] **basil leaves**

CREAMY TOMATO SAUCE
- [ ] **1 tablespoon vegetable oil**
- [ ] **1 onion, finely chopped**
- [ ] **1 clove garlic, crushed**
- [ ] **375 mL/12 fl oz canned tomato soup**
- [ ] **2 tablespoons red wine**
- [ ] **1 tablespoon finely chopped fresh basil**
- [ ] **125 mL/4 fl oz cream (double)**
- [ ] **freshly ground black pepper**

1   Cook tortellini in boiling water in a saucepan following packet directions. Drain, set aside and keep warm.

2   To make sauce, heat oil in a small saucepan and cook onion over a medium heat for 3-4 minutes or until soft. Add garlic, soup, wine and basil, bring to simmering and simmer for 5 minutes. Remove pan from heat, stir in cream and season to taste with black pepper. Spoon sauce over tortellini, top with Parmesan cheese and basil leaves.

Serving suggestion: Accompany with crusty Italian bread.

Fast Fried Rice, Fruity Rice Salad

FAST FRIED RICE

Serves 4

- ☐ **1 tablespoon vegetable oil**
- ☐ **4 spring onions, finely chopped**
- ☐ **2 stalks celery, finely chopped**
- ☐ **2 eggs, lightly beaten**
- ☐ **4 slices ham, finely chopped**
- ☐ **440 g/14 oz canned sweet corn kernels, drained**
- ☐ **300 g/9$^{1}/_{2}$ oz rice, cooked**
- ☐ **2 teaspoons soy sauce**

1 Heat oil in a nonstick frying pan and cook spring onions and celery over a medium heat for 3-4 minutes or until onion is soft. Remove onion mixture from pan and set aside. Pour egg into pan and cook for 2 minutes or until set. Leaving omelette in pan and using an egg slice, chop omelette into small pieces.

2 Add onion mixture, ham, corn, rice and soy sauce to pan and stir to combine. Cook for 1 minute longer or until heated.

FRUITY RICE SALAD

This is a great recipe for using leftovers.

Serves 4

- ☐ **300 g/9$^{1}/_{2}$ oz rice, cooked**
- ☐ **2 small apples, cored and chopped**
- ☐ **4 tablespoons sultanas**
- ☐ **1 green pepper, chopped**
- ☐ **4 tablespoons sunflower seeds**
- ☐ **1 tablespoon finely chopped fresh coriander or parsley**

ORANGE DRESSING
- ☐ **125 mL/4 fl oz orange juice**
- ☐ **2 teaspoons finely grated orange rind**
- ☐ **1 teaspoon finely chopped fresh ginger**
- ☐ **2 teaspoons honey, warmed**

1 Place rice, apples, sultanas, green pepper, sunflower seeds and coriander or parsley in a bowl and toss to combine.

2 To make dressing, place orange juice, orange rind, ginger and honey in a screwtop jar and shake to combine. Pour dressing over rice salad. Serve immediately.

CHEESY BAKED RICE CUSTARD

Serves 4
Oven temperature 180°C, 350°F, Gas 4

- ☐ **30 g/1 oz butter**
- ☐ **2 leeks, sliced**
- ☐ **3 rashers bacon, chopped**
- ☐ **¹/₂ red pepper, finely chopped**
- ☐ **60 g/12 oz short grain rice, cooked**
- ☐ **375 mL/12 fl oz milk**
- ☐ **2 eggs, lightly beaten**
- ☐ **¹/₂ teaspoon dry mustard**
- ☐ **1 teaspoon Worcestershire sauce**
- ☐ **1 tablespoon mayonnaise**
- ☐ **125 g/4 oz grated mature Cheddar**
- ☐ **2 tablespoons finely chopped fresh parsley**
- ☐ **1 teaspoon paprika**

1 Melt butter in a frying pan. Cook leeks, bacon and pepper for 4-5 minutes, or until leeks are soft and bacon brown. Remove pan from heat and stir rice through. Transfer rice mixture to a deep ovenproof dish.
2 Place milk in a saucepan and bring almost to the boil. Remove pan from heat and whisk in eggs, mustard, Worcestershire sauce, mayonnaise, cheese and parsley. Pour milk mixture over rice mixture. Sprinkle lightly with paprika.
3 Place ovenproof dish in a baking dish. Add hot water to baking dish, so it comes halfway up the side of the ovenproof dish. Bake for 25-30 minutes, or until custard firm.

LASAGNE

Serves 6
Oven temperature 190°C, 375°F, Gas 5

- ☐ **9 sheets instant lasagne pasta**
- ☐ **60 g/2 oz grated mature Cheddar**
- ☐ **2 tablespoons grated Parmesan cheese**

MEAT AND MUSHROOM SAUCE
- ☐ **2 teaspoons olive oil**
- ☐ **1 onion, chopped**
- ☐ **2 cloves garlic, crushed**
- ☐ **2 rashers bacon, chopped**
- ☐ **125 g/4 oz button mushrooms, sliced**
- ☐ **500 g/1 lb lean beef mince**
- ☐ **440 g/14 oz canned tomatoes, undrained and mashed**
- ☐ **125 mL/4 fl oz red wine**
- ☐ **¹/₂ teaspoon dried basil**

AUBERGINE AND RICE PIE

Serves 6
Oven temperature 180°C, 350°F, Gas 4

- ☐ **2 large aubergines (eggplant), cut into 5 mm/¹/₄ in slices**
- ☐ **125 mL/4 fl oz olive oil**
- ☐ **1 onion, chopped**
- ☐ **2 cloves garlic, crushed**
- ☐ **500 g/1 lb lean beef mince**
- ☐ **440 g/14 oz canned tomatoes, undrained and mashed**
- ☐ **1 tablespoon finely chopped fresh oregano**
- ☐ **2 tablespoons tomato purée**
- ☐ **freshly ground black pepper**
- ☐ **185 g/6 oz brown rice, cooked**
- ☐ **250 g/8 oz fresh or frozen peas, cooked**
- ☐ **90 g/3 oz grated mature Cheddar**
- ☐ **3 tablespoons grated Parmesan cheese**
- ☐ **4 tablespoons dried breadcrumbs**

1 Brush aubergines (eggplant) with oil. Heat half the remaining oil in a frying pan. Place a single layer of aubergines (eggplant) in pan and cook until golden on each side. Remove and drain on absorbent kitchen paper. Repeat with remaining aubergines (eggplant).
2 Heat remaining oil in pan, cook onion and garlic for 2-3 minutes or until onion is soft. Stir in meat and cook for 6-8 minutes, or until meat browns.
3 Combine tomatoes, oregano, tomato purée and black pepper to taste. Pour into pan. Simmer for 8-10 minutes, or until liquid reduces by half. Remove pan from heat and add rice, peas, Cheddar and Parmesan cheese.
4 Grease a deep, 23 cm/9 in round cake tin. Sprinkle half the breadcrumbs over base and sides of tin. Place a layer of overlapping aubergine (eggplant) slices over base and sides of tin. Spoon meat mixture over aubergines (eggplant). Pack down well using the back of a spoon.
5 Overlap remaining aubergine (eggplant) slices over filling. Sprinkle with remaining breadcrumbs. Bake for 25-30 minutes or until golden brown. Stand 5 minutes before turning out and serving.

Aubergine and Rice Pie,
Cheesy Baked Rice Custard

- ☐ ¹/₂ teaspoon dried oregano
- ☐ 1 teaspoon sugar

SPINACH CHEESE SAUCE
- ☐ 30 g/1 oz butter
- ☐ 2 tablespoons flour
- ☐ 250 mL/8 fl oz milk
- ☐ 125 mL/4 fl oz cream (double)
- ☐ 60 g/2 oz grated mature Cheddar
- ☐ 250 g/8 oz frozen spinach, thawed and drained
- ☐ freshly ground black pepper

1   To make meat sauce, heat oil in a frying pan and cook onion, garlic, bacon and mushrooms for 2-3 minutes, or until onion is soft.
2   Add mince to pan and cook for 4-5 minutes, or until meat browns. Combine tomatoes, wine, basil, oregano and sugar and pour into pan with mince mixture and bring to the boil. Reduce heat, cover and simmer for 35 minutes, or until sauce thickens.
3   To make cheese sauce, melt butter in a saucepan, add flour and cook for 1-2 minutes. Remove pan from heat and stir in milk and cream. Cook over a medium heat, stirring continuously, until sauce boils and thickens.
4   Remove pan from heat and stir in cheese and spinach. Season with black pepper.
5   To assemble lasagne, spread one-third of cheese sauce over base of a lightly greased 18 x 28 cm/7 x 11 in shallow ovenproof dish. Top with 3 lasagne sheets, spread half the meat sauce over, then another third of spinach cheese sauce. Top with another 3 lasagne sheets and remaining meat sauce. Place remaining lasagne sheets over meat sauce and top with remaining cheese sauce.
6   Combine Cheddar and Parmesan cheese and sprinkle over lasagne. Bake for 40 minutes or until golden.

HAM CHEESE AND LEEK PIE

Serves 6
Oven temperature 190°C, 375°F, Gas 5

- ☐ 15 g/¹/₂ oz butter
- ☐ 2 leeks, sliced
- ☐ 185 g/6 oz brown rice, cooked
- ☐ 4 slices ham, chopped
- ☐ 5 eggs
- ☐ 500 mL/16 fl oz milk
- ☐ freshly ground black pepper
- ☐ 60 g/2 oz grated mature Cheddar

- ☐ 1 tablespoon chopped fresh parsley

1   Melt butter in a large frying pan, add leeks and cook, stirring frequently, for 4-5 minutes or until soft. Remove pan from heat, add rice and ham and mix to combine.
2   Spoon rice mixture into a lightly greased 25 cm/10 in ovenproof dish. Place eggs, milk and black pepper to taste in a bowl and whisk to combine. Pour egg mixture over rice mixture, sprinkle with cheese and parsley and bake for 25 minutes or until firm and golden.

Cook's tip: Precious time can be saved by keeping cooked rice or pasta in the refrigerator or freezer. You will then always have the main ingredient for making a rice or pasta salad or a dish such as this one which requires cooked rice.

RICE FRITTERS

Makes 20

- ☐ ¹/₄ teaspoon chilli powder
- ☐ 1 teaspoon garam masala
- ☐ 75 g/2¹/₂ oz wholemeal flour
- ☐ 75 g/2¹/₂ oz besan flour
- ☐ 125 g/4 oz brown rice, cooked
- ☐ 2 eggs, lightly beaten with 185 mL/6 fl oz milk
- ☐ 4 spring onions, finely chopped
- ☐ ¹/₂ small red pepper, finely choppped
- ☐ oil for shallow-frying

1   Sift chilli powder, garam masala and wholemeal and besan flours into a bowl. Mix in rice, then make a well in the centre and gradually stir in egg mixture. Mix to a smooth batter and stir in spring onions and red pepper.
2   Heat oil in a large frying pan and cook spoonfuls of batter for 3-4 minutes each side or until golden. Drain on absorbent kitchen paper and serve immediately.

Besan flour: Besan flour is made from chickpeas and can be found at Asian specialty food stores. Plain flour could be used instead if you wish.

Lasagne

ROSE-SCENTED SAFFRON RICE

Serve this fragrant rice accompaniment with chicken or lamb. Rosewater is available from most health food stores.

Serves 6

- ☐ **500 g/1 lb basmati rice, well washed**
- ☐ **60 g/2 oz ghee**
- ☐ **1 onion, chopped**
- ☐ **250 g/8 oz lamb mince**
- ☐ **1/2 teaspoon mixed spice**
- ☐ **60 g/2 oz currants**
- ☐ **1/2 teaspoon powdered saffron**
- ☐ **2 tablespoons rosewater**
- ☐ **1 litre/1³/4 pt chicken stock**
- ☐ **60 g/2 oz blanched almonds, toasted**

1   Place rice in a large bowl, cover with cold water and set aside for 30 minutes.
2   Heat ghee in a heavy-based frying pan, add onion and cook for 5 minutes or until onion is soft. Increase heat, add lamb and cook until lamb browns. Stir in mixed spice and currants, cook for a further minute, remove pan from heat. Set aside and keep warm.
3   Combine saffron and rosewater. Place chicken stock and 2 teaspoons of rosewater mixture in a large saucepan, bring to the boil. Drain rice and add to the stock. Bring back to the boil, stirring occasionally. Reduce heat, cover and simmer gently for 30 minutes.
4   Fold meat mixture through rice, remove from heat and stand for 5 minutes before serving. To serve, sprinkle with remaining rosewater mixture and top with almonds.

PILAU WITH AUBERGINE

Pilau is a wonderful accompaniment that could easily be a meal on its own. This version with aubergine (eggplant) is particularly tasty and is great served with natural yogurt.

Serves 6

- ☐ **2 aubergines (eggplant), cut into 2.5 cm/1 in cubes**
- ☐ **salt**
- ☐ **60 mL/2 fl oz olive oil**
- ☐ **1 onion, sliced**
- ☐ **440 g/14 oz canned tomatoes, drained and chopped**
- ☐ **2 tablespoons chopped fresh parsley**
- ☐ **1 tablespoon chopped fresh mint**
- ☐ **500 g/1 lb long grain rice, well washed**
- ☐ **750 mL/1¹/4 pt chicken stock**

1   Sprinkle aubergines (eggplant) with salt and set aside for 30 minutes. Rinse under cold running water and pat dry with absorbent kitchen paper.
2   Heat oil in a heavy-based frying pan. Add aubergines (eggplant) and cook until lightly browned. Remove from pan and set aside.
3   Add onion to pan and cook for 4-5 minutes or until onion is soft. Add tomatoes, parsley, mint and aubergines (eggplant) and cook for a further 5 minutes. Stir in rice and chicken stock. Bring to the boil. Reduce heat, cover and simmer for 30 minutes. Allow to stand for 30 minutes before serving.

LONTONG

Lontong are traditionally wrapped in young banana leaves. If these are not readily available, you can successfully substitute aluminium foil. The fried onion flakes that we have used in this recipe can be purchased from Asian food stores.

Serves 6

- ☐ **young banana leaves or aluminium foil**
- ☐ **500 g/1 lb short grain white rice, well washed**
- ☐ **2 tablespoons sweet soy sauce**
- ☐ **2 tablespoons fried onion flakes**

1   If using banana leaves, drop in boiling water to clean and soften. Remove leaves from water and pat dry with absorbent kitchen paper. Brush lightly with a little vegetable oil. Cut leaves or foil into 20 cm/8 in squares.
2   Place a large spoonful of rice in the centre of each square and fold over to completely encase, allowing a little room for expansion during cooking. Tie each parcel with string to secure.
3   Bring a large saucepan of water to the boil, drop in rice bundles and simmer for 1 hour. To serve, drain bundles, unwrap and sprinkle with soy sauce and onion flakes.

ARTICHOKE AND WHITE WINE RISOTTO

Try using asparagus as a substitute for artichokes in this aromatic risotto.

Serves 4

- ☐ **60 g/2 oz butter**
- ☐ **1 onion, chopped**
- ☐ **330 g/10¹/2 oz Arborio or risotto rice**
- ☐ **500 mL/16 fl oz chicken stock**
- ☐ **125 mL/4 fl oz dry white wine**
- ☐ **440 g/14 oz canned artichoke hearts, drained and liquid reserved**
- ☐ **2 tablespoons chopped fresh parsley**
- ☐ **4 thick slices ham, cut into strips**
- ☐ **60 g/2 oz grated Parmesan cheese**
- ☐ **4 cherry tomatoes, quartered**
- ☐ **freshly ground black pepper**

1   Melt butter in a large frying pan, add onion and cook for 5 minutes or until soft.
2   Add rice to pan and cook, stirring frequently, for 5 minutes. Combine stock, wine and reserved artichoke liquid. The total amount of liquid should equal 875 mL/1¹/2 pt. Top up with additional stock, if necessary. Pour one-third of the liquid over the rice and cook over a low heat, stirring, until liquid is absorbed. Continue adding liquid a little at a time and cook, stirring frequently, until all liquid is absorbed.
3   Cut artichokes into quarters. Fold artichokes, parsley, ham, Parmesan cheese and tomatoes into rice. Season to taste with black pepper and serve immediately.

Cook's tip: Arborio rice is an Italian short grain rice from the Po Valley. It is recognisable by the distinctive white spot on each kernel. If it is unavailable, short grain rice can be used instead.

FETTUCCINE WITH WINE AND MUSHROOMS

The perfect way to serve fettuccine – with a magnificent creamy sauce laden with button mushrooms.

Serves 6

- ☐ **500 g/1 lb fettucine**
- ☐ **1 tablespoon olive oil**

CREAMY MUSHROOM SAUCE
- ☐ **1 tablespoon olive oil**
- ☐ **1 large onion, sliced**
- ☐ **2 cloves garlic, crushed**
- ☐ **500 g/1 lb button mushrooms, sliced**
- ☐ **15 g/¹/₂ oz butter**
- ☐ **1 tablespoon flour**
- ☐ **60 mL/2 fl oz white wine**
- ☐ **250 mL/8 fl oz vegetable stock**
- ☐ **125 mL/4 fl oz cream (double)**
- ☐ **2 tablespoons chopped fresh basil**
- ☐ **freshly ground black pepper**
- ☐ **2 tablespoons grated Parmesan cheese**
- ☐ **2 tablespoons snipped fresh chives**

1   Cook fettuccine in boiling water following packet instructions. Drain and toss in oil. Set aside and keep warm.
2   To make sauce, heat oil in a saucepan, add onion and garlic and cook over a medium heat, stirring occasionally, for 10 minutes or until onion is golden. Stir in mushrooms and cook for 2 minutes longer. Remove mushroom mixture from pan and set aside.
3   Melt butter in a clean saucepan, add flour and cook, stirring constantly for 2 minutes. Remove pan from heat and gradually stir in wine and stock. Return pan to heat and cook over a medium heat, stirring constantly, for 5-6 minutes or until sauce boils and thickens. Whisk in cream, then stir in mushroom mixture and basil. Season to taste with black pepper and cook for 3-4 minutes longer or until heated through.
4   To serve, spoon sauce over hot fettuccine and top with Parmesan cheese and chives.

Pilau with Aubergine, Rose-scented Saffron Rice, Lontong

157

BONBONS FILLED WITH CHICKEN AND HERBS

These look wonderful when made with different-coloured pastas. If served as an entreé, this recipe will serve six.

Serves 4

BONBONS
- [ ] **6 sheets fresh plain, tomato- or spinach-flavoured pasta (24 x 27 cm/9½ x 11 in)**
- [ ] **1 egg, lightly beaten**
- [ ] **cream (single) or melted butter for coating**
- [ ] **grated fresh Parmesan cheese**

CHICKEN AND HERB FILLING
- [ ] **200 g/6½ oz cooked chicken meat, finely diced**
- [ ] **60 g/2 oz ham, finely diced**
- [ ] **155 g/5 oz ricotta cheese, drained**
- [ ] **2 tablespoons grated fresh Parmesan cheese**
- [ ] **½ onion, grated**
- [ ] **½ teaspoon finely chopped fresh sage**
- [ ] **½ teaspoon finely chopped fresh oregano**
- [ ] **½ teaspoon finely chopped fresh parsley**
- [ ] **pinch ground nutmeg**
- [ ] **freshly ground black pepper**

1   Cut each pasta sheet into nine rectangles 8 x 9 cm (3 x 3½ in). Trim shorter ends of each rectangle using a zigzag pastry wheel. Set pasta aside and cover with a damp cloth.

2   To make filling, combine chicken, ham, ricotta cheese, Parmesan cheese, onion, sage, oregano, parsley and nutmeg. Season to taste with black pepper.

3   To form bonbons, place a teaspoon of filling in centre of each pasta rectangle. Brush egg down one long side, and fold over pasta to encase filling to form a tube. Press to seal, then pinch and twist trimmed ends tightly, like bonbon wrappers. As each bonbon is formed, set aside, uncovered, to rest.

4   Cook bonbons, a few at a time, in a large saucepan of boiling water for 4-5 minutes or until al dente. Remove with a slotted spoon and pile onto a warmed serving platter. To serve, toss in cream or butter and sprinkle with Parmesan cheese.

Cook's tip: These bonbons are best made with homemade pasta thinly rolled.

For something different you might like to make parcels rather than bonbons. To make parcels, cut 5 cm/2 in circles of pasta and place a teaspoon of filling in the centre of each circle. Gather up edges to form a pouch and pinch together to seal. Cook and serve as described in the recipe.

TAGLIATELLE WITH SPINACH AND MUSHROOMS

Serves 4

- [ ] **500 g/1 lb tomato tagliatelle**
- [ ] **60 g/2 oz butter**
- [ ] **1 clove garlic, crushed**
- [ ] **2 tablespoons Marsala**
- [ ] **250 g/8 oz button mushrooms, sliced**
- [ ] **250 mL/8 fl oz cream (double)**
- [ ] **freshly ground black pepper**
- [ ] **750 g/1½ lb spinach, stalks removed and leaves shredded**
- [ ] **grated Parmesan cheese**

1   Cook tagliatelle in boiling water in a large saucepan following packet directions or until al dente. Drain, set aside and keep warm.

2   Melt butter in a saucepan, add garlic and Marsala and cook over a low heat for 3 minutes or until syrupy. Add mushrooms and cook for 3 minutes longer. Blend in cream and bring to the boil. Season to taste with black pepper.

3   Add pasta to sauce. Toss in spinach and stir to coat. Cook over a low heat for 2-3 minutes or until spinach is heated through. Serve topped with Parmesan cheese.

Tagliatelle with Spinach and Mushrooms,
Open Mushroom Ravioli,
Bonbons filled with Chicken and Herbs

OPEN MUSHROOM RAVIOLI

A stylish approach for a wonderful entrée. A delicious filling is visible between the unjoined sides of pasta.

Serves 4

- ☐ **16 circles plain or tomato fresh pasta, 4-5 cm (1¹/₂-2 in) in diameter**
- ☐ **4 dried mushrooms**
- ☐ **90 mL/3 fl oz hot water**
- ☐ **90 g/3 oz butter**
- ☐ **220 g/7 oz button mushrooms, thinly sliced**
- ☐ **3 tablespoons white port or dry sherry**
- ☐ **3 tablespoons cream (single)**
- ☐ **1¹/₂ tablespoons chicken stock**
- ☐ **pinch ground nutmeg**
- ☐ **freshly ground black pepper**
- ☐ **1 small bunch watercress**
- ☐ **4 tablespoons thick sour cream**

1 Cook pasta circles, a few at a time, in boiling water in a large saucepan for 4-5 minutes or until tender. Remove and lay out in a single layer to dry, on clean teatowels.

2 Place dried mushrooms and hot water in a bowl and set aside to soak for 30 minutes. Drain porcini and chop finely. Reserve liquid.

3 Melt 30 g/1 oz butter in a frying pan and gently cook button mushrooms for 2-3 minutes. Stir in soaked mushrooms and reserved liquid. Blend in port, cream, stock and nutmeg. Season to taste with black pepper. Cook over a medium heat until mixture reduces and thickens. Stir in remaining butter.

4 Place 2 pasta circles on each serving plate. Top each circle with 1-2 tablespoons mushroom mixture, then a few sprigs of watercress. Partially cover with another circle of pasta. Top each ravioli with a dollop of sour cream and garnish with watercress. Serve immediately.

Cook's tip: Dried mushrooms, known as *porcini* in Italy and *cèpes* in France, have a more intense flavour than fresh mushrooms. Dried mushrooms must be reconstituted in warm water before cooking. If cooked for too long they will lose their flavour. Allow 15-20 minutes cooking and the mushrooms will be perfectly tender.

SPINACH TIMBALES WITH PASTA FILLING

Serves 4
Oven temperature 180°C, 350°F, Gas 4

- ☐ **6 large spinach leaves, stalks removed**

PASTA FILLING
- ☐ **2 tablespoons olive oil**
- ☐ **2 small aubergines (eggplant), chopped**
- ☐ **1 onion, chopped**
- ☐ **1 clove garlic, crushed**
- ☐ **1 red pepper, chopped**
- ☐ **2 courgettes (zucchini), chopped**
- ☐ **1 large ripe tomato, peeled and chopped**
- ☐ **2 tablespoons tomato purée**
- ☐ **1 teaspoon hot chilli powder**
- ☐ **3 tablespoons finely chopped pitted black olives**
- ☐ **4 tablespoons small pasta shapes, cooked**
- ☐ **3 tablespoons grated Parmesan cheese**
- ☐ **freshly ground black pepper**

1   Boil, steam or microwave spinach until wilted. Drain well and use to line four greased individual ramekins (250 mL/ 8 fl oz capacity). Allow some leaves to overhang top.
2   To make filling, heat oil in a saucepan, add aubergines (eggplant), onion, garlic, red pepper, courgettes (zucchini) and tomato and cook, stirring occasionally, for 15 minutes or until mixture reduces and thickens. Stir in tomato purée, chilli powder, olives, pasta, Parmesan cheese and black pepper to taste and mix well to combine.
3   Spoon filling into lined ramekins, fold overhanging leaves over filling and cover with greased aluminum foil and bake for 20 minutes. Allow to stand for 5-10 minutes before turning out.

BOWS WITH RICH TOMATO BASIL SAUCE

Serves 2

- ☐ **185 g/6 oz bow pasta**

TOMATO BASIL SAUCE
- ☐ **2 teaspoons olive oil**
- ☐ **1 onion, sliced**
- ☐ **1 clove garlic, crushed**
- ☐ **3 tomatoes, peeled, seeded and chopped**
- ☐ **125 mL/4 fl oz chicken stock**
- ☐ **1 tablespoon tomato purée**
- ☐ **1 tablespoon chopped fresh basil**
- ☐ **2 teaspoons chopped fresh parsley**
- ☐ **1/2 teaspoon sugar**
- ☐ **freshly ground black pepper**
- ☐ **grated Parmeson cheese**

1   Cook pasta in boiling water in a saucepan following packet directions. Drain, set aside and keep warm.
2   To make sauce, heat oil in a saucepan and cook onion and garlic over a medium heat for 3-4 minutes or until onion is soft. Add tomatoes, stock, tomato purée, basil, parsley and sugar and simmer for 10-15 minutes or until reduced and thickened. Season to taste with black pepper. Spoon sauce over pasta. Sprinkle with a little grated fresh Parmesan cheese and extra chopped fresh basil.

Cook's tip: Any leftover sauce can be made into soup. To make, chop 1 small carrot and 1 stalk celery. Place leftover sauce, 250 mL/8 fl oz chicken stock, carrot and celery in a saucepan. Bring to simmering and simmer for 10-15 minutes or until carrot is tender. Season to taste with black pepper.

Bows with Rich Tomato Basil Sauce, Tomato Soup made from leftover Rich Tomato Basil Sauce

RAVIOLI WITH TUNA SAUCE

Serves 4

- ☐ **375 g/12 oz fresh or frozen ravioli with spinach filling**
- ☐ **2 tablespoons grated Parmesan cheese**
- ☐ **fresh dill sprigs**

TUNA SAUCE
- ☐ **2 teaspoons olive oil**
- ☐ **1 onion, finely chopped**
- ☐ **1 clove garlic, crushed**
- ☐ **440 g/14 oz canned tomatoes, undrained and mashed**
- ☐ **1 tablespoon tomato purée**
- ☐ **1 tablespoon dry red wine**
- ☐ **1 teaspoon sugar**
- ☐ **440 g/14 oz canned tuna in spring water, drained and flaked**
- ☐ **1 tablespoon finely chopped fresh parsley**
- ☐ **1 tablespoon finely chopped fresh dill**
- ☐ **freshly ground black pepper**
- ☐ **dill sprigs**

1   Cook ravioli in boiling water in a large saucepan following packet directions. Drain and keep warm.

2   To make sauce, heat oil in a frying pan. Cook onion and garlic for 4-5 minutes or until onion is soft. Stir in tomatoes, tomato purée, wine and sugar. Bring to the boil. Add tuna, parsley and dill, reduce heat and simmer for 10 minutes.

3   Place pasta on a warmed serving platter. Spoon over sauce, sprinkle with Parmesan cheese and garnish with dill sprigs.

SPAGHETTI WITH ASPARAGUS SAUCE

Serves 6

- ☐ **500 g/1 lb spaghetti**
- ☐ **2 tablespoons grated Parmesan cheese**

ASPARAGUS SAUCE
- ☐ **500 g/1 lb fresh asparagus spears, trimmed**
- ☐ **1 tablespoon olive oil**
- ☐ **1 thick slice wholegrain bread, crumbed**
- ☐ **250 mL/8 fl oz evaporated milk**
- ☐ **60 g/2 oz grated mozzarella cheese**
- ☐ **freshly ground black pepper**

1   Cook spaghetti in boiling water in a large saucepan following packet directions.
2   To make sauce, steam, boil or microwave asparagus until tender. Drain and refresh under cold running water. Cut into 3 cm/1¹/₂ in pieces and set aside. Heat oil in a frying pan, add breadcrumbs and cook over a low heat for 2 minutes, stirring all the time. Stir in milk and asparagus, and cook over medium heat for 5 minutes. Mix in cheese and continue to cook until cheese melts. Season to taste with black pepper.
3   Place spaghetti on a warmed serving platter, spoon over sauce and toss gently to combine. Sprinkle with Parmesan cheese and serve immediately.

Spaghetti with Asparagus Sauce, Ravioli with Tuna Sauce

HOT AND SOUR
THAI STIR-FRY

Serves 8

- [ ] **2 tablespoons soy sauce**
- [ ] **1 tablespoon dry sherry**
- [ ] **1 fresh red chilli, seeded and finely chopped**
- [ ] **1 clove garlic, crushed**
- [ ] **500 g/1 lb tofu, cubed and drained**
- [ ] **1 tablespoon vegetable oil**
- [ ] **2 onions, sliced**
- [ ] **1 red pepper, cut into thin strips**
- [ ] **1 green pepper, cut into thin strips**
- [ ] **125 g/4 oz mangetout (snow peas), trimmed**
- [ ] **125 g/4 oz egg noodles, cooked and drained**
- [ ] **2 spring onions, finely chopped**
- [ ] **fresh coriander leaves**

SPICY PEANUT SAUCE
- [ ] **2 cloves garlic, crushed**
- [ ] **125 g/4 oz crunchy peanut butter**
- [ ] **3 tablespoons lime or lemon juice**
- [ ] **3 tablespoons soy sauce**
- [ ] **1 small fresh red chilli, finely chopped**
- [ ] **125 mL/4 fl oz vegetable stock or water**

1   Preheat barbecue to a high heat. Place soy sauce, sherry, chilli and garlic in a bowl, and mix to combine. Add tofu, toss to coat and set aside to marinate for 30 minutes. Drain.

2   To make sauce, place garlic, peanut butter, lime or lemon juice, soy sauce and chilli in a food processor or blender and process to combine. With machine running, slowly add vegetable stock or water and process until combined.

3   Heat oil in a wok or frying pan on barbecue and stir-fry onions and red and green pepper for 4-5 minutes. Using a slotted spoon remove onions and peppers and set aside. Add tofu to wok or frying pan and stir-fry for 1-2 minutes. Return onions and peppers to wok or frying pan, add mangetout (snow peas) and noodles and stir-fry for 3-4 minutes longer. Add peanut sauce and toss to coat noodles and vegetables evenly with sauce. Transfer to a serving platter, garnish with spring onions and coriander leaves. Serve immediately.

Hot and Sour Thai Stir-fry

VEGETABLE PASTA BAKE

Serves 6
Oven temperature 180°C, 350°F, Gas 4

- [ ] **9 wholemeal instant lasagne sheets**
- [ ] **250 g/8 oz silken tofu, beaten until smooth**

VEGETABLE FILLING
- [ ] **1 tablespoon olive oil**
- [ ] **¹/₄ cabbage, shredded**
- [ ] **1 carrot, finely chopped**
- [ ] **1 large green pepper, finely chopped**
- [ ] **1 large red pepper, finely chopped**
- [ ] **315 g/10 oz canned sweet corn kernels, drained**
- [ ] **440 g/14 oz canned peeled tomatoes, undrained and mashed**
- [ ] **5 tablespoons chopped fresh basil**
- [ ] **freshly ground black pepper**

WALNUT TOPPING
- [ ] **125 g/4 oz grated mozzarella cheese**
- [ ] **30 g/1 oz wholemeal breadcrumbs, made from stale bread**
- [ ] **4 tablespoons chopped walnuts**

1   To make filling, heat oil in a saucepan, cook cabbage, carrot, green and red peppers, sweet corn, tomatoes and basil over a medium heat until boiling. Reduce heat and simmer for 15 minutes or until vegetables are soft and mixture reduces and thickens. Season to taste with black pepper.

2   To make topping, combine cheese, breadcrumbs and walnuts in a bowl and set aside.

3   Spread one-third of filling over base of lightly greased 20 x 30 cm/8 x 12 in ovenproof dish. Cover with a layer of lasagne sheets, spread with 75 g/2¹/₂ oz tofu, then one-third of filling mixture. Repeat layers, finishing with lasagne sheets. Spread with remaining tofu and sprinkle with topping. Bake for 30-35 minutes or until tender.

Vegetable Pasta Bake

chapter eight

VEGETABLES ON THE SIDE

Vegetables as a side dish
are an important part of any meal.
They add variety, texture, flavour
and colour and should complement
the main dish. This chapter presents
you with a host of delicious recipes
for vegetable side dishes and
salads that are sure to tempt
even the most reluctant
vegetable eaters.

Tomato and Spinach Stuffed Mushrooms,
Herby Vegetable Salad,
Gipsy Baked Potatoes

TOMATO AND SPINACH STUFFED MUSHROOMS

Serves 6
Oven temperature 200°C, 400°F, Gas 6

- [ ] **6 large flat mushrooms**
- [ ] **3 tablespoons grated mozzarella cheese**
- [ ] **1 tablespoon grated Parmesan cheese**
- [ ] **1 tablespoon finely snipped fresh chives**

SPINACH FILLING
- [ ] **1 tablespoon olive oil**
- [ ] **1 clove garlic, crushed**
- [ ] **3 spring onions, finely chopped**
- [ ] **2 spinach leaves, stalks removed and finely shredded**
- [ ] **1 tablespoon tomato purée**
- [ ] **45 g/1¹/₂ oz breadcrumbs, made from stale bread**
- [ ] **freshly ground black pepper**

1   Wipe mushrooms, remove stalks and finely chop.
2   To make filling, heat 1 teaspoon oil in frying pan, cook garlic and spring onions for 1-2 minutes. Stir in spinach and tomato purée, cook for 2-3 minutes. Fold through breadcrumbs. Season to taste with black pepper.
3   Brush mushroom caps with remaining oil and place on an oven tray. Combine mozzarella and Parmesan cheeses. Spoon filling into mushroom caps, top with cheese mixture, sprinkle with chives and bake for 10-15 minutes.

GIPSY BAKED POTATOES

Serves 4
Oven temperature 180°C, 350°F, Gas 4

- [ ] **2 teaspoons vegetable oil**
- [ ] **1 onion, chopped**
- [ ] **1 clove garlic, crushed**
- [ ] **1 teaspoon finely chopped fresh rosemary**
- [ ] **3 large tomatoes, peeled and chopped**
- [ ] **1 green pepper, diced**
- [ ] **1 teaspoon paprika**
- [ ] **250 mL/8 fl oz chicken stock**
- [ ] **freshly ground black pepper**
- [ ] **2 large potatoes, cut into thick slices**
- [ ] **2 tablespoons finely snipped fresh chives**

1   Heat oil in a frying pan and cook onion, garlic and rosemary for 4-5 minutes or until onion is soft. Add tomatoes, pepper, paprika and chicken stock, bring to the boil and simmer for 10 minutes. Season to taste with black pepper.
2   Arrange potatoes in layers in a lightly greased ovenproof dish, spoon over tomato mixture and bake for 1¹/₂ hours or until cooked through. Sprinkle with chives just prior to serving.

HERBY VEGETABLE SALAD

Serves 4

- [ ] **¹/₄ cauliflower, broken into florets**
- [ ] **1 head broccoli, broken into florets**
- [ ] **1 large carrot, cut into thin strips**
- [ ] **155 g/5 oz mangetout (snow peas), trimmed**
- [ ] **1 red pepper, cut into thin strips**
- [ ] **3 tablespoons lemon juice**
- [ ] **2 teaspoons finely chopped fresh coriander**
- [ ] **2 teaspoons finely chopped fresh rosemary**
- [ ] **freshly ground black pepper**

LEMON VINAIGRETTE
- [ ] **2 tablespoons lemon juice**
- [ ] **1 tablespoon olive oil**
- [ ] **1 clove garlic, crushed**
- [ ] **1 teaspoon wholegrain mustard**

1   Boil, steam or microwave cauliflower, broccoli, carrot and mangetout (snow peas), separately, until just tender. Drain, then refresh under cold water.
2   Drain vegetables well. Toss in a salad bowl with pepper, lemon juice, coriander and rosemary. Season to taste with black pepper. Refrigerate until required.
3   To make vinaigrette, combine all ingredients in a screwtop jar. Shake well to combine. Pour over salad just prior to serving.

COCONUT VEGETABLE SKEWERS

Serves 4

- [ ] **16 button mushrooms**
- [ ] **2 courgettes (zucchini), cut into 8 pieces**
- [ ] **8 whole baby onions, peeled**
- [ ] **16 cherry tomatoes**
- [ ] **125 g/4 oz shredded coconut, toasted**

MINT MARINADE
- [ ] **1 tablespoon finely chopped fresh mint**
- [ ] **2 tablespoons lime or lemon juice**
- [ ] **2 teaspoons honey**
- [ ] **1 tablespoon chilli paste (sambal oelek)**
- [ ] **4 tablespoons coconut milk**

1   To make marinade, place mint, lime or lemon juice, honey, chilli paste (sambal oelek) and coconut milk in a bowl and whisk to combine. Add mushrooms, courgettes (zucchini), onions and tomatoes, toss to coat, cover and set aside to marinate for 1 hour.
2   Drain off marinade and reserve. Thread vegetables onto 8 bamboo skewers, brush with reserved marinade and cook under a medium preheated grill or on a barbecue grill for 10-15 minutes or until vegetables are cooked. Brush with marinade several times during cooking.
3   Remove skewers from heat, roll in coconut and serve immediately.

SWEET POTATO CRISPS

Serves 4

- [ ] **500 g/1 lb sweet potato**
- [ ] **2 tablespoons lemon juice**
- [ ] **oil for deep-frying**
- [ ] **1 tablespoon salt**
- [ ] **1 teaspoon chilli powder or according to taste**
- [ ] **¹/₂ teaspoon caster sugar**

1   Slice potatoes into paper thin slices. Place potato slices and lemon juice in a large bowl, cover with cold water and refrigerate for 2 hours. Drain on absorbent kitchen paper.
2   Heat oil in a large saucepan until a cube of bread dropped in browns in 50 seconds. Cook a few potato slices at a time for 6 minutes or until golden and almost crisp. Remove potato slices from oil, drain on absorbent kitchen paper, set aside and keep warm. Repeat with remaining potatoes.
3   Return cooked potato slices to hot oil and cook until crisp. Remove from oil and drain on absorbent kitchen paper. Place salt, chilli powder and sugar in a small bowl, mix to combine and sprinkle over crisps. Serve immediately.

Alfalfa Potato Salad,
Avocado Salad with Spicy Dressing

AVOCADO SALAD WITH SPICY DRESSING

Serves 4

- ☐ **2 avocados, stoned, peeled and sliced**
- ☐ **2 small tomatoes, cut into wedges**
- ☐ **125 g/4 oz olives, pitted**
- ☐ **1 lettuce, separated into leaves**

SPICY DRESSING

- ☐ **4 tablespoons olive oil**
- ☐ **3 tablespoons lemon juice**
- ☐ **2 tablespoons tomato purée**
- ☐ **1 teaspoon chilli powder**
- ☐ **1/2 teaspoon ground cumin**
- ☐ **freshly ground black pepper**

1   To make dressing, place oil, lemon juice, tomato purée, chilli powder, cumin, and black pepper to taste in a food processor or blender and process until smooth.

2   Place avocados, tomatoes and olives in a bowl, pour dressing over and toss to combine. Cover and place in the refrigerator to marinate for 30 minutes.

3   Arrange lettuce leaves on a serving platter and top with salad.

ALFALFA POTATO SALAD

Serves 6

- ☐ **750 g/1¹/₂ lb potatoes**
- ☐ **1 tablespoon vegetable oil**
- ☐ **2 stalks celery, finely chopped**
- ☐ **1 large cucumber, diced**
- ☐ **2 green peppers, diced**
- ☐ **2 carrots, grated**
- ☐ **1 raw beetroot, grated**
- ☐ **1 small lettuce, leaves torn into bite-sized pieces**
- ☐ **30 g/1 oz alfalfa sprouts**
- ☐ **3 tablespoons mayonnaise**
- ☐ **2 avocados, stoned, peeled and sliced**

1   Boil, steam or microwave washed, unpeeled potatoes until just tender. While still hot, cut into large pieces and place in a bowl. Sprinkle with oil.

2   Add celery, cucumber, green peppers, carrots, beetroot, lettuce, sprouts and mayonnaise to bowl and toss to combine. Top with avocado slices and serve.

You can substitute butter beans or a three bean mix for kidney beans.

Serves 4
Oven temperature 220°C, 425°F, Gas 7

- ☐ **4 medium potatoes**
- ☐ **315 g/10 oz canned red kidney beans**
- ☐ **1 tablespoon tomato purée**
- ☐ **1-2 teaspoons chilli sauce (according to taste)**
- ☐ **paprika**

CARROT BALLS

Serve 4

- ☐ **3 carrots, grated**
- ☐ **2 teaspoons orange rind**
- ☐ **60 g/2 oz grated Swiss cheese**
- ☐ **60 g/2 oz grated Parmesan cheese**
- ☐ **1 tablespoon chopped fresh mint**
- ☐ **2 eggs, lightly beaten**
- ☐ **flour**
- ☐ **185 g/6 oz bran**
- ☐ **3 tablespoons finely chopped almonds**
- ☐ **vegetable oil for cooking**

1   Combine carrots, orange rind, cheeses, mint and half the beaten egg. Season to taste. Shape into balls. Coat with flour, dip in remaining beaten egg and roll in combined bran and almonds.

2   Heat oil in a frying pan. Cook carrot balls until golden brown. Drain on absorbent paper. Serve with mango chutney if desired.

Nutrition tip: An alternative low fat cooking method is to lightly oil a baking dish and place the carrot balls in it. Bake the carrot balls on 200°C/400°F/Gas 6 for 15-20 minutes, turning frequently during the cooking time for a delicious, crusty texture.

Above: Carrot Balls
Right: Pickled Tomatoes and Beans, Potatoes Filled with Chilli Beans

1 Bake scrubbed, unpeeled potatoes for 45 minutes-1hour or until soft but firm. Cool slightly.

2 Cut potatoes in half and scoop out flesh, leaving a thin shell. Mash potato flesh and combine with beans, tomato purée and sauce.

3 Spoon mixture back into potato shells. Dust lightly with paprika and bake at 200°C/ 400°F, Gas 6 until heated through and lightly browned on top.

Microwave it: Potatoes can also be microwaved on HIGH (100%) for 4-5 minutes. Stand for 5 minutes before removing flesh.

PICKLED TOMATOES AND BEANS

This recipe uses canned three bean mix which is made up of a mixture of butter beans, kidney beans and lima beans. Any canned mixed beans can be used as a substitute.

Serves 4

- ☐ 2 tablespoons olive oil
- ☐ 1 clove garlic, crushed
- ☐ 1 tablespoon chopped fresh basil
- ☐ 315 g/10 oz canned three bean mix, drained
- ☐ 250 g/8 oz cherry tomatoes, halved
- ☐ 2½ teaspoons white vinegar
- ☐ ½ teaspoon sugar
- ☐ freshly ground black pepper

1 Heat oil in a frying pan. Cook garlic and basil for 1 minute, stir in beans and tomatoes. Season to taste with black pepper.

2 Cover and simmer for 5-6 minutes. Mix in combined vinegar and sugar. Heat through gently and serve.

GARDEN SALAD WITH CREAMY MAYONNAISE

Serves 4

- [ ] 1 lettuce, leaves separated and torn into pieces
- [ ] 12 cherry tomatoes or tomato wedges
- [ ] 4 hard-boiled eggs, cut into wedges
- [ ] 12 button mushrooms, sliced
- [ ] 60 g/2 oz mangetout (snow peas) or sugar snap peas
- [ ] 1 tablespoon chopped fresh parsley
- [ ] 1 tablespoon chopped fresh basil
- [ ] 1 tablespoon pine nuts, toasted
- [ ] Croutons (see recipe)

YOGURT DRESSING
- [ ] 90 g/3 oz natural yogurt
- [ ] 1 clove garlic, crushed
- [ ] 1 tablespoon white wine vinegar
- [ ] 1 tablespoon snipped fresh chives
- [ ] freshly ground black pepper

1 Arrange lettuce, tomatoes, eggs, mushrooms and mangetout (snow peas) or sugar snap peas on a serving plate. Sprinkle with parsley, basil, pine nuts and Croutons.
2 To make dressing, place yogurt, garlic, vinegar, chives and black pepper to taste in a bowl and whisk to combine. Spoon a little dressing over the salad and serve immediately.

Croutons: To make Croutons, cut crusts from a slice of bread, then lightly brush slice with oil and cut into cubes. Place cubes on a baking tray and bake at 200°C/400°F/Gas 6 for 10-15 minutes or until Croutons are golden and crisp.

SIMPLE GREEN SALAD

Serves 4

- [ ] 1 small lettuce, leaves separated and torn into pieces
- [ ] 1 small cucumber, sliced
- [ ] 1 green pepper, cut into thin strips
- [ ] 4 spring onions, finely chopped
- [ ] 1 tablespoon snipped fresh chives
- [ ] 1 tablespoon finely chopped fresh parsley

VINAIGRETTE
- [ ] 2 tablespoons olive oil
- [ ] 1 tablespoon cider vinegar
- [ ] 1 teaspoon Dijon mustard
- [ ] freshly ground black pepper

1 Arrange lettuce, cucumber, green pepper and spring onions in a salad bowl. Sprinkle with chives and parsley.
2 Place oil, vinegar, mustard and black pepper to taste in a screwtop jar and shake well to combine. Drizzle Vinaigrette over salad and serve immediately.

JULIENNE VEGETABLE SALAD

Serves 4

- [ ] 2 carrots, cut into thin strips
- [ ] 2 courgettes (zucchini), cut into thin strips
- [ ] 2 stalks celery, cut into thin strips
- [ ] 1 teaspoon sesame seeds, toasted

GINGER AND SOY DRESSING
- [ ] 1 teaspoon sesame oil
- [ ] 1 teaspoon grated fresh ginger
- [ ] 2 tablespoons soy sauce
- [ ] 2 tablespoons water
- [ ] 1 teaspoon cider vinegar
- [ ] 1 clove garlic, crushed

1 Arrange carrots, courgettes (zucchini) and celery on a serving plate.
2 To make dressing, place oil, ginger, soy sauce, water, vinegar and garlic in a screwtop jar and shake well to combine. Drizzle dressing over salad and sprinkle with sesame seeds.

From left: Waldorf Salad, Garden Salad with Creamy Mayonnaise, Pesto Pasta Salad, Julienne Vegetable Salad, Simple Green Salad

PESTO PASTA SALAD

This salad can be served warm – keep the pasta warm after cooking.

Serves 4

- ☐ **250 g/8 oz spiral pasta**
- ☐ **12 cherry tomatoes, halved**
- ☐ **4 slices leg ham, cut into thin strips**
- ☐ **125 g/4 oz watercress or snow pea sprouts**

PESTO SAUCE
- ☐ **60 g/2 oz fresh basil leaves**
- ☐ **2 cloves garlic**
- ☐ **2 tablespoons pine nuts**
- ☐ **4 tablespoons olive oil**
- ☐ **6 tablespoons grated fresh Parmesan cheese**
- ☐ **freshly ground black pepper**

1 Cook pasta in a saucepan in boiling water following packet directions. Rinse, drain and set aside to cool.

2 To make sauce, place basil, garlic, pine nuts, and 1 tablespoon oil in a food processor or blender and process until smooth. With machine running, gradually add remaining oil. Mix in Parmesan cheese and season to taste with black pepper.

3 Spoon sauce over pasta and toss to combine. Add tomatoes, ham and watercress or mangetout (snow pea) sprouts to salad and toss.

Cook's tip: This is a wonderful main course salad. To serve as a main course, simply increase the pasta quantity to 500 g/1 lb.

WALDORF SALAD

Serves 4

- ☐ **2 green or red apples, cored and sliced**
- ☐ **2 teaspoons lemon juice**
- ☐ **4 stalks celery, sliced**
- ☐ **2 tablespoons roughly chopped walnuts**
- ☐ **4 tablespoons mayonnaise**
- ☐ **freshly ground black pepper**

Place apples in a bowl, pour lemon juice over and toss to coat. Add celery, walnuts and mayonnaise and toss to combine. Season to taste with black pepper.

CANDIED SWEET POTATO

Serve this sweet vegetable with grilled pork chops.

Serves 6

- ☐ **90 g/3 oz brown sugar**
- ☐ **125 mL/4 fl oz water**
- ☐ **15 g/¹/₂ oz butter**
- ☐ **500 g/1 lb sweet potato, thinly sliced**
- ☐ **2 tablespoons toasted slivered almonds**

1 Combine sugar, water and butter in a nonstick frying pan. Cook over a low heat until butter melts. Add sweet potato, cover and continue to cook over a low heat for 15-20 minutes or until sweet potato is tender.
2 Add almonds and toss lightly to combine.

BEETROOT, ORANGE AND HORSERADISH SALAD

Serves 6

- ☐ **4 cooked beetroot, cut into thin strips**
- ☐ **2 teaspoons grated orange rind**
- ☐ **2 oranges, segmented**

HORSERADISH DRESSING
- ☐ **1¹/₂ tablespoons olive oil**
- ☐ **3 tablespoons cider vinegar**
- ☐ **1 teaspoon dry mustard**
- ☐ **2 teaspoons horseradish relish**
- ☐ **2 teaspoons sugar**

1 Combine beetroot, orange rind and orange segments. Arrange attractively in a salad bowl. Cover and refrigerate for 1-2 hours.
2 To make dressing, combine oil, vinegar, mustard, horseradish and sugar in a screwtop jar. Shake well to combine. Pour over salad just prior to serving.

STIR-FRIED BROCCOLI WITH ALMONDS

A colourful stir-fry that is sure to please the whole family.

Serves 4

- ☐ **2 carrots, cut into matchsticks**
- ☐ **500 g/1 lb broccoli, cut into florets**
- ☐ **2 teaspoons peanut oil**
- ☐ **1 onion, sliced**
- ☐ **1 clove garlic, crushed**
- ☐ **2 teaspoons grated fresh ginger**
- ☐ **2 teaspoons soy sauce**
- ☐ **2 tablespoons toasted almonds**

1 Boil, steam or microwave carrots and broccoli until they just change colour. Drain and refresh under cold running water.
2 Heat oil in a wok or frying pan. Add onion, garlic and ginger and stir-fry for 4-5 minutes. Add carrots, broccoli and soy sauce, and stir-fry for 3-4 minutes longer, or until vegetables are heated through. Just prior to serving toss through almonds.

Nutrition tip: Vegetables of the cabbage family – cabbage, Brussels sprouts, broccoli, cauliflower and turnip – are nutrition 'superstars' and should be included as often as possible. Research has shown that these vegetables contain compounds called indoles and isothiocyanates which can protect against cancer of the bowel. They are also one of the best vegetables for fibre and are high in vitamin C and beta-carotene.

RICOTTA AND HERB COURGETTES

Serves 6
Oven temperature 240°C, 475°F, Gas 8

- ☐ **6 large courgettes (zucchini)**
- ☐ **olive oil**

RICOTTA FILLING
- ☐ **30 g/1 oz breadcrumbs, made from stale bread**
- ☐ **60 g/2 oz grated mozzarella cheese**
- ☐ **125 g/4 oz ricotta cheese**
- ☐ **3 tablespoons grated Parmesan cheese**
- ☐ **1 tablespoon chopped fresh basil**
- ☐ **2 teaspoons chopped fresh oregano**
- ☐ **1 egg white, lightly beaten**

1   Boil, steam or microwave courgettes (zucchini) until just tender. Refresh under cold running water and pat dry with absorbent kitchen paper. Cut almost through each courgette (zucchini) crosswise at 2 cm/³/₄ in intervals, taking care not to cut right through.

2   To make filling, place breadcrumbs, mozzarella cheese, ricotta cheese, Parmesan cheese, basil and oregano in a bowl. Stir in egg white and mix well to combine. Place some filling in each courgette (zucchini) cut. Place courgettes (zucchini) in a lightly oiled baking dish, brush lightly with oil and bake for 15 minutes or until heated through and filling is golden.

Candied Sweet Potato, Stir-fried Broccoli with Almonds, Beetroot, Orange and Horseradish Salad

HOT COLESLAW WITH BRANDY DRESSING

Serves 4

- [ ] **2 rashers bacon, chopped**
- [ ] **1/2 medium cabbage, shredded**
- [ ] **2 green apples, coarsely chopped**
- [ ] **1/2 teaspoon ground nutmeg**

BRANDY DRESSING
- [ ] **1 clove garlic, crushed**
- [ ] **1 tablespoon cider vinegar**
- [ ] **2 tablespoons brandy**
- [ ] **4 tablespoons walnut oil**
- [ ] **freshly ground black pepper**

1 Cook bacon in a heavy-based frying pan until just crisp. Add cabbage and apples and toss well. Cook for 3-4 minutes, then mix in nutmeg. Using a slotted spoon transfer to a warmed bowl and toss to combine.

2 To make dressing, combine garlic, vinegar, brandy, oil and black pepper to taste in a screwtop jar and shake well. Pour over coleslaw and serve.

PUNGENT SPINACH CURRY

This quick spinach curry makes a wonderful dish for a vegetarian meal or for use as an accompaniment to a mild meat dish.

Serves 6

- [ ] **60 g/2 oz ghee or clarified butter**
- [ ] **1 onion, finely chopped**
- [ ] **2 cloves garlic, crushed**
- [ ] **2 small fresh red chillies, finely sliced**
- [ ] **1 teaspoon grated fresh ginger**
- [ ] **500 g/1 lb fresh spinach, stalks removed and leaves shredded**
- [ ] **freshly ground black pepper**

1 Melt ghee or butter in a frying pan. Add onion, garlic, chillies and ginger and cook for 2-3 minutes or until onion is soft.

2 Add spinach, toss to coat with spice mixture and cook for 4-5 minutes or until spinach begins to wilt. Season to taste with black pepper.

CARROT AND GINGER SALAD

Serves 6

- [ ] **3 carrots, grated**
- [ ] **90 g/3 oz sultanas**
- [ ] **60 g/2 oz alfalfa sprouts**
- [ ] **2 tablespoons finely snipped fresh chives**

GREEN GINGER DRESSING
- [ ] **1 tablespoon vegetable oil**
- [ ] **2 tablespoons cider vinegar**
- [ ] **1 tablespoon green ginger wine**
- [ ] **1 teaspoon grated fresh ginger**
- [ ] **freshly ground black pepper**

1 Place carrots and sultanas in a bowl and toss to combine.

2 To make dressing, place oil, vinegar, ginger wine, ginger and black pepper to taste in a screwtop jar and shake well to combine. Spoon dressing over carrot mixture and toss to coat with dressing.

3 Line a large serving platter with alfalfa sprouts, top with carrot mixture and sprinkle with chives.

SALAD SUPREMO

Serves 6

- [ ] **1 cos lettuce, leaves separated and torn into pieces**
- [ ] **250 g/8 oz cherry tomatoes**
- [ ] **1 green pepper, sliced**
- [ ] **4 hard-boiled eggs, quartered**
- [ ] **12 black olives**
- [ ] **2 teaspoons capers**
- [ ] **1 tablespoon olive oil**
- [ ] **125 g/4 oz pepperoni sausage, diced**
- [ ] **2 slices white bread, cut into 1 cm/1/2 in cubes**

OREGANO DRESSING
- [ ] **3 tablespoons cider vinegar**
- [ ] **3 tablespoons vegetable oil**
- [ ] **1/4 teaspoon sugar**
- [ ] **1 clove garlic, crushed**
- [ ] **1 tablespoon chopped fresh oregano or 1 teaspoon dried oregano**
- [ ] **freshly ground black pepper**

1 Arrange lettuce, tomatoes, green pepper, eggs, olives and capers attractively on a large serving platter.

2 Heat oil in a frying pan. Add pepperoni and bread cubes and cook, stirring frequently, for 5 minutes or until bread is crisp and golden. Remove pepperoni and bread from pan and drain on absorbent kitchen paper. Set aside to cool, then sprinkle over salad.

3 To make dressing, place vinegar, oil, sugar, garlic, oregano and black pepper to taste in a screwtop jar and shake well to combine. Drizzle dressing over salad and serve immediately.

CHINESE SESAME SLAW

Serves 6

- [ ] **125 g/4 oz mangetout (snow peas), trimmed**
- [ ] **1/2 Chinese cabbage, finely shredded**
- [ ] **200 g/6 1/2 oz bean sprouts**
- [ ] **4 spring onions, chopped**
- [ ] **1/2 red pepper, cut into strips**
- [ ] **1/2 cucumber, diced**
- [ ] **2 tablespoons sesame seeds, toasted**

SESAME DRESSING
- [ ] **2 teaspoons vegetable oil**
- [ ] **1 teaspoon sesame oil**
- [ ] **2 tablespoons white wine vinegar**
- [ ] **1 tablespoon soy sauce**
- [ ] **freshly ground black pepper**

1 Boil, steam or microwave mangetout (snow peas) until they just change colour. Drain and refresh under cold running water.

2 Place cabbage, bean sprouts, spring onions, red pepper, cucumber and mangetout (snow peas) in a salad bowl.

3 To make dressing, place vegetable oil, sesame oil, vinegar, soy sauce and black pepper to taste in a screwtop jar and shake well to combine. Spoon dressing over salad and toss to combine. Sprinkle with sesame seeds and serve immediately.

PINEAPPLE AND KIWIFRUIT SLAW

Serves 6

- ☐ ¹/₄ **red cabbage, shredded**
- ☐ ¹/₂ **Chinese cabbage, shredded**
- ☐ **440 g/14 oz canned pineapple pieces, drained and juice reserved**
- ☐ **2 kiwifruit, sliced**
- ☐ **1 red pepper, sliced**
- ☐ **1 green pepper, sliced**

CORIANDER AND MINT DRESSING
- ☐ **3 tablespoons grapeseed oil**
- ☐ **2 tablespoons reserved pineapple juice**
- ☐ **3 tablespoons finely chopped fresh coriander**
- ☐ **3 tablespoons finely chopped fresh mint**

1 Combine red and Chinese cabbages, pineapple, kiwifruit and red and green peppers in a salad bowl. Toss lightly, cover and refrigerate until required.
2 To make dressing, combine oil, juice, coriander and mint in a screwtop jar. Shake well to combine all ingredients, pour over slaw and serve.

VEGETABLE SLAW WITH PESTO DRESSING

Serves 6

- ☐ ¹/₂ **savoy cabbage, shredded**
- ☐ **1 large carrot, cut into thin strips**
- ☐ **4 spring onions, chopped**
- ☐ **1 stalk celery, cut into thin strips**
- ☐ **8 radishes, sliced**
- ☐ **1 green pepper, cut into strips**
- ☐ **155 g/5 oz broccoli florets, cooked**

PESTO DRESSING
- ☐ **90 g/3 oz basil leaves**
- ☐ **2 cloves garlic, crushed**
- ☐ **2 tablespoons pine nuts, toasted**
- ☐ **2 tablespoons grated Parmesan cheese**
- ☐ **5 tablespoons mayonnaise**
- ☐ **3 tablespoons natural yogurt**

1 Place cabbage, carrot, spring onions, celery, radishes, pepper and broccoli in a salad bowl. Toss lightly, cover and refrigerate until required.
2 To make dressing, place basil, garlic, pine nuts, Parmesan, mayonnaise and yogurt in a food processor or blender and process until smooth. Pour dressing over slaw and toss lightly.

THREE-CABBAGE HOT SLAW

Serves 6

- ☐ **1 tablespoon vegetable oil**
- ☐ **1 tablespoon sesame oil**
- ☐ **1 clove garlic, crushed**
- ☐ **1 teaspoon grated fresh ginger**
- ☐ **1 fresh red chilli, seeded and chopped**
- ☐ **1 tablespoon sesame seeds**
- ☐ ¹/₄ **red cabbage, shredded**
- ☐ ¹/₄ **Chinese cabbage, shredded**
- ☐ ¹/₄ **savoy cabbage, shredded**

1 Heat vegetable and sesame oils in a wok or frying pan until very hot. Add garlic, ginger, chilli and sesame seeds and stir-fry for 1 minute.
2 Toss in cabbages and stir-fry for 3-4 minutes or until just cooked. The cabbages should still retain their colours and be crisp. Serve immediately.

Pineapple and Kiwifruit Slaw,
Vegetable Slaw with Pesto Dressing,
Three-Cabbage Hot Slaw,
Hot Coleslaw with Brandy Dressing

MANGETOUT BOATS WITH MINTED CREAM CHEESE

Serves 6

- [ ] **18 mangetout (snow peas), trimmed**
- [ ] **125 g/4 oz cream cheese**
- [ ] **30 g/1 oz butter**
- [ ] **60 g/2 oz fresh mint leaves, finely chopped**
- [ ] **1 teaspoon sugar**
- [ ] **1 teaspoon horseradish relish**

1   Drop mangetout (snow peas) into a saucepan of boiling water and cook for 1 minute. Drain and refresh under cold running water. Pat dry on absorbent paper.
2   Beat cream cheese and butter together until smooth. Add mint, sugar and horseradish. Slit mangetout (snow peas) along one edge with a sharp knife or scissors. Spoon or pipe cream cheese mixture into mangetout (snow peas). Refrigerate until firm.

Cook's tip: Mangetout (snow peas) are edible pea pods. To prepare for cooking, top and tail with a sharp knife and pull away strings from older, larger peas. Mangetout (snow peas) can be steamed, boiled, microwaved or stir-fried.

Drop mangetout (snow peas) into boiling water and cook for 1 minute.

Slit mangetout (snow peas) along one edge with a sharp knife or scissors.

Pipe cream cheese into mangetout (snow peas).

BAKED POTATO SKINS

Try baking potato skins instead of deep-frying them – they taste just as good!

Serves 4
Oven temperature 200°C, 400°F, Gas 6

- ☐ **4 large potatoes, scrubbed**
- ☐ **vegetable oil**

RED PEPPER HERBED MAYONNAISE
- ☐ **1 fresh red chilli, seeds removed and chopped**
- ☐ **2 red peppers, roasted and skinned**
- ☐ **1 clove garlic, crushed**
- ☐ **1 tablespoon tomato purée**
- ☐ **250 g/8 oz mayonnaise**
- ☐ **1 tablespoon finely snipped fresh chives**
- ☐ **1 tablespoon finely chopped fresh basil**
- ☐ **freshly ground black pepper**

1 Bake potatoes for about 1 hour or until tender. Cut a slice from the top of each potato and carefully scoop out the flesh with a teaspoon, leaving a wall approximately 5 mm/$^1/_4$ in thick. Brush the inside and skin with oil. Reserve potato flesh for another use.
2 Return potato skins to oven and bake for 15-20 minutes or until crisp and brown.
3 To make mayonnaise, place chilli, peppers and garlic in a food processor or blender and process until peppers are chunky. Combine chilli mixture with tomato purée, mayonnaise, chives and basil. Season to taste with black pepper. Serve potato skins with the mayonnaise.

Hot tip: When handling fresh chillies do not put your hands near your eyes or allow them to touch your lips. To avoid discomfort and burning, wear rubber gloves. Freshly minced chilli is also available from supermarkets.

Cook's tip: Cooked potato flesh can be used to make croquettes, as a topping for a Cottage Pie, or for making Cheesy Potato and Leek Pie.

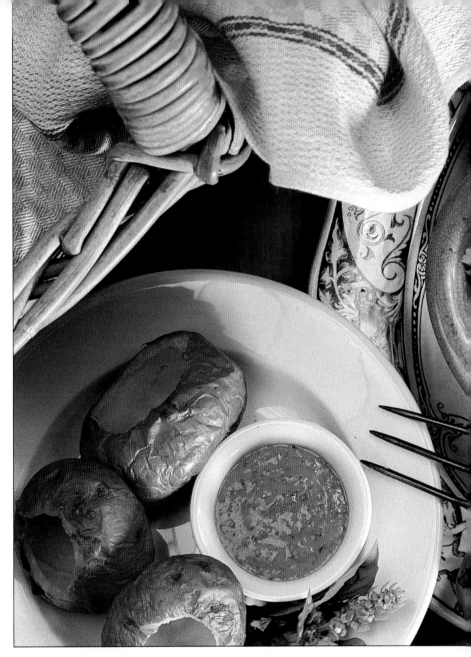

CHEESY POTATO AND LEEK PIE

Serves 6
Oven temperature 220°C, 425°F, Gas 7

- ☐ **125 mL/4 fl oz milk**
- ☐ **3 leeks, trimmed and thinly sliced**
- ☐ **4 potatoes, cooked**
- ☐ **125 g/4 oz ricotta or cottage cheese**
- ☐ **2 eggs, lightly beaten**
- ☐ **1 slice wholegrain bread, crumbed**
- ☐ **4 tablespoons grated Parmesan cheese**
- ☐ **2 teaspoons chopped fresh parsley**

1 Place milk and leeks in a saucepan. Cook over a low heat for 8-9 minutes. Mash potatoes with leeks and milk. Beat in ricotta or cottage cheese and eggs.
2 Spoon potato mixture into a lightly greased 25 cm/10 in pie plate or into six individual gratin dishes. Combine breadcrumbs, Parmesan and parsley and sprinkle over the potato pie.
3 Bake for 30-35 minutes or until pie is puffy and golden.

Microwave it: Leeks can be cooked in milk in your microwave on HIGH (100%) for 4-5 minutes.

CREAMY SPINACH IN COURGETTES

Fresh spinach may be used in place of frozen in this recipe if you wish. Remove the stalks from the spinach, shred the leaves and steam or microwave until wilted, then use as in recipe.

Serves 6
Oven temperature 180°C, 350°F, Gas 4

- ☐ **6 courgettes (zucchini)**
- ☐ **250 g/8 oz frozen spinach, thawed**
- ☐ **2 rashers bacon, chopped**
- ☐ **60 g/2 oz grated mature Cheddar**
- ☐ **paprika**

RICOTTA FILLING
- ☐ **125 g/4 oz ricotta cheese**
- ☐ **1 egg, beaten**
- ☐ **¼ teaspoon ground nutmeg**
- ☐ **freshly ground black pepper**

1 Trim ends from courgettes (zucchini) and boil, steam or microwave until just tender. Drain and cut in half lengthwise. Carefully scoop out centres leaving shells with a little flesh. Set aside. Finely chop scooped out courgette (zucchini) flesh and place in a bowl.
2 Cook bacon in a frying pan for 4-5 minutes or until crisp. Remove bacon from pan and drain on absorbent kitchen paper.
3 Squeeze spinach to remove any excess liquid. Add spinach, ricotta cheese, egg, nutmeg and black pepper to taste to bowl with courgette (zucchini) flesh and mix to combine. Spoon filling into reserved courgette (zucchini) shells, top with bacon and cheese and sprinkle with paprika. Place filled courgettes (zucchini) on a greased baking tray and bake for 15-20 minutes or until cheese melts and is golden.

SWEET POTATO AND ORANGE BAKE

Use orange-fleshed sweet potato to make this dish. Serve with pork, ham or poultry in place of potatoes.

Serves 6
Oven temperature 200°C, 400°F, Gas 6

- ☐ **3 sweet potatoes, sliced**
- ☐ **2 oranges, peeled and sliced**
- ☐ **30 g/1 oz butter, softened**
- ☐ **3 tablespoons brown sugar**
- ☐ **1 teaspoon cornflour**
- ☐ **125 mL/4 fl oz orange juice**
- ☐ **60 g/2 oz slivered almonds**

1 Boil, steam or microwave sweet potatoes until just tender. Drain and arrange in alternate layers with oranges in a lightly greased ovenproof dish.
2 Combine butter, brown sugar, cornflour and orange juice. Pour over potatoes and oranges, sprinkle with almonds and bake for 30 minutes.

Cheesy Potato and Leek Pie, Sweet Potato and Orange Bake, Baked Potato Skins

THE PERFECT CHIP

Serves 4

- [ ] **4 large potatoes**
- [ ] **oil for deep-frying**

1   Cut potatoes into 1 cm/½ in slices, then into strips. Soak strips in cold water for 10 minutes to remove the excess starch. Drain and dry on absorbent kitchen paper.
2   Heat oil in a deep saucepan. Drop a chip into the oil and when it rises to the surface surrounded by bubbles the oil is at the correct temperature for cooking. Drop the chips gradually into the hot oil, or lower them in a wire basket and cook for 6 minutes.
3   Remove chips from oil using a slotted spoon, or by lifting the basket, and drain on absorbent kitchen paper. At this point the chips are blanched and can be left for several hours, or frozen before the final cooking stage.
4   Just prior to serving, reheat the oil and test as above. Cook chips quickly for 3-4 minutes or until golden brown and crisp. Remove from pan with a slotted spoon, drain on absorbent kitchen paper. Season to taste and serve immediately.

Cook's tip: Double-cooking chips ensures crisp golden chips every time. The high water content of potatoes initially reduces the temperature of the oil and double-cooking overcomes this problem. A wire chip basket makes it easier to lower and raise a quantity of chips in hot oil. If cooking a large quantity of chips, cook in batches to prevent overcrowding.

PERFECT MASHED POTATO

Serves 4

- [ ] **4 potatoes, halved**
- [ ] **125 mL/4 fl oz milk**
- [ ] **30 g/1 oz butter, softened**

1   Place potatoes in a saucepan of water, cover and bring to the boil. Cook gently for 20 minutes or until tender.
2   Drain potatoes, then return to pan. Shake pan over low heat to dry. Mash potatoes with a vegetable masher until free of lumps.
3   Stir in milk and butter. Season to taste and beat with a fork until smooth and fluffy.

PERFECT ROAST POTATOES

Serves 4
Oven temperature 180°C, 350°F, Gas 4

- [ ] **4 potatoes**
- [ ] **1 tablespoon vegetable oil**

1   Boil or steam potatoes for 5 minutes. Drain and dry on absorbent kitchen paper. Set aside until cool enough to handle, then cut in half lengthwise. Score the upper rounded surface with a fork; this helps crisp the potatoes during cooking.
2   Brush potatoes with oil and place in a shallow baking dish and bake for 55-60 minutes, turning occasionally during cooking.

Cook's tip: When roasting vegetables use a shallow baking dish, which will allow the vegetables to brown evenly. Other vegetables can be roasted with the potatoes. Cook pumpkin with or without the skin and cut into a similar size as the potatoes. Brown onions are excellent roasted; peel away 1 or 2 layers of skin, leaving a little of the root end intact to hold onions together during cooking.

POTATO AND BEETROOT FLAN

This vibrantly coloured dish will give any meal a lift. It may be served either hot or cold.

Serves 4
Oven temperature 200°C, 400°F, Gas 6

- [ ] **4 potatoes, cooked and mashed (without milk or butter)**
- [ ] **1 large raw beetroot, grated**
- [ ] **1 tablespoon finely chopped fresh dill**
- [ ] **1 tablespoon cream**
- [ ] **1 tablespoon mayonnaise**
- [ ] **2 teaspoons horseradish cream**
- [ ] **freshly ground black pepper**
- [ ] **2 eggs, separated**

1   Combine potatoes, beetroot, dill, cream, mayonnaise, horseradish, black pepper and egg yolks in a mixing bowl.
2   Beat egg whites until stiff peaks form and fold through potato mixture. Spoon mixture into a well-greased 23 cm/9 in flan dish with a removable base. Bake for 25-30 minutes or until firm. Serve warm, or at room temperature, cut into wedges.

BAKED JACKET POTATOES

Serves 4
Oven temperature 180°C, 350°F, Gas 4

- [ ] **4 potatoes**
- [ ] **sour cream or butter for serving**

Scrub and dry potatoes. Prick with a fork, place on a wire rack in a baking dish and bake for 1 hour or until tender. Serve with sour cream or butter.

Cook's tip: Baked potatoes can be placed in the oven and cooked with other dishes. If the other food you are cooking requires a slightly lower or higher temperature your baked potatoes will happily cook along with it taking just a little shorter or longer time as the case may be.

BACON AND BANANA POTATO CAKES

Serves 4

- [ ] **4 potatoes, cooked and mashed (without milk or butter)**
- [ ] **1 small green apple, grated**
- [ ] **1 tablespoon mayonnaise**
- [ ] **2 teaspoons chopped fresh mint**
- [ ] **3 tablespoons flour**

FILLING
- [ ] **4 rashers bacon, finely chopped**
- [ ] **1 banana, sliced**

COATING
- [ ] **flour**
- [ ] **1 egg, lightly beaten**
- [ ] **125 g/4 oz dried breadcrumbs**
- [ ] **oil for cooking**

1   Combine potato, apple, mayonnaise, mint and flour. Divide potato mixture into sixteen equal portions and form into patties.
2   To make filling, cook bacon in a nonstick frying pan for 2-3 minutes or until crisp. Set aside to cool slightly. Place a spoonful of bacon on eight of the patties. Top with banana slices and remaining potato patties. Mould potato patties to completely seal filling.
3   To coat, cover patties lightly with flour, dip in egg then breadcrumbs. Refrigerate for 30 minutes.
4   Heat oil in a frying pan and cook patties, two at a time, until golden brown on both sides. Remove from pan and drain on absorbent kitchen paper. Set aside and keep warm. Cook remaining patties.

BACON AND CREAMED CORN FILLED POTATOES

You will require only half the potato flesh for this recipe. Reserve the remaining flesh for another use. Leftover potato can be made into potato cakes or croquettes, or can be pan cooked.

Serves 4
Oven temperature 180°C, 350°F, Gas 4

☐ **4 potatoes, baked in their jackets**
☐ **4 rashers bacon, chopped**
☐ **125 g/4 oz canned creamed sweet corn**
☐ **2 tablespoons sour cream**
☐ **pinch chilli powder**
☐ **60 g/2 oz grated mature Cheddar**

1　Cut potatoes in half, scoop out flesh, leaving a 1 cm/¹/₂ in thick shell. Reserve the flesh and set aside.
2　Cook the bacon in a nonstick frying pan for 2-3 minutes or until crisp. Mash half the potato flesh and combine with bacon, corn, sour cream and chilli powder. Spoon mixture into potato shells, top with cheese.
3　Place potatoes on an oven tray and bake for 15 minutes or until cheese melts.

Top: Potato and Beetroot Flan
Centre: Baked Jacket Potatoes, Bacon and Creamed Corn Filled Potatoes
Bottom: Bacon and Banana Potato Cakes

PEAR AND SPINACH SALAD

Serves 6

- ☐ **500 g/1 lb spinach, stalks removed and shredded**
- ☐ **2 spring onions, sliced**
- ☐ **3 slices ham, cut into thin strips**
- ☐ **2 pears, cored, peeled and diced**

LEMON MUSTARD DRESSING
- ☐ **2 tablespoons lemon juice**
- ☐ **1 tablespoon wholegrain mustard**
- ☐ **2 teaspoons sugar**
- ☐ **1 teaspoon dried tarragon leaves**
- ☐ **2 tablespoons olive oil**
- ☐ **125 mL/4 fl oz vegetable oil**

1 Combine spinach, onions, ham and pears in a large glass serving dish. Toss gently.
2 To make dressing, combine lemon juice, mustard, sugar, tarragon and oils in a screwtop jar and shake until well mixed. Pour dressing over spinach salad and serve.

POTATO NEST WITH CARROT PUREE

For something different try using sweet potatoes in place of the potatoes in this recipe, accompany them with parsnip purée and substitute lemon juice for the orange juice.

Serves 6
Oven temperature 180°C, 350°F, Gas 4

POTATO NEST
- ☐ **4 large potatoes**
- ☐ **2 egg yolks**
- ☐ **¼ teaspoon nutmeg**
- ☐ **60 g/2 oz butter**
- ☐ **freshly ground black pepper**

CARROT PUREE
- ☐ **6 large carrots**
- ☐ **185 mL/6 fl oz chicken stock**
- ☐ **2 tablespoons orange juice**
- ☐ **¼ teaspoon ground nutmeg**

1 To make nest, cook potatoes in a saucepan of boiling water until tender. Drain and return to pan. Toss over heat for 2-3 minutes to dry. Remove from heat and mash well. Stir in egg yolks, nutmeg and half the butter. Season to taste with black pepper.
2 Spoon mixture into a piping bag and pipe a decorative border around the edge of an ovenproof dinner plate. Spoon any leftover potato into the centre of plate. Brush with remaining butter, melted, and bake for 20 minutes.
3 To make purée, place carrots and stock in a saucepan, bring to the boil, cover and simmer for 10 minutes or until carrots are tender. Cool slightly. Purée carrot mixture in a food processor until smooth. Return mixture to the pan. Add orange juice and nutmeg. Stir over low heat until heated through. Spoon purée into centre of potato nest and serve.

TOMATO AND CHEESE FRITTERS

These fritters are delicious served with choko pickles or your favourite chutney. Serve hot for a party snack, or as a tasty side dish at your next barbecue.

Serves 6

- ☐ 75 g/2½ oz bran
- ☐ 60 g/2 oz grated Swiss cheese
- ☐ 2 tablespoons chopped fresh basil
- ☐ ½ teaspoon caraway seeds
- ☐ 3 medium, partially ripe tomatoes
- ☐ 60 g/2 oz flour, seasoned with freshly ground pepper
- ☐ 2 eggs, beaten
- ☐ oil for shallow-frying

1   Combine bran, cheese, basil and caraway seeds. Cut tomatoes into 5 mm/ ¼ in slices. Coat with seasoned flour, dip in egg, then coat with bran mixture.

2   Heat oil in a frying pan. Cook tomato slices until golden brown. Drain on absorbent kitchen paper.

TWO PEA SALAD

Serves 5

- ☐ 500 g/1 lb frozen peas
- ☐ 155 g/5 oz mangetout (snow peas), trimmed
- ☐ 1 small onion, thinly sliced

LEMON DRESSING
- ☐ 1 clove garlic, crushed
- ☐ 2 tablespoons vegetable oil
- ☐ 2 teaspoons lemon juice
- ☐ freshly ground black pepper

1   Boil or microwave peas until just cooked. Drain and place in a salad bowl. Boil, steam or microwave mangetout (snow peas) until they just change colour. Drain and place in salad bowl with peas in salad bowl. Add onions to bowl.

2   To make dressing, place garlic, oil, lemon juice and black pepper to taste in a screwtop jar and shake well to combine. Spoon dressing over salad and toss to combine. Set aside to cool to room temperature before serving.

Left: Potato Nest with Carrot Purée, Pear and Spinach Salad
Below: Tomato and Cheese Fritters

ARTICHOKE SALAD WITH PESTO DRESSING

Serves 6

- [ ] **500 g/1 lb watercress, washed**
- [ ] **440 g/14 oz canned artichoke hearts, drained**
- [ ] **4 tomatoes, peeled and diced**
- [ ] **125 g/4 oz mozzarella cheese, sliced**

PESTO DRESSING
- [ ] **60 g/2 oz fresh basil leaves**
- [ ] **3 tablespoons olive oil**
- [ ] **1 clove garlic, crushed**
- [ ] **3 tablespoons grated fresh Parmesan cheese**
- [ ] **2 tablespoons pine nuts, toasted**

1 Break watercress into small pieces and place in a bowl. Arrange artichokes, tomatoes and mozzarella cheese over watercress.
2 To make dressing, place basil, oil, garlic, Parmesan cheese and pine nuts in a food processor or blender and process until smooth. Drizzle over salad and toss gently to coat salad ingredients.

SPINACH AND RAISINS ALLA LIGURIA

Serves 4

- [ ] **500 g/1 lb spinach, stalks removed**
- [ ] **30 g/1 oz butter**
- [ ] **1 clove garlic, crushed**
- [ ] **4 slices prosciutto, chopped**
- [ ] **3 tablespoons raisins, chopped**
- [ ] **1 tablespoon chopped fresh thyme**
- [ ] **freshly ground black pepper**
- [ ] **3 tablespoons pine nuts, toasted**

1 Boil, steam or microwave spinach until just tender. Drain well and chop roughly.
2 Heat butter in a frying pan. Cook garlic and prosciutto, stirring, for 1 minute. Add spinach, raisins and thyme and cook, stirring, for 2-3 minutes longer or until heated through. Season to taste with black pepper and transfer to a serving dish. Sprinkle with pine nuts and serve immediately.

MILANESE-STYLE FENNEL

This dish can be made a day ahead of serving then reheated when required.

Serves 6
Oven temperature 200°C, 400°F, Gas 6

- [ ] **2 large fennel bulbs, trimmed and cut into 1 cm/$^1/_2$ in strips**

WHITE SAUCE
- [ ] **30 g/1 oz butter**
- [ ] **2 tablespoons flour**
- [ ] **375 mL/12 fl oz milk**
- [ ] **$^1/_4$ teaspoon ground nutmeg**
- [ ] **freshly ground black pepper**

CHEESY TOPPING
- [ ] **60 g/2 oz breadcrumbs, made from stale bread**
- [ ] **3 tablespoons grated fresh Parmesan cheese**
- [ ] **30 g/1 oz butter, melted**
- [ ] **paprika**

1 Boil, steam or microwave fennel until tender. Drain and set aside.
2 To make sauce, melt butter in a saucepan, add flour and cook, stirring, for 1 minute. Remove from heat and gradually stir in milk. Cook over a medium heat, stirring constantly, until sauce boils and thickens. Add nutmeg and season to taste with black pepper.
3 To make topping, combine breadcrumbs, Parmesan cheese and butter. Arrange fennel in a shallow ovenproof dish, pour sauce over and sprinkle with topping. Dust with paprika and bake for 15-20 minutes or until browned.

Microwave it: To make the sauce in the microwave, melt butter in a microwave-safe jug, stir in flour then gradually stir in milk. Cook on HIGH (100%) for 3 minutes, or until sauce boils and thickens. Stir twice during cooking.

ITALIAN BEAN HOTPOT

This recipe is quick and easy to prepare. Served with fresh crusty bread and a salad it makes a perfect luncheon or supper dish.

Serves 6

- [ ] **2 tablespoons olive oil**
- [ ] **2 cloves garlic, crushed**
- [ ] **1 onion, sliced**
- [ ] **1 tablespoon chopped fresh sage, or 1 teaspoon dried sage leaves**
- [ ] **2 x 315 g/10 oz canned cannellini beans, drained**
- [ ] **440 g/14 oz canned peppers, drained and thinly sliced**
- [ ] **440 g/14 oz canned tomatoes, undrained and chopped**
- [ ] **440 g/14 oz canned tomato purée**
- [ ] **2 courgettes (zucchini), sliced**
- [ ] **freshly ground black pepper**
- [ ] **3 tablespoons grated fresh Parmesan cheese**

1 Heat oil in a frying pan and cook garlic, onion and sage for 4-5 minutes or until onion is soft.
2 Stir in beans, peppers, tomatoes, tomato purée and zucchini (courgettes). Bring to the boil, reduce heat and simmer, uncovered, for 15 minutes or until mixture reduces and thickens. Season to taste with black pepper and sprinkle with Parmesan cheese.

Cook's tip: You can use dried cannellini beans for this recipe if you wish, but you will need to cook them first.

Italian Bean Hotpot, Spinach and Raisins Alla Liguria, Artichoke Salad with Pesto Dressing, Milanese-Style Fennel

CAULIFLOWER
AU GRATIN

Serves 4
Oven temperature 180°C, 350°F, Gas 4

- [ ] **1 small cauliflower, broken into florets**
- [ ] **375 mL/12 fl oz milk**
- [ ] **1¹/₂ tablespoons cornflour blended with 3 tablespoons water**
- [ ] **1 teaspoon wholegrain mustard**
- [ ] **3 tablespoons natural yogurt**
- [ ] **freshly ground black pepper**
- [ ] **60 g/2 oz crushed cornflakes**
- [ ] **3 tablespoons grated mature Cheddar**
- [ ] **15 g/¹/₂ oz butter, melted**
- [ ] **paprika**

1   Steam, boil or microwave cauliflower until just tender. Drain and set aside.
2   Place milk in a saucepan and cook over a medium heat until almost at boiling point. Remove pan from heat and stir in cornflour mixture. Return pan to heat and cook over a medium heat until sauce boils and thickens, stirring constantly.
3   Combine mustard and yogurt. Remove sauce from heat and blend in yogurt mixture. Season to taste with black pepper. Spread half the sauce over the base of an ovenproof dish. Top with cauliflower and remaining sauce.
4   Combine cornflakes, cheese and butter. Sprinkle on top of cauliflower. Dust lightly with paprika and bake for 15-20 minutes or until golden brown.

Place milk in a saucepan and cook over a medium heat until almost boiling. Remove pan from heat and stir in cornflour mixture.

Combine cornflakes, cheese and butter and sprinkle over cauliflower.

SPICY ASPARAGUS WITH PINE NUTS

This recipe makes a delicious entrée. Use bacon instead of salami for a less spicy flavour.

Serves 4

- ☐ 500 g/1 lb fresh asparagus spears, trimmed and cut into 5 cm/2 in pieces
- ☐ 15 g/¹/₂ oz butter
- ☐ 60 g/2 oz pine nuts
- ☐ 125 g/4 oz hot Italian salami, cut into 5 mm/¹/₄ in cubes
- ☐ 2 tablespoons chopped fresh basil
- ☐ 3 tablespoons grated fresh Parmesan cheese

1   Steam or microwave asparagus until just tender. Drain and rinse under cold running water to refresh, then drain again and set aside.

2   Heat butter in a frying pan and cook pine nuts and salami until lightly browned. Add asparagus and basil and cook, stirring constantly, for 1 minute or until heated through. Sprinkle with Parmesan cheese and serve immediately.

RADICCHIO ANCHOVY SALAD

Serves 6

- ☐ 1 radicchio, washed and leaves separated
- ☐ ¹/₂ bunch curly endive, washed and leaves separated
- ☐ 1 chicory (witloof), washed and leaves separated
- ☐ 8 radishes, washed and sliced
- ☐ 3 tablespoons chopped fresh Italian flat leaf parsley

ANCHOVY DRESSING
- ☐ 60 mL/2 fl oz olive oil
- ☐ 60 mL/2 fl oz lemon juice
- ☐ 60 mL/2 fl oz dry white wine
- ☐ 3 anchovy fillets, drained and chopped
- ☐ 1 clove garlic, crushed
- ☐ ¹/₂ teaspoon sugar

1   Arrange radicchio, endive and chicory (witloof) attractively on a large platter. Top with radishes and parsley.

2   To make dressing, place oil, lemon juice, wine, anchovies, garlic and sugar in a food processor or blender and process until smooth. Just before serving, drizzle dressing over salad.

FENNEL AND ORANGE SALAD

Serves 6

- ☐ 1 bunch curly endive, leaves separated and washed
- ☐ 1 small fennel bulb, cut into thin strips
- ☐ 3 oranges, segmented
- ☐ 1 onion, sliced
- ☐ 20 black olives

ORANGE DRESSING
- ☐ 4 tablespoons olive oil
- ☐ 3 tablespoons white wine vinegar
- ☐ 1 tablespoon chopped fresh fennel leaves
- ☐ ¹/₂ teaspoon grated orange rind
- ☐ ¹/₂ teaspoon sugar
- ☐ freshly ground black pepper

1   Place endive on a large serving platter. Arrange fennel, oranges, onion and olives attractively over endive.

2   To make dressing, place oil, vinegar, fennel leaves, orange rind, sugar and black pepper to taste in a screwtop jar. Shake well to combine. Pour dressing over salad and serve immediately.

Fennel: The aniseed-flavoured fennel – also known as 'Florence fennel' or 'finocchio' – was much esteemed by the Romans, who used it to flavour many of their dishes.

The feathery leaves and aromatic seeds add zing to vegetables, salad dressings, pickles and sauces, and taste delicious as a traditional accompaniment to fish.

Fennel has a strong aniseed flavour but you will find when it is cooked that it loses its aniseed flavour.

SPICY VEGETABLES

Use any vegetables you like for this dish, however you will find this combination perfect. Remember not to overcook your vegetables when stir-frying or they will become soggy and lose many of their valuable vitamins.

Serves 4

- ☐ 3 tablespoons groundnut (peanut) oil
- ☐ 2 onions, cut into eighths
- ☐ 1 teaspoon grated fresh ginger
- ☐ 200 g/6¹/₂ oz oyster mushrooms, sliced
- ☐ 1 small head broccoli, broken into florets
- ☐ ¹/₂ Chinese cabbage, shredded
- ☐ 1 large carrot, cut into thin strips
- ☐ 2 stalks celery, sliced diagonally
- ☐ 250 g/8 oz mangetout (snow peas)
- ☐ 60 mL/2 fl oz chicken stock

HONEY AND SOY SAUCE
- ☐ 1 tablespoon sesame oil
- ☐ 1 tablespoon soy sauce
- ☐ 2 teaspoons honey
- ☐ 1 teaspoon lemon juice

1   Heat oil in a wok or large frying pan, add onion and stir-fry for 4-5 minutes or until golden. Add ginger and mushrooms and stir-fry for 1 minute longer.

2   Add broccoli, cabbage, carrot, celery, mangetout (snow peas) and stock to pan and stir-fry for 4-5 minutes or until vegetables just change colour and are just tender.

3   To make sauce, place sesame oil, soy sauce, honey and lemon juice in a small bowl and whisk to combine. Pour sauce over vegetables in pan and stir-fry for 1-2 minutes longer or until heated through. Serve immediately.

Radicchio Anchovy Salad, Fennel and Orange Salad, Spicy Asparagus with Pine Nuts

189

MARINATED MUSHROOMS

These mushrooms make an excellent accompaniment to a meal, or a low-kilojoule snack.

Serves 4

- [ ] **500 g/1 lb button mushrooms, stems removed**
- [ ] **1/2 red pepper, diced**
- [ ] **1/2 green pepper, diced**

HERB DRESSING
- [ ] **1 clove garlic, crushed**
- [ ] **1 tablespoon vegetable oil**
- [ ] **3 tablespoons red wine vinegar**
- [ ] **1 tablespoon finely chopped fresh parsley**
- [ ] **1 tablespoon finely snipped fresh chives**
- [ ] **freshly ground black pepper**

1   Place mushrooms and peppers in a bowl.
2   To make dressing, place garlic, oil, vinegar, parsley, chives and black pepper to taste in a screwtop jar. Shake well to combine and pour over mushrooms and peppers. Cover, refrigerate and marinate for about 2 hours before serving.

ITALIAN GREEN BEAN SALAD

Serves 4

- [ ] **500 g/1 lb green beans, topped and tailed**
- [ ] **6 spring onions, finely chopped**
- [ ] **3 tomatoes, peeled and chopped**
- [ ] **8 black olives, pitted**
- [ ] **freshly ground black pepper**

LEMON AND HERB DRESSING
- [ ] **1 tablespoon olive oil**
- [ ] **3 tablespoons lemon juice**
- [ ] **1 clove garlic, crushed**
- [ ] **1 tablespoon chopped fresh parsley**
- [ ] **1 tablespoon finely snipped fresh chives**
- [ ] **1 teaspoon finely chopped fresh rosemary**
- [ ] **1 teaspoon finely chopped fresh thyme**

1   Boil, steam or microwave beans until just tender. Refresh under cold running water.
2   Place beans, spring onions, tomatoes and olives in a salad bowl.

3 To make dressing, place oil, lemon juice, garlic, parsley, chives, rosemary and thyme in a screwtop jar. Shake well to combine and pour over salad. Season with black pepper to taste and toss.

TOMATO AND BASIL SALAD

You might like to try a combination of cherry tomatoes and little yellow teardrop tomatoes to make this aromatic tomato salad look even more attractive.

Serves 6

- ☐ 750 g/1¹/₂ lb ripe tomatoes, peeled and sliced
- ☐ 4 tablespoons finely chopped fresh basil
- ☐ 2 tablespoons grated Parmesan cheese
- ☐ freshly ground black pepper

WHITE WINE VINEGAR DRESSING
- ☐ 1 clove garlic, crushed
- ☐ 1 tablespoon olive oil
- ☐ 3 tablespoons white wine vinegar

1 Arrange overlapping tomato slices on a serving platter and sprinkle with basil leaves.

2 To make dressing, place garlic, oil and vinegar in a screwtop jar. Shake well to combine and sprinkle over tomatoes. Just before serving, sprinkle tomato salad with Parmesan cheese. Season with black pepper to taste.

STIR-FRIED VEGETABLES

Serves 6

- ☐ 1 tablespoon vegetable oil
- ☐ 1 onion, sliced
- ☐ 1 clove garlic, crushed
- ☐ 1 teaspoon finely grated fresh ginger
- ☐ 1 carrot, thinly sliced
- ☐ 1 green pepper, diced
- ☐ 2 stalks celery, sliced
- ☐ 300 g/9¹/₂ oz mushrooms, sliced
- ☐ 100 g/3¹/₂ oz mangetout (snow peas), topped and tailed
- ☐ ¹/₂ cabbage, shredded
- ☐ 350 g/11 oz canned baby sweet corn
- ☐ 1 tablespoon soy sauce

1 Heat oil until hot in a wok or frying pan. Add onion, garlic and ginger and stir-fry for 2-3 minutes. Toss in carrot, green pepper

and celery, and cook for 4-5 minutes.
2 To vegetable mixture, add mushrooms and mangetout (snow peas). Stir-fry for 1-2 minutes, or until mangetout (snow peas) are just tender. Stir in cabbage, sweet corn and soy sauce, and cook for 3-4 minutes. Serve immediately.

TOMATO, COURGETTE AND ONION BAKE

Serves 4

- ☐ 1 tablespoon olive oil
- ☐ 2 large onions, sliced into rings
- ☐ 1 clove garlic, crushed
- ☐ 1 green pepper, diced
- ☐ 1 teaspoon dried mixed herbs
- ☐ 100 g/3¹/₂ oz mushrooms, sliced
- ☐ 440 g/14 oz canned tomatoes, undrained and mashed
- ☐ 1 tablespoon tomato purée
- ☐ 1 tablespoon cornflour blended with 125 mL/4 fl oz water
- ☐ 3 courgettes (zucchini), thickly sliced

CHEESY TOPPING
- ☐ 30 g/1 oz breadcrumbs, made from stale bread
- ☐ 2 tablespoons grated mature Cheddar

1 Heat oil in a saucepan and cook onions, garlic, green pepper and herbs for 2-3 minutes or until onion is soft. Add mushrooms and cook for 5 minutes longer.
2 Stir in tomatoes and tomato purée, and cook until mixture boils. Stir in cornflour mixture and cook till sauce thickens.
3 Boil, steam or microwave courgettes (zucchini) until just tender. Place courgettes (zucchini) in a shallow ovenproof dish and pour over tomato sauce. Top with breadcrumbs and cheese.
4 Place under a preheated grill and cook for 5 minutes or until top is golden.

Far left: Italian Green Bean Salad, Tomato and Basil Salad, Marinated Mushrooms
Left: Tomato, Courgette and Onion Bake, Stir-fried Vegetables

COOKED AND RAW BEETROOT SALAD

The cooked and raw beetroot in this salad have quite different textures and make a very interesting combination.

Serves 4

- ☐ **1 large cooked beetroot, grated**
- ☐ **1 large raw beetroot, grated**
- ☐ **2 green apples, cut into thin strips**
- ☐ **fresh dill sprigs**

DILL DRESSING
- ☐ **2 tablespoons lemon juice**
- ☐ **4 tablespoons vegetable oil**
- ☐ **1 tablespoon finely chopped fresh dill**
- ☐ **freshly ground black pepper**

1   Place cooked and raw beetroot and apples in a salad bowl.
2   To make dressing, place lemon juice, oil, dill and black pepper to taste in a screwtop jar and shake well to combine. Spoon dressing over beetroot and apples and toss to coat all ingredients with dressing. Top with dill sprigs and serve.

VEGETABLES FRITTERS WITH HERB DRESSING

Serves 4

- ☐ **¹/₂ small cauliflower, cut into florets**
- ☐ **1 aubergine (eggplant)**
- ☐ **salt**
- ☐ **1 large red pepper, cut into strips**
- ☐ **cornflour**

BATTER
- ☐ **75 g/2¹/₂ oz flour**
- ☐ **3 tablespoons self-raising flour**
- ☐ **250 mL/8 fl oz water**
- ☐ **1 egg, lightly beaten**
- ☐ **oil for deep-frying**

HERB DRESSING
- ☐ **125 mL/4 fl oz Italian dressing**
- ☐ **1 tablespoon chopped fresh basil**
- ☐ **1 tablespoon chopped fresh oregano**
- ☐ **1 small fresh red chilli, seeded and chopped**

1   Steam, boil or microwave cauliflower until just tender. Drain well and set aside.

Cut aubergine (eggplant) in half lengthwise and slice into 1 cm/¹/₂ in slices. Sprinkle with salt and set aside for 30 minutes. Rinse aubergine (eggplant) under cold running water and pat dry with absorbent kitchen paper. Cut aubergine (eggplant) into strips.
2   Toss cauliflower, aubergine (eggplant) and red pepper in cornflour. Shake off any excess cornflour and set aside.
3   To make batter, place flour, self-raising flour, water and egg in a food processor or blender and process until smooth. Heat oil in a large saucepan until a cube of bread dropped in browns in 50 seconds. Dip vegetables in batter and cook a few at a time until golden. Remove from oil and drain on absorbent kitchen paper.
4   To make dressing, place Italian dressing, basil, oregano and chilli in a screwtop jar and shake well to combine. Serve with hot vegetables.

ROAST PEPPER SALAD

A colourful, strongly flavoured salad, this dish is the perfect accompaniment to grilled meats. If yellow peppers are unavailable, make the salad using three green and three red. If possible the salad stand for 2-3 hours before serving to allow the flavours to develop fully.

Serves 6

- ☐ **2 red peppers**
- ☐ **2 green peppers**
- ☐ **2 yellow peppers**

BASIL DRESSING
- ☐ **12 fresh basil leaves, chopped**
- ☐ **1 clove garlic, crushed**
- ☐ **125 mL/4 fl oz olive oil**
- ☐ **3 tablespoons red wine vinegar**
- ☐ **freshly ground black pepper**

1   Cut red, green and yellow peppers into quarters, remove seeds and cook, skin side up, under a high preheated grill for 10 minutes or until skins blister and char. Remove peppers from grill, place in a plastic food bag, seal and set aside for 10 minutes or until cool enough to handle. Remove skins, cut peppers into strips and place in a salad bowl.
2   To make dressing, place basil, garlic, oil, vinegar and black pepper to taste in a screwtop jar and shake well to combine. Pour dressing over peppers and toss to combine. Cover and refrigerate until ready to serve.

BRUSSELS SPROUTS AND ALMONDS IN TANGY SAUCE

Serves 4

- ☐ **500 g/1 lb Brussels sprouts**
- ☐ **3 tablespoons toasted almond flakes**

TANGY SAUCE
- ☐ **30 g/1 oz butter, melted**
- ☐ **2 tablespoons brown sugar**
- ☐ **3 teaspoons cornflour**
- ☐ **¹/₂ teaspoon prepared mustard**
- ☐ **1 small onion, finely chopped**
- ☐ **3 tablespoons white vinegar**

1   Boil, steam or microwave Brussels sprouts until tender. Drain and keep warm.
2   Combine butter, sugar, cornflour, mustard, onion and vinegar in a saucepan. Cook, stirring, until sauce boils and thickens. Pour over Brussels sprouts, with toasted almonds and serve.

Cook's tip: When steaming vegetables of different textures together, place the vegetable that will take longer to cook on the bottom of the steamer where it will cook more rapidly.

MOULDED TOMATO RISOTTO

Serves 6
Oven temperature 200°C, 400°F, Gas 6

- ☐ **3 tablespoons olive oil**
- ☐ **2 onions, chopped**
- ☐ **500 g/1 lb quick-cook brown rice**
- ☐ **440 g/14 oz canned tomatoes, undrained and mashed**
- ☐ **3 tablespoons tomato purée**
- ☐ **1 litre/1³/₄ pt boiling chicken stock**
- ☐ **90 g/3 oz butter**
- ☐ **100 g/3¹/₂ oz grated Parmesan cheese**
- ☐ **freshly ground black pepper**
- ☐ **2 tablespoons chopped fresh basil**
- ☐ **courgette (zucchini) ribbons for garnish**

1   Heat oil in a frying pan and cook onions until golden. Add rice, tossing to coat grains. Pour in combined tomatoes, tomato purée and boiling stock. Stir over heat until rice is cooked and all of the liquid has been absorbed.

2   Fold through butter, Parmesan, black pepper to taste and basil. Spoon into a well-greased ovenproof bowl. Cover and bake for 10-15 minutes. Turn out onto a serving plate and decorate top with courgette (zucchini) ribbons.

Cook's tip: To make courgette (zucchini) ribbons, cut long thin slices from top to base of courgette (zucchini) using a vegetable peeler.

Right: Moulded Tomato Risotto
Above: Brussels Sprouts and Almonds in Tangy Sauce

chapter nine

SWEET REWARDS

Whether as an occasional
treat or an everyday occurrence,
dessert is the crowning glory of any
meal. Next time you are considering
what to give the family for dessert ,
why not try Turkish Syllabub or
Orange and Lemon Delicious
Pudding? The range of recipes
in this chapter ensures that
you never have to wonder
about what to serve
for dessert again.

Sour Cream Apple Pie

SOUR CREAM APPLE PIE

Serves 8
Oven temperature 200°C, 400°F, Gas 6

- ☐ **315 g/10 oz prepared sweet shortcrust pastry**
- ☐ **2 tablespoons apricot jam**

APPLE FILLING
- ☐ **75 g/2¹/₂ oz butter**
- ☐ **3 Granny Smith apples, cored, peeled and sliced**
- ☐ **2 tablespoons brown sugar**

CARAMEL SAUCE
- ☐ **60 g/2 oz sugar**
- ☐ **4 teaspoons water**
- ☐ **60 mL/2 fl oz cream (double)**
- ☐ **30 g/1 oz butter, cut into small pieces**

SOUR CREAM TOPPING
- ☐ **500 g/1 lb sour cream**
- ☐ **4 teaspoons caster sugar**
- ☐ **1 teaspoon vanilla essence**

1   Roll pastry out and line a greased, deep 18 cm/7 in fluted flan tin with a removable base. Prick pastry base with a fork. Line pastry case with nonstick baking paper, weigh down with uncooked rice and cook for 10 minutes. Remove rice and paper and bake for 8-10 minutes longer or until pastry is golden. Place jam in a small saucepan and bring to the boil. As soon as the pastry case is cooked, brush with boiling jam and return to the oven for 3-4 minutes longer. Set pastry case aside to cool completely.

2   To make filling, melt half the butter in a large frying pan and add half the apple slices, sprinkle with half the sugar and cook, turning slices until they are tender. Remove apple slices to a plate and repeat with remaining butter, apple slices and sugar. Layer apple slices evenly in pastry case.

3   To make sauce, place sugar and water in a heavy-based saucepan and cook over a low heat, stirring until sugar dissolves. Bring to the boil and boil without stirring for 8 minutes or until mixture is a caramel colour. Occasionally brush down sides of pan with a pastry brush dipped in cold water. Reduce heat, stir in cream and continue stirring until sauce is smooth. Mix in butter and set aside to cool slightly. Using a large spoon, drizzle caramel over apples in pastry case.

4   To make topping, place sour cream, sugar and vanilla essence in a bowl and mix to combine. Spoon sour cream mixture over apples and spread out carefully, using the back of a spoon, taking mixture just to rim of pie. Reduce oven temperature to 180°C/350°F/Gas 4 and bake pie for 5-7 minutes. Allow to cool at room temperature, then refrigerate for several hours or overnight before serving.

RASPBERRY MOUSSE FLAN

Serves 8
Oven temperature 200°C, 400°F, Gas 6

ALMOND PASTRY
- ☐ **155 g/5 oz flour**
- ☐ **2 tablespoons caster sugar**
- ☐ **15 g/¹/₂ oz ground almonds**
- ☐ **125 g/4 oz butter, cut into small pieces**
- ☐ **1 egg yolk, lightly beaten**
- ☐ **2-3 tablespoons water, chilled**

RASPBERRY MOUSSE FILLING
- ☐ **90 g/3 oz raspberries**
- ☐ **2 eggs, separated**
- ☐ **60 g/2 oz caster sugar**
- ☐ **125 mL/4 fl oz cream (double), whipped**
- ☐ **8 teaspoons gelatine dissolved in 125 mL/4 fl oz hot water, cooled to room temperature**
- ☐ **500 g/1 lb mixed berries of your choice**

1   To make pastry, place flour, sugar and almonds in a food processor and process to combine. Add butter and process until mixture resembles fine breadcrumbs. With machine running, add egg yolk and enough water to form a soft dough. Turn pastry onto a floured surface and knead lightly until smooth. Wrap in plastic food wrap and refrigerate for 30 minutes.

2   Roll out pastry on a lightly floured surface and line a lightly greased, deep 20 cm/8 in fluted flan tin with a removable base. Refrigerate for 15 minutes. Line pastry case with nonstick baking paper, weigh down with uncooked rice and bake for 10 minutes. Remove rice and paper and cook for 10 minutes longer or until pastry case is lightly browned and cooked.

3   To make filling, place raspberries in a food processor or blender and purée. Push purée through a sieve, to remove seeds. Place egg yolks and sugar in a bowl and beat until thick and creamy. Place egg whites in a separate bowl and beat until stiff peaks form.

4   Fold whipped cream and egg whites into the egg yolk mixture. Then fold 4

tablespoons of egg mixture into raspberry purée. Fold half the gelatine mixture into the raspberry mixture and the remainder into the egg mixture.

5   Place large spoonfuls of egg mixture into pastry case, then top with small spoonfuls of raspberry mixture. Repeat until both mixtures are used and pastry case is two-thirds full. Run a spatula through the mousse to swirl the mixtures. Refrigerate for 2 hours or until mousse is firm. Just prior to serving, top the flan with mixed berries.

STEAMED PEAR PUDDING WITH CARAMEL SAUCE

Serves 8

- ☐ 3 pears, cored, peeled and finely chopped
- ☐ 125 mL/4 fl oz water
- ☐ 1¹/₂ tablespoons sugar
- ☐ 45 g/1¹/₂ oz butter
- ☐ 3 tablespoons caster sugar
- ☐ 2 eggs
- ☐ 90 g/3 oz self-raising flour, sifted
- ☐ 4 tablespoons milk

CARAMEL SAUCE
- ☐ 185 g/6 oz sugar
- ☐ 3 tablespoons water
- ☐ 45 g/1¹/₂ oz unsalted butter, cut into pieces
- ☐ 155 mL/5 fl oz cream (double)

1 Place pears, water and sugar in a saucepan and cook over a medium heat for 10 minutes, or until pears are just tender. Remove pan from heat and set aside to cool.

2 Place butter and caster sugar in a bowl and beat until light and fluffy. Add eggs one at a time, beating well after each addition. Sift flour over mixture and fold in with milk.

3 Strain pears and fold into batter. Pour batter into a greased 1.5 litre/2¹/₂ pt capacity pudding basin. Cover with a round of lightly greased baking paper, then aluminium foil and pudding basin lid.

4 Place basin in a large saucepan with enough boiling water to come halfway up the side of the basin and bring to the boil. Reduce heat and simmer for 1¹/₂ hours or until pudding is firm, replacing water if necessary as the pudding cooks. Allow to stand 5 minutes before turning out.

5 To make sauce, place sugar and water in a heavy-based saucepan and cook over a medium heat, stirring, until sugar dissolves and mixture caramelises and is a deep amber colour. Remove pan from heat, add butter a piece at a time, stirring until melted. Return sauce to heat, pour in cream and cook, stirring, for 2 minutes. Remove from heat and set aside to cool. Serve sauce with pudding.

ROCKY ROAD ICE CREAM

Serves 6

- ☐ 1 litre/1³/₄ pt vanilla ice cream, softened
- ☐ 2 x 60 g/2 oz chocolate-coated Turkish delight bars, chopped
- ☐ 10 pink marshmallows, chopped
- ☐ 5 white marshmallows, chopped
- ☐ 4 tablespoons shredded coconut, toasted
- ☐ 6 red glacé cherries, chopped
- ☐ 6 green glacé cherries, chopped
- ☐ 2 x 45 g/1¹/₂ oz chocolate-coated scorched peanut bars, chopped

Place ice cream in a large mixing bowl, fold in Turkish delight, pink and white marshmallows, coconut, red and green cherries and peanut bars. Spoon mixture into a freezerproof container, cover and freeze until firm.

Serving suggestion: Place scoops of ice cream in individual bowls and serve with wafers.

Raspberry Mousse Flan

BRANDY GRAPE FLAN

Serves 8
Oven temperature 200°C, 400°F, Gas 6

- ☐ **155 g/5 oz prepared shortcrust pastry, thawed**

GRAPE FILLING
- ☐ **250 g/8 oz cream cheese**
- ☐ **2 tablespoons bottled lemon butter**
- ☐ **1 tablespoon icing sugar**
- ☐ **500 g/1 lb large green grapes**

APRICOT GLAZE
- ☐ **3 tablespoons apricot jam**
- ☐ **1¹/₂ tablespoons water**
- ☐ **2 teaspoons brandy**

1   Line a lightly greased 20 cm/8 in flan tin with pastry. Line pastry case with nonstick baking paper, weigh down with uncooked rice and bake for 10 minutes. Remove rice and paper. Reduce temperature to 180°C/350°F/Gas 4 and bake 15-20 minutes longer or until pastry is lightly browned. Cool. Set aside to cool.
2   To make filling, place cream cheese in a bowl and beat until soft. Mix in lemon butter and icing sugar. Spread cream cheese mixture over the base of pastry case.
3   Wash grapes and separate from stems. Cut in half and remove seeds. Arrange grapes in a decorative pattern over cream cheese mixture.
4   To make glaze, heat apricot jam and water in a saucepan, stirring until jam melts. Push through a sieve. Stir in brandy and cool slightly. Brush glaze over grapes and chill flan until ready to serve.

Line a lightly greased 20 cm/8 in flan tin with pastry.

Arrange grapes in a decorative pattern over cream cheese mixture.

Brush glaze over grapes and chill flan until ready to serve.

198

RUM BREAD AND BUTTER PUDDING

This is an exotic version of a family favourite. Allowing the pudding to stand for an hour before baking will give a light crusty dessert.

Serves 6
Oven temperature 180°C, 350°F, Gas 4

- ☐ **3 tablespoons sultanas**
- ☐ **3 tablespoons raisins**
- ☐ **2 tablespoons dark rum**
- ☐ **3 eggs**
- ☐ **3 egg yolks**
- ☐ **170 g/5¹/₂ oz caster sugar**
- ☐ **750 mL/1¹/₄ pt milk**
- ☐ **250 mL/8 fl oz cream (double)**
- ☐ **2 teaspoons vanilla essence**
- ☐ **1 tablespoon finely grated orange rind**
- ☐ **12 slices buttered bread, crusts removed and slices cut into quarters**
- ☐ **1 teaspoon ground cinnamon**

1   Place sultanas and raisins in a bowl, pour over rum and set aside to soak for 30 minutes.

2   Combine eggs, egg yolks and 100 g/ 3¹/₂ oz sugar in a mixing bowl and beat until light and fluffy. Place milk and cream in a saucepan and cook over a medium heat, stirring constantly, until almost boiling. Remove pan from heat and set aside to cool slightly. Pour milk mixture into egg mixture and beat until combined. Blend in vanilla essence and orange rind.

3   Place one-third of the bread slices, buttered side up, in a greased 2 litre/3¹/₂ pt capacity ovenproof dish. Top with half sultana mixture. Repeat with remaining bread and sultana mixture, finishing with a layer of bread, buttered side facing up.

4   Pour egg mixture evenly over bread in dish. Combine remaining sugar with cinnamon and sprinkle over pudding. Bake for 1 hour or until a knife inserted in the centre comes out clean.

Cook's note: The rum may be omitted from this pudding.

Rum Bread and Butter Pudding

ORANGE AND LEMON DELICIOUS PUDDING

*One of those magic puddings –
as the pudding cooks it separates
to give a layer of fluffy sponge over a
tangy citrus sauce.*

Serves 6
Oven temperature 180°C, 350°F, Gas 4

- [ ] **220 g/7 oz caster sugar**
- [ ] **125 g/4 oz butter, softened**
- [ ] **60 g/2 oz self-raising flour**
- [ ] **1 tablespoon finely grated lemon rind**
- [ ] **1 tablespoon finely grated orange rind**
- [ ] **2 tablespoons lemon juice**
- [ ] **2 tablespoons orange juice**
- [ ] **2 eggs, separated**
- [ ] **250 mL/8 fl oz milk**

1 Place sugar and butter in a bowl and beat until light and fluffy. Mix in flour, lemon rind, orange rind, lemon juice and orange juice.

2 Place egg yolks and milk in a small bowl and whisk to combine. Mix into citrus mixture.

3 Beat egg whites until stiff peaks form then fold into batter. Spoon into a greased 1 litre/1³/₄ pt capacity ovenproof dish. Place ovenproof dish in a baking dish with enough boiling water to come halfway up the side of ovenproof dish. Bake for 45 minutes or until pudding is cooked. Serve hot with cream or ice cream.

Orange and Lemon Delicious Pudding

LIQUEUR FRUIT SALAD

Serves 4

- [ ] ½ pineapple, cubed
- [ ] 440 g/14 oz canned lychees, drained
- [ ] 250 g/8 oz raspberries
- [ ] 4 mandarins, segmented
- [ ] 125 mL/4 fl oz champagne or sparkling white wine, chilled

ORANGE SYRUP
- [ ] 1 tablespoon finely grated orange rind
- [ ] 1 tablespoon finely grated lemon rind
- [ ] 125 g/4 oz caster sugar
- [ ] 250 mL/8 fl oz water
- [ ] 125 mL/4 fl oz fresh orange juice
- [ ] 60 mL/2 fl oz orange-flavoured liqueur
- [ ] 2 tablespoons passion fruit pulp

1 To make syrup, place orange rind, lemon rind, sugar and water in a saucepan and cook over a low heat until sugar dissolves. Bring to the boil and boil rapidly for 5 minutes. Remove from heat and set aside to cool completely. Strain syrup and discard rinds. Stir in orange juice, liqueur and passion fruit pulp.
2 Place pineapple, lychees, raspberries and mandarin segments in a bowl, pour syrup over fruit, cover and set aside to macerate overnight. To serve, drain fruit, place in a serving bowl and pour champagne over.

COFFEE SPONGE PUFFS

Serves 6
Oven temperature 180°C, 350°F, Gas 4

- [ ] 2 eggs
- [ ] 125 g/4 oz caster sugar
- [ ] 4 tablespoons self-raising flour, sifted
- [ ] 4 tablespoons cornflour
- [ ] icing sugar

COFFEE CUSTARD FILLING
- [ ] 250 mL/8 fl oz milk
- [ ] 1 tablespoon instant coffee powder
- [ ] 3 egg yolks
- [ ] 60 g/2 oz caster sugar
- [ ] 1½ tablespoons flour
- [ ] 125 mL/4 fl oz cream (double), whipped

1 Place eggs in a mixing bowl and beat until thick and creamy. Add sugar a little at a time, beating well after each addition until mixture thickens and sugar dissolves. This will take about 10 minutes.
2 Sift flour and cornflour together then fold through egg mixture in two batches. Spoon heaped tablespoons of mixture onto lightly greased baking trays, leaving about 5 cm/2 in between each puff. Bake for 8-10 minutes or until puffs are golden. Transfer puffs to a wire rack to cool.
3 To make filling, place milk and coffee in a saucepan and heat until almost boiling. Whisk together egg yolks, sugar and flour until thick and creamy. Gradually whisk milk mixture into egg mixture. Return mixture to saucepan and heat, stirring, until mixture thickens. Remove from heat and set aside to cool. Fold whipped cream through mixture.
4 Spread filling over flat side of half the puffs and top with remaining puffs. Dust tops with icing sugar and serve immediately.

CASSATA SICILIANA

A simple do-ahead dinner party dessert that looks spectacular when decorated with extra glacé fruit. It is best prepared a day before serving.

Serves 8

- [ ] 500 g/1 lb ricotta cheese
- [ ] 250 g/8 oz sugar
- [ ] 2 tablespoons chopped pistachios
- [ ] 3 tablespoons chopped glacé fruit
- [ ] ¼ teaspoon ground cinnamon
- [ ] 60 g/2 oz dark chocolate, grated
- [ ] 2 tablespoons almond-flavoured liqueur
- [ ] 20 cm/8 in round sponge cake, cut into 1 cm/¼ in slices

ALMOND TOPPING
- [ ] 250 mL/8 fl oz cream (double)
- [ ] 1 tablespoon almond-flavoured liqueur
- [ ] selection glacé fruit

1 Beat ricotta and sugar together until light and fluffy. Divide mixture in half. Fold pistachios and chopped fruit through half of mixture. Mix cinnamon, chocolate and liqueur into other half. Cover and set aside.
2 Line base and sides of a 20 cm (8 in) bowl or mould with plastic food wrap, then with three-quarters of cake slices. Fill with ricotta mixture and cover with remaining cake. Cover and freeze for 2 hours or overnight.
3 When mixture is set pour chocolate mixture over, return to freezer and freeze until set.
4 To make topping, whip cream and liqueur together until soft peaks form. Just prior to serving, turn out cassata, spread completely with cream and decorate with glacé fruit.

SICILIAN ROLL

Serves 8
Oven temperature 180°C, 350°F, Gas 4

- [ ] 3 eggs
- [ ] 125 g/4 oz caster sugar
- [ ] 90 g/3 oz self-raising flour, sifted
- [ ] 2 tablespoons hot milk
- [ ] 125 mL/4 fl oz cream (double), whipped
- [ ] 60 g/2 oz chocolate, grated

RICOTTA FILLING
- [ ] 250 g/8 oz ricotta cheese
- [ ] 4 tablespoons icing sugar
- [ ] ½ teaspoon vanilla essence
- [ ] 1 tablespoon crème de cacao
- [ ] 30 g/1 oz chocolate, grated
- [ ] 1 tablespoon chopped glacé fruit

1 Place eggs in a large mixing bowl and beat until thick and creamy. Add sugar a little at a time, beating well after each addition until sugar dissolves and mixture thickens. Fold in flour alternately with milk.
2 Spoon mixture into a lightly greased and lined 25 x 30 cm/10 x 12 in shallow cake tin and bake for 12-15 minutes or until firm. Turn out onto a sheet of baking paper, remove lining paper and trim edges of cake. Roll up from the narrow end, using baking paper to lift and guide roll. Stand for 5 minutes, then unroll and allow to cool.
3 To make filling, place ricotta cheese, icing sugar, vanilla and crème de cacao in a mixing bowl and beat until well combined. Fold chocolate and glacé fruit through mixture and spread over cake. Reroll and transfer to a serving platter. Spread with cream and decorate with grated chocolate.

Cassata Siciliana, Sicilian Roll, Coffee Sponge Puffs

APRICOT ALMOND
SHORTCAKE

Serves 8
Oven temperature 180°C, 350°F, Gas 4

- ☐ **125 g/4 oz butter**
- ☐ **125 g/4 oz sugar**
- ☐ **1 egg**
- ☐ **90 g/3 oz self-raising flour, sifted**
- ☐ **90 g/3 oz flour, sifted**

ALMOND APRICOT FILLING
- ☐ **45 g/1¹/₂ oz butter**
- ☐ **2 tablespoons caster sugar**
- ☐ **1 egg yolk**
- ☐ **90 g/3 oz ground almonds**
- ☐ **2 teaspoons flour**
- ☐ **440 g/14 oz canned apricots, drained**

ALMOND TOPPING
- ☐ **410 g/13 oz ground almonds**
- ☐ **5 tablespoons caster sugar**
- ☐ **6 eggs, separated**
- ☐ **2 tablespoons almond-flavoured liqueur**
- ☐ **250 g/8 oz apricot jam, warmed and sieved**

☐ **60 g/2 oz flaked almonds, toasted**

1   Place butter and sugar in a large mixing bowl and beat until light and creamy. Add egg and beat well, stir in self-raising and plain flours. Turn out onto a lightly floured surface and knead lightly until smooth. Divide mixture into two equal portions and refrigerate for 30 minutes.

2   Roll out each portion between sheets of plastic food wrap or greaseproof paper to a 20 cm/8 in circle. Press one circle dough into a greased and lined 20 cm/8 in deep cake tin.

3   To make filling, place butter, sugar and egg yolk in a small bowl and beat until light and fluffy. Stir in almonds and flour. Place apricots in a food processor or blender and process until smooth. Swirl apricots through almond mixture. Take care not to overmix. Spread mixture over dough in cake tin, leaving a small border around edge. Place second circle of dough over apricot mixture and press edges together. Brush with water and bake for 35-40 minutes. Stand 15 minutes before turning out on a wire rack to cool.

4   To make topping, place almonds and sugar in a mixing bowl. Combine egg yolks

and liqueur in a small bowl, then gradually stir into almond mixture. Remove one-third of mixture and set aside. Add 1 tablespoon of unbeaten egg white to remaining mixture and spread over sides and top of shortcake. Add a little more egg white if mixture is difficult to spread.

5   Add 2 tablespoons of unbeaten egg white to reserved almond mixture and spoon into a piping bag fitted with a large star nozzle. Pipe lines in a zigzag pattern over top and pipe small rosettes around the edge. Place cake on an oven tray and bake at 250°C/500°F/Gas 9 for 8-10 minutes or until top is lightly browned. Spoon two-thirds of jam between zigzag piping and set aside for 10 minutes to cool slightly. Spread sides with remaining jam and coat with toasted almonds. Cool cake completely before cutting.

Apricot Almond Shortcake

204

SUMMER WINE JELLY

Almost any fresh fruit can be used to make this dessert. You should avoid pineapple, pawpaw and kiwifruit as they contain an enzyme which prevents the jelly from setting.

Serves 8

- ☐ **4 apricots, stoned and halved**
- ☐ **200 g/6½ oz green grapes**
- ☐ **250 g/8 oz strawberries, hulled and halved**
- ☐ **250 g/8 oz fresh or canned cherries, stoned**
- ☐ **60 g/2 oz gelatine dissolved in 125 mL/4 fl oz hot water, cooled**
- ☐ **500 mL/16 fl oz sweet white wine**
- ☐ **500 mL/16 fl oz apple juice**
- ☐ **90 mL/3 fl oz melon liqueur or additional apple juice**

1 Place apricots, grapes, strawberries and cherries in a bowl and toss to combine.
2 Place gelatine mixture, wine, apple juice and melon liqueur or additional apple juice in a bowl and mix to combine. Pour one-quarter of the wine mixture into a lightly oiled 1 litre/1¾ pt capacity mould and top with one-quarter of the fruit. Place in refrigerator to set.
3 Repeat with remaining liquid and fruit. When jelly is set, unmould and serve garnished with extra fruit if desired.

Unmoulding a gelatine dessert: Moulded gelatine desserts need to be loosened before you try to turn them out. This is easily done by placing the mould in warm water for a few seconds. After removing mould from water dry the base and tip the mould sideways, while at the same time gently pulling the mixture away from the edge of the mould. This breaks the airlock. Rinse a serving plate with cold water and place upside down on top of the mould. Then, holding firmly, quickly turn over both mould and plate and give a sharp shake. The dessert should fall onto the plate. If it refuses to move, place a hot, wet cloth over the base of the mould for 10-20 seconds. Wetting the plate means that you can easily move the dessert if it does not land in the centre when you unmould it.

Summer Wine Jelly

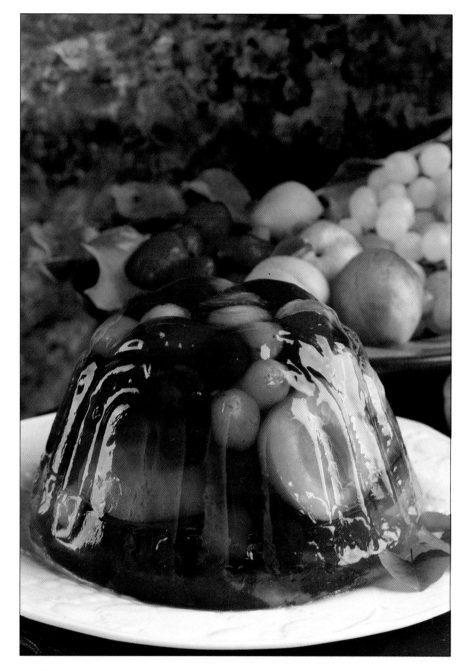

TURKISH SYLLABUB

Serve this tangy dessert on its own in pretty glass dishes, or as a topping for fruit salad.

Serves 4

- ☐ **250 mL/8 fl oz cream (double)**
- ☐ **1 tablespoon honey**
- ☐ **250 g/8 oz natural yogurt**
- ☐ **1 tablespoon raw sugar**

Place cream and honey in a bowl and whip until thick. Fold in yogurt, spoon into individual serving glasses and sprinkle with sugar. Chill for 2-3 hours before serving.

BANANA ICE CREAM

Serves 4

- ☐ **6 large ripe bananas, chopped**
- ☐ **250 mL/8 fl oz vegetable oil**
- ☐ **2 tablespoons honey**
- ☐ **6 tablespoons milk powder**
- ☐ **250 mL/8 fl oz water**
- ☐ **2 tablespoons fine carob powder**

Place bananas, oil, honey, milk powder, water and carob powder in a food processor or blender and process until smooth. Pour into a freezerproof container, cover and freeze until firm.

STRIPED ROULADE WITH APRICOT MOUSSE FILLING

This impressive roulade may look very grand but it is in fact easy to make. Follow our step-by-step recipe and see just how easy it really is.

Serves 6
Oven temperature 200°C, 400°F, Gas 6

- ☐ **60 g/2 oz self-raising flour, sifted**
- ☐ **2 tablespoons cocoa, sifted**
- ☐ **4 eggs**
- ☐ **5 tablespoons caster sugar**

APRICOT MOUSSE FILLING
- ☐ **1 tablespoon gelatine**
- ☐ **3 tablespoons apricot nectar**
- ☐ **440 g/14 oz canned apricots, drained and 3 tablespoons liquid reserved**
- ☐ **3 eggs, separated**
- ☐ **4 tablespoons caster sugar**
- ☐ **1 tablespoon brandy**
- ☐ **1 tablespoon Cointreau**
- ☐ **125 mL/4 fl oz cream (double)**

1 Place 2 tablespoons flour and cocoa in a mixing bowl and the remaining flour in another.
2 Beat eggs and sugar until thick and creamy. Divide mixture evenly between two bowls. Fold cocoa mixture through egg mixture in one bowl and fold flour mixture through the remaining egg mixture.
3 Place chocolate and plain cake batters into two separate piping bags fitted with 2 cm/³/₄ in plain nozzles. Pipe lines of chocolate mixture, 2 cm/³/₄ in apart, diagonally across a greased and lined Swiss roll tin. Then pipe plain mixture in lines between chocolate strips. Bake for 8-10 minutes, or until cake is cooked through and springy to touch.
4 Turn roulade out onto a damp teatowel sprinkled with caster sugar. Roll up with teatowel from short end and allow to cool.
5 To make filling, sprinkle gelatine over apricot nectar in a small bowl, place it over a small saucepan of simmering water and stir until gelatine dissolves. Set aside to cool at room temperature. Place apricots and reserved liquid in a food processor or blender and process until smooth. Beat egg yolks and sugar in a bowl until thick and creamy. Stir in apricot purée, gelatine

mixture, brandy and Cointreau. Beat cream until soft peaks form, fold into apricot mixture. Beat egg whites until soft peaks form, fold into apricot mixture. Refrigerate

for 2-3 hours, or until mixture is almost set. Unroll roulade and spread with filling. Reroll and refrigerate until filling is set.

Pipe lines of chocolate mixture 2 cm/³/₄ in apart diagonally across a greased and lined Swiss roll tin. Then pipe plain mixture between chocolate stripes.

Turn roulade onto a damp teatowel sprinkled with caster sugar, and roll up from short end.

Unroll roulade, spread with filling, and reroll. Refrigerate until filling is set.

RHUBARB FOOL WITH ORANGE BISCUITS

Serves 8
Oven temperature 190°C, 375°F, Gas 5

- [ ] **750 g/1½ lb rhubarb, trimmed and cut into 1 cm/½ in pieces**
- [ ] **250 g/8 oz brown sugar**
- [ ] **¼ teaspoon ground cloves**
- [ ] **½ teaspoon vanilla essence**
- [ ] **2 tablespoons lemon juice**
- [ ] **2 tablespoons orange juice**
- [ ] **185 mL/6 fl oz cream (double)**
- [ ] **100 g/3½ oz natural yogurt**

ORANGE BISCUITS
- [ ] **75 g/2½ oz unsalted butter**
- [ ] **60 g/2 oz caster sugar**
- [ ] **1 egg**
- [ ] **1½ teaspoons finely grated orange rind**
- [ ] **90 g/3 oz flour**

1 Place rhubarb, sugar, cloves, vanilla essence and lemon and orange juices in a saucepan. Bring to the boil, then reduce heat and simmer, stirring occasionally, for 15 minutes or until rhubarb is soft and mixture thick. Spoon rhubarb mixture into a bowl, cover and chill.

2 Place cream in a bowl and beat until soft peaks form. Fold yogurt into cream, then fold in chilled rhubarb mixture to give a marbled effect. Spoon into individual serving glasses and chill.

3 To make biscuits, place butter and sugar in a mixing bowl and beat until light and creamy. Add egg and orange rind and beat well to combine. Stir in flour.

4 Place teaspoons of mixture, 5 cm/2 in apart, on lightly greased baking trays and bake for 10 minutes or until golden. Cool biscuits on trays for 1 minute before removing to wire racks to cool completely. Accompany each fool with two or three biscuits.

APPLE PUDDING WITH RICOTTA CREAM

The Ricotta Cream served with this pudding is a delicious alternative to cream. You might like to try it as an accompaniment to other desserts.

Serves 4
Oven temperature 200°C, 400°F, Gas 6

- [ ] **6 green apples, cored, peeled and cut into 1 cm/½ in slices**
- [ ] **100 g/3½ oz raisins**
- [ ] **60 g/2 oz pine nuts, toasted**
- [ ] **250 mL/8 fl oz orange juice**
- [ ] **90 g/3 oz honey**

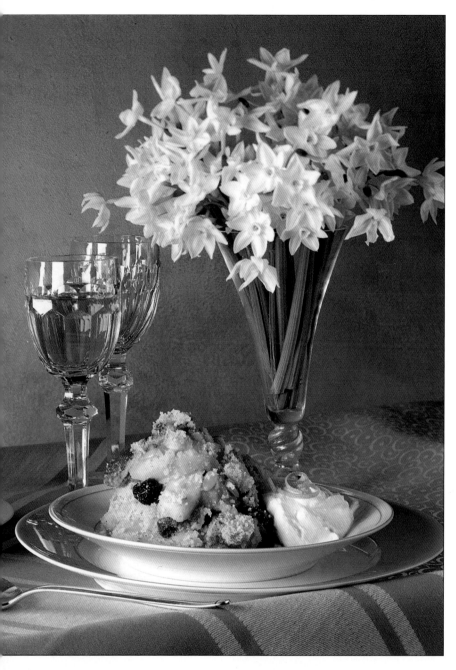

INDIVIDUAL SUMMER PUDDINGS

Fresh or frozen berries can be used to make this dessert.

Serves 4

- ☐ 100 g/3¹/₂ oz caster sugar
- ☐ 500 mL/16 fl oz water
- ☐ 875 g/1³/₄ lb mixed berries, such as raspberries, strawberries, blueberries or blackberries
- ☐ 14 slices bread, crusts removed

BERRY SAUCE
- ☐ 155 g/5 oz mixed berries, such as raspberries, strawberries, blueberries or blackberries
- ☐ 2 tablespoons icing sugar
- ☐ 1 tablespoon fresh lemon juice
- ☐ 2 tablespoons water

1   Place sugar and water in a saucepan and cook over a low heat, stirring constantly, until sugar dissolves. Bring to the boil, reduce heat, add berries and simmer for 4-5 minutes or until fruit is soft, but still retains its shape. Remove from heat. Drain, reserving liquid, and set aside to cool.

2   Cut 8 circles of bread with a pastry cutter. Line the base of four 125 mL/4 fl oz capacity ramekins with 4 rounds of the bread. Cut remaining bread slices into fingers and line the sides of ramekins, trimming bread to fit if necessary. Spoon fruit into ramekins and enough reserved liquid to moisten bread well, then cover with remaining bread circles. Reserve any remaining liquid. Cover tops of ramekins with aluminium foil, top with a weight, and refrigerate overnight.

3   To make sauce, place berries, icing sugar, lemon juice and water in a food processor or blender and process until puréed. Push mixture through a sieve to remove seeds and chill until required.

4   Turn puddings onto individual serving plates, spoon sauce over or pass separately.

Serving suggestion: Garnish with additional berries and natural yogurt.

- ☐ ¹/₂ teaspoon ground cinnamon
- ☐ 6 whole cloves
- ☐ 1 tablespoon finely grated orange rind
- ☐ 60 g/2 oz ground almonds

RICOTTA CREAM
- ☐ 100 g/3¹/₂ oz fresh ricotta cheese
- ☐ 100 g/3¹/₂ oz cottage cheese
- ☐ 1-2 tablespoons milk
- ☐ 1-2 tablespoons caster sugar

1   Layer apples, raisins and pine nuts in a shallow ovenproof dish. Pour over orange juice, drizzle with honey, then sprinkle with cinnamon, cloves, orange rind and almonds. Cover dish with aluminium foil and bake for 35-40 minutes or until apples are tender.

2   To make cream, place ricotta and cottage cheese in a food processor or blender and process until smooth. Add a little milk if the mixture is too thick and sweeten with sugar to taste.

Serving suggestion: Serve this dessert hot or cold with a little Ricotta Cream.

Left: Individual Summer Puddings
Above: Apple Pudding with Ricotta Cream, Rhubarb Fool with Orange Biscuits

BANANA FRITTERS WITH CARAMEL SAUCE

Fruit fritters are always popular, especially with children. You might like to make these using other fruits, such as apples, peaches or canned pineapple rings.

Serves 4

- [ ] 4 large firm bananas, cut in half then split lengthwise
- [ ] 2 tablespoons lime juice
- [ ] oil for cooking

BATTER
- [ ] 125 g/4 oz self-raising flour, sifted
- [ ] 1 egg, lightly beaten
- [ ] 125 mL/4 fl oz milk
- [ ] 2 tablespoons caster sugar
- [ ] 1 egg white

CARAMEL SAUCE
- [ ] 125 g/4 oz sugar
- [ ] 125 mL/4 fl oz water
- [ ] 125 mL/4 fl oz cream (double)
- [ ] 2 teaspoons whisky (optional)

1   To make batter, place flour in a mixing bowl and make a well in the centre. Combine egg, milk and caster sugar and mix into flour mixture to make a batter of a smooth consistency. Set aside to stand for 10 minutes.

2   To make sauce, place sugar and water in a saucepan and cook over a low heat, stirring constantly, until sugar dissolves. Bring to the boil, then reduce heat and simmer, without stirring, for 5 minutes or until mixture is golden.

3   Remove pan from heat and carefully stir in cream and whisky, if using. Return pan to a low heat and cook, stirring carefully, until combined. Remove pan from heat and set aside to cool.

4   Beat egg white until soft peaks form, then fold into batter.

5   Heat oil in a large saucepan. Brush bananas with lime juice and dip in batter to coat. Drain off excess batter and cook bananas in hot oil for 2-3 minutes or until golden. Drain on absorbent kitchen paper. Serve immediately with sauce.

FRUITY BREAD AND BUTTER PUDDING

The fruitiest bread and butter pudding you will ever have. This version of the traditional English pudding uses sultanas, apples and fruit loaf to make it extra fruity.

Serves 8
Oven temperature 180°C, 350°F, Gas 4

- ☐ **60 g/2 oz butter**
- ☐ **90 g/3 oz brown sugar**
- ☐ **90 g/3 oz sultanas**
- ☐ **¹/₂ teaspoon ground cinnamon**
- ☐ **440 g/14 oz canned sliced apples**
- ☐ **12 thick slices fruit loaf, buttered and crusts removed**
- ☐ **3 eggs**
- ☐ **310 mL/10 fl oz milk**
- ☐ **185 mL/6 fl oz cream (double)**
- ☐ **¹/₂ teaspoon vanilla essence**

1   Melt butter in a frying pan and add sugar and cook over a medium heat, stirring constantly, until sugar dissolves. Stir in sultanas, cinnamon and apples, toss to combine and cook for 1-2 minutes longer. Remove pan from heat and set aside to cool.

2   Cut bread slices into triangles and arrange one-third, buttered side up, in the base of a greased ovenproof dish. Top with half the apple mixture and another layer of bread triangles. Spoon over remaining apple mixture and top with bread triangles and arrange remaining slices around the edges.

3   Place eggs, milk, cream and vanilla essence in a mixing bowl and beat until well combined. Pour carefully over bread and apples in dish. Place dish in a baking dish with enough water to come halfway up the sides of ovenproof dish. Bake for 45-50 minutes or until pudding is firm and top is golden.

JAFFA SELF-SAUCING PUDDING

Chocolate and orange combine in this recipe to make the most wonderful self-saucing pudding you will ever taste.

Serves 8
Oven temperature 180°C, 350°F, Gas 4

- ☐ **125 g/4 oz butter**
- ☐ **2 teaspoons finely grated orange rind**
- ☐ **170 g/5¹/₂ oz caster sugar**
- ☐ **2 eggs**
- ☐ **100 g/3¹/₂ oz chocolate chips**
- ☐ **185 g/6 oz self-raising flour, sifted**
- ☐ **125 mL/4 fl oz orange juice**

CHOCOLATE SAUCE
- ☐ **30 g/1 oz cocoa powder**
- ☐ **100 g/3¹/₂ oz caster sugar**
- ☐ **375 mL/12 fl oz boiling water**

1   Place butter and orange rind in a large mixing bowl and beat until light and fluffy. Gradually add sugar, beating well after each addition until mixture is creamy.

2   Beat in eggs one at a time. Toss chocolate chips in flour, then fold flour mixture and orange juice, alternately, into batter. Spoon batter into a greased ovenproof dish.

3   Sift together cocoa powder and sugar over batter in dish, then carefully add boiling water. Bake for 40 minutes or until pudding is firm.

Fruity Bread and Butter Pudding, Banana Fritters with Caramel Sauce, Jaffa Self-saucing Pudding

PEAR AND WALNUT UPSIDE-DOWN PUDDING

Serves 8
Oven temperature 180°C, 350°F, Gas 4

- ☐ **3 tablespoons demerara sugar**
- ☐ **2 x 440 g/14 oz canned pear halves, drained and 250 mL/8 fl oz syrup reserved**
- ☐ **8 red glacé cherries, halved**
- ☐ **250 g/8 oz butter, softened**
- ☐ **4 eggs**
- ☐ **250 g/8 oz self-raising flour**
- ☐ **220 g/7 oz caster sugar**
- ☐ **125 g/4 oz chopped walnuts**
- ☐ **3 tablespoons maple syrup**

1   Sprinkle base of a greased and lined, deep 23 cm/9 in round cake tin with demerara sugar. Arrange pears and cherries over base.

2   Place butter, eggs, flour and caster sugar in food processor and process until smooth. Stir in walnuts. Carefully spoon batter over pears and cherries in tin and bake for 1-1¼ hours, or until cooked when tested with a skewer.

3   Place maple syrup and reserved pear juice in a small saucepan and cook over a medium heat until syrup is reduced by half.

4   Turn pudding onto a serving plate and pour syrup over. Serve hot or warm with cream or ice cream if desired.

Sprinkle base of cake tin with demerara sugar. Arrange pears and cherries over base.

Carefully spoon batter over pears and cherries in tin.

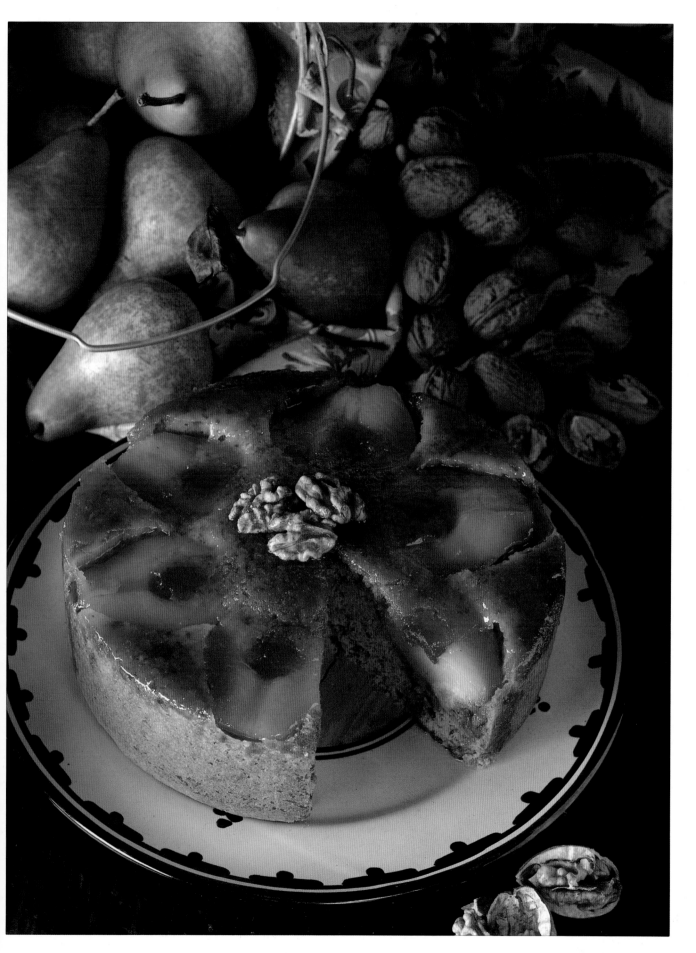

CREAMY BERRY RICE

Serves 4

- [ ] **100 g/3½ oz short grain rice**
- [ ] **125 g/4 oz blueberries**
- [ ] **125 g/4 oz raspberries**
- [ ] **4 tablespoons natural yogurt**
- [ ] **3 tablespoons berry-flavoured yogurt**
- [ ] **185 mL/6 fl oz evaporated milk**
- [ ] **1 tablespoon honey**
- [ ] **½ teaspoon ground mixed spice**

1   Cook rice in a large saucepan of boiling water for 10-12 minutes, or until tender. Drain and rinse under cold running water.
2   Place rice, blueberries, raspberries, natural yogurt, berry-flavoured yogurt, evaporated milk, honey and mixed spice in a bowl and mix to combine. Spoon into individual serving dishes and chill.

Variation: You might like to use chopped drained, canned fruits such peaches, pears or apricots in place of the berries and a complementary-flavoured fruit yogurt in place of the berry yogurt.

CHERRY PEACH CRUMBLES

Serves 4
Oven temperature 180°C, 350°F, Gas 4

- [ ] **440 g/14 oz canned pitted black cherries, drained and 125 mL/ 4 fl oz juice reserved**
- [ ] **440 g/14 oz canned sliced peaches, drained and 125 mL/ 4 fl oz juice reserved**
- [ ] **2 teaspoons cornflour blended with 2 tablespoons cherry brandy**

ALMOND TOPPING
- [ ] **60 g/2 oz crushed macaroons**
- [ ] **1 tablespoon brown sugar**
- [ ] **2 tablespoons chopped flaked almonds**

1   Spoon cherries and peaches into four individual ovenproof dishes. Place reserved cherry and peach juices and cornflour mixture into a saucepan and cook over a medium heat, stirring constantly, until mixture thickens slightly. Pour over fruit.
2   To make topping, place macaroons, sugar and almonds in a bowl and mix to combine. Sprinkle topping over fruit and bake for 10-15 minutes or until topping is golden and fruit is heated through.

ALMOND CHEESECAKE

Serves 8
Oven temperature 150°C, 300°F, Gas 2

- [ ] **170 g/5½ oz caster sugar**
- [ ] **60 g/2 oz butter, softened**
- [ ] **500 g/1 lb cream cheese**
- [ ] **3 tablespoons flour, sifted**
- [ ] **2 tablespoons honey**
- [ ] **5 eggs, separated**
- [ ] **125 mL/4 fl oz cream (double)**
- [ ] **1 teaspoon vanilla essence**
- [ ] **75 g/2½ oz blanched almonds, finely chopped**

BROWN SUGAR TOPPING
- [ ] **3 tablespoons brown sugar**
- [ ] **3 tablespoons finely chopped blanched almonds**
- [ ] **1 teaspoon ground cinnamon**

1   To make topping, place brown sugar, almonds and cinnamon in a bowl and mix to combine. Set aside.
2   Place caster sugar and butter in a bowl and beat until light and fluffy. Add cream cheese and beat until mixture is creamy. Add flour, honey and egg yolks and beat well to combine, then fold in cream and vanilla. Place egg whites in a bowl and beat until stiff peaks form. Fold egg whites and almonds into cream cheese mixture.
3   Spoon into a greased and lined 25 cm/ 1 in springform tin. Sprinkle with topping and cook for 1½ hours or until just firm. Leave cheesecake to cool in turned off oven.

Cook's note: This cheesecake will sink a little on cooling.

APPLE AND RHUBARB CRUMBLE

Serves 4
Oven temperature 180°C, 350°F, Gas 4

- [ ] **8 stalks rhubarb, cut into 5 cm/ 2 in pieces**
- [ ] **4 cooking apples, cored, peeled and sliced**
- [ ] **100 g/3½ oz caster sugar**
- [ ] **125 mL/4 fl oz water**
- [ ] **3 tablespoons orange juice**

HAZELNUT CRUMBLE
- [ ] **100 g/3½ oz ground hazelnuts**
- [ ] **45 g/1½ oz rolled oats**
- [ ] **3 tablespoons desiccated coconut**
- [ ] **4 tablespoons flour**
- [ ] **3 tablespoons brown sugar**
- [ ] **¼ teaspoon ground cinnamon**
- [ ] **90 g/3 oz butter, chopped into small pieces**

1   Place rhubarb, apples, caster sugar, water and orange juice in a saucepan and cook over a medium heat, stirring constantly, until sugar dissolves. Bring to the boil, then reduce heat, cover and simmer for 10 minutes or until fruit is tender. Spoon fruit mixture into a 750 mL/1¼ pt capacity ovenproof dish.
2   To make crumble, combine hazelnuts, oats, coconut, flour, brown sugar and cinnamon in a bowl. Rub in butter using fingertips until mixture resembles coarse breadcrumbs. Sprinkle crumble over fruit mixture and bake for 20-25 minutes.

COLLEGE PUDDING

College Pudding, the first pudding to be boiled in a cloth, was served to Cambridge University students in 1617.

Serves 4

- [ ] **3 tablespoons strawberry jam**
- [ ] **60 g/2 oz butter, softened**
- [ ] **3 tablespoons caster sugar**
- [ ] **1 egg, lightly beaten**
- [ ] **½ teaspoon vanilla essence**
- [ ] **125 g/4 oz flour**
- [ ] **1 teaspoon baking powder**
- [ ] **4 tablespoons milk**

1   Place jam in the base of a greased and base-lined 1 litre/1¾ pt pudding basin.
2   Place butter and sugar in a mixing bowl and beat until creamy. Add egg and vanilla essence and beat until light and fluffy.
3   Sift together flour and baking powder. Fold flour mixture and milk, alternately, into egg mixture. Spoon batter into prepared basin.
4   Cover top of pudding with a greased round of baking paper, then seal with lid. Place basin in a large saucepan with enough boiling water to come halfway up the sides of basin. Cook over a medium heat for 1½ hours or until cooked when tested with a skewer. Add more boiling water to pan during cooking, if necessary.

Almond Cheesecake, Apple and Rhubarb Crumble, College Pudding

TRIPLE-CHOCOLATE TERRINE

This wonderful dessert fulfils every chocoholic's dream. It takes a little time to prepare, but is well worth the effort.

Serves 10
Oven temperature 180°C, 350°F, Gas 4

BUTTER CAKE
- ☐ **125 g/4 oz butter**
- ☐ **1 teaspoon vanilla essence**
- ☐ **100 g/3¹/₂ oz caster sugar**
- ☐ **2 eggs**
- ☐ **125 g/4 oz self-raising flour, sifted**
- ☐ **90 mL/3 fl oz milk**

DARK CHOCOLATE FUDGE FILLING
- ☐ **125 g/4 oz butter**
- ☐ **2 tablespoons icing sugar**
- ☐ **90 g/3 oz dark chocolate, melted and cooled**
- ☐ **250 mL/8 fl oz cream (double), chilled**

MILK CHOCOLATE MOUSSE
- ☐ **200 g/6¹/₂ oz milk chocolate, chopped**
- ☐ **125 g/4 oz unsalted butter**
- ☐ **2 eggs**
- ☐ **2 tablespoons caster sugar**
- ☐ **250 mL/8 fl oz cream (double)**
- ☐ **1 tablespoon dark rum**
- ☐ **6 teaspoons gelatine dissolved in 2 tablespoons hot water, cooled**

WHITE CHOCOLATE GLAZE
- ☐ **250 g/8 oz white chocolate**
- ☐ **100 g/3¹/₂ oz unsalted butter**

1   To make cake, place butter and vanilla essence in a mixing bowl and beat until light and fluffy. Gradually add sugar, beating well after each addition, until mixture is creamy. Beat in eggs one at a time. Fold flour and milk, alternately, into butter mixture. Spoon mixture into a greased and lined 11 x 21 cm/4¹/₂ x 8¹/₂ in loaf tin and bake for 20-25 minutes or until cooked when tested with a skewer. Stand in tin for 5 minutes, then turn onto a wire rack to cool.

2   To make fudge filling, beat butter and icing sugar until creamy. Fold in chocolate,

then cream. Refrigerate until required.

3   To make mousse, place chocolate and butter in a saucepan and cook over a low heat, stirring constantly, until well blended. Remove from heat and set aside to cool. Place eggs and sugar in a bowl and beat until thick and creamy. Fold in chocolate mixture, cream, rum and gelatine mixture.

4   To assemble terrine, cut cake horizontally into three layers. Spread 2 layers with fudge filling and place one of these layers, filling side upwards, in the base of an 11 x 21 cm/4¹/₂ x 8¹/₂ in loaf tin lined with plastic food wrap. Top with half

the chocolate mousse and refrigerate for 10 minutes or until almost set. Place the second layer of filling-topped cake over the mousse with filling facing upwards. Top with remaining mousse and refrigerate until almost set. Place remaining cake layer on top and refrigerate until set.

5   To make glaze, place chocolate and butter in a small saucepan and cook over a low heat, stirring constantly, until well blended. Set aside and cool slightly. Turn terrine onto a wire rack, trim edges, pour glaze over to cover and allow to set.

Spread 2 layers of cake with fudge filling and place one of these layers, filling side upwards, in the base of a loaf tin lined with plastic food wrap. Top with half the chocolate mousse and refrigerate.

Turn terrine onto a wire rack, pour glaze over to cover and allow to set.

RHUBARB AND APPLE TART

Rhubarb and apple combine to give a new twist to a traditional recipe.

Serves 10
Oven temperature 200°C, 400°F, Gas 6

PASTRY
- ☐ **125 g/4 oz flour, sifted**
- ☐ **2 teaspoons icing sugar, sifted**
- ☐ **90 g/3 oz butter, cubed**
- ☐ **4 teaspoons iced water**

RHUBARB AND APPLE FILLING
- ☐ **6 stalks rhubarb, chopped**
- ☐ **2 tablespoons sugar**
- ☐ **3 green apples, cored, peeled and sliced**
- ☐ **30 g/1 oz butter**
- ☐ **125 g/4 oz cream cheese**
- ☐ **90 g/3 oz sugar**
- ☐ **1 teaspoon vanilla essence**
- ☐ **1 egg**

1 To make pastry, place flour and icing sugar in a bowl and rub in butter, using your fingertips, until mixture resembles coarse breadcrumbs. Add water and knead to a smooth dough. Wrap in plastic food wrap and refrigerate for 30 minutes.

2 Roll out pastry on a lightly floured surface and line a greased 23 cm/9 in fluted flan tin with removable base. Line pastry case with nonstick baking paper and weigh down with uncooked rice. Bake for 15 minutes. Remove rice and paper and cook for 5 minutes longer.

3 To make filling, poach or microwave rhubarb until tender. Drain well, stir in sugar and set aside to cool. Melt butter in a frying pan and cook apples for 3-4 minutes. Remove apples from pan and set aside to cool.

4 Place cream cheese, sugar, vanilla essence and egg in a bowl and beat until smooth. Spoon rhubarb into pastry case, then top with cream cheese mixture and arrange apple slices attractively on the top. Reduce oven temperature to 180°C/350°F/ Gas 4 and cook for 40-45 minutes or until filling is firm.

Cook's tip: The pastry for this tart can be made in the food processor if you wish. Place flour, icing sugar and butter in a food processor and process until mixture resembles coarse breadcrumbs. With machine running, add water and continue to process until a smooth dough forms.

COFFEE NUT PIE

This version of the traditional American Mud Pie is sure to be popular as a dessert or as a special afternoon tea treat.

Serves 6

- ☐ **220 g/7 oz plain chocolate biscuits, crushed**
- ☐ **125 g/4 oz butter, melted**

COFFEE FILLING
- ☐ **1 litre/1³/₄ pt vanilla ice cream, softened**
- ☐ **2 teaspoons instant coffee powder dissolved in 4 teaspoons hot water and cooled**

CHOC-NUT TOPPING
- ☐ **125 mL/4 fl oz evaporated milk**
- ☐ **100 g/3¹/₂ oz caster sugar**
- ☐ **200 g/6¹/₂ oz dark chocolate**
- ☐ **60 g/2 oz chopped pecans or walnuts**

1 Place crushed biscuits and butter in a bowl and mix well to combine. Press biscuit mixture into a shallow 23 cm/9 in dish.

2 To make filling, place ice cream and coffee mixture in a bowl and mix to combine. Spoon over biscuit base and place in freezer.

3 To make topping, place evaporated milk, sugar and chocolate in a saucepan and cook over a low heat, stirring, until chocolate is melted and mixture is smooth. Stir in pecans or walnuts, allow to cool, then pour topping over filling and freeze until firm.

Decorating suggestion: Top with chocolate caraques and whipped cream.

Coffee Nut Pie, Rhubarb and Apple Tart

FRENCH CHRISTMAS LOG

Serves 10
Oven temperature 180°C, 350°F, Gas 4

- ☐ **5 eggs**
- ☐ **100 g/3¹/₂ oz caster sugar**
- ☐ **60 g/2 oz dark chocolate, melted and cooled**
- ☐ **60 g/2 oz self-raising flour**
- ☐ **6 teaspoons cocoa powder**
- ☐ **icing sugar**

RUM FILLING
- ☐ **185 mL/6 fl oz cream (double)**
- ☐ **1 tablespoon icing sugar**
- ☐ **1 tablespoon dark rum**

GANACH ICING
- ☐ **185 g/6 oz dark chocolate**
- ☐ **170 mL/5¹/₂ fl oz cream (double)**
- ☐ **30 g/1 oz unsalted butter**

CHOCOLATE MUSHROOMS
- ☐ **1 egg white**
- ☐ **¹/₂ teaspoon vinegar**
- ☐ **75 g/2¹/₂ oz caster sugar**
- ☐ **1 teaspoon cornflour**
- ☐ **30 g/1 oz dark chocolate, melted**
- ☐ **1 teaspoon cocoa powder**

1   Place eggs in a mixing bowl and beat until fluffy. Gradually add sugar, beating well after each addition, until thick and creamy. Beat in chocolate. Sift together flour and cocoa powder and fold into egg mixture. Pour mixture into a greased and lined 26 x 32 cm/10¹/₂ x 12³/₄ in Swiss roll tin and bake for 10-12 minutes or until just firm. Turn cake onto a damp teatowel dusted with cocoa powder, remove baking paper and roll up cake from short end. Allow to stand for 2-3 minutes, then unroll, cover with a second damp teatowel and set aside to cool.
2   To make filling, place cream, icing sugar and rum in a mixing bowl and beat until soft peaks form. Cover and chill until required.
3   To make icing, place chocolate, cream and butter in a saucepan and cook over a low heat, stirring constantly, until mixture is well combined. Remove from heat and chill until mixture is almost set, but of a spreadable consistency. Beat mixture until thick, then chill until required.
4   To make mushrooms, place egg white and vinegar in a small mixing bowl and beat until soft peaks form. Gradually add sugar, beating well after each addition, until stiff peaks form and mixture is thick and glossy. Fold in cornflour. Spoon mixture into a piping bag fitted with a plain nozzle and pipe seven button shapes for the tops

of the mushrooms and small knobs for the stems onto a greased and lined baking tray. Reduce oven temperature to 120°C/250°F/Gas ¹/₂ and bake for 30 minutes or until meringues are crisp and dry. Allow to cool on tray, then join tops and stems, using a little melted chocolate, to make mushrooms. Sprinkle with cocoa powder.
5   To assemble log, spread cake with filling and roll up. Spread log with icing and mark with a spatula to show textured bark. Decorate with mushrooms and dust with icing sugar.

Serving suggestion: Decorate serving plate with any remaining mushrooms. Cut into slices and serve with vanilla ice cream, if desired.

ICED CHRISTMAS PUDDING

This pudding is also delicious made with chocolate ice cream in place of the vanilla.

Serves 10-12

- ☐ **60 g/2 oz sultanas**
- ☐ **60 g/2 oz currants**
- ☐ **60 g/2 oz raisins, chopped**
- ☐ **30 g/1 oz red glacé cherries, chopped**
- ☐ **30 g/1 oz green glacé cherries, chopped**
- ☐ **30 g/1 oz mixed peel**
- ☐ **60 mL/2 fl oz brandy**
- ☐ **1 litre/1³/₄ pt vanilla ice cream, softened**
- ☐ **125 mL/4 fl oz cream (double)**
- ☐ **60 g/2 oz flaked almonds, toasted**
- ☐ **30 g/1 oz chocolate chips**

1   Place sultanas, currants, raisins, red and green cherries and brandy in a bowl and mix to combine. Cover and set aside to macerate overnight.
2   Place ice cream and cream in a large bowl, stir in fruit mixture, almonds and chocolate chips and mix well to combine.
3   Spoon ice cream mixture into a 2 litre/3¹/₂ pt capacity pudding basin lined with plastic food wrap, cover and freeze until required.
4   To serve, remove covering, immerse in hot water and turn pudding onto a chilled serving plate. Serve immediately.

TRADITIONAL CHRISTMAS PUDDING

Serves 10-12

- ☐ **500 g/1 lb sultanas**
- ☐ **250 g/8 oz raisins**
- ☐ **60 g/2 oz mixed peel**
- ☐ **125 g/4 oz glacé apricots, chopped**
- ☐ **125 g/4 oz glacé cherries, halved**
- ☐ **125 g/4 oz blanched almonds**
- ☐ **185 mL/ 6 fl oz brandy**
- ☐ **250 g/8 oz butter, softened**
- ☐ **90 g/3 oz brown sugar**
- ☐ **1 tablespoon finely grated orange rind**
- ☐ **4 eggs**
- ☐ **4 teaspoons orange juice**
- ☐ **125 g/4 oz flour**
- ☐ **1 teaspoon ground cinnamon**
- ☐ **¹/₂ teaspoon ground mixed spice**
- ☐ **¹/₂ teaspoon ground nutmeg**
- ☐ **240 g/7¹/₂ oz breadcrumbs made from stale bread**

1   Combine sultanas, raisins, mixed peel, apricots, cherries, almonds and brandy in a bowl and set aside.
2   Place butter, sugar and orange rind in a large mixing bowl and beat until creamy. Add eggs one at a time, beating well after each addition. Mix in orange juice.
3   Sift together flour, cinnamon, mixed spice and nutmeg. Fold flour mixture, fruit mixture and breadcrumbs into butter mixture.
4   Spoon pudding mixture into a 2 litre/3¹/₂ pt capacity pudding basin lined with an oven bag. Seal oven bag with string, place a piece of aluminium foil over pudding and seal with pudding basin lid. Place basin in a large saucepan with enough water to come halfway up the side of the basin. Boil for 4¹/₂-5¹/₂ hours or until pudding is cooked through. Serve hot, warm or cold with whipped cream or vanilla ice cream.

Cook's tip: If the pudding is not to be eaten immediately it may be stored in the refrigerator, wrapped in the oven bag, then reheated by reboiling in the pudding basin for 1 hour.

Traditional Christmas Pudding,
French Christmas Log

RASPBERRY CHOCOLATE TRUFFLE CAKES

These rich little chocolate cakes filled with a raspberry cream and served with a bittersweet chocolate sauce are a perfect finale to any dinner party. Follow the step-by-step instructions and you will see just how easy this spectacular dessert is.

Serves 8
Oven temperature 180°C, 350°F, Gas 4

- [ ] **60 g/2 oz cocoa powder, sifted**
- [ ] **250 mL/8 fl oz boiling water**
- [ ] **125 g/4 oz butter**
- [ ] **390 g/12¹/₂ oz caster sugar**
- [ ] **1¹/₂ tablespoons raspberry jam**
- [ ] **2 eggs**
- [ ] **200 g/6¹/₂ oz self-raising flour, sifted**
- [ ] **410 g/13 oz dark chocolate, melted**
- [ ] **raspberries for garnishing**

RASPBERRY CREAM
- [ ] **125 g/4 oz raspberries, puréed and sieved**
- [ ] **125 mL/4 fl oz cream (double), whipped**

CHOCOLATE SAUCE
- [ ] **125 g/4 oz dark chocolate**
- [ ] **125 mL/4 fl oz water**
- [ ] **60 g/2 oz caster sugar**
- [ ] **1 teaspoon brandy (optional)**

1   Combine cocoa powder and boiling water. Mix to dissolve and set aside to cool.
2   Place butter, sugar and jam in a bowl and beat until light and fluffy. Beat in eggs one at a time, adding a little flour with each egg. Fold remaining flour and cocoa mixture, alternately, into creamed mixture.
3   Spoon mixture into eight lightly greased 125 mL/4 fl oz capacity ramekins or large muffin tins. Bake for 20-25 minutes or until cakes are cooked when tested with a skewer. Cool for 5 minutes then turn onto wire racks to cool. Turn cakes upside down and scoop out centre leaving a 1 cm/¹/₂ in shell. Spread each cake with chocolate to cover top and sides, then place right way up on a wire rack.
4   To make cream, fold raspberry purée into cream. Spoon cream into a piping bag fitted with a large nozzle. Carefully turn cakes upside down and pipe in cream to fill cavity. Place right way up on individual serving plates.
5   To make sauce, place chocolate and water in a small saucepan and cook over a low heat for 4-5 minutes or until chocolate melts. Add sugar and continue cooking, stirring constantly, until sugar dissolves. Bring just to the boil, then reduce heat and simmer, stirring, for 2 minutes. Set aside to cool for 5 minutes, then stir in brandy, if using. Cool sauce to room temperature.

To serve: Decorate plates with sauce.

Turn cakes upside down and scoop out centre of each cake leaving a 1 cm/ ¹/₂ in shell.

Carefully turn chocolate-coated cakes upside down and pipe in cream to fill cavity.

223

PEACH AND BLACKBERRY COBBLER

Serves 6
Oven temperature 180°C, 350°F, Gas 4

- [ ] **2 x 440 g/14 oz canned sliced peaches, drained**
- [ ] **440 g/14 oz canned blackberries, drained**
- [ ] **4 teaspoons cornflour blended with 60 mL/2 fl oz water**
- [ ] **1 tablespoon brown sugar**

COBBLER DOUGH
- [ ] **30 g/1 oz flour**
- [ ] **60 g/2 oz self-raising flour**
- [ ] **2 tablespoons caster sugar**
- [ ] **60 g/2 oz butter**
- [ ] **1 egg, lightly beaten**
- [ ] **2 teaspoons milk**

1   To make dough, sift together flour and self-raising flour into a mixing bowl. Stir in caster sugar. Rub in butter, using fingertips, until mixture resembles fine breadcrumbs. Make a well in the centre of the flour mixture and mix in egg and milk to form a soft dough.
2   Arrange peaches and blackberries in a greased, shallow ovenproof dish and pour over cornflour mixture. Drop heaped spoonfuls of batter around edge of fruit mixture and sprinkle with brown sugar. Bake for 30-35 minutes or until cobbler topping is golden.

Serving suggestion: Delicious served with fresh berries and whipped cream.

CHOCOLATE MALTED SELF-SAUCING PUDDING

This wonderful pudding makes enough for everyone to enjoy second helpings.

Serves 8
Oven temperature 180°C, 350°F, Gas 4

- [ ] **125 g/4 oz flour**
- [ ] **125 g/4 oz self-raising flour**
- [ ] **1 teaspoon baking powder**
- [ ] **3 tablespoons cocoa powder**
- [ ] **3 tablespoons malted milk powder**
- [ ] **220 g/7 oz caster sugar**
- [ ] **250 mL/8 fl oz milk**
- [ ] **2 eggs, beaten**

CHOCOLATE SAUCE
- [ ] **100 g/3 1/2 oz dark chocolate, chopped into small pieces**
- [ ] **500 mL/16 fl oz hot water**
- [ ] **30 g/1 oz butter**
- [ ] **170 g/5 1/2 oz brown sugar**
- [ ] **3 tablespoons cocoa powder, sifted**
- [ ] **2 tablespoons cornflour**
- [ ] **malted milk powder**

1   Sift together flour, self-raising flour, baking powder, cocoa powder and malted milk powder into a large bowl. Stir in caster sugar. Place milk and eggs in a separate bowl and whisk to combine. Stir milk mixture into flour mixture and mix well to combine. Spoon batter into a greased 2 litre/3 1/2 pt capacity ovenproof dish.
2   To make sauce, place chocolate, water and butter in a saucepan and cook over a low heat, stirring constantly until chocolate melts.
3   Place brown sugar, cocoa powder and cornflour in a mixing bowl, pour in chocolate mixture and mix well to combine. Spoon sauce evenly over batter and bake for 45-50 minutes or until firm. Just prior to serving dust top of pudding with malted milk powder.

RUM CHERRY CREAM

Serves 6

- [ ] **185 g/6 oz cherries, stoned and halved**
- [ ] **3 tablespoons dark rum**
- [ ] **125 g/4 oz sugar**
- [ ] **155 g/5 oz ricotta cheese**
- [ ] **375 g/12 oz cream cheese, softened**
- [ ] **75 mL/2 1/2 fl oz sour cream**

PLUM SAUCE
- [ ] **4 large dark plums, skinned, stoned and halved**
- [ ] **200 g/6 1/2 oz loganberries**
- [ ] **2 tablespoons icing sugar**

1   Place cherries, 2 tablespoons rum and 1 tablespoon sugar in a bowl and set aside to macerate for 1 hour. Drain and dry cherries on absorbent kitchen paper.
2   Press ricotta cheese through a sieve and set aside. Place cream cheese in a bowl and beat until soft and creamy. Beat in ricotta cheese, sour cream and remaining sugar and rum. Continue to beat until well combined.
3   Line six ramekins with damp muslin and half fill with cheese mixture. Arrange cherries over the mixture and top with remaining mixture. Cover and refrigerate overnight.

4   To make sauce, place plums, berries and icing sugar in a food processor or blender and process until smooth. Push purée through a sieve and refrigerate. To serve, spoon sauce onto serving plates. Turn out creams, remove muslin and place in centre of plates.

APPLE AND BERRY CRUMBLE

Blueberries have been used to make this delicious crumble, but you might like to try blackberries, raspberries or strawberries instead.

Serves 6
Oven temperature 180°C, 350°F, Gas 4

- [ ] **60 g/2 oz caster sugar**
- [ ] **125 mL/4 fl oz water**
- [ ] **4 green apples, cored, peeled and sliced**
- [ ] **440 g/14 oz canned blueberries, drained**

CRUMBLE TOPPING
- [ ] **250 g/8 oz crushed shortbread biscuits**
- [ ] **45 g/1 1/2 oz unsalted butter, softened**
- [ ] **4 tablespoons ground almonds**
- [ ] **2 tablespoons demerara sugar**
- [ ] **1/2 teaspoon ground cinnamon**
- [ ] **1 egg yolk**
- [ ] **1 1/2 tablespoons cream (double)**

1   Place sugar and water in a saucepan and cook over a medium heat, stirring constantly, until sugar dissolves. Bring to the boil, then add apples and cook over a low heat for 8-10 minutes or until apples are tender. Remove from heat and set aside to cool.
2   Drain apples and combine with blueberries. Spoon apple mixture into a greased, shallow ovenproof dish.
3   To make topping, place crushed biscuits, butter, almonds, sugar, cinnamon, egg yolk and cream in a mixing bowl and mix until just combined. Sprinkle topping over apple mixture and bake for 20-25 minutes or until golden.

Serving suggestion: This crumble is delicious served with natural yogurt or fruit-flavoured yogurt.

Apple and Berry Crumble,
Peach and Blackberry Cobbler

chapter ten

⎯⎯⎯⎯ ● ⎯⎯⎯⎯

THE FRESH OUTDOORS

Barbecues and picnics
*are a great way for family
and friends to spend time together
and enjoy each other's company
in an informal atmosphere. These
recipes are sure to make your
next outdoor meal a
great success.*

*Garlic Baked Potatoes,
Seafood Kebabs,
Curried Chicken Kebabs*

CURRIED CHICKEN KEBABS

Serves 6

- ☐ **750 g/1¹/₂ lb chicken breast fillets, skin removed, cut into 2.5 cm/1 in cubes**
- ☐ **12 skewers, lightly oiled**

LIME CURRY GLAZE
- ☐ **315 g/10 oz lime marmalade**
- ☐ **2 tablespoons Dijon mustard**
- ☐ **2 teaspoons curry powder**
- ☐ **1 tablespoon lime juice**

1   To make glaze, place marmalade, mustard, curry powder and lime juice in a small saucepan and cook over a medium heat, stirring, for 3 minutes or until ingredients are combined. Remove from heat and set aside to cool.

2   Thread chicken cubes onto skewers. Place skewers in a shallow glass or ceramic dish, spoon glaze over, cover and set aside to marinate at room temperature for 1 hour.

3   Remove chicken from glaze and reserve any remaining glaze. Cook kebabs on a lightly oiled preheated barbecue, brushing kebabs with reserved glaze and turning frequently, for 8-10 minutes or until cooked.

GARLIC BAKED POTATOES

These potatoes are the perfect accompaniment to any barbecue.

Serves 6

- ☐ **6 large potatoes, scrubbed**
- ☐ **3 teaspoons olive oil**
- ☐ **1 tablespoon finely chopped fresh rosemary**
- ☐ **freshly ground black pepper**
- ☐ **6 cloves garlic, halved**

1   Using an apple corer, carefully remove a plug from each potato, making sure not to go right through the potato. Reserve the plugs.

2   Combine oil, rosemary and black pepper to taste. Fill hole in each potato with two garlic halves and a little oil mixture. Cut off two-thirds of each plug and discard. Replace remaining plug in potato and wrap potatoes in aluminium foil. Cook potatoes on a preheated barbecue for 1 hour or until tender.

SEAFOOD KEBABS

Serves 4

- ☐ **8 mussels, removed from shells**
- ☐ **1 large white fish fillet, cut into 8 x 2 cm/³/₄ in cubes**
- ☐ **8 large uncooked prawns, shelled and deveined, tails left intact**
- ☐ **8 scallops**
- ☐ **1 salmon fillet, cut into 8 x 2 cm/³/₄ in cubes**
- ☐ **8 skewers, lightly oiled**

CHILLI LIME GLAZE
- ☐ **60 mL/2 fl oz olive oil**
- ☐ **2 fresh red chillies, seeds removed and finely chopped**
- ☐ **1 clove garlic, crushed**
- ☐ **60 mL/2 fl oz lime juice**

1   Alternately thread a mussel, a piece of white fish, a prawn, a scallop and a piece of salmon onto a skewer. Repeat with remaining seafood and skewers.

2   To make glaze, place oil, chillies, garlic and lime juice in a small bowl and mix to combine. Brush kebabs with glaze and cook on a lightly oiled preheated barbecue, turning frequently and brushing with remaining glaze, until seafood changes colour and is cooked through. Serve immediately.

GRILLED TROUT WITH APPLE STUFFING

Serves 4

- ☐ **4 small trout, cleaned with head and tail intact**
- ☐ **olive oil**

APPLE STUFFING
- ☐ **30 g/1 oz butter**
- ☐ **1 small onion, chopped**
- ☐ **1 apple, cored and finely chopped**
- ☐ **30 g/1 oz breadcrumbs, made from stale bread**
- ☐ **1 teaspoon lemon juice**
- ☐ **1 tablespoon finely chopped fresh mint**
- ☐ **2 teaspoons finely chopped fresh parsley**
- ☐ **freshly ground black pepper**

1   To make stuffing, melt butter in a frying pan, add onion and cook for 5 minutes or until transparent. Place apple and breadcrumbs in a bowl, add onion, lemon

juice, mint, parsley and black pepper to taste and mix to combine.

2   Fill cavity of each trout with stuffing. Secure openings using toothpicks and lightly brush outside of each trout with oil. Cook trout on a preheated medium barbecue for 5-8 minutes each side or until flesh flakes with tested with a fork.

SAVOURY BREAD

Garlic and herb breads are easy to make and can be prepared in advance and frozen if you wish.

Serves 8

- ☐ **1 large French stick**

FLAVOURED BUTTER
- ☐ **125 g/4 oz butter, softened**
- ☐ **2 cloves garlic crushed; or 2 tablespoons finely chopped fresh herbs – choose from rosemary, parsley, thyme, chives**
- ☐ **freshly ground black pepper**

1   Slice bread on a slight diagonal at 2 cm/³/₄ in intervals almost all the way through so that the slices remain joined at the base.

2   To make Flavoured Butter, place butter, garlic or herbs, and black pepper to taste in a food processor and process to combine.

3   Spread one side of each slice of bread with Flavoured Butter. Wrap loaf in a double thickness of aluminium foil and heat on a preheated barbecued for 15-20 minutes or until bread is hot.

MARSHMALLOW SURPRISES

Eat with care – these delicious morsels are very hot when first assembled.

Serves 10

- ☐ **20 plain biscuits**
- ☐ **20 white marshmallows**
- ☐ **20 pink marshmallows**
- ☐ **20 squares chocolate, broken into 10 pieces**

1 Top 10 biscuits with a chocolate piece.
2 Thread 1 white and 1 pink marshmallow onto a long-handled fork or skewer and toast slowly over a preheated low barbecue so that the marshmallow is hot and gooey in the centre. Using a spoon, push marshmallows onto chocolate-topped biscuits and top with remaining biscuits. Press biscuits together and eat!

PUFF TOMATO AND MUSHROOM PIZZA

This easy pizza will keep hunger pangs at bay while your food is cooking on the barbecue.

Serves 8
Oven temperature 200°C, 400°F, Gas 6

- ☐ **375 g/12 oz prepared puff pastry**
- ☐ **60 g/2 oz grated Parmesan cheese**
- ☐ **125 g/4 oz grated mozzarella cheese**
- ☐ **1 onion, finely sliced**
- ☐ **200 g/6¹/₂ oz mushrooms, sliced**
- ☐ **3 tomatoes, cut into 1 cm/¹/₂ in slices**
- ☐ **10 black olives, pitted**
- ☐ **2 teaspoons chopped fresh oregano or ¹/₂ teaspoon dried oregano**
- ☐ **2 teaspoons chopped fresh thyme, or ¹/₂ teaspoon dried thyme**

1 Roll out pastry to fit a greased 26 x 32 cm/10¹/₂ x 12³/₄ in Swiss roll tin. Sprinkle pastry with Parmesan and mozzarella cheeses, then top with onion, mushrooms, tomatoes and olives. Sprinkle with oregano and thyme.
2 Bake for 30 minutes or until pastry is puffed and golden. Serve hot, warm or cold.

Puff Tomato and Mushroom Pizza

FOIL-WRAPPED CHICKEN BREASTS

Serves 6

- [ ] **60 g/2 oz butter**
- [ ] **1 small onion, chopped**
- [ ] **1 clove garlic, crushed**
- [ ] **125 g/4 oz breadcrumbs, made from stale bread**
- [ ] **3 tablespoons finely chopped fresh parsley**
- [ ] **freshly ground black pepper**
- [ ] **6 chicken breast fillets, skinned and pounded**

1   Melt 15 g/½ oz butter in a small frying pan, add onion and garlic and cook over a medium heat for 3-4 minutes or until onion is soft.
2   Place breadcrumbs in a bowl, add onion mixture and parsley. Melt remaining butter and mix into breadcrumb mixture. Season to taste with black pepper.
3   Cut six pieces of heavy-duty aluminium foil large enough to enclose chicken breast fillets. Brush foil lightly with oil and place a fillet on each piece of foil. Top one half of each fillet with some stuffing and fold fillet over to enclose. Wrap foil around chicken to form a tight parcel so that juice will not escape during cooking.
4   Place foil parcels on a preheated medium barbecue and cook, turning halfway through cooking, for 10-15 minutes or until chicken is cooked and tender.

Cook's tip: If you do not have heavy-duty aluminium foil, use a double thickness of ordinary foil instead.

VEGETABLE AND SALAD ROLL-UPS

Serves 4

- [ ] **4 wholemeal pitta bread rounds**
- [ ] **4 tablespoons mayonnaise**
- [ ] **8 lettuce leaves, shredded**
- [ ] **2 tomatoes, sliced**
- [ ] **1 beetroot, grated**

SOYA PATTIES
- [ ] **60 g/2 oz wholemeal breadcrumbs, made from stale bread**
- [ ] **440 g/14 oz canned soya beans, drained and roughly mashed**
- [ ] **1 carrot, grated**
- [ ] **1 courgette (zucchini), grated**
- [ ] **2 tablespoons tomato purée**
- [ ] **½ teaspoon ground cumin**
- [ ] **1 egg white**

1   To make patties, place breadcrumbs, soya beans, carrot, courgette (zucchini), tomato purée, cumin and egg white in a bowl and mix to combine. Shape mixture into 12 small patties and cook in a nonstick frying pan, for 3 minutes each side or until golden brown. Set aside and keep warm.
2   Spread bread rounds with mayonnaise. Top with lettuce, tomato, beetroot and patties. Roll up bread to form a cylinder and serve immediately.

TORTELLINI SALAD

Serves 4

- [ ] **750 g/1½ lb mixed-coloured tortellini**
- [ ] **250 g/8 oz asparagus, cut into 5 cm/2 in pieces**
- [ ] **200 g/6½ oz mangetout (snow peas), trimmed**
- [ ] **1 lettuce**
- [ ] **1 red pepper, sliced**
- [ ] **250 g/8 oz yellow cherry tomatoes**
- [ ] **125 mL/4 fl oz Italian dressing**

1   Cook tortellini in boiling water in a large saucepan, following packet directions. Drain, rinse under cold water and set aside to cool.
2   Boil, steam or microwave asparagus and mangetout (snow peas) separately until tender. Refresh under cold running water and set aside to cool.
3   Arrange lettuce, red pepper, tomatoes, tortellini, asparagus and mangetout (snow peas) in a large serving bowl. Pour dressing over and serve immediately.

Do ahead: Cook the pasta and vegetables for this salad in advance and store in the refrigerator for up to 2 days. The salad then only takes minutes to assemble.

FRESH HERB AND CHICKEN BURGERS

Serves 4

- [ ] **4 chicken breast fillets, approximately 125 g/4 oz each**
- [ ] **4 round, wholegrain bread rolls, halved and toasted**
- [ ] **12 cherry tomatoes, sliced**
- [ ] **8 lettuce leaves**

HERB MAYONNAISE
- [ ] **4 tablespoons mayonnaise**
- [ ] **2 teaspoons snipped fresh chives**
- [ ] **2 teaspoons chopped fresh parsley**

1   To make mayonnaise, place mayonnaise, chives and parsley in a bowl and mix to combine.
2   Heat a large nonstick frying pan and cook chicken for 4-5 minutes each side or until golden and tender. Place a chicken breast on base of each roll. Top with tomato and lettuce. Spoon mayonnaise over and top with remaining roll halves.

Serving suggestion: Serve with coleslaw and fresh fruit.

TRI-POTATO SALAD

Serves 4

- [ ] **12 baby new potatoes**
- [ ] **500 g/1 lb orange sweet potato, cubed**
- [ ] **500 g/1 lb white sweet potato, cubed**
- [ ] **1 small onion, chopped**
- [ ] **250 g/8 oz ham, chopped**

MUSTARD HERB DRESSING
- [ ] **5 tablespoons mayonnaise**
- [ ] **3 tablespoons natural yogurt**
- [ ] **2 teaspoons wholegrain mustard**
- [ ] **2 tablespoons snipped fresh chives**

1   Boil, steam or microwave new potatoes and orange and white sweet potatoes separately, until tender. Drain, set aside and keep warm.
2   Heat a nonstick frying pan and cook onion and ham for 3 minutes or until onion is soft.
3   Place potatoes in a large serving bowl and toss onion mixture through.
4   To make dressing, place mayonnaise, yogurt, mustard and chives in a bowl and mix to combine. Spoon over warm salad and serve.

Serving suggestion: A salad of oranges and onions tossed in French Dressing is a good accompaniment for this salad.

Tortellini Salad, Tri-Potato Salad, Fresh Herb and Chicken Burgers, Vegetable and Salad Roll-Ups

BLUE CHEESE CAESAR SALAD

If cos lettuce is unavailable iceberg lettuce can be used instead.

Serves 10

- ☐ **90 mL/3 fl oz olive oil**
- ☐ **2 slices bread, crusts removed and cut into 1 cm/¹/₂ in cubes**
- ☐ **2 rashers bacon, chopped**
- ☐ **1 cos lettuce, washed, leaves separated, torn into large pieces**
- ☐ **60 g/2 oz pine nuts, toasted**
- ☐ **125 g/4 oz grated Parmesan cheese**

BLUE CHEESE DRESSING
- ☐ **90 g/3 oz Stilton or blue cheese**
- ☐ **2 tablespoons natural yogurt**
- ☐ **2 tablespoons sour cream**
- ☐ **90 mL/3 fl oz cream (double)**
- ☐ **2 tablespoons lemon juice**
- ☐ **freshly ground black pepper**

1   To make croutons, heat oil in a frying pan and cook bread over a medium-high heat, tossing frequently, for 1-2 minutes or until golden on all sides. Remove from pan and drain on absorbent kitchen paper.
2   Place bacon in a nonstick frying pan and cook over a medium heat for 3-4 minutes or until crisp. Remove from pan and drain on absorbent kitchen paper.
3   To make dressing, place Stilton or blue cheese, yogurt, sour cream, cream, lemon juice and black pepper to taste in a food processor or blender and process until smooth.
4   Place lettuce, bacon, croutons and pine nuts in a serving bowl, pour dressing over and toss. Sprinkle with Parmesan cheese and serve immediately.

CHICKEN WITH CREAMY PESTO STUFFING

Serves 10

- ☐ **3 x 1.5 kg/3 lb chickens**

CREAMY PESTO STUFFING
- ☐ **90 g/3 oz basil leaves**
- ☐ **60 g/2 oz pine nuts**
- ☐ **60 g/2 oz finely grated Parmesan cheese**
- ☐ **250 g/8 oz cream cheese, softened**

1   To make stuffing, place basil leaves, pine nuts and Parmesan cheese in a food processor and process to finely chopped. Stir basil mixture into cream cheese.
2   Cut through backbone of each chicken. Remove both halves of backbone, then turn chicken over and press to flatten.
3   Using your fingers or the handle of a wooden spoon, loosen skin over breasts, thighs and legs of chicken. Push stuffing under loosened skin, then thread skewers through wings and legs of chickens.
4   Cook chicken on a lightly oiled preheated medium barbecue for 15-20 minutes each side or until chicken is cooked through.

When is the chicken cooked? To test your chicken for doneness pierce the thickest part of the chicken at the thigh joint and when the juices run clear the bird is cooked.

BROWN ALE DAMPER

Makes a 20 cm/8 in damper

- ☐ **250 g/8 oz self-raising flour**
- ☐ **315 g/10 oz wholemeal self-raising flour**
- ☐ **1 teaspoon salt**
- ☐ **45 g/1¹/₂ oz butter**
- ☐ **500 mL/16 fl oz beer**

1   Sift together self-raising flour, wholemeal self-raising flour and salt into a bowl. Return husks to bowl. Rub in butter using fingertips until mixture resembles coarse breadcrumbs. Make a well in the centre of the flour mixture and pour in beer. Using a round-bladed knife, mix to form a soft dough.
2   Turn dough onto a lightly floured surface and knead until smooth. Shape dough into a 20 cm/8 in round and place on a double thickness of oiled aluminium foil large enough to completely encase damper. Score dough into wedges using a sharp knife. Lightly dust with flour and wrap foil loosely around damper to completely enclose. Cook on a preheated barbecue, turning several times, for 1 hour or until cooked through. Serve warm, broken into pieces, with butter if desired.

Brown Ale Damper, Chicken with Creamy Pesto Stuffing, Blue Cheese Caesar Salad

1 Bring vegetable stock to the boil and pour over couscous. Set aside to stand for 10 minutes, then drain.

2 Combine couscous, carrot, pepper, tomato, cucumber and avocado in a bowl.

3 To make dressing, place oil, rind, juice, mustard, honey and basil in a screwtop jar. Shake well to combine. Pour over salad and toss. Just prior to serving, sprinkle with almonds.

Couscous: Couscous is a fine semolina made from wheat that originated in North Africa, however variations on the traditional dish can be found in Sicily, France and even Brazil, where it is 'cuscuz' rather than couscous.

It is readily available in packages, much the same as rice, and is served as an accompaniment to a meal.

SPICY PEA PARATHAS

Serves 4

- ☐ **250 g/8 oz wholemeal flour**
- ☐ **250 g/8 oz white flour**
- ☐ **30 g/1 oz butter**
- ☐ **250 mL/8 fl oz warm water, approximately**

POTATO AND PEA FILLING
- ☐ **1 large potato, cooked and mashed**
- ☐ **45 g/1$^1/_2$ oz split peas, cooked and mashed**
- ☐ **125 g/4 oz ricotta cheese**
- ☐ **2 teaspoons coriander seeds**
- ☐ **2 teaspoons cumin seeds**
- ☐ **1$^1/_2$ tablespoons sweet fruit chutney**

1 Sift wholemeal and white flours into a large bowl. Rub in butter, make a well in the centre and gradually add enough water to form a soft dough. Knead on a lightly floured surface until smooth.

2 To make filling, place potato, split peas, ricotta cheese, coriander and cumin seeds, and chutney in a bowl. Mix well to combine.

3 Divide dough into eight portions and roll into small flat rounds. Place a spoonful of filling in the centre of each round. Mould dough around filling to enclose.

4 Cook parathas on a lightly greased preheated barbecue plate, or in a frying pan, for 4 minutes each side or until golden.

Couscous Salad

EGG SALAD WITH HERB DRESSING

Serves 6

- ☐ **lettuce leaves**
- ☐ **6 hard-boiled eggs, quartered**
- ☐ **12 cherry tomatoes**
- ☐ **1 avocado, stoned, peeled and sliced**
- ☐ **24 black olives**

FRESH HERB DRESSING
- ☐ **250 g/8 oz natural yogurt**
- ☐ **2 tablespoons chopped fresh parsley**
- ☐ **1 tablespoon chopped fresh mint**
- ☐ **1 tablespoon snipped fresh chives**
- ☐ **2 tablespoons apple juice**
- ☐ **freshly ground black pepper**

1 To make dressing, place yogurt, parsley, mint, chives and apple juice in a food processor or blender, and process until dressing is combined and green in colour. Season to taste with black pepper.

2 Arrange lettuce leaves, eggs, tomatoes, avocado slices and olives attractively on a serving platter and just prior to serving spoon over dressing.

COUSCOUS SALAD

This salad would be perfect for your next 'al fresco' meal.

Serves 4

- ☐ **250 mL/8 fl oz vegetable stock or water**
- ☐ **200 g/6$^1/_2$ oz couscous**
- ☐ **1 carrot, thinly sliced**
- ☐ **1 red pepper, chopped**
- ☐ **1 tomato, chopped**
- ☐ **1 small cucumber, cubed**
- ☐ **1 avocado, stoned, peeled and cubed**
- ☐ **30 g/1 oz flaked almonds, toasted**

DRESSING
- ☐ **1 tablespoon olive oil**
- ☐ **1 teaspoon grated lime rind**
- ☐ **2 tablespoons lime juice**
- ☐ **1 teaspoon wholegrain mustard**
- ☐ **1 tablespoon honey**
- ☐ **1 tablespoon chopped fresh basil**

MARINATED AUBERGINE AND TOMATO SALAD

Using basil, garlic and balsamic vinegar, this salad combines the flavours of Italy. Serve as a starter, as part of an antipasto platter or take it on a picnic. It is delicious served with pitta bread and yogurt.

Serves 6

- [ ] **6 baby aubergines (eggplant), cut lengthwise into 1 cm/1/2 in slices**
- [ ] **olive oil**
- [ ] **3 tomatoes, peeled and thinly sliced**
- [ ] **4 tablespoons finely chopped fresh basil**
- [ ] **freshly ground black pepper**

DRESSING
- [ ] **3 tablespoons balsamic vinegar**
- [ ] **1 tablespoon olive oil**
- [ ] **2 cloves garlic, crushed**

1 Brush each aubergine (eggplant) slice generously with oil and cook under a preheated grill for 4-5 minutes each side or until golden and tender.

2 To make dressing, place vinegar, oil and garlic in a screwtop jar. Shake well to combine.

3 Place a layer of warm aubergine (eggplant) slices in a shallow ceramic or glass dish. Top with a layer of tomato slices. Sprinkle with a tablespoon of dressing, a tablespoon of basil and season with black pepper to taste. Repeat layers until all aubergines (eggplant) and tomatoes are used. Cover and refrigerate for at least 2 hours.

Cook's tip: If the aubergine (eggplant) appears to be drying out during cooking, brush with a little more olive oil. This salad is even better if left to marinate overnight.

MARINATED LEG OF LAMB

Your butcher will butterfly the leg in minutes for you.

Serves 6

- [ ] **1.5-2 kg/3-4 lb leg of lamb, butterflied**
- [ ] **freshly ground black pepper**

LEMON HERB MARINADE
- [ ] **2 cloves garlic, crushed**
- [ ] **60 mL/2 fl oz olive oil**
- [ ] **60 mL/2 fl oz lemon juice**
- [ ] **1 tablespoon finely chopped fresh marjoram or 1 teaspoon dried marjoram**
- [ ] **1 tablespoon finely chopped fresh thyme or 1 teaspoon dried thyme**

1 Lay lamb out flat and season well with black pepper. Place in a shallow glass or ceramic dish.

2 To make marinade, place garlic, oil, lemon juice, marjoram and thyme in a small bowl and mix to combine. Pour marinade over lamb, cover and allow to marinate for 3-4 hours or overnight.

3 Remove lamb from marinade and reserve marinade. Place lamb on a lightly oiled preheated medium barbecue grill and cook, turning several times and basting with reserved marinade for 15-25 minutes or until cooked to your liking.

*Spicy Pea Parathas,
Marinated Aubergine and Tomato Salad*

MIXED SAUSAGE
AND ONION GRILL

Buy a selection of your favourite sausages for this mixed grill. Mild or hot Italian sausages, bratwurst, knackwurst, pork, beef, or some of the more exotic flavours such as lamb and mint or turkey and sage are all delicious choices.

Serves 6

- [ ] **12 sausages of different varieties**
- [ ] **12 baby new potatoes, scrubbed**
- [ ] **3 red onions, cut into quarters**
- [ ] **12 skewers, lightly oiled**
- [ ] **olive oil**

1   Parboil sausages. Drain and set aside to cool, then refrigerate.
2   Boil, steam or microwave potatoes until just tender.
3   Thread 2 onion quarters onto 6 of the skewers, then brush with oil. Cook on a preheated lightly oiled barbecue, turning halfway through cooking, for 15-20 minutes or until onions are golden and tender.
4   Thread 2 potatoes onto each of the remaining skewers and brush with oil. Cook on barbecue, turning halfway through cooking, for 10-15 minutes or until potatoes are golden and heated through.
5   Cook sausages on lightly oiled barbecue for 10-15 minutes or until sausages are golden and crisp on the outside and heated through.

Serving suggestion: Serve with a selection of mustards and sauces.

CHAR-GRILLED
VEGETABLE SLICES

Serves 6

- [ ] **125 mL/4 fl oz olive oil**
- [ ] **1 clove garlic, crushed**
- [ ] **1 large aubergine (eggplant), cut lengthwise into thick slices**
- [ ] **3 large courgettes (zucchini), cut lengthwise into thick slices**
- [ ] **2 red peppers, cut into quarters, seeds removed and sliced**
- [ ] **3 large firm tomatoes, cut into thick slices**
- [ ] **freshly ground black pepper**

1   Place oil and garlic in a small bowl and whisk to combine. Brush aubergine (eggplant) slices, courgette (zucchini) slices, red pepper slices and tomato slices with oil mixture.
2   Cook aubergine (eggplant), courgette (zucchini) and red pepper slices on a lightly oiled preheated barbecue, turning frequently, for 4-5 minutes or until almost cooked. Add tomato slices to barbecue and cook all vegetables for 2-3 minutes longer.

BARBECUE A SAUSAGE

Children and adults alike love sausages cooked on a barbecue. With the huge variety now available from butchers, specialty shops and delicatessens, you need have no fear of sausages ever being dull.

- [ ] **required number of sausages**

1   To cook perfect barbecued sausages they should be parboiled first. This ensures that they will be cooked on the inside and golden on the outside and that some of the fat will be removed.
2   To parboil sausages, place them in a saucepan, cover with water and bring slowly to the boil, then reduce heat and simmer for 5 minutes. Drain and set aside to cool. When cool, cover and refrigerate for several hours or overnight.
3   Cook sausages on a lightly oiled preheated barbecue, turning several times, for 10 minutes or until golden and heated through.

Mixed Sausage and Onion Grill,
Char-grilled Vegetable Slices

PITTA CRISPS

These easy-to-make snacks are great to nibble on while waiting for the barbecue food to cook.

Serves 10
Oven temperature 200°C, 400°F, Gas 6

- ☐ **6 pitta bread**
- ☐ **4 tablespoons vegetable oil**
- ☐ **60 g/2 oz grated Parmesan cheese**
- ☐ **2 teaspoons paprika**
- ☐ **¹/₂ teaspoon chilli powder**

1   Split each pitta bread in half, horizontally, brush with oil and place on baking trays.
2   Place Parmesan cheese, paprika and chilli in a small bowl and mix to combine. Sprinkle bread with cheese mixture and bake for 15 minutes or until bread is crisp. Allow bread to cool, then break into pieces.

HAM AND CHEESE SKEWERS

Grilled ham and cheese sandwiches on a skewer!

Makes 10 skewers

- ☐ **250 g/8 oz sliced ham, cut into strips 3 cm/1¹/₄ in wide**
- ☐ **375 g/12 oz mature Cheddar cut into 1 cm/¹/₂ in cubes**
- ☐ **1 loaf wholegrain bread, cut into 1 cm/¹/₂ in cubes**
- ☐ **10 skewers, lightly oiled**

1   Wrap ham strips around cheese cubes. Thread ham-wrapped cheese cubes and bread cubes, alternately, on to skewers.
2   Cook on a lightly oiled preheated barbecue grill, turning frequently, for 4-5 minutes or until bread is toasted and cheese just starts to melt.

BEST EVER HAMBURGERS

Serve the patties and rolls separately and allow people to make their own hamburger using the salad bar ingredients.

Makes 10 burgers

- ☐ **10 wholemeal rolls, split in half**

MEAT PATTIES
- ☐ **1 kg/2 lb lean beef mince**
- ☐ **1 onion, finely chopped**
- ☐ **1 carrot, grated**
- ☐ **60 g/2 oz breadcrumbs, made from stale bread**
- ☐ **1 tablespoon Worcestershire sauce**
- ☐ **1 tablespoon tomato sauce**
- ☐ **dash chilli sauce, according to taste**
- ☐ **2 tablespoons finely chopped fresh parsley**
- ☐ **freshly ground black pepper**

1   To make patties, place beef, onion, carrot, breadcrumbs, Worcestershire sauce, tomato sauce, chilli sauce, parsley and black pepper to taste in a bowl, and mix to combine.
2   Wet hands and shape meat mixture into ten patties. Place patties on a tray, cover and refrigerate until ready to cook.
3   Cook patties on a lightly oiled preheated barbecue plate (griddle), or in a lightly oiled frying pan on the barbecue, for 4-5 minutes each side or until cooked to your liking, pressing down with a spatula during cooking. Toast rolls on barbecue.

Burgers with onions: Onions can be cooked at the same time as the burgers. Allowing 1 onion for every 2 people, slice onions and cook with a little oil on barbecue plate (griddle) or in a frying pan.

Hamburgers with hidden fillings: It is fun and easy to make hamburgers that hold a surprise. Cheese is always a popular hidden ingredient – you might like to try mature Cheddar, mozzarella or blue cheese. Simply cut cheese into 2.5 cm/1 in cubes and, when shaping your pattie, place cheese in centre of pattie and shape meat around it.

CHILLI HONEY DRUMSTICKS

Serves 10

- ☐ **10 chicken drumsticks**

CHILLI HONEY MARINADE
- ☐ **125 mL/4 fl oz lemon juice**
- ☐ **170 g/5¹/₂ oz honey**
- ☐ **1 clove garlic, crushed**
- ☐ **pinch chilli powder**

1 To make marinade, place lemon juice, honey, garlic and chilli powder in a bowl and mix to combine.

2 Place drumsticks in a shallow glass or ceramic dish, pour marinade over and toss to coat. Cover and marinate in the refrigerator for at least 2 hours, or overnight, turning several times during marinating.

3 Drain drumsticks and reserve marinade. Cook drumsticks on a lightly oiled preheated barbecue, brushing frequently with marinade for 10-15 minutes or until chicken is tender.

SALAD BAR

Arranging a salad bar that includes bowls of salad ingredients and toppings for potatoes is a great way of allowing people to assemble their own hamburgers, make their own salads and choose their favourite toppings for baked potatoes.
Quantities will vary depending on who you are feeding, but remember that appetites seem to increase outdoors.

SALAD BOWLS
☐ **mixed lettuce leaves**
☐ **tomato slices or halved cherry tomatoes**
☐ **beetroot slices**
☐ **sliced cucumbers**
☐ **mature Cheddar slices**
☐ **sliced red and green peppers**
☐ **hard-boiled eggs, sliced**
☐ **chopped spring onions**
☐ **sliced raw mushrooms**
☐ **grated raw carrot**

POTATO TOPPERS
☐ **snipped chives**
☐ **sour cream**
☐ **bacon pieces**
☐ **grated mature Cheddar**

PICKLES AND SAUCES
☐ **tomato sauce**
☐ **mustard pickle**
☐ **barbecue sauce**
☐ **Worcestershire sauce**
☐ **selection of mustards**

FRUIT AND NUTS
Fruit and nuts provide a healthy and delicious snack to eat while waiting for the barbecued food and make a good alternative for dessert.

☐ **melon slices**
☐ **orange segments**
☐ **kiwifruit slices**
☐ **fresh pineapple wedges or slices**
☐ **bananas, whole or sliced and tossed in lemon juice**
☐ **apples, whole or cubed and tossed in lemon juice**
☐ **selection dried fruit and nuts**

Chilli Honey Drumsticks, Ham and Cheese Skewers, Pitta Crisps

MARINATED
MUSHROOM SALAD

Serves 10

- ☐ **4 tablespoons olive oil**
- ☐ **2 cloves garlic, crushed**
- ☐ **750 g/1½ lb small button mushrooms, trimmed**
- ☐ **2 tablespoons red wine vinegar**
- ☐ **1 tablespoon lemon juice**
- ☐ **3 tablespoons chicken stock**
- ☐ **1 tablespoon chopped fresh basil**
- ☐ **2 tablespoons chopped fresh parsley**

1   Heat oil in a frying pan and cook garlic and mushrooms for 2-3 minutes. Reduce heat, add vinegar, lemon juice and stock, and simmer for 1 minute.
2   Stir in basil and parsley and set aside to cool. Cover cooled mushroom mixture and refrigerate until required.

BARBECUED CHIPS

Serves 10

- ☐ **500 g/1 lb potatoes, cut crosswise into 5 mm/¼ in slices**
- ☐ **500 g/1 lb parsnips, cut lengthwise into 5 mm/¼ in slices**
- ☐ **500 g/1 lb sweet potatoes, cut crosswise into 5 mm/¼ in slices**
- ☐ **3 tablespoons olive oil**
- ☐ **4 onions, chopped**

1   Blanch potato, parsnip and sweet potato slices in a large saucepan of boiling water for 2 minutes. Drain, rinse under cold running water and drain on absorbent kitchen paper.
2   Heat oil in a large frying pan on a preheated barbecue and cook onions for 15-20 minutes or until golden and crisp. Add potato, parsnip and sweet potato slices and cook for 10 minutes or until chips are tender.

Barbecued Chips, Marinated Mushroom Salad, Vegetable Burgers

240

VEGETABLE BURGERS

Makes 10 burgers

- ☐ **10 wholemeal rolls, split**
- ☐ **10 lettuce leaves**

MIXED VEGETABLE PATTIES
- ☐ **500 g/1 lb broccoli, chopped**
- ☐ **500 g/1 lb courgettes (zucchini), chopped**
- ☐ **250 g/8 oz carrots, chopped**
- ☐ **2 onions, finely chopped**
- ☐ **2 cloves garlic, crushed**
- ☐ **3 tablespoons chopped fresh parsley**
- ☐ **185 g/6 oz dried breadcrumbs**
- ☐ **60 g/2 oz flour, sifted**
- ☐ **freshly ground black pepper**

SPICY TOMATO SAUCE
- ☐ **1 tablespoon olive oil**
- ☐ **1 onion, finely chopped**
- ☐ **1 clove garlic, crushed**
- ☐ **1 fresh red chilli, seeded and finely chopped**
- ☐ **1 green pepper, finely chopped**
- ☐ **440 g/14 oz canned tomatoes, undrained and mashed**
- ☐ **freshly ground black pepper**

1 To make patties, boil, steam or microwave broccoli, courgettes (zucchini) and carrots until tender. Drain, rinse under cold running water and pat dry.

2 Place broccoli, courgettes (zucchini), carrots, onions, garlic and parsley in a food processor and process until puréed. Transfer vegetable mixture to a mixing bowl, add breadcrumbs and flour, season to taste with black pepper and mix to combine. Cover and refrigerate for 30 minutes.

3 Shape mixture into ten patties. Place on a tray lined with nonstick baking paper, cover and refrigerate until required.

4 To make sauce, heat oil in a saucepan and cook onion, garlic, chilli and green pepper for 5 minutes or until onion and green pepper are soft. Add tomatoes, bring mixture to the boil, then reduce heat and simmer for 15-20 minutes or until sauce thickens. Season to taste with black pepper.

5 Cook patties on a lightly oiled preheated medium barbecue plate (griddle) or in a lightly oiled frying pan on a preheated barbecue for 3-4 minutes each side. Toast rolls on barbecue. Place a lettuce leaf, a pattie and a spoonful of sauce on the bottom half of each roll, top with remaining roll half and serve immediately.

SMOKED CHICKEN SALAD WITH GINGER DRESSING

A pretty salad with a fresh taste that is easy to make and travels well. Put the salad in the serving bowl to marinate on the way to your picnic.

Serves 6

- ☐ 1 x 1-1.5 kg/2-3 lb smoked chicken, meat removed and broken into bite-sized pieces
- ☐ 4 spring onions, finely chopped
- ☐ 1 small red pepper, thinly sliced
- ☐ 1 small fresh red chilli, seeded and thinly sliced
- ☐ 1 tablespoon chopped fresh coriander
- ☐ 1 tablespoon chopped fresh mint
- ☐ freshly ground black pepper

ORANGE AND GINGER DRESSING
- ☐ 3 tablespoons olive oil
- ☐ 2 tablespoons white wine vinegar
- ☐ 2 tablespoons orange juice
- ☐ 1 teaspoon wholegrain mustard
- ☐ 1 teaspoon brown sugar
- ☐ 1 teaspoon finely grated fresh ginger

1   Place chicken, spring onions, red pepper, chilli, coriander and mint in a serving bowl. Season to taste with black pepper.
2   To make dressing, place oil, vinegar, orange juice, mustard, sugar and ginger in a screwtop jar and shake well to combine. Pour over chicken mixture and toss to combine. Cover and refrigerate.

BAKED CAMEMBERT AND GORGONZOLA LOAF

Bake this loaf within the hour before you leave for your picnic. It is wrapped in foil and will stay warm.

Serves 6
Oven temperature 180°C, 350°F, Gas 4

- ☐ 23 cm/9 in round loaf of bread
- ☐ 375 g/12 oz Camembert cheese, thinly sliced
- ☐ 200 g/6¹/₂ oz Gorgonzola cheese, thinly sliced
- ☐ 3 pears, cored, peeled and thinly sliced
- ☐ 3 fresh dates, thinly sliced

1   Slice top from bread and scoop out centre, leaving a 2.5 cm/1 in shell. Top and centre of bread can be reserved and made into breadcrumbs for use later.
2   Place a layer of Camembert cheese slices over base of bread and top loaf with a layer of Gorgonzola cheese and a layer of pear slices. Repeat layers, finishing with a layer of pears. Wrap loaf in a sheet of aluminium foil and bake for 30 minutes.
3   Remove from oven, open foil and top loaf with dates. While still hot, rewrap for transportation to picnic. Serve directly from the foil.

BROWNIES

Makes 24
Oven temperature 180°C, 350°F, Gas 4

- ☐ 125 g/4 oz dark chocolate, roughly chopped
- ☐ 125 g/4 oz unsalted butter, roughly chopped
- ☐ 1 teaspoon vanilla essence
- ☐ 2 eggs
- ☐ 220 g/7 oz caster sugar
- ☐ 125 g/4 oz flour
- ☐ ¹/₄ teaspoon baking powder
- ☐ 125 g/4 oz walnuts, chopped

CHOCOLATE FUDGE ICING
- ☐ 200 g/6¹/₂ oz dark chocolate, melted
- ☐ 60 g/2 oz butter, melted

1   Melt chocolate and butter in a saucepan over a low heat, taking care not to overheat. Remove from heat and stir in vanilla essence.
2   Beat eggs and sugar together until thick and creamy. Fold through chocolate mixture. Sift flour and baking powder over chocolate mixture. Sprinkle walnuts over chocolate mixture, then fold in using a spatula.
3   Spoon mixture into a greased and lined 20 cm/8 in square shallow cake tin. Smooth top using a spatula. Bake for 25-30 minutes, or until only just set. Cool in tin on a wire rack.
4   To make icing, combine chocolate and butter in a mixing bowl and beat until well blended. Spread over brownie and set aside to firm. Cut into squares to serve.

Baked Camembert and Gorgonzola Loaf, Brownies, Smoked Chicken Salad with Ginger Dressing

BARBECUED LEG OF LAMB WITH LEMON HERB BUTTER

Serves 8

- ☐ **1 boned leg of lamb**
- ☐ **2 cloves garlic, cut into slivers**
- ☐ **2 sprigs fresh rosemary**
- ☐ **freshly ground black pepper**

LEMON HERB BUTTER
- ☐ **125 g/4 oz butter, softened**
- ☐ **2 teaspoons grated lemon rind**
- ☐ **1 tablespoon chopped fresh basil**
- ☐ **1 tablespoon chopped fresh parsley**
- ☐ **1 tablespoon lemon juice**
- ☐ **1 teaspoon sweet chilli sauce**

1 Trim meat of excess fat. Make three deep slashes on top of meat with a sharp knife and tuck slivers of garlic and rosemary leaves into each. Sprinkle liberally with black pepper.

2 To make herb butter, combine butter, rind, basil, parsley, lemon juice and sauce and mix well.

3 Barbecue or grill lamb over a gentle heat, basting with herb butter until tender.

POTATO SALAD AND AVOCADO DRESSING

Serves 6

- ☐ **1 kg/2 lb baby new potatoes, scrubbed**
- ☐ **2 tablespoons chopped fresh parsley**
- ☐ **6 hard-boiled eggs, quartered**
- ☐ **1 onion, sliced**

AVOCADO DRESSING
- ☐ **1 avocado, peeled and stoned**
- ☐ **1 clove garlic, crushed**
- ☐ **1 tablespoon lemon juice**
- ☐ **125 g/4 oz sour cream**
- ☐ **2 drops Tabasco sauce**
- ☐ **1 teaspoon honey**

1 Boil or steam potatoes until tender. Drain and place potatoes in a salad bowl with parsley, eggs and onion.

2 To make dressing, process avocado, garlic, lemon juice, sour cream, sauce and honey in a food processor or blender until smooth.

Nutrition tip: Try natural yogurt in recipes instead of sour cream. If using in hot food, stir through at the end of cooking and do not allow to boil or it will go grainy.

GLAZED FRUIT KEBABS

Serves 4

- ☐ **220 g/7 oz canned pineapple pieces**
- ☐ **1 cooking apple, cored, peeled and cubed**
- ☐ **2 large bananas, thickly sliced**
- ☐ **250 g/8 oz strawberries, washed and hulled**
- ☐ **2 kiwifruit, cubed**
- ☐ **1 orange, segmented**

ORANGE GLAZE
- ☐ **125 mL/4 fl oz orange juice**
- ☐ **1 tablespoon honey**
- ☐ **1 tablespoon orange-flavoured liqueur**
- ☐ **2 teaspoons cornflour**

1 Thread fruit pieces onto eight oiled wooden skewers, alternating the pieces attractively.

2 To make the glaze, combine ingredients in a saucepan. Cook over a medium heat for 2-3 minutes until glaze boils and thickens.

3 Barbecue or grill kebabs over a gentle heat, turning and brushing frequently with glaze.

COOK'S TIP

When using wooden skewers, don't forget to soak them in cold water for at least an hour before using under grill or over a barbecue, as they can burn.

Barbecued Leg of Lamb with Lemon Herb Butter, Potato Salad and Avocado Dressing, Glazed Fruit Kebabs

BARBECUED STEAK SANDWICHES

Marinated steak, barbecued and placed between slices of grilled bread makes the best steak sandwiches you will ever taste.

Serves 6

- ☐ **6 lean rump steaks, cut 1 cm/¹/₂ in thick**
- ☐ **3 onions, thinly sliced**
- ☐ **12 thick slices wholemeal or grain bread**
- ☐ **olive oil**

GINGER WINE MARINADE
- ☐ **250 mL/8 fl oz red wine**
- ☐ **125 mL/4 fl oz olive oil**
- ☐ **1 clove garlic, crushed**
- ☐ **2 teaspoons grated fresh ginger**

1 To make marinade, place wine, oil, garlic and ginger in a bowl and mix to combine. Place steaks in a shallow glass or ceramic dish. Pour marinade over, cover, and marinate at room temperature for 2-3 hours or overnight in the refrigerator.

2 Cook onions on a lightly oiled preheated barbecue plate (griddle) or in a lightly oiled frying pan on a preheated barbecue for 10-15 minutes or until golden. Drain steaks and cook on lightly oiled barbecue for 3-5 minutes each side or until cooked to your liking.

3 Lightly brush bread slices with oil and cook on a preheated barbecue grill for 1-2 minutes each side or until lightly toasted. To assemble sandwiches, top 6 toasted bread slices with steak, onions and remaining bread slices.

Cook's tip: You may like to add some salad ingredients to your sandwiches. Mustard or relish is also a tasty addition.

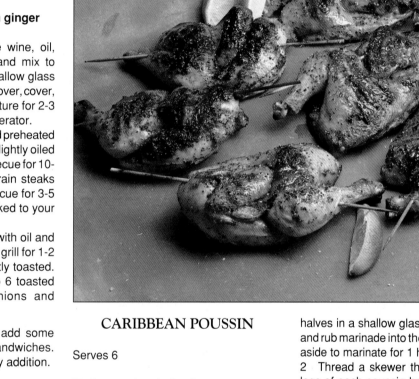

CARIBBEAN POUSSIN

Serves 6

- ☐ **3 poussins, halved**
- ☐ **2 tablespoons cracked black peppercorns**
- ☐ **1 teaspoon ground coriander**

LIME MARINADE
- ☐ **3 tablespoons white rum**
- ☐ **2 teaspoons finely grated lime rind**
- ☐ **1 tablespoon lime juice**
- ☐ **2 tablespoons honey**
- ☐ **2 cloves garlic, crushed**
- ☐ **1 teaspoon grated fresh ginger**

1 To make marinade, place rum, lime rind, lime juice, honey, garlic and ginger in a bowl and mix to combine. Place poussin halves in a shallow glass or ceramic dish and rub marinade into them. Cover and set aside to marinate for 1 hour.

2 Thread a skewer through wings and legs of each poussin half and brush with any remaining marinade. Combine black peppercorns and coriander and press onto skin of birds. Cook on a lightly oiled preheated barbecue grill, turning frequently for 15-20 minutes or until birds are cooked through.

Cook's tip: This is also a delicious way to prepare and cook chicken pieces. Instead of using poussins, simply use chicken pieces and prepare and marinate as in this recipe – the cooking time for the chicken pieces will be about the same as for the poussins. You should cook them until the juices run clear.

Left: Barbecued Steak Sandwiches
Above: Caribbean Poussin

chapter eleven

BAKED TO PERFECTION

Chocolate Cake, Brownies
and Dundee Cake are all family
favourites and are just three of the
sumptuous recipes you will find in
this chapter. When you cook these
and the other delicious home-
baked goodies you are sure
to draw compliments from
family and friends.

Chocolate Shortbread, Quick Brownies,
White Choc-Chip Chocolate Cake

249

QUICK NUT FUDGE CAKE

Makes a 20 cm/8 in round cake
Oven temperature 180°C, 350°F, Gas 4

- ☐ **125 g/4 oz butter, melted**
- ☐ **250 g/8 oz brown sugar**
- ☐ **2 eggs, lightly beaten**
- ☐ **1 teaspoon vanilla essence**
- ☐ **30 g/1 oz cocoa powder, sifted**
- ☐ **250 g/8 oz self-raising flour, sifted**
- ☐ **60 g/2 oz chopped walnuts**

CHOCOLATE BUTTER ICING
- ☐ **125 g/4 oz butter, softened**
- ☐ **100 g/3¹/₂ oz dark chocolate, melted and cooled**
- ☐ **2 egg yolks**
- ☐ **75 g/2¹/₂ oz icing sugar, sifted**

1   Place butter, brown sugar, eggs and vanilla essence in a large mixing bowl and mix to combine. Stir in cocoa powder, flour and walnuts. Mix well to combine.
2   Spoon batter into a greased and lined 20 cm/8 in round cake tin and bake for 35-40 minutes or until cake is cooked when tested with a skewer. Stand cake in tin for 5 minutes before turning onto a wire rack to cool.
3   To make icing, place butter in a mixing bowl and beat until light and fluffy. Add chocolate, egg yolks and icing sugar and beat until smooth. Spread icing over cold cake.

CHOCOLATE SHORTBREAD

Melt-in-the-mouth chocolate-flavoured shortbread.

Makes 30
Oven temperature 160°C, 325°F, Gas 3

- ☐ **250 g/8 oz butter, softened**
- ☐ **75 g/2¹/₂ oz icing sugar**
- ☐ **125 g/4 oz flour**
- ☐ **125 g/4 oz cornflour**
- ☐ **30 g/1 oz cocoa powder**

1   Place butter and icing sugar in a mixing bowl and beat until mixture is creamy. Sift together flour, cornflour and cocoa powder. Stir flour mixture into butter mixture.
2   Turn dough onto a floured surface and knead lightly until smooth. Roll spoonfuls of mixture into balls, place on greased baking trays and flatten slightly with a fork. Bake for 20-25 minutes or until firm. Allow to cool on trays.

WHITE CHOC-CHIP CHOCOLATE CAKE

A rich chocolate cake studded with white chocolate chips and topped with creamy white chocolate frosting.

Makes a 23 cm/9 in round cake
Oven temperature 180°C, 350°F, Gas 4

- ☐ **125 g/4 oz butter, softened**
- ☐ **220 g/7 oz caster sugar**
- ☐ **1 teaspoon vanilla essence**
- ☐ **2 eggs**
- ☐ **170 g/5¹/₂ oz self-raising flour**
- ☐ **30 g/1 oz cocoa powder**
- ☐ **¹/₂ teaspoon baking powder**
- ☐ **250 mL/8 fl oz milk**
- ☐ **200 g/6¹/₂ oz white chocolate, chopped**

WHITE CHOCOLATE FROSTING
- ☐ **125 g/4 oz butter, softened**
- ☐ **100 g/3¹/₂ oz white chocolate, melted and cooled**
- ☐ **2 egg yolks**
- ☐ **75 g/2¹/₂ oz icing sugar, sifted**

1   Place butter, sugar and vanilla essence in a mixing bowl and beat until mixture is creamy. Add eggs one at a time beating well after each addition.
2   Sift together flour, cocoa powder and baking powder. Fold flour mixture and milk, alternately, into butter mixture, then fold in chocolate.
3   Spoon batter into a greased and lined 23 cm/9 in round cake tin and bake for 30-35 minutes or until cooked when tested with a skewer. Stand in tin for 5 minutes before turning onto a wire rack to cool completely.
4   To make frosting, place butter in a mixing bowl and beat until light and fluffy. Add chocolate, egg yolks and icing sugar and beat until smooth. Spread frosting over top and sides of cold cake.

QUICK BROWNIES

Makes 25
Oven temperature 180°C, 350°F, Gas 4

- ☐ **155 g/5 oz butter, softened**
- ☐ **170 g/5¹/₂ oz honey, warmed**
- ☐ **4 teaspoons water**
- ☐ **2 eggs, lightly beaten**
- ☐ **220 g/7 oz self-raising flour, sifted**
- ☐ **125 g/4 oz brown sugar**
- ☐ **125 g/4 oz dark chocolate, melted and cooled**
- ☐ **icing sugar**

1   Place butter, honey, water, eggs, flour, sugar and chocolate in a food processor and process until ingredients are combined.
2   Spoon batter into a greased and lined 23 cm/9 in square cake tin and bake for 30-35 minutes or until cooked when tested with a skewer. Stand cake in tin for 5 minutes before turning onto a wire rack to cool. Dust cold cake with icing sugar and cut into squares.

MELTING CHOCOLATE

➤ Chocolate melts more rapidly if broken into small pieces.
➤ Keep the container in which the chocolate is being melted, uncovered and completely dry. Covering can cause condensation and just one drop of water will ruin the chocolate.
➤ The melting process should occur slowly, as chocolate scorches if overheated.
➤ Chocolate 'seizes' if it is overheated or if it comes in contact with water or steam. Seizing results in the chocolate tightening and becoming a thick mass that will not melt.
➤ To rescue seized chocolate stir in a little cream or vegetable oil until the chocolate becomes smooth again.
➤ To melt chocolate, place in a bowl and set aside. Fill a saucepan with enough water to come just under the bowl; the water should not touch the bowl when it is placed in the saucepan. Bring water to the boil, then remove from heat and place chocolate over the hot water. Stand off the heat, stirring chocolate occasionally until it melts and is of a smooth consistency. Cool at room temperature.
➤ Chocolate can be melted quickly and easily in the microwave. Place chocolate in a microwave-safe glass or ceramic dish and cook on HIGH (100%) for 2 minutes per 375 g/12 oz chocolate. When melting chocolate in the microwave oven you will find that it tends to hold its shape, so always stir it before additional heating. If the chocolate is not completely melted, cook for an extra 30 seconds, then stir again.

BASIC BISCUITS

Makes 40
Oven temperature 180°C, 350°F, Gas 4

- ☐ **125 g/4 oz butter**
- ☐ **1 teaspoon vanilla essence**
- ☐ **185 g/6 oz caster sugar**
- ☐ **1 egg**
- ☐ **125 g/4 oz flour, sifted**
- ☐ **125 g/4 oz self-raising flour, sifted**

1 Cream butter, sugar and vanilla essence until light and fluffy. Add egg and beat well. Fold in flour and self-raising flour, cover and refrigerate for 2 hours.
2 Roll heaped teaspoonfuls of mixture into balls. Place onto a greased baking tray, spacing well apart to allow for spreading. Flatten each biscuit slightly with a fork and bake for 12-15 minutes or until golden brown. Allow to cool on tray for a few minutes then transfer to a wire rack to finish cooling.

Variations

Spicy Fruit Cookies: Replace 4 tablespoons of the caster sugar with 4 tablespoons brown sugar. Sift 2 teaspoons of cinnamon, 1 teaspoon of mixed spice and 1 teaspoon of ginger with the flour. Roll out mixture and cut 16 rounds with a biscuit cutter. Place teaspoonfuls of fruit mince on half the rounds and cover with remaining rounds. Press the edges lightly to seal and bake for 20-25 minutes, or until golden brown.

Three-Chocolate Cookies: Add 45 g/1½ oz finely chopped dark chocolate, 45 g/1½ oz finely chopped milk chocolate and 45 g/1½ oz finely chopped white chocolate to the biscuit mixture after beating in the egg. Place spoonfuls of mixture on a greased baking tray and bake for 12-15 minutes or until golden brown.

Creamy Jam Drops: Roll mixture into balls and flatten slightly. Make indents in the centre of each round and fill with a small amount of cream cheese and top with a teaspoon of blackberry jam, or a jam of your choice. Be careful not to fill the holes too much, or the jam will overflow during cooking. Bake for 12-15 minutes, or until golden brown.

DATE WRAPS

Makes 20
Oven temperature 160°C, 325°F, Gas 3

- ☐ **20 dried dates, pitted**
- ☐ **4 tablespoons brandy**
- ☐ **1 quantity Basic Biscuits**

1 Soak dates in brandy for 30 minutes, then drain.
2 Divide biscuit dough into 20 equal portions. Mould each portion around a date. Place on a greased baking tray and bake for 20-25 minutes, or until golden brown.

Basic Biscuits, Spicy Fruit Cookies, Three-Chocolate Cookies, Creamy Jam Drops, Date Wraps

COFFEE SANDWICH CAKE

Layers of light sponge sandwiched together with a liqueur cream and topped with a coffee icing. All this cake needs is a wonderful cup of coffee to accompany it.

Makes an 18 cm/7 in sandwich cake
Oven temperature 160°C, 325°F, Gas 3

- ☐ **250 g/8 oz butter, softened**
- ☐ **220 g/7 oz caster sugar**
- ☐ **6 eggs, lightly beaten**
- ☐ **250 g/8 oz self-raising flour, sifted**
- ☐ **4 teaspoons baking powder**

COFFEE ICING
- ☐ **60 g/2 oz butter, softened**
- ☐ **125 g/4 oz icing sugar, sifted**
- ☐ **¹/₂ teaspoon ground cinnamon**
- ☐ **2 teaspoons instant coffee powder dissolved in 2 teaspoons hot water, cooled**

LIQUEUR CREAM
- ☐ **1 tablespoon coffee-flavoured liqueur**
- ☐ **125 mL/4 fl oz cream (double), whipped**

1 Place butter and sugar in a food processor and process until creamy. Add eggs, flour and baking powder and process until all ingredients are combined. Spoon batter into two greased and lined 18 cm/7 in sandwich tins and bake for 30-35 minutes or until golden. Turn onto a wire rack to cool.

2 To make icing, place butter, icing sugar, cinnamon and coffee mixture in a food processor and process until fluffy.

3 To make filling, fold liqueur into whipped cream. Spread filling over one cake and top with remaining cake. Spread icing over top of cake.

Cook's tip: To make a nonalcoholic version of this dessert dissolve 1 teaspoon instant coffee powder in 1 teaspoon hot water, cool, then fold into cream in place of the liqueur.

Coffee Sandwich Cake

SPICED GINGER DROPS

Ginger lovers won't be able to get enough of these spicy cookies.

Makes 30
Oven temperature 180°C, 350°F, Gas 4

- ☐ **125 g/4 oz flour, sifted**
- ☐ **¹/₄ teaspoon ground ginger**
- ☐ **¹/₄ teaspoon ground mixed spice**
- ☐ **¹/₄ teaspoon ground cinnamon**
- ☐ **¹/₂ teaspoon bicarbonate of soda**
- ☐ **60 g/2 oz butter, cut into pieces**
- ☐ **90 g/3 oz brown sugar**
- ☐ **2¹/₂ tablespoons golden syrup, warmed**
- ☐ **1¹/₂ tablespoons finely chopped glacé ginger or stem ginger in syrup**

1   Place flour, ground ginger, mixed spice, cinnamon and bicarbonate of soda in a large mixing bowl. Rub in butter until mixture resembles fine breadcrumbs. Stir in sugar, golden syrup and glacé or stem ginger.

2   Turn dough onto a lightly floured surface and knead to form a soft dough. Roll rounded teaspoons of mixture into balls and place 3 cm/1¹/₄ in apart on greased baking trays. Bake for 10-15 minutes or until golden. Transfer biscuits to wire racks to cool.

Spiced Ginger Drops

DUNDEE CAKE

This traditional Scottish recipe, dating right back to the eighteenth century, is characterised by the almonds that decorate the top of the cake.

Makes a 20 cm/8 in round cake
Oven temperature 150°C, 300°F, Gas 2

- ☐ **250 g/8 oz butter, softened**
- ☐ **1 teaspoon rum essence**
- ☐ **220 g/7 oz caster sugar**
- ☐ **4 eggs, lightly beaten**
- ☐ **250 g/8 oz flour**
- ☐ **1 teaspoon baking powder**
- ☐ **3 tablespoons cornflour**
- ☐ **250 g/8 oz sultanas**
- ☐ **250 g/8 oz currants**
- ☐ **125 g/4 oz mixed peel**
- ☐ **125 g/4 oz slivered almonds**
- ☐ **60 g/2 oz glacé cherries, halved**
- ☐ **2 teaspoons finely grated orange rind**
- ☐ **1 tablespoon orange juice**
- ☐ **45 g/1½ oz blanched almonds**

Spoon mixture into a greased and lined deep 20 cm/8 in round cake tin.

1   Place butter and rum essence into a large mixing bowl and beat until light and fluffy. Gradually add sugar, beating well after each addition until mixture is creamy.
2   Add eggs one at a time, beating well after each addition. Sift together flour, baking powder and cornflour, then fold into butter mixture.
3   Stir in sultanas, currants, mixed peel, slivered almonds, cherries, orange rind and orange juice. Spoon mixture into a greased and lined deep 20 cm/8 in round cake tin. Decorate top of cake with almonds, arranged in circles, and bake for 2½-3 hours, or until cooked when tested with a skewer. Set aside to cool in tin before turning out.

Decorate the top of the cake with almonds, arranged in circles.

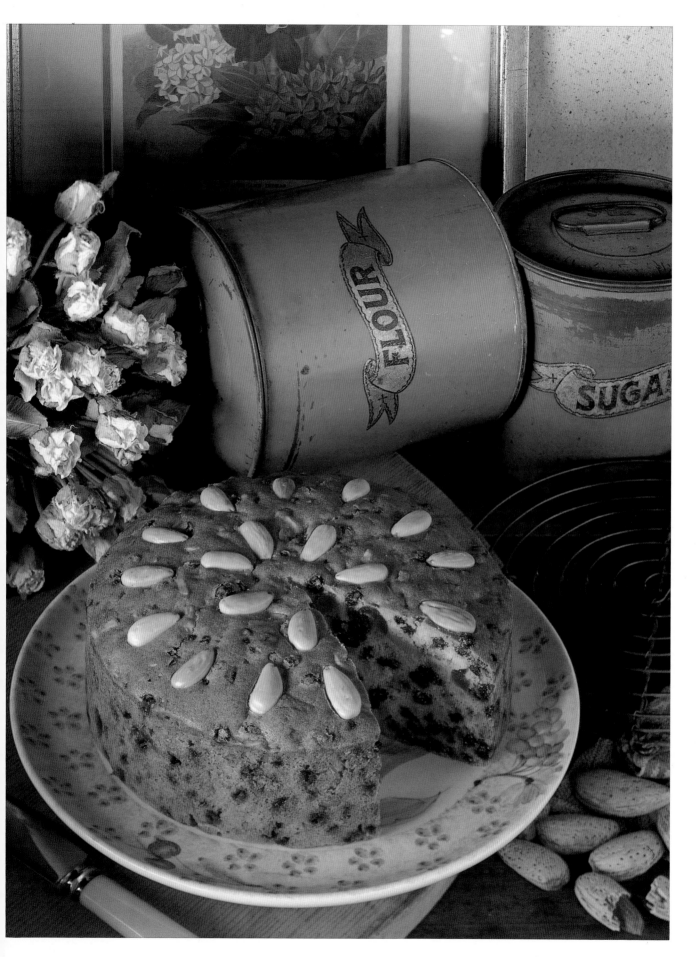

TANGY APPLE AND APRICOT LOAF

An easily prepared moist loaf that is great for picnics and lunch boxes.

Makes an 11 x 21 cm/4½ x 8½ in loaf
Oven temperature 180°C, 350°F, Gas 4

- ☐ **155 g/5 oz dried apricots, chopped**
- ☐ **125 g/4 oz dried apples, chopped**
- ☐ **2 teaspoons finely grated lemon rind**
- ☐ **2 tablespoons lemon juice**
- ☐ **170 mL/5½ fl oz water**
- ☐ **185 g/6 oz brown sugar**
- ☐ **60 g/2 oz butter**
- ☐ **185 g/6 oz wholemeal self-raising flour, sifted**
- ☐ **60 g/2 oz self-raising flour, sifted**

1 Place apricots, apples, lemon rind, lemon juice, water, sugar and butter in a saucepan, bring to the boil and simmer for 5 minutes. Remove pan from heat and set aside to cool for 5 minutes.
2 Stir wholemeal and self-raising flours into fruit mixture. Spoon batter into greased and lined 11 x 21 cm/ 4½ x 8½ in loaf tin and bake for 1 hour or until cooked when tested with a skewer. Cool loaf in tin for 15 minutes before turning onto a wire rack to cool completely.

ORANGE AND LIME YOGURT SYRUP CAKE

Serves 10
Oven temperature 180°C, 350°F, Gas 4

- ☐ **125 g/4 oz butter**
- ☐ **1 teaspoon grated lime rind**
- ☐ **3 teaspoons grated orange rind**
- ☐ **220 g/7 oz caster sugar**
- ☐ **3 eggs**
- ☐ **200 g/6½ oz self-raising flour, sifted**
- ☐ **125 g/4 oz natural yogurt**

LIME AND ORANGE SYRUP
- ☐ **2 tablespoons lime juice**
- ☐ **3 tablespoons orange juice**
- ☐ **3 tablespoons sugar**

1 Place butter, and lime and orange rinds in a large mixing bowl and beat until light and creamy. Add sugar a little at a time, beating well after each addition.
2 Beat in eggs one at a time and mix well. Fold through flour alternately with yogurt. Spoon mixture into a greased 20 cm/8 in ring tin and bake for 30-35 minutes or until cooked. Stand in cake tin for 5 minutes, then turn out onto a wire rack with a tray underneath.
3 To make syrup, place lime juice, orange juice and sugar in a saucepan. Cook over a medium heat, stirring constantly, until sugar dissolves. Bring mixture to the boil without stirring, and boil for 3 minutes. Remove from heat and pour hot syrup over hot cake. Set aside to cool.

WHOLEMEAL CHERRY AND ALMOND BREAD

An eye-catching, tasty bread that can be served while still warm. Great to serve with coffee in place of dessert.

Makes 30 slices
Oven temperature 180°C, 350°F, Gas 4

- ☐ **2 eggs**
- ☐ **125 g/4 oz caster sugar**
- ☐ **155 g/5 oz whole blanched almonds**
- ☐ **125 g/4 oz whole red glacé cherries**
- ☐ **125 g/4 oz self-raising flour, sifted**
- ☐ **125 g/4 oz wholemeal flour, sifted**

1 Place eggs and sugar in a bowl and beat with an electric beater for 6 minutes or until mixture is thick and creamy. Stir in almonds, cherries, self-raising and wholemeal flours.
2 Spread mixture into a greased and lined 7 x 26 cm/3 x 10½ in bar tin and bake for 30-35 minutes or until firm and browned. Cool bread in tin for 15 minutes before turning onto a wire rack to cool completely. Wrap in foil and leave overnight.
3 Cut bread into 3 mm/⅛ in slices using a sharp knife. Place slices on oven trays in single layers and bake for 10 minutes or until bread is lightly browned.

Cook's tip: If you have an electric knife, it is ideal for cutting this loaf.

STRAWBERRY TARTS

The wicked jam and moreish topping will make these tarts disappear in no time.

Makes 24
Oven temperature 200°F, 400°F, Gas 6

- ☐ **125 g/4 oz butter**
- ☐ **60 g/2 oz sugar**
- ☐ **1 egg**
- ☐ **2 teaspoons milk**
- ☐ **250 g/8 oz self-raising flour, sifted**
- ☐ **185 g/6 oz strawberry jam**

COCONUT TOPPING
- ☐ **60 g/2 oz sugar**
- ☐ **60 g/2 oz desiccated coconut**
- ☐ **1 egg**

1   Place butter and sugar in a bowl and beat until light and fluffy. Mix in egg and milk, then flour, mixing to form a dough. Turn out onto a lightly floured surface and roll out thinly, cut into rounds using a 7.5 cm/3 in cutter and place in lightly greased patty tins. Top with a spoonful of jam.
2   To make topping, place sugar, coconut and egg in a bowl and mix well. Place a spoonful of topping on each tart and bake for 10-15 minutes, or until tops are golden and bases are cooked.

Variations
You might like to change the filling and/or topping for the Strawberry Tarts.
Lemon Tarts: Replace strawberry jam with lemon butter. Top with topping and cook as for Strawberry Tarts.
Orange Tarts: Remove rind and pith from 2 oranges and chop orange flesh. Use in place of strawberry jam. Top with topping and cook as for Strawberry Tarts.
Marmalade Tarts: Replace strawberry jam with marmalade. Top with a rolled oats topping. To make rolled oats topping, place 60 g/2 oz rolled oats, 60 g/2 oz brown sugar, 60 g/2 oz wholemeal self-raising flour in a bowl and stir in 90 g/3 oz butter, melted. Sprinkle over tarts and cook as for Strawberry Tarts.
Jam Tarts: To make plain jam tarts, fill the tarts with a jam of your choice and omit topping. Cook as for Strawberry Tarts.

Wholemeal Cherry and Almond Bread, Strawberry Tarts, Orange and Lime Yogurt Syrup Cake

CHILLI SOUP BISCUITS

Makes 16 biscuits
Oven temperature 220°C, 425°F, Gas 7

- [ ] **2 rashers bacon, finely chopped**
- [ ] **250 g/8 oz flour**
- [ ] **3 teaspoons baking powder**
- [ ] **1/2 teaspoon salt**
- [ ] **90 g/3 oz butter**
- [ ] **90 g/3 oz grated mature Cheddar**
- [ ] **2 small fresh red chillies, seeded and finely chopped**
- [ ] **170 mL/5 1/2 fl oz milk**
- [ ] **30 g/1 oz butter, melted**

1 Cook bacon in a nonstick frying pan over a medium high heat for 3-4 minutes or until crisp. Remove from pan and drain on absorbent kitchen paper.
2 Sift together flour, baking powder and salt into a mixing bowl. Rub in butter with fingertips until mixture resembles coarse breadcrumbs.
3 Stir bacon, cheese and chillies into flour mixture. Add milk and mix to form a soft dough. Turn onto a floured surface and knead lightly with fingertips until smooth.
4 Using heel of hand, gently press dough out to 1 cm/1/2 in thick. Cut out rounds using a 5 cm/2 in pastry cutter. Place on a greased baking tray and brush with melted butter. Bake for 12-15 minutes or until golden brown. Remove from tray and cool on a wire rack or serve warm spread with butter.

HERB ROLLS

Spring onions and herbs have been added to this soda bread recipe. The dough is then formed into rolls to make the quickest herb-flavoured rolls ever.

Makes 12 rolls
Oven temperature 180°C, 350°F, Gas 4

- [ ] **90 g/3 oz butter**
- [ ] **8 spring onions, finely chopped**
- [ ] **315 g/10 oz flour**
- [ ] **125 g/4 oz self-raising flour**
- [ ] **3 teaspoons baking powder**
- [ ] **1/2 teaspoon bicarbonate of soda**
- [ ] **4 teaspoons sugar**
- [ ] **1 tablespoon finely chopped fresh parsley**
- [ ] **1 tablespoon finely chopped fresh basil**
- [ ] **125 mL/4 fl oz buttermilk or milk**
- [ ] **3 eggs, lightly beaten**
- [ ] **1 egg, beaten with 1 1/2 teaspoons olive oil**

1 Melt butter in a frying pan and cook spring onions over a medium heat for 2-3 minutes or until onions are soft. Remove from heat and set aside.
2 Sift together flour and self-raising flour, baking powder and bicarbonate of soda into a large mixing bowl. Stir in sugar, parsley and basil. Combine milk, eggs and onion mixture and mix into flour mixture to form a firm dough.
3 Turn onto a floured surface and knead lightly until smooth. Divide dough into twelve portions and roll each into a ball then place on greased and floured baking trays. Brush each roll with egg and oil mixture and bake for 30-35 minutes or until cooked through.

SODA BREAD

A loaf for when you need bread unexpectedly. Soda bread is made with bicarbonate of soda rather than yeast so requires no rising. It is best eaten slightly warm.

Serves 8
Oven temperature 200°C, 400°F, Gas 6

- [ ] **500 g/1 lb flour**
- [ ] **1 teaspoon bicarbonate of soda**
- [ ] **1 teaspoon salt**
- [ ] **45 g/1 1/2 oz butter**
- [ ] **500 mL/16 fl oz buttermilk or milk**

1 Sift together flour, bicarbonate of soda and salt into a mixing bowl. Rub in butter using fingertips until mixture resembles coarse breadcrumbs. Make a well in the centre of the flour mixture and pour in milk. Using a round-ended knife, mix to form a soft dough.
2 Turn dough onto a floured surface and knead lightly until smooth. Shape into an 18 cm/7 in round and place on a greased and floured baking tray. Score dough into eighths using a sharp knife. Dust lightly with flour and bake for 35-40 minutes or until loaf sounds hollow when tapped on the base.

Serving suggestion: Wonderful spread with lashings of treacle or golden syrup.

Herb Rolls, Soda Bread, Chilli Soup Biscuits

GINGERBREAD UPSIDE-DOWN CAKE

Makes a 20 cm/8 in ring cake
Oven temperature 180°C, 350°F, Gas 4

- ☐ **60 g/2 oz dried apricots**
- ☐ **60 g/2 oz butter, softened**
- ☐ **90 g/3 oz brown sugar**
- ☐ **4 tablespoons chopped pecan nuts**

GINGERBREAD CAKE
- ☐ **125 g/4 oz flour, sifted**
- ☐ **60 g/2 oz self-raising flour, sifted**
- ☐ **$\frac{1}{2}$ teaspoon bicarbonate of soda**
- ☐ **3 teaspoons ground ginger**
- ☐ **$\frac{1}{2}$ teaspoon ground nutmeg**
- ☐ **90 g/3 oz brown sugar**
- ☐ **125 g/4 oz golden syrup**
- ☐ **125 mL/4 fl oz water**
- ☐ **125 g/4 oz butter**

1   Place apricots in a bowl, cover with boiling water, cover bowl and set aside to soak for 30 minutes. Drain and set aside. Place butter and sugar in a small bowl and beat until smooth. Spread butter mixture over the base of a greased and lined 20 cm/8 in ring tin. Sprinkle with pecans and top with apricots, cut side up.

2   To make gingerbread, place flour and self-raising flour, bicarbonate of soda, ginger, nutmeg and sugar in a large bowl and mix to combine. Place golden syrup, water and butter in a saucepan and cook over a low heat, stirring, until butter is melted and ingredients are combined. Remove pan from heat and set aside to cool for 5 minutes. Pour golden syrup mixture into dry ingredients and mix well to combine. Spoon gingerbread into prepared tin and bake for 35-40 minutes or until cake is cooked when tested with a skewer. Allow cake to stand for 15 minutes before turning out.

COFFEE KISSES

The dough for these coffee-flavoured biscuits is similar to a shortbread – making it perfect for piping. Follow the step-by-step instructions and see just how easy these biscuits are to make.

Makes 25
Oven temperature 180°C, 350°F, Gas 4

- ☐ **250 g/8 oz butter, softened**
- ☐ **100 g/3¹/₂ oz icing sugar, sifted**
- ☐ **2 teaspoons instant coffee powder dissolved in 1 tablespoon hot water, cooled**
- ☐ **250 g/8 oz flour, sifted**
- ☐ **45 g/1¹/₂ oz dark chocolate, melted**
- ☐ **icing sugar**

1 Place butter and icing sugar in a large mixing bowl and beat until light and fluffy. Stir in coffee mixture and flour.
2 Spoon mixture into a piping bag fitted with a medium star nozzle and pipe 2 cm/³/₄ in rounds of mixture 2 cm/³/₄ in apart on greased baking trays. Bake for 10-12 minutes or until lightly browned. Stand on trays for 5 minutes before removing to wire racks to cool completely.
3 Join biscuits with a little melted chocolate, then dust with icing sugar.

Spoon mixture into a piping bag fitted with a medium star nozzle.

Pipe 2 cm/ ³/₄ in rounds of mixture 2 cm/³/₄ in apart on greased baking trays.

Join biscuits with a little melted chocolate, then dust with icing sugar.

MUESLI SLICE

Makes 24
Oven temperature 160°C, 325°F, Gas 3

- [ ] **60 g/2 oz butter**
- [ ] **3 tablespoons honey**
- [ ] **2 eggs, lightly beaten**
- [ ] **250 g/8 oz natural yogurt**
- [ ] **250 g/8 oz ricotta cheese**
- [ ] **45 g/1¹/₂ oz desiccated coconut**
- [ ] **45 g/1¹/₂ oz flaked almonds**
- [ ] **125 g/4 oz chopped raisins**
- [ ] **155 g/5 oz wholemeal flour, sifted and husks returned**
- [ ] **3 tablespoons sesame seeds**

1 Place butter and honey in a mixing bowl and beat to combine. Gradually mix in eggs and yogurt, then stir in ricotta cheese, coconut, almonds, raisins, flour and sesame seeds.
2 Pour mixture into a lightly greased and lined shallow 18 x 28 cm/7 x 11 in cake tin and bake for 35-40 minutes, or until firm and golden brown. Cool slice in tin.

SPEEDY DATE SLICE

Makes 24
Oven temperature 180°C, 350°F, Gas 4

- [ ] **90 g/3 oz butter**
- [ ] **185 g/6 oz raw (muscovado) sugar**
- [ ] **1 egg**
- [ ] **155 g/5 oz chopped dried dates**
- [ ] **125 g/4 oz self-raising flour**
- [ ] **60 g/2 oz muesli**
- [ ] **2 tablespoons sunflower seeds**
- [ ] **1 tablespoon poppy seeds**
- [ ] **2 tablespoons chopped pumpkin seeds**
- [ ] **125 g/4 oz natural yogurt**

LEMON ICING
- [ ] **2 teaspoons butter**
- [ ] **2 tablespoons hot water**
- [ ] **4 tablespoons lemon juice**
- [ ] **350 g/11 oz icing sugar, sifted**

1 Place butter and raw (muscovado) sugar in a small mixing bowl and beat until light and fluffy. Beat in egg, then stir in dates, flour, muesli, sunflower seeds, poppy seeds, pumpkin seeds and yogurt.
2 Spoon mixture into a lightly greased and lined shallow 18 x 28 cm/7 x 11 in cake tin and bake for 25 minutes, or until firm and golden brown. Cool in tin.

3 To make icing, melt butter in hot water and combine with lemon juice. Add icing sugar and beat until smooth. Spread evenly over cooled slice. Allow icing to set then cut into fingers or squares.

OATY BISCUITS

Makes 15
Oven temperature 180°C, 350°F, Gas 4

- [ ] **60 g/2 oz butter**
- [ ] **3 tablespoons brown sugar**
- [ ] **1 teaspoon vanilla essence**
- [ ] **1 egg**
- [ ] **90 g/3 oz rolled oats**
- [ ] **3 tablespoons wheat germ**
- [ ] **75 g/2¹/₂ oz wholemeal self-raising flour, sifted and husks returned**
- [ ] **3 tablespoons chopped pecans**
- [ ] **3 tablespoons chopped dates**

ICING
- [ ] **2 teaspoons butter**
- [ ] **3 tablespoons hot water**
- [ ] **155 g/5 oz icing sugar, sifted**
- [ ] **few drops pink food colouring**

1 Place butter in a small mixing bowl and beat until light and fluffy. Add brown sugar and vanilla essence and beat to combine. Add egg and beat to combine.
2 Stir in oats, wheat germ, flour, pecans and dates and mix well.
3 Place spoonfuls of mixture onto lightly greased baking trays and bake for 10 minutes or until golden brown. Remove biscuits from trays and cool on a wire rack.
4 To make icing, melt butter in hot water. Combine with icing sugar and beat until smooth. Colour with food colouring and place a drop of icing on each biscuit.

WHOLEHEARTED ROCKCAKES

Makes 20
Oven temperature 180°C, 350°F, Gas 4

- [ ] **315 g/10 oz wholemeal self-raising flour, sifted and husks returned**
- [ ] **¹/₂ teaspoon ground cinnamon**
- [ ] **4 tablespoons raw (muscovado) sugar**
- [ ] **125 g/4 oz butter**
- [ ] **125 g/4 oz raisins, chopped**

- [ ] **30 g/1 oz dried apples, chopped**
- [ ] **1 egg, lightly beaten**
- [ ] **4 tablespoons milk**

1 Place flour, cinnamon and sugar in a large mixing bowl. Rub in butter with fingertips. Stir in raisins and apples, then gradually add egg and enough milk to make a thick dough.
2 Place large spoonfuls of mixture onto greased baking trays and bake for 12-15 minutes, or until cooked through and golden brown.

MINCEMEAT SHORTCAKE

Serves 8
Oven temperature 180°C, 350°F, Gas 4

- [ ] **250 g/8 oz self-raising flour**
- [ ] **125 g/4 oz butter**
- [ ] **125 g/4 oz caster sugar**
- [ ] **1 egg, beaten**
- [ ] **1 tablespoon lemon juice**
- [ ] **200 g/6¹/₂ oz prepared mincemeat**
- [ ] **1 egg white, lightly beaten**
- [ ] **extra caster sugar**

1 Place flour in a food processor and process to sift. Add butter and process until mixture resembles fine breadcrumbs. Add sugar, egg and lemon juice and process to make a firm dough. Turn dough onto a lightly floured surface and knead briefly. Wrap dough in plastic food wrap and refrigerate for 30 minutes.
2 Divide dough into two equal portions. Roll one portion out to line the base and sides of a lightly greased 20 cm/8 in round shallow cake tin. Spread mincemeat over base.
3 Roll out remaining dough to make a 21 cm/8¹/₂ in circle and place over mincemeat. Press edges together, brush with egg white, sprinkle with extra caster sugar and bake for 30-35 minutes or until cooked. Stand for 10 minutes before turning out onto a wire rack to cool.

Wholehearted Rockcakes, Speedy Date Slice, Oaty Biscuits, Muesli Slice

BASIC FRUIT MIXTURE

This basic fruit mixture is designed for those who wish to make the most of their time during the Christmas season. Make the mixture up to one month in advance and store it in an airtight container, in the refrigerator. This amount of mixture is sufficient to make a Christmas cake, a pudding and twenty-four mince pies. You may like to use brandy or sweet sherry in place of the melon liqueur.

- [ ] **1 kg/2 lb sultanas, chopped**
- [ ] **375 g/12 oz currants**
- [ ] **170 g/5¹/₂ oz raisins, chopped**
- [ ] **30 g/1 oz mixed peel, chopped**
- [ ] **155 g/5 oz pitted dried dates, chopped**
- [ ] **170 g/5¹/₂ oz dried apricots, chopped**
- [ ] **155 g/5 oz pitted prunes, chopped**
- [ ] **250 g/8 oz glacé cherries, quartered**
- [ ] **155 g/5 oz glacé pineapple, chopped**
- [ ] **¹/₂ honeydew melon, peeled, seeded and chopped**
- [ ] **75 g/2¹/₂ oz angelica, chopped**
- [ ] **350 g/11 oz golden syrup**
- [ ] **250 mL/8 fl oz melon-flavoured liqueur**

Place sultanas, currants, raisins, mixed peel, dates, apricots, prunes, cherries, pineapple, honeydew and angelica in a large mixing bowl. Stir in golden syrup and liqueur and mix well to combine. Cover tightly with plastic food wrap and stand overnight, or transfer to an airtight container and store in the refrigerator until required.

MINCE PIES

Makes 24
Oven temperature 180°C, 350°F, Gas 4

FRUIT FILLING
- [ ] **2 tablespoons golden syrup**
- [ ] **125 g/4 oz butter, frozen and grated**
- [ ] **¹/₄ quantity Basic Fruit Mixture**

ALMOND PASTRY
- [ ] **250 g/8 oz flour**
- [ ] **125 g/4 oz butter, chilled and cut into small pieces**
- [ ] **170 g/5¹/₂ oz caster sugar**
- [ ] **60 g/2 oz ground almonds**
- [ ] **3 drops almond essence**
- [ ] **4-5 tablespoons iced water**

1 To make filling, place golden syrup, butter and fruit mixture in a bowl and mix to combine. Set aside.

2 To make pastry, sift flour into a bowl. Rub in butter with fingertips until mixture resembles fine breadcrumbs. Stir in sugar, almonds, almond essence and enough water to mix to a firm dough. Wrap pastry in plastic food wrap and refrigerate for 30 minutes.

3 Roll out pastry to 3 mm/¹/₈ in thick and cut twenty-four 7 cm/3 in rounds and twenty-four 6 cm/2¹/₂ in rounds, using metal pastry cutters. Place large pastry rounds in lightly greased patty tins. Spoon in filling and top with smaller pastry rounds. Press edges together and bake for 15-20 minutes or until pastry is golden and crisp. Stand in tins for 10 minutes before removing to a wire rack to cool.

Cook's tip: Mince pies are delicious served warm or at room temperature dusted with icing sugar.

SPICY SYRUP CHRISTMAS CAKE

Makes a 23 cm/9 in square cake
Oven temperature 160°C, 325°F, Gas 3

- [ ] **250 g/8 oz butter**
- [ ] **425 g/13¹/₂ oz semolina**
- [ ] **5 eggs, lightly beaten**
- [ ] **220 g/7 oz caster sugar**
- [ ] **2 teaspoons mixed spice**
- [ ] **1 teaspoon grated orange rind**
- [ ] **¹/₂ quantity Basic Fruit Mixture**

ORANGE SYRUP
- [ ] **1 orange**
- [ ] **375 mL/12 fl oz water**
- [ ] **375 g/12 oz sugar**
- [ ] **1 cinnamon stick**

1 Place butter in a large bowl and beat until light and creamy. Add semolina and beat in eggs one at a time, beating well after each addition.

2 Add caster sugar a little at a time, beating well after each addition. Stir in mixed spice, orange rind and fruit mixture. Mix well to combine. Spoon mixture into a 23 cm/9 in lined, square cake tin and bake for 2¹/₂-3 hours or until cooked when tested with a skewer.

3 To make syrup, cut 2-3 thin slices of rind from the orange using a vegetable peeler. Place water, sugar, cinnamon stick and orange peel in a saucepan and cook over a medium heat, stirring constantly until sugar dissolves. Bring syrup to the boil without stirring, then reduce heat and simmer for 10 minutes. Set aside to cool slightly, then strain.

4 Pour syrup over cooked hot cake and set aside. Allow cake to completely cool in cake tin.

Preparing the cake tin: To achieve a good, evenly shaped Christmas cake, line your cake with heavy-duty aluminium foil, placing the shiny side against the tin. Cut three strips of newspaper or brown paper 2.5 cm/1 in wider than the depth of the cake tin. Position these strips around the outside of the tin and secure in place with string. The paper acts an insulator and prevents the outside of the cake from burning.

STEAMED CHRISTMAS PUDDING

Serves 8

- [ ] **250 g/ 8 oz butter, softened**
- [ ] **100 g/3¹/₂ oz semolina**
- [ ] **3 eggs, lightly beaten**
- [ ] **4 tablespoons golden syrup**
- [ ] **140 g/4¹/₂ oz rye breadcrumbs, made from stale bread**
- [ ] **220 g/7 oz ground hazelnuts or almonds**
- [ ] **¹/₄ quantity Basic Fruit Mixture**

1 Place butter in a bowl and beat until light and fluffy. Add semolina, eggs and golden syrup and beat well to combine. Fold in breadcrumbs, hazelnuts or almonds and fruit mixture.

2 Spoon pudding mixture into a large well-greased pudding basin. Cover with a large piece of greased aluminium foil. If the basin has a lid, place the lid over the foil and bring surplus foil up over it. If the basin has no lid, tie the foil securely in position, using string. Lower pudding into a large saucepan containing sufficient boiling water to come halfway up the side of the basin and cook for 4 hours. Add more boiling water as required during the cooking. On completion of cooking remove and set aside to cool to room temperature. Refrigerate in basin for up to six weeks. On the day of serving steam for 1 hour then turn out and serve.

Cook's tip: Christmas pudding is delicious

served with Hard Brandy Sauce. This can be made up to 3 months in advance and frozen, or it will keep in the refrigerator for up to a week. To make, place 125 g/4 oz softened butter in a bowl and beat until light and fluffy. Add 350 g/11 oz sifted icing sugar a little at a time, beating well after each addition until mixture is light and fluffy. Beat in 2 tablespoons brandy. Store and use as required.

VICTORIA SANDWICH CAKE

Makes a 20 cm/8 in round cake
Oven temperature 180°C, 350°F, Gas 4

- [ ] **4 eggs**
- [ ] **170 g/5¹/₂ oz caster sugar**
- [ ] **125 g/4 oz self-raising flour**
- [ ] **1 tablespoon cornflour**
- [ ] **4 tablespoons warm water**
- [ ] **1¹/₂ tablespoons melted butter**
- [ ] **1 tablespoon icing sugar, sifted**

JAM AND CREAM FILLING
- [ ] **155 g/5 oz strawberry or raspberry jam**
- [ ] **125 mL/4 fl oz cream (double), whipped**
- [ ] **1 tablespoon icing sugar**

1   Place eggs in a bowl and beat until thick and creamy. Gradually add sugar, beating well after each addition. Continue beating until mixture becomes thick. This will take about 10 minutes.

2   Sift together flour and cornflour over egg mixture and fold in. Stir in water and melted butter.

3   Divide mixture evenly between two greased and lined 20 cm/8 in round sandwich tins and bake for 20-25 minutes or until cake shrinks away slightly from sides of tin and springs back when touched with the fingertips. Stand in cake tin for 5 minutes before turning onto a wire rack to cool completely.

4   To assemble, spread one sponge cake with jam, then top with whipped cream and remaining sponge cake. Sprinkle top of cake with icing sugar and serve.

Passion Fruit Sandwich Cake: Spread one sponge cake with lemon butter, then top with whipped cream and remaining sponge cake. Spread top of cake with passion fruit icing. To make icing, combine 15 g/¹/₂ oz softened butter and 75 g/2¹/₂ oz passion fruit pulp with 155 g/5 oz sifted icing sugar, sifted and mix with enough water to make icing of spreadable consistency.

SCONES

Makes 12
Oven temperature 220°C, 425°F, Gas 7

- [ ] **250 g/8 oz self-raising flour**
- [ ] **1 teaspoon baking powder**
- [ ] **2 teaspoons sugar**
- [ ] **45 g/1¹/₂ oz butter**
- [ ] **1 egg**
- [ ] **125 mL/4 fl oz milk**

1   Sift together flour and baking powder into a large mixing bowl. Stir in sugar, then rub in butter using fingertips until mixture resembles coarse breadcrumbs.

2   Whisk together egg and milk. Make a well in centre of flour mixture and pour in egg mixture. Mix to form a soft dough, turn onto a floured surface and knead lightly.

3   Press dough out to a 2 cm/1³/₄ in thickness, using palm of hand. Cut out scones using a floured 5 cm/2 in cutter. Avoid twisting the cutter or the scones will rise unevenly.

4   Arrange close together on a greased and lightly floured baking tray or in a 20 cm/8 in shallow cake tin. Brush with a little milk and bake for 12-15 minutes or until golden brown.

Scones

FIG PINWHEEL BISCUITS

Pinwheel biscuits always look impressive and are very easy to make. Just follow the step-by-step instructions for making these delicious biscuits that wrap a spiced dough around a wonderful fig and almond filling.

Makes 50
Oven temperature 180°C, 350°F, Gas 4

- ☐ **170 g/5¹/₂ oz butter**
- ☐ **170 g/5¹/₂ oz brown sugar**
- ☐ **1 egg**
- ☐ **¹/₂ teaspoon vanilla essence**
- ☐ **375 g/12 oz flour**
- ☐ **¹/₂ teaspoon bicarbonate of soda**
- ☐ **¹/₄ teaspoon ground cinnamon**
- ☐ **¹/₄ teaspoon ground nutmeg**
- ☐ **2 tablespoons milk**

FIG AND ALMOND FILLING
- ☐ **250 g/8 oz dried figs, finely chopped**
- ☐ **60 g/2 oz sugar**
- ☐ **125 mL/4 fl oz water**
- ☐ **¹/₂ teaspoon ground mixed spice**
- ☐ **30 g/1 oz almonds, finely chopped**

1 To make filling, place figs, sugar, water and mixed spice in a saucepan and bring to the boil. Reduce heat and cook, stirring, for 2-3 minutes or until mixture is thick. Remove from heat and stir in almonds. Set aside to cool.

2 Place butter in a large mixing bowl and beat until light and fluffy. Gradually add sugar, beating well after each addition until mixture is creamy. Beat in egg and vanilla essence.

3 Sift together flour, bicarbonate of soda, cinnamon and nutmeg. Beat milk and half the flour mixture into butter mixture. Stir in remaining flour mixture. Turn dough onto a lightly floured surface and knead lightly. Roll into a ball, wrap in plastic food wrap and refrigerate for 30 minutes.

4 Divide dough into two portions. Roll out one portion to a 20 x 28 cm/8 x 11 in rectangle and spread with filling. Roll up from the long side, like a Swiss roll. Repeat with remaining dough and filling. Wrap rolls in plastic food wrap and refrigerate for 15 minutes or until you are ready to cook the biscuits.

5 Cut rolls into 1 cm/¹/₂ in slices. Place slices on greased baking trays and cook for 10-12 minutes. Stand biscuits on trays for 1 minute before removing to a wire rack to cool completely.

Freeze it: The uncooked rolls can be frozen if you wish. When you have unexpected guests or the biscuit barrel is empty, these biscuits are great standbys.

Divide dough into two portions. Roll out one portion to a 20 x 28 cm/8 x 11 in rectangle and spread with filling.

Roll up dough from the long side, like a Swiss roll. Wrap rolls in plastic food wrap.

Cut rolls into 1 cm/ ¹/₂ in slices and place on greased baking trays.

BASIC BUTTER CAKE

Add interest to the cake stall by cooking cakes in differently shaped tins. The following recipe works perfectly using the cake tins and cooking times we have given in the chart.

- ☐ **125 g/4 oz butter**
- ☐ **1 teaspoon vanilla essence**
- ☐ **185 g/6 oz caster sugar**
- ☐ **2 eggs**
- ☐ **185 g/6 oz flour, sifted**
- ☐ **1½ teaspoons baking powder**
- ☐ **125 mL/4 fl oz milk**

1 Cream butter and vanilla essence in a small mixing bowl until light and fluffy. Add sugar gradually, beating well after each addition.

2 Beat in eggs one at a time and fold in. Combine flour and baking powder alternately with milk. Spoon mixture into prepared cake pan.

3 Bake according to size of cake tin you have chosen. Stand for 5 minutes before turning onto a wire rack to cook completely. When cooked, ice with frosting or icing of your choice.

Variations

Apple cake: Spread two-thirds of the cake mixture into the prepared cake tin. Top with 200 g/6½ oz stewed apple, then remaining cake mixture. Bake according to cake tin size. Stand 10 minutes before turning out.

Orange cake: Replace vanilla essence with 2 teaspoons grated orange rind when creaming butter. Substitute 4 tablespoons orange juice for milk. Bake according to cake tin size. Stand 5 minutes before turning out.

Coffee cake: Replace vanilla essence with 1 tablespoon instant coffee dissolved in 1 tablespoon boiling water. Cool then cream with butter. Bake according to cake tin size. Stand 5 minutes before turning out.

Coconut cake: Replace vanilla essence with ½ teaspoon coconut essence and add 45 g/1½ oz desiccated coconut with flour and baking powder. Bake according to cake tin size. Stand 5 minutes before turning out.

Banana cake: Omit milk and add 3 small very ripe mashed bananas to creamed butter and egg mixture. Combine flour, baking powder and 1 teaspoon bicarbonate of soda and fold into butter and egg mixture. Bake according to cake tin size. Stand 5 minutes before turning out.

Basic Butter Cake, Apple Cake, Coffee Cake

Cook's tip: Test your cake just before the end of cooking time. Insert a skewer into the thickest part of the cake. If it comes away clean, your cake is cooked. If there is still cake mixture on the skewer, cook 5 minutes more then test again.

Alternatively, you can gently press the top of cake with your fingertips. When cooked, the depression will spring back quickly. When the cake starts to leave the sides of tin, it is also a good indication that cake is cooked.

PREPARATION
AND COOKING TIMES

TIN SIZE	PREPARATION	TEMPERATURE	COOKING TIME (minutes)
20 cm/8 in ring tin	Grease and line	180°C, 350°F, Gas 4	40
20 cm/8 in deep round tin	Grease and line	180°C, 350°F, Gas 4	50
20 cm/8 in baba tin	Lightly grease	180°C, 350°F, Gas 4	40
11 x 21 cm/4¹/₂ x 8 in loaf tin	Grease and line	180°C, 350°F, Gas 4	60
24 patty tins	Paper patty cake cases	200°C, 400°F, Gas 6	15

LEMON CREAM CHEESE FROSTING

- [ ] 125 g/4 oz cream cheese
- [ ] 1 teaspoon grated lemon rind
- [ ] 250 g/8 oz icing sugar, sifted
- [ ] 2 teaspooons lemon juice

Beat cream cheese in a small mixing bowl until creamy. Add lemon rind, icing sugar and lemon juice and mix well.

Cook's tip: To soften cream cheese, leave at room temperature. To soften in the microwave, remove foil wrap, place in a microwave-safe dish and cook on HIGH (100%) for 20 seconds.

CHOCOLATE FROSTING

- [ ] 90 g/3 oz butter
- [ ] 250 g/8 oz icing sugar, sifted
- [ ] 1 tablespoon cocoa powder, sifted
- [ ] 2 tablespoons cream

Beat butter in a small bowl until creamy. Add icing sugar, cocoa powder and cream. Beat until frosting is of a spreadable consistency.

Coconut Cake, Banana Cake,
Orange Cake

COFFEE FROSTING

- [ ] 60 g/2 oz butter
- [ ] 250 g/8 oz icing sugar, sifted
- [ ] 2 teaspoons instant coffee powder, dissolved in 1 tablespoon boiling water

Beat butter in a small mixing bowl until creamy. Add icing sugar and cooled coffee mixture and beat until frosting is of a spreadable consistency.

ORANGE CREAM FROSTING

- [ ] 60 g/2 oz cream cheese
- [ ] 2 tablespoons cream
- [ ] 1 teaspoon grated orange rind
- [ ] 250 g/8 oz icing sugar, sifted

Beat cream cheese, cream and orange rind in a small mixing bowl until creamy. Add icing sugar and beat until smooth.

Cook's tip: Butter icing can be used as a filling for cakes or made to a thicker consistency for piping.

EASY BERRY BREAD

*Finding an ingredient hidden inside a
loaf of bread or a cake is always fun.
To make sure the berries stay hidden in
this Easy Berry Bread during cooking
do not overfill the bread.
Follow these simple step-by-step
instructions and make this
Easy Berry Bread.*

Makes an 18 cm/7 in round
Oven temperature 220°C, 425°F, Gas 7

- [ ] **375 g/12 oz self-raising flour**
- [ ] **1 teaspoon baking powder**
- [ ] **1½ teaspoons ground mixed spice**
- [ ] **1½ tablespoons sugar**
- [ ] **30 g/1 oz butter**
- [ ] **125 mL/4 fl oz milk**
- [ ] **170 mL/5½ fl oz water**
- [ ] **200 g/6½ oz raspberries**
- [ ] **1 tablespoon caster sugar**
- [ ] **4 teaspoons milk**

1   Sift together flour, baking powder and
mixed spice into a mixing bowl. Add sugar
and rub in butter using fingertips until
mixture resembles coarse breadcrumbs.
2   Make a well in the centre of flour mixture
and, using a round-ended knife, mix in milk
and water. Mix to form a soft dough.
3   Turn dough onto a floured surface and
knead lightly until smooth. Divide dough
into two portions and flatten each into an
18 cm/7 in round. Sprinkle raspberries and
sugar over surface of one round leaving
2.5 cm/1 in around edge. Brush edge with
a little milk and place remaining round on
top. Seal edges securely using fingertips.
4   Place on a greased and lightly floured
baking tray. Brush surface with milk and
bake for 10 minutes. Reduce oven
temperature to 180°C/350°F/Gas 4 and
bake for 20-25 minutes longer or until
cooked through.

*Make a well in the centre
of flour mixture and,
using a round-ended
knife, mix in milk and
water to form a soft
dough.*

*Divide dough into
two portions and
flatten each into an
18 cm/7 in
round. Sprinkle
raspberries and
sugar over one
round leaving
2.5 cm/1 in
around edge.*

*Place remaining round
on top and seal edges
securely using
fingertips.*

COCONUT CAKE

This light moist sponge-type cake, covered with a white frosting and topped with shredded coconut is a must for any afternoon tea.

Makes a 23 cm/9 in round cake
Oven temperature 180°C, 350°F, Gas 4

- [ ] **125 g/4 oz butter, softened**
- [ ] **1 teaspoon vanilla essence**
- [ ] **220 g/7 oz caster sugar**
- [ ] **3 egg whites**
- [ ] **250 g/8 oz self-raising flour, sifted**
- [ ] **185 mL/6 fl oz milk**
- [ ] **90 g/3 oz shredded coconut**

FLUFFY FROSTING
- [ ] **125 mL/4 fl oz water**
- [ ] **315 g/10 oz sugar**
- [ ] **3 egg whites**
- [ ] **1 teaspoon lemon juice**

1   Place butter and vanilla essence in a mixing bowl and beat until light and fluffy. Gradually add caster sugar, beating well after each addition until mixture is creamy.
2   Beat in egg whites, one at a time. Fold flour and milk, alternately, into creamed mixture. Divide batter evenly between two greased and lined 23 cm/9 in sandwich tins and bake for 25-30 minutes or until cakes are cooked when tested with a skewer. Stand in tins for 5 minutes before turning onto a wire rack to cool.
3   To make frosting, place water and sugar in a saucepan and cook over a medium heat, without boiling, stirring constantly until sugar dissolves. Brush any sugar from sides of pan using a pastry brush dipped in water. Bring syrup to the boil and boil rapidly for 3-5 minutes, without stirring, or until syrup reaches the soft ball stage (115°C/239°F on a sweet thermometer). Place egg whites in a mixing bowl and beat until soft peaks form. Continue beating while pouring in syrup in a thin stream a little at a time. Continue beating until all syrup is used and frosting will stand in stiff peaks. Beat in lemon juice.
4   Spread one cake with a little frosting and sprinkle with 2 tablespoons coconut, then top with remaining cake. Spread remaining frosting over top and sides of cake and sprinkle with remaining coconut.

Cook's tip: This cake looks pretty when decorated with edible flowers such as violets, rose petals or borage.

OATY CHOC-CHIP BISCUITS

A large biscuit that is ideal for lunch boxes or as an after-school or after-work treat.

Makes 25
Oven temperature 190°C, 375°F, Gas 5

- [ ] **125 g/4 oz butter, softened**
- [ ] **¹/₂ teaspoon vanilla essence**
- [ ] **125 g/4 oz brown sugar**
- [ ] **1 egg**
- [ ] **¹/₂ teaspoon bicarbonate of soda dissolved in 4 teaspoons warm water**
- [ ] **90 g/3 oz flour, sifted**
- [ ] **140 g/4¹/₂ oz rolled oats**
- [ ] **45 g/1¹/₂ oz desiccated coconut**
- [ ] **185 g/6 oz chocolate chips**
- [ ] **75 g/2¹/₂ oz raisins**

1   Place butter, vanilla essence and sugar in a mixing bowl and beat until light and creamy. Beat in egg, bicarbonate of soda mixture and flour.
2   Stir in oats, coconut, chocolate chips and raisins. Place rounded tablespoons of mixture 10 cm/4 in apart on greased baking trays. Using a knife, spread out each mound of mixture to form a thin round, 7.5 cm/3 in in diameter. Bake for 8-10 minutes or until golden. Transfer to wire racks to cool.

ORANGE COCONUT LOAF

Makes an 11 x 21 cm/4¹/₂ x 8¹/₂ in loaf
Oven temperature 180°C, 350°F, Gas 4

- [ ] **220 g/7 oz caster sugar**
- [ ] **90 g/3 oz butter, softened**
- [ ] **1 teaspoon vanilla essence**
- [ ] **3 teaspoons finely grated orange rind**
- [ ] **185 mL/6 fl oz coconut milk**
- [ ] **3 egg whites**
- [ ] **200 g/6¹/₂ oz self-raising flour, sifted**
- [ ] **1 teaspoon baking powder**

1   Place sugar, butter, vanilla essence and orange rind in a food processor and process until combined. Add coconut milk, egg whites, flour and baking powder and process until just combined and smooth.
2   Pour batter into a greased and lined 11 x 21 cm/4¹/₂ x 8¹/₂ in loaf tin and bake for 35-40 minutes or until cooked when tested with a skewer. Stand for 5 minutes in tin before turning onto a wire rack to cool.

LIME AND COCONUT COOKIES

The tang of lime and the unique flavour and texture of coconut combine to make these wonderful cookies.

Makes 35
Oven temperature 180°C, 350°F, Gas 4

- [ ] **125 g/4 oz butter, chopped**
- [ ] **170 g/5¹/₂ oz brown sugar**
- [ ] **1 teaspoon vanilla essence**
- [ ] **1 egg**
- [ ] **125 g/4 oz flour**
- [ ] **60 g/2 oz self-raising flour**
- [ ] **90 g/3 oz rolled oats**
- [ ] **45 g/1¹/₂ oz desiccated coconut**
- [ ] **2 teaspoons finely grated lime rind**
- [ ] **2 tablespoons lime juice**

1   Place butter, sugar, vanilla essence, egg, flour and self-raising flour, rolled oats, coconut, lime rind and lime juice in a food processor and process until well combined.
2   Place heaped spoonfuls of mixture on greased baking trays and bake for 12-15 minutes or until lightly browned. Cool on wire racks.

GOLDEN OAT BISCUITS

Golden, crunchy and delicious, these biscuits won't last long.

Makes 30
Oven temperature 180°C, 350°F, Gas 4

- [ ] **90 g/3 oz rolled oats**
- [ ] **125 g/4 oz flour, sifted**
- [ ] **90 g/3 oz desiccated coconut**
- [ ] **250 g/8 oz sugar**
- [ ] **4 teaspoons golden syrup, warmed**
- [ ] **125 g/4 oz butter, melted**
- [ ] **2 tablespoons boiling water**
- [ ] **1 teaspoon bicarbonate of soda**

1   Place oats, flour, coconut and sugar in a large mixing bowl. Combine golden syrup, butter, water and bicarbonate of soda.
2   Pour golden syrup mixture into dry ingredients and mix well to combine. Place spoonfuls of mixture 3 cm/1¹/₄ in apart on greased baking trays and bake for 10-15 minutes or until biscuits are just firm. Stand on trays for 3 minutes before transferring to wire racks to cool.

*Golden Oat Biscuits,
Lime and Coconut Cookies*

APRICOT DANISH PASTRIES

Makes 8
Oven temperature 220°C, 425°F, Gas 7

- ☐ **300 g/9¹/₂ oz prepared or ready-rolled puff pastry sheets**
- ☐ **8 canned apricot halves, drained**
- ☐ **1 quantity Apricot Glaze (below)**

1   Roll out pastry to 3 mm/¹/₈ in thick. Cut into eight 10 cm/4 in squares. Make four 5 cm/2 in cuts, starting from each corner and cutting towards the centre of each pastry square.
2   Fold one half of each corner to centre and place an apricot over the top. Repeat with remaining pastry squares and apricots.
3   Place pastries on greased baking trays and bake for 15-20 minutes or until puffed and golden. Brush hot pastries with glaze. Cool pastries on a wire rack.

SWEET CHEESE PASTRIES

Makes 8
Oven temperature 220°C, 425°F, Gas 7

- ☐ **300 g/9¹/₂ oz prepared or ready-rolled puff pastry sheets**
- ☐ **1 tablespoon water**
- ☐ **1 quantity Apricot Glaze**

CREAM CHEESE FILLING
- ☐ **200 g/6¹/₂ oz cream cheese**
- ☐ **1 egg yolk**
- ☐ **2 tablespoons caster sugar**

1   To make filling, place cream cheese, egg yolk and sugar in a food processor or blender and process until smooth.
2   Roll out pastry to 3 mm/¹/₈ in thick and cut into eight 12 cm/4³/₄ in squares. Spread filling over half the pastry rectangle leaving a 1 cm/¹/₂ in border. Brush edge with a little water and fold pastry over to enclose filling. Press edges firmly together to seal. Cut six slits 3 cm/1¹/₄ in in length along joined edges of pastry. Repeat with remaining pastry rectangles and filling.

3   Place pastries on greased baking trays and bake for 15-20 minutes or until puffed and golden. Brush hot pastries with glaze. Cool pastries on a wire rack.

CHERRY SQUARES

Makes 8
Oven temperature 220°C, 425°F, Gas 7

- ☐ **300 g/9¹/₂ oz prepared or ready-rolled puff pastry sheets**
- ☐ **1 quantity Apricot Glaze**

CHERRY FILLING
- ☐ **750 g/1¹/₂ lb bottled, pitted morello cherries, drained**
- ☐ **60 g/2 oz caster sugar**
- ☐ **1 teaspoon ground cinnamon**

1   To make filling, combine cherries, sugar and cinnamon in a bowl. Set aside.
2   Roll out pastry to 3 mm/¹/₈ in thick and cut into eight 12 cm/4³/₄ in squares. Roll in edges to form a narrow rim, then place a spoonful of filling in centre of each pastry square.
3   Place pastries on greased baking trays and bake for 15-20 minutes or until puffed and golden. Brush hot pastries with glaze. Cool pastries on a wire rack.

APRICOT GLAZE

- ☐ **155 g/5 oz apricot jam**
- ☐ **4 teaspoons water**

Place jam and water in a small saucepan and cook over a high heat until mixture boils. Remove from heat and use as required.

From top: Sweet Cheese Pastries, Apricot Danish Pastries, Cherry Squares

BEST EVER
CHOCOLATE CAKE

Makes a 20 cm/8 in round cake
Oven temperature 180°C, 350°F, Gas 4

- ☐ **90 g/3 oz cocoa powder**
- ☐ **375 mL/12 fl oz boiling water**
- ☐ **185 g/6 oz butter**
- ☐ **440 g/14 oz caster sugar**
- ☐ **2 tablespoons raspberry jam**
- ☐ **3 eggs**
- ☐ **300 g/9^1/$_2$ oz self-raising flour**

CHOCOLATE MOCHA ICING
- ☐ **125 g/4 oz butter**
- ☐ **330 g/10^1/$_2$ oz icing sugar, sifted**
- ☐ **1^1/$_2$ tablespoons cocoa powder, sifted**
- ☐ **2 teaspoons instant coffee**
- ☐ **2 tablespoons milk**

DECORATION
- ☐ **glacé cherries**
- ☐ **silver dragees**

1   Combine cocoa powder and boiling water, and mix to dissolve. Allow to cool completely.

2   Cream butter, sugar and jam until light and fluffy. Beat in eggs one at a time, adding a little flour with each egg. Fold in remaining flour and cocoa mixture alternately.

3   Spoon mixture into two greased and lined 20 cm/8 in sandwich tins and bake for 35 minutes or until cooked.

4   To make icing, place butter in a small mixing bowl. Beat until creamy. Add icing sugar a little at a time, beating well after each addition. Combine cocoa powder and coffee and mix to a smooth paste with milk, then whisk into icing.

5   Ice cake when cold and decorate with glacé cherries and silver dragees.

Spread one layer of cake with icing.

Top with second cake layer. Cover top and sides of cake with icing.

Decorate cake with glacé cherries and silver dragees.

chapter twelve

•

JUST A SNACK

A *little taste of something delicious is 'good for the soul' . . . not to mention children's morning break at school, mid-afternoon in a frantic office, or whenever time is short and food is needed.*

Fruity Banana and Camembert Muffins, Chilli Bean Tacos, French Onion Rolls

FRENCH ONION ROLLS

Serves 4
Oven temperature 200°C, 400°F, Gas 6

- [ ] 4 wholemeal rolls
- [ ] 15 g/¹/₂ oz butter
- [ ] 1 large onion, sliced
- [ ] 2 eggs, lightly beaten
- [ ] 125 g/4 oz sour cream
- [ ] 3 tablespoons evaporated milk
- [ ] ¹/₂ teaspoon ground nutmeg
- [ ] 1 teaspoon horseradish cream
- [ ] freshly ground black pepper
- [ ] 125 g/4 oz grated mature Cheddar

1   Cut tops from rolls and scoop out centres, leaving about 1 cm/¹/₂ in thick shell. Place rolls on a baking tray and set aside.
2   Melt butter in a frying pan and cook onion for 4-5 minutes or until golden. Divide onion between rolls.
3   Place eggs, sour cream, milk, nutmeg and horseradish cream in a bowl. Mix to combine and season to taste with black pepper. Spoon egg mixture into rolls, top with cheese and bake for 20-25 minutes or until firm.

TOMATO AND MOZZARELLA PIZZA SUBS

Serves 2

- [ ] 2 long wholemeal rolls, split and toasted
- [ ] 2 tablespoons tomato purée
- [ ] 1 small onion, chopped
- [ ] 1 tablespoon finely chopped fresh basil
- [ ] 4 olives, pitted and sliced
- [ ] 1 tablespoon pine nuts
- [ ] 30 g/1 oz grated mozzarella cheese
- [ ] freshly ground black pepper

1   Spread each roll half with tomato purée. Top with onion, then sprinkle with basil, olives, pine nuts and cheese. Season to taste with black pepper.
2   Cook under a preheated grill for 4-5 minutes or until cheese melts and topping is golden.

PITTA PIZZA ROLL-UPS

Makes 6
Oven temperature 220°C, 425°F, Gas 7

- [ ] 3 tablespoons tomato purée
- [ ] 2 tablespoons chopped fresh basil
- [ ] 3 tablespoons chopped pitted olives
- [ ] 6 large pitta bread rounds
- [ ] 200 g/6¹/₂ oz mushrooms, chopped
- [ ] 1 small red pepper, sliced
- [ ] 1 onion, chopped
- [ ] 200 g/6¹/₂ oz ricotta cheese
- [ ] 200 g/6¹/₂ oz grated mozzarella cheese

1   Place tomato purée, basil and olives in a bowl and mix to combine. Divide mixture into six portions and spread over pitta bread rounds. Top with mushrooms, red pepper, onion and ricotta cheese. Roll up tightly and secure with a toothpick.
2   Place rolls on a baking tray, sprinkle with mozzarella cheese and bake for 15-20 minutes or until cheese melts and rolls are heated through.

CHILLI BEAN TACOS

Serves 4
Oven temperature 180°C, 350°F, Gas 4

- [ ] 440 g/14 oz canned red kidney beans, drained and rinsed
- [ ] 1 teaspoon ground cumin
- [ ] 1 tomato, peeled and chopped
- [ ] 1 teaspoon chilli sauce
- [ ] 8 taco shells
- [ ] 4 lettuce leaves, shredded
- [ ] grated mature Cheddar

1   Place kidney beans, cumin, tomato and chilli sauce in a saucepan and cook over a medium heat for 3-4 minutes or until heated through.
2   Arrange taco shells on a baking tray and heat for 5 minutes or until heated through. Fill taco shells with bean mixture. Top with shredded lettuce and cheese. Serve immediately.

CHEESY CHICKEN PASTIES

Makes 10 pasties
Oven temperature 200°C, 400°F, Gas 6

- [ ] 375 g/12 oz prepared shortcrust pastry
- [ ] 2 tablespoons milk

CHICKEN FILLING
- [ ] 30 g/1 oz butter
- [ ] 1 clove garlic, crushed
- [ ] 2 boneless chicken breast fillets, chopped
- [ ] 8 button mushrooms, sliced
- [ ] 6 stalks asparagus, chopped
- [ ] 2 tablespoons sour cream
- [ ] 60 g/2 oz grated mature Cheddar
- [ ] 2 tablespoons grated Parmesan cheese
- [ ] 1 tablespoon chopped fresh parsley
- [ ] freshly ground black pepper

1   Roll out pastry to 3 mm/¹/₈ in thick and, using an upturned saucer as a guide, cut out ten 13 cm/5¹/₄ in circles.
2   To make filling, melt 15 g/¹/₂ oz butter in a frying pan, add garlic and chicken and cook for 3-4 minutes or until chicken is just cooked. Remove chicken mixture from pan and set aside to cool. Melt remaining butter in pan, add mushrooms and asparagus and cook over a high heat for 3-4 minutes or until asparagus is tender crisp. Remove vegetable mixture from pan and set aside to cool.
3   Combine chicken mixture, vegetable mixture, sour cream, mature Cheddar, Parmesan cheese, parsley and black pepper to taste. Place a spoonful of mixture in the centre of each pastry round and brush edges of pastry with a little water. Draw edges together over top of filling, press to seal and crimp edges with fingertips to form a fluted pattern.
4   Brush pastry parcels with a little milk, place on a greased oven tray and bake for 20-25 minutes or until golden and heated through.

MIDDLE EASTERN POCKET SANDWICHES

Pitta bread makes a wonderful container for holding all kinds of your favourite fillings. We have filled our pocket bread with refreshing cucumber salad, exotic lettuce leaves and succulent chunks of lean roast lamb.

Serves 4

- ☐ **4 wholemeal pitta breads**
- ☐ **lettuce leaves**
- ☐ **500 g/1 lb lean roast lamb, cut into 1 cm/¹/₂ in chunks**
- ☐ **fresh mint sprigs for garnish**

CUCUMBER AND YOGURT SALAD
- ☐ **1 cucumber, chopped**
- ☐ **3 spring onions, finely chopped**
- ☐ **60 g/2 oz finely chopped fresh mint leaves**
- ☐ **300 g/9¹/₂ oz natural yogurt**
- ☐ **1 tablespoon lemon juice**
- ☐ **¹/₂ teaspoon chilli sauce, or according to taste**
- ☐ **freshly ground black pepper**

1   Cut pitta breads in half and carefully open. Line each half with lettuce leaves.
2   To make salad, place cucumber, spring onions and mint in a bowl. Mix together yogurt, lemon juice and chilli sauce. Pour over cucumber salad and fold gently to combine. Season to taste with black pepper.
3   Spoon salad and lamb into pitta pockets. Serve with fresh mint sprigs.

SMOKED SALMON ON RYE

Makes 4 sandwiches

- ☐ **155 g/5 oz thinly sliced smoked salmon**
- ☐ **4 slices rye bread**
- ☐ **juice ¹/₂ lemon**
- ☐ **¹/₂ red onion, cut into thin slices**
- ☐ **8 thin slices cucumber**
- ☐ **4 teaspoons drained capers**
- ☐ **4 thin slices lemon**
- ☐ **freshly ground black pepper**
- ☐ **fresh dill sprigs for garnish**

1   Arrange salmon on bread slices and sprinkle with a little lemon juice.
2   Place onion on salmon. Arrange cucumber, capers and lemon slices attractively on top. Season with plenty of freshly ground black pepper and garnish with dill sprigs. Serve with a tossed green salad.

AVOCADO AND CHICKEN ON PUMPERNICKEL

Makes 4 open sandwiches

- ☐ **1 large avocado, stoned and peeled**
- ☐ **juice 1 lemon**
- ☐ **4 slices pumpernickel bread**
- ☐ **155 g/5 oz watercress**
- ☐ **fresh mint sprigs for garnish**

CHICKEN SALAD
- ☐ **300 g/9¹/₂ oz cooked chicken, chopped**
- ☐ **2 spring onions, finely chopped**
- ☐ **1 tablespoon pine nuts**
- ☐ **1 teaspoon finely chopped fresh mint**
- ☐ **2 tablespoons mayonnaise**

1   Cut avocado into 12 slices and sprinkle with lemon juice.
2   To make chicken salad, combine chicken, spring onions, pine nuts, mint and mayonnaise in a bowl.
3   Divide watercress between bread slices and top with chicken salad. Arrange three avocado slices on top of chicken salad and garnish with mint sprigs.

FRUITY BANANA AND CAMEMBERT MUFFINS

Serves 4

- ☐ **1 large banana, sliced**
- ☐ **¹/₂ green apple, chopped**
- ☐ **¹/₂ stalk celery, sliced**
- ☐ **3 tablespoons chopped pecan nuts**
- ☐ **2 teaspoons desiccated coconut**
- ☐ **2 tablespoons mayonnaise**
- ☐ **4 fruit muffins, halved and buttered**
- ☐ **125 g/4 oz Camembert cheese, sliced**

Combine banana, apple, celery, pecans, coconut and mayonnaise. Spoon onto muffin halves and top with Camembert slices. Grill under a medium heat until cheese melts. Serve immediately.

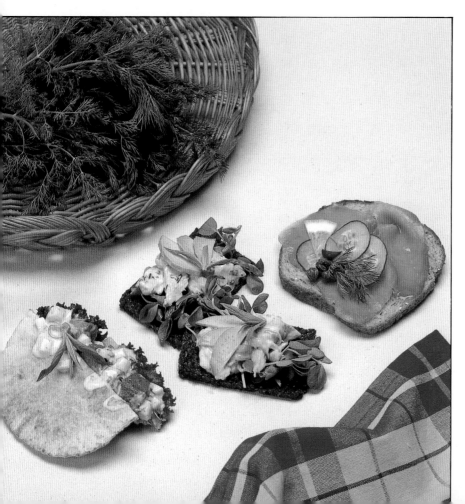

*Smoked Salmon on Rye,
Avocado and Chicken on Pumpernickel,
Middle Eastern Pocket Sandwiches*

SALMON TOASTIES

This easy snack uses store-cupboard ingredients and is just as delicious made with canned tuna.

Makes 2 toasties
Oven temperature 200°C, 400°F, Gas 6

- ☐ 155 g/5 oz canned pink salmon, drained
- ☐ 60 g/2 oz sour cream
- ☐ 2 teaspoons lemon juice
- ☐ 2 teaspoons chopped fresh dill or parsley
- ☐ freshly ground black pepper
- ☐ 15 g/¹/₂ oz butter
- ☐ 4 slices bread, crusts removed

1 Place salmon, sour cream, lemon juice, dill or parsley and black pepper to taste in a small bowl and mix to combine. Lightly butter bread on one side.

2 Spread half of the salmon mixture over unbuttered side of 2 slices of bread. Cover with remaining bread slices, buttered side up. Secure sides with wooden cocktail sticks or toothpicks.

3 Place on a greased baking tray and bake for 10 minutes or until bread is crisp and golden.

Cook's tip: If you do not have any sour cream, mayonnaise or natural yogurt can be used instead.

NACHOS

Serves 4
Oven temperature 200°C, 400°F, Gas 6

- ☐ 155 g/5 oz corn chips
- ☐ 2 tomatoes, peeled and finely chopped
- ☐ 125 g/4 oz grated mozzarella cheese
- ☐ 125 g/4 oz grated mature Cheddar

AVOCADO TOPPING

- ☐ 2 small avocados, peeled and chopped
- ☐ 2 teaspoons lemon juice
- ☐ 1 small onion, grated
- ☐ 2 cloves garlic, crushed
- ☐ 1 teaspoon chilli sauce

1 Layer corn chips, tomatoes, mozzarella cheese and Cheddar in an ovenproof dish, finishing with a layer of Cheddar and bake for 10-15 minutes or until cheese melts and is golden.

2 To make topping, place avocados, lemon juice, onion, garlic and chilli sauce in a food processor or blender and process until smooth. Spoon into centre of hot corn chips and serve immediately.

HAM AND CORN TRIANGLES

Makes 4 triangles
Oven temperature 180°C, 350°F, Gas 4

- ☐ 2 slices bread
- ☐ 15 g/¹/₂ oz butter, melted

CORN TOPPING

- ☐ 60 g/2 oz canned creamed sweet corn
- ☐ 1 spring onion, finely chopped
- ☐ 1 slice canned pineapple, chopped
- ☐ 1 slice ham, finely chopped
- ☐ 60 g/2 oz grated mature Cheddar

1 Cut each slice of bread in half diagonally and brush both sides with butter. Place bread triangles on a baking tray and bake for 5 minutes or until crisp.

2 Top toasted triangles with sweet corn, spring onion, pineapple, ham and cheese. Bake for 5 minutes or until cheese is melted and golden.

From left: Open Focaccia Sandwich, Ham and Corn Triangles, Salmon Toasties

OPEN FOCACCIA SANDWICH

For something different use any of your favourite breads, spreads, meats and vegetables to make this sandwich.

Makes 1 serving

- ☐ **1 piece focaccia bread, halved and buttered**
- ☐ **4 slices roast beef or lamb**
- ☐ **¼ avocado, peeled and sliced**
- ☐ **4 cherry tomatoes, sliced**
- ☐ **1 teaspoon finely chopped fresh rosemary (optional)**
- ☐ **4 slices Swiss cheese**
- ☐ **freshly ground black pepper**

To assemble sandwiches, top focaccia with beef or lamb, avocado and tomatoes then sprinkle with rosemary (if used) and top with Swiss cheese. Season to taste with black pepper.

Toasted Focaccia Sandwich: Toasted, this sandwich is a wonderful light evening meal. Toast focaccia slices under a preheated grill on both sides before buttering. Prepare as in recipe then place under a preheated medium grill and cook for 3-4 minutes or until heated and cheese is melted.

Cook's tip: Why not use a bread that you have not tried before to make this sandwich. There are many breads available from bread shops, supermarkets and delicatessens. You might try using white bread, wholemeal bread, wholegrain bread, rye bread, sandwich rolls, baguettes/ French rolls, pitta bread, crispbread or bagels. Remember that bread freezes well so you can buy a whole loaf and any leftover can be frozen to use at a later date.

SALMON SCROLLS

Smoked salmon with a tasty filling makes a perfect treat. Or you might like to serve these scrolls with a mixed lettuce and fresh herb salad as a starter or light meal.

Serves 2

- ☐ 4 slices smoked salmon
- ☐ 1 tablespoon chopped fresh parsley
- ☐ 2 teaspoons chopped fresh dill

CREAM CHEESE FILLING
- ☐ 125 g/4 oz cream cheese
- ☐ 2 tablespoons sour cream
- ☐ 2 teaspoons wholegrain mustard
- ☐ 2 teaspoons lemon juice
- ☐ freshly ground black pepper

1 Place salmon in a rectangle shape on a piece of plastic food wrap.
2 To make filling, beat together cream cheese, sour cream, mustard, lemon juice and black pepper to taste. Spread evenly over salmon slices and sprinkle with parsley and dill.
3 Roll up salmon widthwise, like a Swiss roll, cover and refrigerate until firm. To serve, cut into 1 cm/¹/₂ in rounds.

AUBERGINE DIP WITH FRESH VEGETABLES

Serves 4
Oven temperature 200°C, 400°F, Gas 6

- ☐ 1 large aubergine (eggplant)
- ☐ 4 tablespoons natural yogurt
- ☐ 2 tablespoons lemon juice
- ☐ 3 tablespoons chopped fresh parsley
- ☐ 2 cloves garlic, crushed
- ☐ 2 tablespoons olive oil
- ☐ 1 tablespoon tahini paste
- ☐ fresh parsley sprigs
- ☐ paprika
- ☐ selection crisp vegetables such as mangetout (snow peas), carrot sticks, cauliflower florets and radishes

1 Prick aubergine (eggplant) in several places with a fork and place in an ovenproof dish. Bake for 40-45 minutes or until tender. Set aside until cool enough to handle.
2 Peel skin off aubergine (eggplant) and roughly chop flesh. Place aubergine (eggplant) flesh, yogurt, lemon juice,

parsley, garlic, oil and tahini paste in a food processor or blender and process until smooth. Transfer to a bowl and garnish with parsley sprigs and paprika. Serve with vegetables.

FRUITY APRICOT COOKIES

Makes 25
Oven temperature 180°C, 350°F, Gas 4

- ☐ 125 g/4 oz butter
- ☐ 125 g/4 oz brown sugar
- ☐ ¹/₂ teaspoon ground cinnamon
- ☐ 1 egg
- ☐ 60 g/2 oz self-raising flour
- ☐ 75 g/2¹/₂ oz wholemeal self-raising flour
- ☐ 15 g/¹/₂ oz wheat germ
- ☐ 4 tablespoons desiccated coconut
- ☐ 45 g/1¹/₂ oz rolled oats
- ☐ 90 g/3 oz dried apricots, chopped
- ☐ 60 g/2 oz dried apples, chopped
- ☐ 3 tablespoons currants

1 Place butter and sugar in a mixing bowl and beat until light and fluffy. Stir in egg, then fold in self-raising and wholemeal self-raising flours, wheat germ, coconut, rolled oats, apricots, apples and currants. Mix to combine ingredients.
2 Roll spoonfuls of mixture into balls, place on lightly greased baking trays and flatten slightly with a fork. Bake for 10-12 minutes, or until biscuits are firm. Remove from oven and cool on tray.

ENERGY BARS

Great to have on hand as after work or school snacks, or tuck them into your bag for a quick boost of energy during the day.

Makes 20

- ☐ 60 g/2 oz puffed rice cereal
- ☐ 75 g/2¹/₂ oz bran flakes, lightly crushed
- ☐ 75 g/2¹/₂ oz shredded coconut
- ☐ 60 g/2 oz dried apricots, chopped
- ☐ 30 g/1 oz dried apples, chopped
- ☐ 60 g/2 oz glacé pineapple, chopped
- ☐ 90 g/3 oz sultanas
- ☐ 1 teaspoon ground cinnamon
- ☐ 90 g/3 oz brown sugar
- ☐ 90 g/3 oz butter

- ☐ 185 g/6 oz honey
- ☐ 125 mL/4 fl oz coconut milk

1 Place rice cereal, bran flakes, coconut, apricots, apples, pineapple, sultanas and cinnamon in a bowl and mix to combine.
2 Place brown sugar, butter, honey and coconut milk in a small saucepan and cook over a low heat, stirring, until sugar and honey melt and all ingredients combine. Bring to the boil, reduce heat and simmer for 5 minutes or until mixture is thick and syrupy. Pour over dry ingredients and mix well. Press into a greased and lined 15 x 25 cm/6 x 10 in shallow cake tin and refrigerate until set. Cut into bars and store in an airtight container.

RICE CAKES WITH THREE TOPPINGS

Each topping is enough for 4 rice cakes

- ☐ 4 rice cakes

FRUITY TOPPING
- ☐ 3 tablespoons strawberry jam
- ☐ 2 bananas, sliced
- ☐ 2 tablespoons sunflower seeds

Spread rice cakes with jam, top with banana slices and sprinkle with sunflower seeds.

NUTTY CHEESE TOPPING
- ☐ 2 tablespoons peanut butter
- ☐ 125 g/4 oz cottage cheese
- ☐ 1 apple, cored and sliced

Spread rice cakes with peanut butter, top with cottage cheese and apple slices.

SALMON TOPPING
- ☐ 220 g/7 oz canned salmon, drained
- ☐ 3 tablespoons natural yogurt or sour cream
- ☐ 2 teaspoons lemon juice
- ☐ 2 teaspoons French mustard
- ☐ freshly ground black pepper
- ☐ 30 g/1 oz bean sprouts

Mix together salmon, yogurt or sour cream, lemon juice, mustard and black pepper to taste. Place sprouts on rice cakes and top with salmon mixture.

Top shelf from left: Fruity Apricot Cookies, Energy Bars, Rice Cakes with Three Toppings
Bottom shelf from left: Salmon Scrolls, Aubergine Dip with Fresh Vegetables

CROSTINI

*This super-quick snack can be topped
with olives and red pepper just before
serving if you wish.*

Serves 2

- ☐ 1 clove garlic, crushed
- ☐ 8 black olives, pitted and finely
  chopped
- ☐ 1 tablespoon capers, finely
  chopped
- ☐ 4 tablespoons olive oil
- ☐ 4 slices wholemeal bread,
  crusts removed and slices cut
  in half
- ☐ 90 g/3 oz mozzarella cheese,
  thinly sliced

1   Place garlic, olives, capers and 1
tablespoon oil in a food processor or blender
and process until smooth. Spread garlic
mixture over half the bread slices. Top with
cheese and remaining bread slices.
2   Brush top of each sandwich with oil
and cook under a preheated grill until lightly
browned. Turn over, brush with remaining
oil and grill until brown.

EGG AND MUSTARD
HAM ROLLS

*In this recipe the eggs are baked in the
oven. These rolls make a great snack
or a delicious brunch.*

Serves 4
Oven temperature 180°C, 350°F, Gas 4

- ☐ 4 wholemeal rolls
- ☐ 2 tablespoons wholegrain
  mustard
- ☐ 15 g/$^1/_2$ oz butter
- ☐ 45 g/1$^1/_2$ oz button mushrooms,
  sliced
- ☐ 1 onion, chopped
- ☐ 45 g/1$^1/_2$ oz thin ham slices, cut
  into strips
- ☐ freshly ground black pepper
- ☐ 4 eggs
- ☐ 60 g/2 oz grated mature Cheddar

1   Cut a slice from the top of each bread
roll, set aside and reserve. Scoop out the
centre, leaving a thin shell and reserve
crumbs for another use. Spread inside of
each roll with mustard.
2   Melt butter in a frying pan and cook

mushrooms and onion for 2-3 minutes over
a medium heat. Add ham and cook for 2
minutes longer. Divide the mixture between
the rolls and sprinkle with black pepper to
taste.
3   Break an egg into a small bowl, then
slide it into a roll. Repeat with remaining
eggs and rolls. Sprinkle with cheese and
replace the tops.
4   Place rolls on a baking tray and bake
for 25 minutes or until egg whites are firm.

Variations
Egg and Spinach Rolls: Replace
wholegrain mustard with tomato purée,
and mushrooms and onion with 6 chopped
spinach leaves. Prepare as directed. You
may also like to sprinkle the cheese with
chopped fresh oregano before baking.

Egg and Mustard Ham Rolls

TURKEY TRIANGLES

Makes 4 triangles
Oven temperature 220°C, 425°F, Gas 7

- ☐ **155 g/5 oz prepared puff pastry**

TURKEY FILLING
- ☐ **4 slices smoked turkey, chopped**
- ☐ **2 tablespoons sour cream**
- ☐ **1 tablespoon cranberry sauce**
- ☐ **2 teaspoons snipped fresh chives**
- ☐ **freshly ground black pepper**

1 Roll out pastry to 3 mm/¹/₈ in thick and cut into four 12.5 cm/5 in squares.
2 To make filling, place turkey, sour cream, cranberry sauce and chives in a small bowl and mix to combine. Place a spoonful of filling in the centre of each pastry square. Fold opposite pastry corners together to form a triangle. Brush edges with a little water and press together, using a fork to seal and make a decorative edge. Place on a greased baking tray and bake for 15 minutes or until pastry is puffed and golden.

PEANUT DIP

This peanut dip is great served with vegetable crudités.

Makes 250 g/8 oz

- ☐ **1 tablespoon groundnut (peanut) oil**
- ☐ **1 clove garlic, crushed**
- ☐ **1 onion, chopped**
- ☐ **1 teaspoon chilli sauce**
- ☐ **5 tablespoons crunchy peanut butter**
- ☐ **125 mL/4 fl oz water**
- ☐ **125 g/4 oz natural yogurt**
- ☐ **freshly ground black pepper**

Heat oil in a frying pan, add garlic and onion and cook for 4-5 minutes or until onion is soft. Add chilli sauce, peanut butter and water and mix well to combine. Bring to the boil, then remove pan from heat, stir in yogurt and season to taste with black pepper. Serve hot, warm or at room temperature.

SPICED ALMONDS

Serves 6

- ☐ **¹/₂ teaspoon chilli powder**
- ☐ **¹/₄ teaspoon ground cumin**
- ☐ **¹/₂ teaspoon ground coriander**
- ☐ **185 g/6 oz blanched almonds**

1 Place chilli, cumin and coriander in a small nonstick saucepan and cook over a low heat for 1 minute. Add almonds, toss with spices and cook for 3-5 minutes longer or until almonds are golden.
2 Remove pan from heat and set aside to cool. Serve warm or at room temperature as a snack or with drinks.

Peanut Dip, Spiced Almonds

289

MELON CUPS WITH YOGURT DRESSING

Serves 4

- [ ] **2 small melons, halved and seeds removed**
- [ ] **2 nectarines, stoned and sliced**
- [ ] **155 g/5 oz strawberries, hulled and sliced**
- [ ] **155 g/5 oz black grapes**

YOGURT DRESSING
- [ ] **185 g/6 oz natural yogurt**
- [ ] **1 tablespoon honey**
- [ ] **1 kiwifruit, roughly chopped**

1 To make dressing, place yogurt, honey and kiwifruit in a bowl and mix to combine.
2 Place melon halves on individual serving plates. Fill with nectarines, strawberries and grapes. Spoon dressing over fruit in melon halves and chill.

FRENCH TOASTED SANDWICHES

Serves 4

- [ ] **8 slices brown bread, crusts removed**
- [ ] **4 slices lean ham, finely chopped**
- [ ] **315 g/10 oz canned asparagus tips, drained and mashed**
- [ ] **125 g/4 oz grated Swiss cheese**
- [ ] **3 eggs, well beaten**
- [ ] **5 tablespoons milk**

1 Roll bread slices out flat using a rolling pin. Layer half of each slice, diagonally, with ham, asparagus and cheese. Fold uncovered half over filling and press flat. Secure with toothpicks to enclose filling.
2 Combine egg and milk in a shallow dish. Dip each filled bread triangle in egg mixture and cook in a preheated nonstick frying pan until golden brown on both sides. Serve immediately.

FRUIT AND NUT MUFFINS

Serves 2

- [ ] **2 muffins, halved and toasted**

FRUIT AND NUT TOPPING
- [ ] **4 tablespoons ricotta cheese**
- [ ] **1 tablespoon currants**
- [ ] **1 tablespoon chopped raisins**
- [ ] **1 teaspoon grated orange rind**
- [ ] **2 tablespoons chopped pecan nuts**

Place ricotta cheese, currants, raisins and orange rind in a bowl. Mix to combine and spread over muffin halves. Sprinkle with pecan nuts and serve.

Cook's tip: Use wholemeal or mixed grain muffins to increase your fibre intake.

PEACHES AND CREAM MUFFINS

Serves 2

- [ ] **2 muffins, halved and toasted**

PEACHES AND CREAM TOPPING
- [ ] **4 tablespoons cottage cheese**
- [ ] **pulp of 1 passion fruit**
- [ ] **2 peaches, stoned and sliced**

Combine cottage cheese and passion fruit pulp in a bowl. Spread mixture over muffin halves, top with peach slices and serve.

TURKEY MUFFINS

Serves 2

- [ ] **2 muffins, halved and toasted**

TURKEY TOPPING
- [ ] **1 tomato, sliced**
- [ ] **2 slices cooked turkey breast**
- [ ] **3 tablespoons grated mature Cheddar**
- [ ] **freshly ground black pepper**

Place tomato slices on muffin halves. Top with turkey slices, cheese and black pepper to taste. Place under a preheated grill until heated through.

Melon Cups with Yogurt Dressing

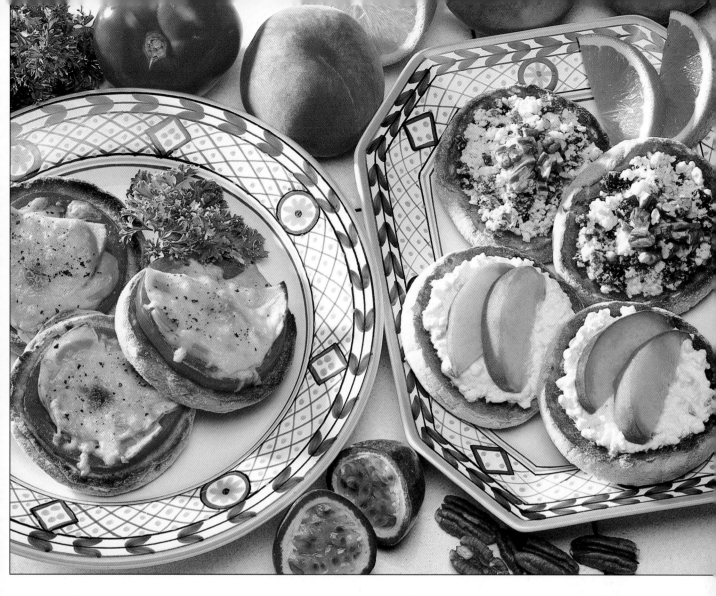

Turkey Muffins, Fruit and Nut Muffins, Peaches and Cream Muffins

SPRING OMELETTE

Serves 2

- ☐ **15 g/¹/₂ oz butter**
- ☐ **4 eggs, lightly beaten**
- ☐ **3 tablespoons milk**
- ☐ **freshly ground black pepper**
- ☐ **3 tablespoons grated mature Cheddar**

VEGETABLE FILLING
- ☐ **15 g/¹/₂ oz butter**
- ☐ **2 spring onions, finely chopped**
- ☐ **6 button mushrooms, sliced**
- ☐ **¹/₂ small red pepper, sliced**
- ☐ **1 teaspoon chopped fresh coriander**

1 To make filling, melt butter in a nonstick frying pan and cook spring onions, mushrooms, red pepper and coriander for 2 minutes or until tender. Remove vegetables from pan, set aside and keep warm.
2 To make omelette, melt butter in a clean nonstick frying pan. Combine eggs, milk and black pepper to taste in a bowl. Pour into pan and cook over a low heat until almost set. Top half the omelette with filling, then sprinkle with cheese. Fold omelette over, cut into half, slide onto serving plates and serve immediately.

chapter thirteen

PRESERVED FOR FLAVOUR

I*f you have never ventured
into preserving, why not start by
trying some of these mouthwatering
recipes. Preserves are not only a great
way of storing excess produce, but
they also make wonderful gifts
for family and friends.*

*Top shelf; Spicy Apple Chutney,
Cinnamon Pears in Brandy, Corn and
Mustard Seed Relish
Bottom shelf; Pickled Dill Cucumbers,
Pickled Onions*

CINNAMON PEARS
IN BRANDY

Makes 3.5-4 litres/6-7 pt

- [ ] **8 small pears, peeled, halved and cored with stems left intact**
- [ ] **3 tablespoons lemon juice**
- [ ] **250 g/8 oz sugar**
- [ ] **375 mL/12 fl oz water**
- [ ] **1 cinnamon stick, broken into pieces**
- [ ] **2 teaspoons finely grated lime rind**
- [ ] **375 mL/12 fl oz brandy**

1 Place pears in a large bowl, add lemon juice and just enough water to cover pears.
2 Place sugar and water in a large heavy-based saucepan and cook over a low heat, stirring until sugar dissolves. Bring to the boil without stirring.
3 Drain pears and add to pan with cinnamon stick and lime rind. Cook over a low heat until pears are just tender.
4 Arrange pears in hot sterilised jars. Stir brandy into sugar syrup, then pour over pears to completely cover. Seal and store in a cool dark place.

PICKLED DILL
CUCUMBERS

Makes 5-6 litres/8-10½ pt

- [ ] **3 kg/6 lb gherkins or small pickling cucumbers, trimmed**
- [ ] **salt**
- [ ] **2.5 litres/4 pt white wine vinegar**
- [ ] **1 tablespoon black mustard seeds**
- [ ] **½ teaspoon whole black peppercorns**
- [ ] **4 whole cloves**
- [ ] **4 sprigs fresh dill**

1 Place gherkins or cucumbers on sheets of absorbent kitchen paper and sprinkle with salt. Set aside to stand for 2-3 hours. Rinse under cold running water and pat dry on absorbent kitchen paper. Place gherkins or cucumbers in a heatproof bowl.
2 Place vinegar, mustard seeds, peppercorns, cloves and dill in a large saucepan and bring to the boil. Pour mixture over gherkins or cucumbers in bowl and set aside to stand overnight.
3 Remove cloves. Place gherkins or cucumbers and liquid in a large saucepan and cook over a medium heat until gherkins or cucumbers are just tender. Remove pan from heat and set aside to cool. Pack gherkins or cucumbers and liquid into hot sterilised jars. Seal and store in a cool dark place.

PICKLED ONIONS

Makes 4 litres/7 pt

- [ ] **2 kg/4 lb pickling onions, unpeeled**
- [ ] **750 g/1½ lb salt**

PICKLING VINEGAR
- [ ] **1.5 litres/2½ pt white wine vinegar**
- [ ] **1 tablespoon salt**
- [ ] **2 teaspoons ground ginger**
- [ ] **6 whole cloves**
- [ ] **2 fresh red chillies, cut in half**
- [ ] **2 teaspoons yellow mustard seeds**
- [ ] **6 whole black peppercorns**
- [ ] **2 bay leaves**

1 Place onions and salt in a bowl. Add enough water to cover onions and set aside to stand for 2 days. Stir occasionally during standing time.
2 Drain onions and discard liquid. Peel onions and cover with boiling water. Set aside to stand for 3 minutes, then drain and repeat twice more using additional boiling water. Pack onions into hot sterilised jars and set aside.
3 To make vinegar, place white wine vinegar, salt, ginger, cloves, chillies, mustard seeds, peppercorns and bay leaves in a large saucepan. Bring to the boil, then reduce heat and simmer for 10 minutes. Cool slightly, then pour liquid over onions in jars and seal. Store in a cool dark place for 2 months before using.

SPICY APPLE CHUTNEY

Makes 2 x 250 g/8 oz jars

- [ ] **2 tablespoons vegetable oil**
- [ ] **1 clove garlic, crushed**
- [ ] **1 teaspoon grated fresh ginger**
- [ ] **2 fresh red chillies, seeded and chopped**
- [ ] **2 tablespoons mustard seeds**
- [ ] **1 teaspoon mixed spice**
- [ ] **1 teaspoon ground turmeric**
- [ ] **15 whole black peppercorns**
- [ ] **2 teaspoons ground cumin**
- [ ] **8 large cooking apples, cored, peeled and sliced**
- [ ] **170 mL/5½ fl oz white vinegar**
- [ ] **125 g/4 oz sugar**

1 Heat oil in a large saucepan and cook garlic, ginger and chillies over a medium heat for 2-3 minutes. Combine mustard seeds, mixed spice, turmeric, peppercorns and cumin, add to pan and cook for 3-4 minutes longer.
2 Add apples, vinegar and sugar to pan and simmer, uncovered, for 1 hour or until thick. Pour chutney into hot sterilised jars and seal when cold.

CORN AND
MUSTARD SEED RELISH

Makes 3 x 500 g/1 lb jars

- [ ] **1 large onion, finely chopped**
- [ ] **500 mL/16 fl oz white wine vinegar**
- [ ] **100 g/3½ oz caster sugar**
- [ ] **1 tablespoon curry powder**
- [ ] **1 teaspoon ground turmeric**
- [ ] **2 teaspoons yellow mustard seeds**
- [ ] **2 tablespoons grated fresh ginger**
- [ ] **2 x 440 g/14 oz canned sweet corn kernels, drained**
- [ ] **1 carrot, finely chopped**
- [ ] **2 stalks celery, chopped**
- [ ] **1 red pepper, chopped**
- [ ] **2 tablespoons cornflour, blended with 5 tablespoons water**
- [ ] **freshly ground black pepper**

1 Place onion in a saucepan and add enough water to cover onion. Bring to the boil, remove from heat, drain and set aside.
2 Place vinegar, sugar, curry powder, turmeric, mustard seeds and ginger in a clean saucepan. Bring to the boil, then reduce heat and simmer for 3-4 minutes.
3 Add sweet corn kernels, carrot, celery, red pepper and onion to pan. Bring to the boil, then reduce heat and simmer for 15 minutes.
4 Stir in cornflour mixture and cook over a medium heat, stirring constantly, for 5 minutes or until mixture boils and thickens. Season to taste with black pepper. Spoon relish into hot sterilised jars. Seal when cool and store in a cool dark place.

HERB VINEGARS

Flavoured vinegars add extra zest to any savoury dish, pickle or salad that calls for vinegar. Use fresh herbs such as basil, tarragon, thyme or rosemary. For something different, you might like to use red or white wine vinegar. Homemade flavoured vinegars make wonderful gifts.

Makes 1 litre/1³/₄ pt

- ☐ **125 g/4 oz fresh herbs of your choice**
- ☐ **1 litre/1³/₄ pt vinegar**

1   Wash herbs and pat dry. Crush slightly.
2   Place herbs in a bottle and add vinegar. Seal and leave in a warm place, like a sunny windowsill, for 3-4 weeks.
3   Strain vinegar through muslin. Place a fresh herb sprig in a clean, pretty bottle and add vinegar. Seal and label.

PICKLED PEPPPERS

Makes 1 x 500 g/1 lb jar

- ☐ **2 onions, sliced**
- ☐ **2 red peppers, sliced**
- ☐ **2 green peppers, sliced**
- ☐ **2 yellow peppers, sliced**
- ☐ **2 tablespoons coarse cooking salt**
- ☐ **1 fresh red chilli, finely chopped**
- ☐ **2 bay leaves**
- ☐ **375 mL/12 fl oz white wine vinegar**
- ☐ **1 teaspoon black mustard seeds**
- ☐ **2 teaspoons pink peppercorns**
- ☐ **185 g/6 oz sugar**

1   Combine onions, red, green and yellow peppers and salt in large bowl. Cover and let stand overnight.
2   Rinse vegetables under cold running water. Drain and pat dry on absorbent paper. Arrange attractively in a sterilised jar with the red chilli and bay leaves.

3   Combine vinegar, mustard seeds, peppercorns and sugar in a saucepan. Cook over a medium heat without boiling, stirring constantly until sugar dissolves. Bring to the boil, then reduce heat and simmer, uncovered, for 3 minutes. Pour over vegetables in jars and seal while hot.

BEETROOT, ORANGE AND APPLE CHUTNEY

This chutney is delicious with cheese and cold lamb.

Makes 4 x 375 g/12 oz jars

- ☐ **1 kg/2 lb beetroot, stems and leaves removed**
- ☐ **250 g/8 oz sugar**
- ☐ **1 onion, finely chopped**
- ☐ **500 mL/16 fl oz red wine vinegar**
- ☐ **1 teaspoon ground allspice**
- ☐ **2 large Granny Smith apples, cored, peeled and chopped**
- ☐ **1 orange, segmented**

1   Place beetroot in a large saucepan and cover with water. Cover pan, bring to the boil, then reduce heat and simmer for 1 hour or until beetroot is tender. Drain and set aside until cool enough to handle. Peel beetroot and dice.
2   Place sugar, onion, vinegar and allspice in a saucepan and cook over a medium heat, without boiling, stirring constantly until sugar dissolves.
3   Bring sugar mixture to the boil, reduce heat, add apples and simmer for 15-20 minutes or until apples pulp. Stir in beetroot and orange and cook for 5 minutes longer. Spoon chutney into hot sterilised jars. Cover and label when cold.

A selection of Herb Vinegars

BOCCONCINI MARINATED WITH HERBS

Serve bocconcini sliced with assorted salad leaves and a little of the marinade spooned over.

Serves 8

- ☐ **500 g/1 lb fresh bocconcini, drained and dried**
- ☐ **3 cloves garlic, peeled**
- ☐ **2 sprigs fresh oregano**
- ☐ **2 sprigs fresh thyme**
- ☐ **1 sprig fresh parsley**
- ☐ **1 bay leaf**
- ☐ **3 small fresh red chillies**
- ☐ **200 mL/6¹/₂ fl oz extra virgin olive oil**

Place bocconcini, garlic, oregano, thyme, parsley, bay leaf and chillies in a sterilised jar. Cover with olive oil. Seal jar and refrigerate for up to 2 weeks.

Cook's tip: Bocconcini are small balls of fresh mozzarella cheese. If they are unavailable you can use fresh mozzarella cut into cubes instead.

CHICK PEAS IN GARLIC OIL

Makes 1 x 500 mL/16 fl oz jar

- ☐ **185 g/6 oz dried chick peas**
- ☐ **300 mL/9¹/₂ fl oz olive oil**
- ☐ **4 cloves garlic, crushed**
- ☐ **freshly ground black pepper**
- ☐ **3 tablespoons lemon juice**
- ☐ **3 tablespoons chopped fresh parsley**

1   Place chick peas in a small saucepan and cover with cold water. Bring to the boil, then turn off heat, cover and soak for 1 hour. Drain and cover with fresh cold water. Cover pan and cook over a low heat for 2-3 hours or until chick peas are tender. Drain well.

2   Heat oil in a frying pan, add garlic and chick peas and cook, stirring constantly, until chick peas are lightly browned. Season to taste with black pepper and mix in lemon juice and parsley. Pack into a warm sterilised jar, seal and refrigerate until required.

SICILIAN PRESERVED AUBERGINE

*Serve preserved aubergine (eggplant)
as part of an antipasto selection,
or as a vegetable accompaniment
to cooked meats.*

Makes 1 litre/1³/₄ pt

- ☐ **1 kg/2 lb baby aubergines (eggplant), cut lengthwise into thin strips**
- ☐ **3 tablespoons salt**
- ☐ **2 tablespoons finely chopped fresh mint**
- ☐ **3 cloves garlic, crushed**
- ☐ **1 teaspoon finely chopped fresh oregano**
- ☐ **2 tablespoons red wine vinegar**
- ☐ **3 small fresh red chillies, seeded and sliced**
- ☐ **410 mL/13 fl oz extra virgin olive oil**

1   Sprinkle aubergine (eggplant) slices
with salt and set aside to stand for 2 hours.
Rinse and pat dry.
2   Combine aubergines (eggplant), mint,
garlic, oregano and 1 tablespoon vinegar.
Layer aubergines (eggplant) and chillies in
a warm sterilised jar. Press down firmly
and add remaining vinegar and enough
olive oil to cover. Seal and refrigerate until
required.

ROASTED PEPPERS IN OLIVE OIL

*Roasting peppers gives them a
succulent, sweet taste. This can be
done over coals, a gas flame or
under the grill.*

Makes 1 x 600 mL/1 pt jar

- ☐ **4 red peppers, roasted until black**
- ☐ **4 yellow peppers, roasted until black**
- ☐ **2 teaspoons salt**
- ☐ **3 cloves garlic, peeled**
- ☐ **200 mL/6¹/₂ fl oz extra virgin olive oil**

1   Cut peppers in half, remove seeds and
skin. Slice into large pieces.
2   Sprinkle peppers with salt and pack
into a warm sterilised jar. Add garlic cloves
and cover with oil. Allow to settle, cover
and refrigerate until required.

SPICED OLIVES

*Serve these olives as part of an
antipasto platter, to top pizzas, or in
salads for an extra-special flavour.*

Makes 1 x 600 mL/1 pt jar

- ☐ **500 g/1 lb Kalamata olives**
- ☐ **2 cloves garlic, chopped**
- ☐ **3 small fresh red chillies, chopped**
- ☐ **2 tablespoons chopped fresh parsley**
- ☐ **3 bay leaves**
- ☐ **200 mL/6¹/₂ fl oz extra virgin olive oil**

Combine olives, garlic, chillies and parsley.
Place olive mixture and bay leaves in a
warm sterilised jar. Cover with olive oil,
seal and refrigerate until required.

*Spiced Olives, Roasted Peppers in Olive Oil,
Bocconcini Marinated with Herbs, Sicilian
Preserved Aubergine*

CHILLI SAMBAL

Use this sambal as a dipping sauce or keep in a jar in the refrigerator to add some quick flavour to your recipes.

Makes 1 x 125 g/4 oz jar

- ☐ **25 small fresh red chillies, stalks removed**
- ☐ **2 cloves garlic**
- ☐ **1 small onion, chopped**
- ☐ **2 tablespoons brown sugar**
- ☐ **185 mL/6 fl oz water**
- ☐ **1 teaspoon cornflour**
- ☐ **2 tablespoons white vinegar**

1   Place whole chillies, garlic and onion in a food processor or blender and process to make a paste. Transfer to a small saucepan and stir in sugar, water, cornflour and vinegar. Bring to the boil, reduce heat and simmer until thickened.

2   Remove from heat and set aside to cool. Transfer to a warm sterilised jar. Seal and label when cold. Store in the refrigerator until required.

Preserving tips: Always use clean unchipped jars.

Remove any old labels by soaking.

The jars must be sterilised before filling or the preserve will go mouldy. To sterilise jars, wash in hot water then warm in the oven at a low temperature until dry. Remember that the lids must also be sterilised.

Jars should be warm when adding the hot preserve. Cold jars will crack or break if a hot mixture is suddenly added to them.

MINT CHUTNEY

A food processor makes the preparation of this chutney very easy. The chutney will keep for up to a week in the refrigerator, however it will lose its colour after the first day

Makes 1 x 125 g/4 oz jar

- ☐ **125 g/4 oz fresh mint sprigs**
- ☐ **3 fresh green chillies, seeds removed and chopped**
- ☐ **3 spring onions, chopped**
- ☐ **2 teaspoons sugar**
- ☐ **¹/₂ teaspoon salt**
- ☐ **1 tablespoon vinegar**

1   Remove mint leaves from stalks. Wash and dry.

2   Place mint leaves, chillies, spring onions, sugar, salt and vinegar in a food processor or blender and process until smooth.

3   Transfer to a warm sterilised jar. Seal and store in the refrigerator until required.

DATE AND ORANGE CHUTNEY

A delicious sweet chutney that can also be made using fresh figs rather than dates if you wish.

Makes 2 x 250 g/8 oz jars

- ☐ **250 g/8 oz fresh dates, pitted and chopped**
- ☐ **1 orange, chopped**
- ☐ **1 teaspoon grated fresh ginger**
- ☐ **60 g/2 oz raisins**
- ☐ **1 tablespoon brown sugar**
- ☐ **75 mL/2¹/₂ fl oz cider vinegar**
- ☐ **75 mL/2¹/₂ fl oz water**

1   Place dates, orange, ginger, raisins, sugar, vinegar and water in a saucepan and cook, stirring occasionally, over a low heat for 20 minutes.

2   Transfer to warm sterilised jars, seal and label when cold. Store in the refrigerator until required.

Date and Orange Chutney, Chilli Sambal, Mint Chutney, Chilli Pickled Cabbage

CHILLI PICKLED CABBAGE

Traditional Kim Chee is made months in advance and is placed in large stone jars to mature. This simplified version is ready after one week.

Makes 1 x 1.2 litres/2 pt jar

- ☐ **1 kg/2 lb Chinese cabbage, coarsely chopped**
- ☐ **1 tablespoon salt**
- ☐ **2 spring onions, chopped**
- ☐ **2 cloves garlic, crushed**
- ☐ **1 tablespoon sambal oelek (chilli paste)**
- ☐ **2 teaspoons grated fresh ginger**
- ☐ **125 mL/4 fl oz light soy sauce**
- ☐ **125 mL/4 fl oz white vinegar**
- ☐ **¹/₂ teaspoon sesame oil**

1   Sprinkle cabbage with salt and set aside for 4 hours.
2   Press cabbage to remove excess liquid. Add spring onions, garlic, sambal oelek (chilli paste), ginger, soy sauce and vinegar, and stir to combine.
3   Place into a large, warm, sterilised jar, seal and leave in a cool place for at least 1 day before using to allow flavours to develop.
4   Sprinkle with the sesame oil to serve.

MIDDLE EASTERN PEACH

An exotic pickle that combines the flavours of lush peaches with spices of the Middle East.

Makes 1 x 375 g/12 oz jar

- ☐ **1¹/₂ teaspoons tamarind paste**
- ☐ **375 mL/12 fl oz white wine vinegar**
- ☐ **500 g/1 lb fresh peaches, peeled and sliced**
- ☐ **1 tablespoon grated fresh ginger**
- ☐ **3 teaspoons ground coriander**
- ☐ **3 cloves garlic, crushed**
- ☐ **125 g/4 oz sugar**
- ☐ **2 small fresh red chillies**

1   Dissolve tamarind paste in 125 mL/ 4 fl oz vinegar. Place peaches, ginger, coriander, garlic, tamarind mixture, remaining vinegar, sugar and chillies in a saucepan. Bring to the boil, stirring, until sugar is dissolved.
2   Reduce heat and simmer without stirring for 20 minutes. Transfer to warm, sterilised jars. Seal and label when cold.

CURRIED AUBERGINE PICKLE

Blend your own spices to create this perky pickle. Adjust the amount of chilli according to the degree of hotness you desire.

Makes 3 x 500 g/16 oz jars

- ☐ **4 small fresh red chillies, seeded and chopped**
- ☐ **5 cloves garlic**
- ☐ **1 tablespoon grated fresh ginger**
- ☐ **1¹/₂ tablespoons mustard seeds**
- ☐ **2 teaspoons ground turmeric**
- ☐ **2 teaspoons garam masala**
- ☐ **250 mL/8 fl oz vegetable oil**
- ☐ **1.5 kg/3 lb aubergines (eggplant), cut into 2 cm/³/₄ in cubes**
- ☐ **¹/₂ teaspoon salt**
- ☐ **125 g/4 oz brown sugar**
- ☐ **185 mL/6 fl oz white vinegar**

1   Blend chillies, garlic, ginger, mustard seeds, turmeric and garam masala to a paste in a food processor or blender.
2   Heat oil in a frying pan and cook spice paste for 1 minute. Add aubergines (eggplant), toss to coat with spice paste. Reduce heat, cover and cook until aubergines (eggplant) are tender. Add salt, sugar and vinegar and simmer, uncovered, until thickened.
3   Transfer to warm sterilised jars. Allow to cool and skim off any oil that rises to the surface. Seal and label when cold.

Curried Aubergine Pickle, Middle Eastern Peach

THREE-FRUIT MARMALADE

The name 'marmalade' comes from the Portuguese word for quince. The original marmalade was a quince jelly from Portugal which was taken to England in the fourteenth century.

Makes 3 x 500 g/1 lb jars

- ☐ **2 large oranges**
- ☐ **2 limes**
- ☐ **1 large grapefruit**
- ☐ **1 litre/1³/₄ pt water**
- ☐ **1.75 kg/3¹/₂ lb sugar**

1 Cut oranges, limes and grapefruit in half, then slice thinly, discarding seeds. Place fruit in a large bowl and add water. Cover and stand overnight.
2 Transfer fruit and water to a large saucepan and bring to the boil, then reduce heat and simmer, uncovered, for 1 hour or until fruit is soft.
3 Add sugar, stirring constantly without boiling, until sugar dissolves. Bring to the boil and cook, uncovered, without stirring, for 45 minutes or until marmalade gels when tested.
4 Stand 10 minutes before pouring marmalade into hot sterilised jars. Seal when cold.

MIXED-BERRY JAM

Makes 4 x 250 g/8 oz jars

- ☐ **750 g/1¹/₂ lb mixed fresh berries**
- ☐ **250 mL/8 fl oz water**
- ☐ **750 g/1¹/₂ lb sugar**
- ☐ **3 tablespoons lemon juice**

1 Place berries, water, sugar and lemon juice in a large saucepan and cook over a low heat, stirring until sugar dissolves.
2 Bring to the boil, then reduce heat and simmer for 30-35 minutes or until jam gels when tested.
3 Stand for 10 minutes, then pour into hot sterilised jars. Seal when cold.

PLUM JAM

This jam is delicious as a cake or tart filling.

Makes 4 x 250 g/8 oz jars

- ☐ **1 kg/2 lb blood plums halved and stoned**
- ☐ **250 mL/8 fl oz water**
- ☐ **1 kg/2 lb sugar**
- ☐ **15 g/¹/₂ oz butter**

1 Place plums and water in a large saucepan and bring to the boil. Reduce heat, cover and simmer for 15-20 minutes or until fruit is soft and pulpy.
2 Add sugar and cook, stirring constantly without boiling, until sugar dissolves. Bring jam to the boil and cook, uncovered, for 20-30 minutes or until jam gels when tested. Stir in butter.
3 Stand jam for 10 minutes, before spooning into hot sterilised jars. Seal and label when cold.

Setting test: To test the set or gel of a jam, remove the pan from heat and allow the bubbles to subside. Drop a spoonful of jam onto a chilled saucer and set aside at room temperature to cool. The jam should form a skin that will wrinkle when pushed with your finger. If the jam does not pass the setting test, return to heat and boil for a few minutes longer, then retest. Remember to remove the pan from the heat while testing the jam or it will continue to cook.

STRAWBERRY JAM

Makes 4 x 250 g/8 oz jars

- ☐ **1 kg/2 lb strawberries, washed and hulled**
- ☐ **1 kg/2 lb sugar**
- ☐ **125 mL/4 fl oz lemon juice**
- ☐ **185 mL/6 fl oz water**

1 Place strawberries, sugar, lemon juice and water in a large saucepan and cook over a low heat, stirring until sugar dissolves.
2 Bring to the boil and cook, without stirring, for 40-45 minutes or until jam gels when tested.
3 Pour jam into hot sterilised jars. Seal and label when cold.

Sealing and labelling preserves: Preserves should be covered immediately after potting or when completely cold. Never cover when just warm as that creates conditions ideal for the growth of mould. If you are going to allow the jam to cool before covering, place a clean cloth over the jars to prevent dust falling on the surface of the jam.

LEMON BUTTER

Lemon butter, curd or honey seems to have originated from the curd tarts, known as cheesecakes, of the seventeeth century.

Makes 1 x 250 g/8 oz jar

- ☐ **2 eggs**
- ☐ **125 g/4 oz sugar**
- ☐ **5 tablespoons lemon juice**
- ☐ **1 tablespoon finely grated lemon rind**
- ☐ **30 g/1 oz butter**

1 Place eggs and sugar in a heatproof bowl and beat lightly. Stir in lemon juice, lemon rind and butter.
2 Place bowl over a saucepan of simmering water and cook, stirring constantly, for 15 minutes or until mixture thickens.
3 Pour into hot sterilised jars. Seal and label when cold.

BRANDIED APRICOTS

Makes 3 x 250 g/8 oz jars

- ☐ **500 g/1 lb sugar**
- ☐ **250 mL/8 fl oz water**
- ☐ **1 kg/2 lb apricots, halved and stoned**
- ☐ **¹/₄ teaspoon ground nutmeg**
- ☐ **250 mL/8 fl oz brandy**

1 Place sugar and water in a large saucepan and cook over a medium heat, stirring constantly, until sugar dissolves. Add apricots and nutmeg, bring to simmering and simmer until apricots are just tender.
2 Using a slotted spoon remove apricots from liquid and pack tightly into hot sterilised jars. Bring syrup to the boil and boil for 8 minutes or until reduced by half and golden.
3 Half fill each jar with brandy, then add syrup to within 2 cm/³/₄ in of the top. Seal and label when cold.

Lemon Butter, Mixed-Berry Jam, Plum Jam, Three-Fruit Marmalade, Strawberry Jam

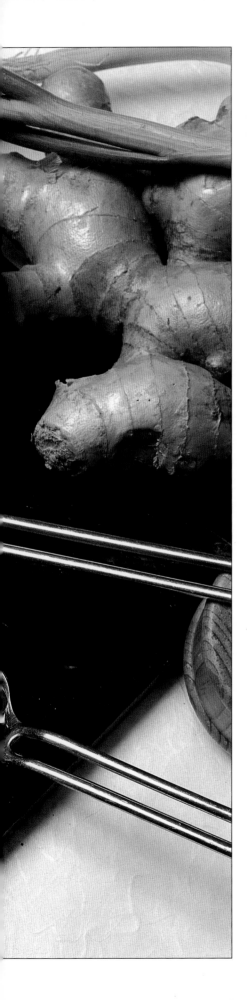

chapter fourteen

BASIC RECIPES

In this chapter you will find
recipes for stocks, sauces and
dressings that will add that special
something to your cooking. Many of the
sauces are delicious spooned over
steamed vegetables, while the stocks
provide the basis for tasty
homemade soups.

Italian Green Sauce with Basil,
Creamy Mustard Sauce,
Mexican Chilli Sauce,
Spicy Peanut Satay Sauce

CORIANDER PESTO

A delicious sauce for pasta, an excellent addition to soup, or just serve it as a dip.

Makes about 250 mL/8 fl oz

- [ ] **3 large bunches fresh coriander**
- [ ] **2 cloves garlic, crushed**
- [ ] **60 g/2 oz pine nuts**
- [ ] **125 mL/4 fl oz olive oil**
- [ ] **60 g/2 oz grated Parmesan cheese**

Place coriander leaves, garlic and pine nuts in a food processor or blender and process until finely chopped. With machine running, slowly pour in the oil and process until smooth. Add cheese and process to blend.

ITALIAN GREEN SAUCE WITH BASIL

Wonderful with hot pasta!

Makes 250 mL/8 fl oz

- [ ] **2 small bunches fresh basil**
- [ ] **3 spring onions, finely chopped**
- [ ] **2 cloves garlic, crushed**
- [ ] **1 tablespoon capers, drained and rinsed**
- [ ] **155 mL/5 fl oz olive oil**
- [ ] **1 tablespoon lemon juice**
- [ ] **freshly ground black pepper.**

Place basil leaves, spring onions, garlic and capers in a food processor or blender and process until smooth. With machine running, slowly pour in oil, then lemon juice, and continue to process until well blended. Season to taste with black pepper.

SPICY PEANUT SATAY SAUCE

Makes 375 mL/12 fl oz

- [ ] **2 tablespoons groundnut (peanut) oil**
- [ ] **315 g/10 oz roasted peanuts, finely chopped**
- [ ] **2 cloves garlic, crushed**
- [ ] **1 onion, finely chopped**
- [ ] **1/2 teaspoon chilli powder**
- [ ] **1 tablespoon brown sugar**
- [ ] **2 tablespoons soy sauce**
- [ ] **1/4 teaspoon five spice powder**
- [ ] **500 mL/16 fl oz coconut milk**

1 Heat oil in a saucepan and cook peanuts, garlic, onion and chilli powder, stirring for 3-4 minutes.
2 Add sugar, soy sauce and five spice powder, reduce heat and pour in coconut milk. Simmer for 5-10 minutes, stirring occasionally. If sauce becomes too thick, thin with a little milk.

CREAMY MUSTARD SAUCE

Best made just before serving, this superbly tangy sauce is great poured over steamed vegetables.

Makes about 250 mL/8 fl oz

- [ ] **315 mL/10 fl oz cream (single)**
- [ ] **1 1/2 tablespoons wholegrain mustard**
- [ ] **1 clove garlic, crushed**
- [ ] **3 tablespoons vegetable stock**
- [ ] **1 tablespoon finely snipped fresh chives or finely chopped parsley**
- [ ] **freshly ground black pepper**

Place cream in a small saucepan and bring to the boil. Boil rapidly until reduced by a quarter. Stir in mustard, garlic and vegetable stock. Simmer for 5-10 minutes, stirring frequently, until sauce reduces and thickens a little. Stir in chives or parsley and season to taste with pepper. Serve immediately.

MEXICAN CHILLI SAUCE

Makes about 500 mL/16 fl oz

- [ ] **2 tablespoons sesame oil**
- [ ] **3 small fresh red chillies, seeded and finely chopped**
- [ ] **3 small fresh green chillies, seeded and finely chopped**
- [ ] **3 cloves garlic, crushed**
- [ ] **2 onions, finely chopped**
- [ ] **1 tablespoon finely chopped fresh coriander**
- [ ] **440 g/14 fl oz canned tomatoes, undrained and mashed**
- [ ] **1 teaspoon brown sugar**
- [ ] **1/2 teaspoon ground cinnamon**
- [ ] **1/4 teaspoon ground cloves**
- [ ] **1/4 teaspoon ground root ginger**
- [ ] **2 tablespoons lemon juice**
- [ ] **3 tablespoons water**

Heat oil in a frying pan and cook red and green chillies, garlic, onions and coriander for 2-3 minutes. Stir in tomatoes, sugar, cinnamon, cloves, ginger, lemon juice and water and simmer for 10-15 minutes or until sauce reduces and thickens.

LIME AND LEMON SAUCE

Serve this sauce spooned over grilled fish or chicken or steamed vegetables.

Makes 500 mL/16 fl oz

- [ ] **60 g/2 oz butter**
- [ ] **1 clove garlic, crushed**
- [ ] **1 1/2 tablespoons cornflour blended with 3 tablespoons water**
- [ ] **500 mL/16 fl oz vegetable stock**
- [ ] **1 tablespoon lemon juice**
- [ ] **1 tablespoon lime juice**
- [ ] **1/2 teaspoon grated lime rind**
- [ ] **1/2 teaspoon grated lemon rind**
- [ ] **1/4 teaspoon ground turmeric**

Melt butter in a saucepan, add garlic and cook over a medium heat for 1 minute. Stir in cornflour mixture, stock, lemon juice, lime juice, lemon rind, lime rind and turmeric and cook, stirring constantly, for 4-5 minutes or until sauce boils and thickens.

BARBECUE SAUCE

This sauce can be served hot, warm or cold and is the perfect accompaniment for any barbecued or grilled foods.

Makes 250 mL/8 fl oz

- [ ] **1 tablespoon vegetable oil**
- [ ] **1 onion, chopped**
- [ ] **1 clove garlic, crushed**
- [ ] **1 teaspoon dry mustard**
- [ ] **1 tablespoon Worcestershire sauce**
- [ ] **1 tablespoon brown sugar**
- [ ] **3 tablespoons tomato sauce**
- [ ] **1 teaspoon chilli sauce**
- [ ] **185 mL/6 fl oz beef stock**
- [ ] **freshly ground black pepper**

Heat oil in a saucepan, add onion and garlic and cook for 3-4 minutes or until onion is soft. Stir in mustard, Worcestershire sauce, sugar, tomato sauce, chilli sauce and stock and bring to the boil. Reduce heat and simmer for 8-10 minutes or until sauce reduces and thickens slightly. Season to taste with black pepper.

SWEET AND SOUR BARBECUE SAUCE

A sweet and sour sauce is always a popular accompaniment for chicken and pork, but is also delicious served with sausages and fish.

Makes 500 mL/16 fl oz

- ☐ **1 tablespoon vegetable oil**
- ☐ **1 small onion, chopped**
- ☐ **1 red pepper, chopped**
- ☐ **1 tablespoon soy sauce**
- ☐ **2 tablespoons honey**
- ☐ **1 tablespoon tomato purée**
- ☐ **2 tablespoons cornflour**
- ☐ **125 mL/4 fl oz cider vinegar**
- ☐ **125 mL/4 fl oz chicken stock or water**
- ☐ **440 g/14 oz canned pineapple pieces, drained**

1 Heat oil in a saucepan, add onion and red pepper and cook for 4-5 minutes or until soft. Place soy sauce, honey, tomato purée, cornflour and vinegar in a small bowl and mix to combine.
2 Stir cornflour mixture into vegetables, then stir in stock or water and cook over a medium heat, stirring constantly, for 2-3 minutes or until sauce boils and thickens. Stir in pineapple pieces and cook for 2-3 minutes longer.

APPLE AND HORSERADISH SAUCE

Delicious served with beef and sausages, this condiment also makes an interesting accompaniment for barbecued or grilled fish.

Makes 250 mL/8 fl oz

- ☐ **125 mL/4 fl oz cream (double)**
- ☐ **1 green apple, cored and grated**
- ☐ **3 tablespoons horseradish relish**
- ☐ **freshly ground black pepper**

Place cream in a bowl and whip until soft peaks form. Fold in apple and horseradish relish and season to taste with black pepper.

EASY HOLLANDAISE SAUCE

Hollandaise sauce is normally made in the top of a double boiler by slowly adding the melted butter to the egg mixture. In this easy version no cooking is required if you make sure that the butter is hot and bubbling when you add it to the egg mixture.

Makes 250 mL/8 fl oz

- ☐ **3 egg yolks**
- ☐ **2 tablespoons lemon juice**
- ☐ **125 g/4 oz butter**
- ☐ **freshly ground black pepper**

Place egg yolks and lemon juice in a food processor or blender and process until light and frothy. Melt butter until it is hot and bubbling. With food processor running, slowly pour in hot, melted butter and process until thick. Season to taste with black pepper and serve immediately.

Microwave it: Hollandaise sauce can be quickly and easily made in the microwave. Place egg yolks and lemon juice in a small jug and whisk to combine. Melt butter in a separate jug, then whisk into egg yolk mixture and cook on MEDIUM (50%), stirring every minute, for $1^{1}/_{2}$ minutes or until sauce thickens.

TARTARE SAUCE

Makes 250 mL/8 fl oz

- ☐ **250 mL/8 fl oz mayonnaise**
- ☐ **2 tablespoons finely chopped gherkin**
- ☐ **1 tablespoon finely chopped fresh parsley**
- ☐ **1 tablespoon chopped fresh dill**
- ☐ **freshly ground black pepper**

Place mayonnaise, gherkin, capers, parsley, dill and black pepper to taste in a bowl and mix well to combine.

STIRRED EGG CUSTARD

Makes 375 mL/12 fl oz

- ☐ **185 mL/6 fl oz milk, scalded**
- ☐ **1 tablespoon sugar**
- ☐ **3 eggs, lightly beaten**
- ☐ **185 mL/6 fl oz cream (single)**
- ☐ **$^{1}/_{2}$ teaspoon vanilla essence**

1 Place milk and sugar in a small saucepan and cook over a low heat, stirring constantly, for 3-4 minutes or until sugar dissolves.
2 Place eggs in a heatproof bowl, place bowl over a saucepan of simmering water and gradually stir in milk mixture, then cream. Cook, stirring constantly, until custard evenly coats the back of a wooden spoon.
3 Remove bowl from saucepan and place in iced water to stop the cooking process. Stir in vanilla essence and use custard as desired.

CREME ANGLAISE

Créme Anglaise is a light custard sauce which is great served warm or chilled with fruit desserts and puddings.

Makes 250 mL/8 fl oz

- ☐ **3 egg yolks**
- ☐ **$1^{1}/_{2}$ tablespoons sugar**
- ☐ **300 mL/$9^{1}/_{2}$ fl oz milk, scalded**
- ☐ **$^{1}/_{2}$ teaspoon vanilla essence**

1 Place egg yolks and sugar in a heatproof bowl and mix to combine. Place bowl over a saucepan of simmering water and beat until a ribbon trail forms.
2 Gradually stir in milk and vanilla essence, then transfer mixture to a heavy-based saucepan and cook over a low heat, stirring in a figure-eight pattern, until custard thickens and coats the back of a wooden spoon. Do not allow the custard to boil.
3 Remove pan from heat, place in a bowl of ice, and stir until custard cools a little. Strain through a fine sieve if necessary and use as desired.

WHITE SAUCE

This classic sauce is the base in many sauces. Add 60 g/2 oz grated cheese for a cheese sauce or 2 tablespoons finely chopped fresh parsley to make parsley sauce. Or make a curry sauce with 2 teaspoons curry powder and ¹/₂ onion, chopped. For mushroom sauce, simply add 60 g/2 oz sliced mushrooms cooked for about 5 minutes in butter.

Makes 250 mL/8 fl oz

- ☐ **15 g/¹/₂ oz butter**
- ☐ **2 tablespoons flour**
- ☐ **250 mL/8 fl oz milk**

1   Melt butter in a saucepan. Stir in flour and cook for 1 minute, stirring contantly.
2   Gradually stir in milk and cook over a medium heat until sauce boils and thickens. Season to taste if desired.

Microwave it: To make White Sauce, melt butter in a microwave-safe jug, mix in flour, gradually add milk and cook on HIGH (100%) for 3-4 minutes or until thickened. Stir after 1¹/₂ minutes.

ONION AND HERB YOGURT SAUCE

Serve this low-kilojoule sauce poured over vegetables as a delicious alternative to white sauce.

Makes 315 mL/10 fl oz

- ☐ **1 tablespoon olive oil**
- ☐ **1 onion, finely chopped**
- ☐ **¹/₄ teaspoon ground coriander**
- ☐ **2 tablespoons flour**
- ☐ **125 mL/4 fl oz oz reduced-fat milk**
- ☐ **185 g/6 oz natural yogurt**
- ☐ **1 tablespoon finely chopped fresh basil**
- ☐ **1 tablespoon finely chopped fresh parsley**
- ☐ **1 tablespoon finely snipped fresh chives**
- ☐ **freshly ground black pepper**

1   Heat oil in a saucepan and cook onion and coriander for 4-5 minutes or until onion is soft. Stir in flour and gradually mix in milk. Reduce heat and cook until sauce thickens.
2   Mix in yogurt, basil, parsley and chives and stir over a low heat until heated through. Season to taste with black pepper.

GREEN SAUCE

This sauce is a colourful addition to meals that seem to be a little bland in colour. Try it with vegetables such as cauliflower. It is also delicious served with poultry or fish.

Makes 250 mL/8 fl oz

- ☐ **30 g/1 oz fresh parsley, chopped**
- ☐ **2 tablespoons chopped fresh basil**
- ☐ **4 tablespoons snipped fresh chives**
- ☐ **250 mL/8 fl oz milk**
- ☐ **15 g/¹/₂ oz butter**
- ☐ **2 tablespoons flour**
- ☐ **1 tablespoon grated Parmesan cheese**
- ☐ **freshly ground black pepper**

1   In a food processor or blender, purée parsley, basil and chives with a little of the milk to make a green paste. Mix in remaining milk.
2   Melt butter in saucepan, stir in flour and cook for 1 minute. Blend in milk mixture and cook until sauce boils and thickens, stirring frequently during cooking.
3   Stir in cheese and season to taste with black pepper.

COCKTAIL SAUCE

This sauce is delicious served with seafood. It will keep in the refrigerator for up to 2 days.

Makes 250 mL/8 fl oz

- ☐ **250 mL/8 fl oz tomato sauce**
- ☐ **1 tablespoon Worcestershire sauce**
- ☐ **1 teaspoon horseradish relish**
- ☐ **1 teaspoon cider vinegar**
- ☐ **1 teaspoon prepared mustard**
- ☐ **1 tablespoon lemon juice**
- ☐ **3-4 drops Tabasco sauce or to taste**
- ☐ **2 tablespoons cream (double)**

1   Place tomato sauce, Worcestershire sauce, horseradish relish, vinegar, mustard and lemon juice in a bowl and whisk to combine.
2   Season to taste with Tabasco sauce and stir in cream. Cover and chill until required.

FRESH TOMATO SAUCE

Serve this sauce with any boiled, steamed or microwaved vegetables. Top with breadcrumbs and Parmesan cheese and place under a hot grill to create a tomato-flavoured gratin. Use six fresh large tomatoes in summer when they are plentiful. You may need to add a tablespoon of tomato purée for extra flavour.

Makes 375 mL/12 fl oz

- ☐ **1 tablespoon olive oil**
- ☐ **1 onion, sliced**
- ☐ **1 clove garlic, crushed**
- ☐ **¹/₂ green pepper, sliced**
- ☐ **440 g/14 oz canned, peeled tomatoes, mashed**
- ☐ **125 mL/4 fl oz white wine**
- ☐ **1 teaspoon dried mixed herbs**
- ☐ **freshly ground black pepper**

1   Heat oil in a saucepan and cook onion, garlic and green pepper for 4-5 minutes until onion is soft. Stir in tomatoes and wine and simmer for 5 minutes.
2   Add herbs and season to taste with black pepper. Simmer for a further 20 minutes or until sauce reduces.

Microwave it: Fresh Tomato Sauce is made in about 15 minutes in the microwave. In a large microwave-safe jug, cook onion and garlic in oil on HIGH (100%) for 2-3 minutes Add remaining ingredients. Cook on HIGH (100%) for a further 10-15 minutes or until sauce reduces and thickens.

HOT CURRY SAUCE

As a topping for baked potatoes or as an accompaniment to steamed vegetables, this easy-to-prepare sauce makes a tasty change.

Makes 500 mL/16 fl oz

- ☐ **6 courgettes (zucchini), peeled and chopped**
- ☐ **1 tablespoon vegetable oil**
- ☐ **1 onion, chopped**
- ☐ **1 teaspoon curry powder**
- ☐ **¹/₂ teaspoon chilli sauce**
- ☐ **1 tablespoon chutney or relish**

1 Boil, steam or microwave courgettes (zucchini) until tender. Drain and set aside.
2 Heat oil in a frying pan, add onion and curry powder and cook for 4-5 minutes or until onion is soft.
3 Place courgettes (zucchini), onion mixture, chilli sauce and chutney in a food processor or blender and process until smooth. Pour into a saucepan and cook over a low heat, stirring, for 4-5 minutes or until sauce is heated through.

CAMEMBERT SAUCE

This creamy fondue-like sauce will dress up the plainest vegetable. Try it poured over courgettes (zucchini), broccoli, potatoes or pumpkin. It is also a great way to use up that odd piece of Camembert or Brie left in the fridge.

Makes 185 mL/6 fl oz

- ☐ **15 g/¹/₂ oz butter**
- ☐ **1 tablespoon flour**
- ☐ **125 mL/4 fl oz milk**
- ☐ **3 tablespoons white wine**
- ☐ **75 g/2¹/₂ oz Camembert or Brie cheese, rind removed**
- ☐ **freshly ground black pepper**

1 Melt butter in a small saucepan. Stir in flour and cook for 1 minute. Blend in milk and cook until sauce boils and thickens, stirring frequently during cooking.
2 Stir in wine and cheese. Season to taste with black pepper, and cook over a low heat until cheese melts.

Microwave it: In a microwave-safe jug, melt butter. Stir in flour and milk. Cook on HIGH (100%) for 2 minutes or until sauce thickens. Stir after 1 minute. Mix in wine and cheese. Cook 1 minute on MEDIUM (50%) or until cheese melts.

From top: Camembert Sauce, Fresh Tomato Sauce, White Sauce, Green Sauce, Onion and Herb Yogurt Sauce

YOGURT DRESSING

This dressing makes a great lower kilojoule (calorie) alternative to mayonnaise. Try it on potato salad or coleslaw.

Makes 250 mL/8 fl oz

- ☐ **185 g/6 oz natural yogurt**
- ☐ **1 clove garlic, crushed (optional)**
- ☐ **2 tablespoons white wine vinegar**
- ☐ **2 tablespoons snipped fresh chives**

Combine yogurt, garlic, vinegar and chives in a bowl. Whisk well to combine.

Variations
Mint Yogurt Dressing: Prepare Yogurt Dressing as directed. Mix in 2 tablespoons finely chopped fresh mint.
Curried Yogurt Dressing: Prepare Yogurt Dressing. Blend in a teaspoon of curry powder and a dash of chilli sauce.
Thousand Island Yogurt Dressing: Prepare Yogurt Dressing, omitting garlic. Mix in 2 tablespoons chopped green olives, 2 finely sliced spring onions, 1 finely chopped hard-boiled egg, 1 tablespoon finely chopped green pepper, 1 tablespoon tomato purée and 1/2 teaspoon chilli sauce.

VINAIGRETTE

Makes 250 mL/8 fl oz

- ☐ **185 mL/6 fl oz olive oil**
- ☐ **3 tablespoons cider vinegar**
- ☐ **1 tablespoon Dijon mustard**
- ☐ **freshly ground black pepper**

Place oil, vinegar and mustard in a screwtop jar. Season to taste with black pepper. Shake well to combine.

Variations
Walnut or Hazelnut Dressing: Replace olive oil with 4 tablespoons walnut or hazelnut oil and 100 mL/3½ fl oz vegetable oil.
Lemon Herb Vinaigrette: Replace vinegar with 3 tablespoons lemon juice, add 60 g/2 oz mixed chopped fresh herbs. Suggested herbs include basil, parsley, chives, rosemary, thyme or tarragon.

GINGER AND SOY DRESSING

If possible, make earlier in the day to allow the flavours to develop.

Makes 250 mL/8 fl oz

- ☐ **1 tablespoon sesame oil**
- ☐ **1 tablespoon grated fresh ginger**
- ☐ **125 mL/4 fl oz soy sauce**
- ☐ **125 mL/4 fl oz water**
- ☐ **1 tablespoon cider vinegar**
- ☐ **1 clove garlic, crushed (optional)**

Combine sesame oil, ginger, soy, water, vinegar and garlic in a screwtop jar. Shake well to combine. Stand 15 minutes before using.

ORIENTAL MAYONNAISE

Serve as a dipping sauce for lightly cooked fresh vegetables such as asparagus spears, celery and carrot sticks, or spoon over hot vegetables.

Makes 375 mL/12 fl oz

- ☐ **1 clove garlic, crushed**
- ☐ **2 teaspoons grated fresh ginger**
- ☐ **4 tablespoons soy sauce**
- ☐ **2 tablespoons cider vinegar**
- ☐ **2 tablespoons brown sugar**
- ☐ **1 teaspoon fennel seeds**
- ☐ **2 egg yolks**
- ☐ **1/2 teaspoon dry mustard powder**
- ☐ **185 mL/6 fl oz vegetable oil**
- ☐ **2 teaspoons sesame oil**
- ☐ **1/2 teaspoon hot chilli sauce**

1   Place garlic, ginger, soy sauce, vinegar, sugar and fennel seeds in a small saucepan and bring to the boil. Reduce heat and simmer, uncovered, for 10 minutes or until mixture reduces by half. Remove from heat and strain to remove fennel seeds. Set aside to cool.
2   Combine egg yolks and mustard powder in food processor or blender. Process until just combined. With the machine running, pour in vegetable and sesame oils in a steady stream. Process until mayonnaise thickens.
3   Add soy mixture and process to combine. Mix in chilli sauce to taste.

APPLE AND HERB DRESSING

Use this dressing as a low-fat, low-kilojoule (calorie) alternative to traditional French dressing or try it as a tasty dressing on rice salad.

Makes 375 mL/12 fl oz

- ☐ **250 mL/8 fl oz unsweetened apple juice**
- ☐ **3 tablespoons apple cider vinegar**
- ☐ **1 clove garlic, crushed**
- ☐ **1 tablespoon finely snipped fresh chives**
- ☐ **2 tablespoons finely chopped fresh parsley**
- ☐ **freshly ground black pepper**

Place apple juice, vinegar, garlic, chives, parsley and black pepper to taste in a screwtop jar and shake well to combine.

TOFU MAYONNAISE

This delicious mayonnaise made from tofu is a cholesterol-free alternative to traditional mayonnaise.

Makes 375 mL/12 fl oz

- ☐ **250 g/8 oz tofu**
- ☐ **1 teaspoon Dijon mustard**
- ☐ **3 tablespoons cider vinegar**
- ☐ **125 mL/4 fl oz olive oil**
- ☐ **freshly ground black pepper**

1   Place tofu, mustard and 1 tablespoon vinegar in food processor or blender and process until smooth.
2   With machine running, slowly add 2 tablespoons oil then 1 tablespoon vinegar. Continue in this way until all the oil and vinegar are used. Season to taste with black pepper.

LOW-OIL VINAIGRETTE

Makes 250 mL/8 fl oz

- [ ] **4 tablespoons olive oil**
- [ ] **170 mL/5$^{1}/_{2}$ fl oz cider vinegar**
- [ ] **$^{1}/_{2}$ teaspoon dry mustard powder**
- [ ] **cayenne pepper**
- [ ] **freshly ground black pepper**

Combine oil, vinegar and mustard in a screwtop jar. Season to taste with cayenne and black pepper. Shake well to combine.

MAYONNAISE

Makes 375 mL/12 fl oz

- [ ] **2 egg yolks**
- [ ] **$^{1}/_{4}$ teaspoon dry mustard powder**
- [ ] **250 mL/8 fl oz olive oil**
- [ ] **2 tablespoons lemon juice or white wine vinegar**
- [ ] **freshly ground black pepper**

1   Place egg yolks and mustard in a food processor.
2   With machine running, slowly pour in olive oil, and process until mixture thickens. Blend in lemon juice or vinegar and season to taste with black pepper.

Variations
Green Herbed Mayonnaise: Purée 30 g/1 oz basil leaves, 2 tablespoons fresh parsley, 12 chives and 1 clove garlic. Prepare as above using vinegar, not lemon juice.
Blue Cheese Mayonnaise: Blend 100 g/3$^{1}/_{2}$ oz blue cheese into prepared mayonnaise

From top: Mayonnaise, Oriental Mayonnaise, Yogurt Dressing, Vinaigrette, Low-Oil Vinaigrette, Ginger and Soy Dressing

BEEF STOCK

This recipe will make a rich stock. If you wish, the meat can be omitted and just the bones used.

Makes 2 litres/3¹/₂ pt

- ☐ **500 g/1 lb shin beef, diced**
- ☐ **500 g/1 lb marrow bones, cut into pieces**
- ☐ **1 onion, quartered**
- ☐ **2 carrots, roughly chopped**
- ☐ **4 stalks celery, roughly chopped**
- ☐ **fresh herbs of your choice**
- ☐ **¹/₂ teaspoon whole black peppercorns**
- ☐ **3 litres/5 pt cold water**

1   Place beef, bones, onion, carrots, celery, herbs, peppercorns and water in a large saucepan and bring to the boil. Reduce heat and simmer, stirring occasionally, for 2 hours
2   Strain stock and refrigerate overnight.
3   Skim fat from the surface and use as required.

Keeping stock: Stock will keep in the refrigerator for 3-4 days or in the freezer for 12 months. As stock really does not keep very well, except in the freezer, it is better to freeze it even if you are only keeping it for a few days.

CHICKEN STOCK

Makes 2 litres/3¹/₂ pt

- ☐ **1 chicken carcass, skin removed and trimmed of all visible fat**
- ☐ **1 onion, quartered**
- ☐ **2 carrots, roughly chopped**
- ☐ **4 stalks celery, roughly chopped**
- ☐ **fresh herbs of your choice**
- ☐ **¹/₂ teaspoon whole black peppercorns**
- ☐ **3 litres/5 pt cold water**

1   Place chicken carcass, onion, carrots, celery, herbs, peppercorns and water in a large saucepan and bring to the boil. Reduce heat and simmer, stirring occasionally, for 2 hours.
2   Strain stock and refrigerate overnight.
3   Skim fat from the surface and use stock as required.

Freeze it: Freeze stock in 125 mL/4 fl oz or 250 mL/8 fl oz portions for easy use at a later date. It is also a good idea to freeze some stock in ice cube trays for those

times when you require only one or two tablespoons of stock. Remember to remove the stock from the trays once frozen and place it in a freezer bag or it will evaporate and you will be left with nothing. The trays in which the stock has been frozen are no longer suitable for ice as the stock taints the trays and the flavour will be absorbed by the ice cubes.

FISH STOCK

Fish stock is even better if you can include the shells of lobster, prawns or crab in it. When making fish stock it is important that the cooking time is no longer than 20 minutes as the bones and trimming become bitter and impart an unpleasant taste.

Makes 2 litres/3¹/₂ pt

- ☐ **fish bones, skin and seafood shells, the quantity and type used is not important**
- ☐ **1 large onion, quartered**
- ☐ **1 large carrot, roughly chopped**
- ☐ **4 stalks celery, roughly chopped**
- ☐ **1 bay leaf**
- ☐ **1 sprig fresh thyme**
- ☐ **¹/₂ teaspoon whole black peppercorns**
- ☐ **3 litres/5 pt cold water**

1   Place fish trimmings, onion, carrot, celery, bay leaf, thyme, peppercorns and water in a large saucepan and bring to the boil. Reduce heat and simmer for 20 minutes.
2   Strain stock and use as required.

VEGETABLE STOCK

This is a wonderful vegetable stock and well worth the effort. It will add a delicious flavour to any dish, and is a must for any vegetarian cook.

Makes 2 litres/3¹/₂ pt

- ☐ **2 large onions, quartered**
- ☐ **2 large carrots, roughly chopped**
- ☐ **1 head celery, leaves included, roughly chopped**
- ☐ **1 bunch parsley, stalks included**
- ☐ **¹/₂ teaspoon whole black peppercorns**
- ☐ **2.5 litres/4 pt cold water**

1   Place onions, carrots, celery, parsley, peppercorns and water in a large saucepan. Bring to the boil, reduce heat and simmer, stirring occasionally, for 30 minutes.
2   Remove stock from heat and allow to cool. Place stock in a food processor or blender and process to purée. Push vegetable mixture through a sieve. Discard solids and use liquid as required.

Cook's tip: Do not add salt when making stock, especially if you do not know how it is to be used. Salting stock can lead to a dish that is too salty if you reduce the stock or if you are using other salty ingredients.

MICROWAVE CHICKEN STOCK

The microwave is particularly good for making small quantities of stock. The chicken carcass remaining after a roast is ideal for making stock.

Makes 1.5 litres/2¹/₂ pt

- ☐ **1 chicken carcass**
- ☐ **1 onion, chopped**
- ☐ **1 carrot, chopped**
- ☐ **2 stalks celery, chopped**
- ☐ **1 tablespoon chopped fresh parsley**
- ☐ **1 teaspoon chopped fresh thyme or ¹/₂ teaspoon dried thyme**
- ☐ **¹/₂ teaspoon whole black peppercorns**
- ☐ **cold water**

1   Place chicken carcass, onion, carrot, celery, parsley, thyme and peppercorns in a large microwave-safe dish. Cover with water and cook, uncovered, on HIGH (100%) for 45 minutes.
2   Strain stock and refrigerate overnight.
3   Skim fat from the surface and use as required.

Cook's tip: Beef, fish and vegetable stock can be made in the microwave in much the same way as chicken stock. Just remember that beef stock requires a little longer cooking and fish stock should not be cooked for more than 20 minutes.

RICH SHORTCRUST PASTRY

Rich shortcrust pastry can be used for both sweet and savoury pies.

- ☐ **250 g/8 oz flour, sifted**
- ☐ **185 g/6 oz butter, chilled and cut into small cubes**
- ☐ **1 egg yolk, lightly beaten**
- ☐ **3-4 tablespoons chilled water**

1　Place flour in a bowl and rub in butter using your fingertips until mixture resembles coarse breadcrumbs.
2　Mix in egg yolk and enough water to form a soft dough with a metal spatula or round-ended knife.
3　Turn dough onto a lightly floured surface and knead gently until smooth. Wrap in plastic food wrap and refrigerate for 30 minutes. Roll out and use as desired.

ALMOND PASTRY CASES

Bake these pastry cases and serve filled with lemon butter or your favourite jam as an afternoon tea treat.

Oven temperature 200°C, 400°F, Gas 6

- ☐ **250 g/8 oz flour, sifted**
- ☐ **3 tablespoons caster sugar**
- ☐ **185 g/6 oz butter, chilled and cut into small cubes**
- ☐ **1 egg yolk, lightly beaten with a few drops vanilla essence**
- ☐ **3-4 tablespoons chilled water**
- ☐ **3 tablespoons ground almonds**

1　Place flour and sugar in a bowl and mix to combine. Add butter and rub in using your fingertips until mixture resembles coarse breadcrumbs.
2　Mix in egg yolk mixture and enough water to form a soft dough with a metal spatula or round-ended knife. Turn onto a lightly floured surface and knead gently until smooth. Wrap in plastic food wrap and refrigerate for 30 minutes.
3　On a lightly floured surface roll pastry out to 3 mm/$\frac{1}{8}$ in thick, sprinkle with almonds and cut out rounds, using a 5 cm/2 in pastry cutter.
4　Place rounds in lightly greased patty tins, prick bases with a fork and bake for 15-20 minutes or until golden. Remove cases from tins and cool on a wire rack.

CHEESE PASTRY

Cheese pastry makes a tasty pastry for savoury pies. Omit the mustard and pepper and this pastry is perfect with apples and pears.

- ☐ **90 g/3 oz grated mature Cheddar**
- ☐ **1½ teaspoons dry mustard**
- ☐ **½ teaspoon cayenne pepper**
- ☐ **250 g/8 oz flour, sifted**
- ☐ **185 g/6 oz butter, chilled and cut into small cubes**
- ☐ **1 egg yolk, lightly beaten**
- ☐ **3-4 tablespoons chilled water**

1　Place cheese, mustard, cayenne pepper and flour in a bowl and mix to combine. Rub butter in using your fingertips until mixture resembles coarse breadcrumbs.
2　Mix in egg yolk and enough water to form a soft dough with metal spatula or round-ended knife.
3　Turn dough onto a lightly floured surface and knead gently until smooth. Wrap in plastic food wrap and refrigerate for 30 minutes. Roll out and use as desired.

FOOD PROCESSOR PASTRY

The food processor is great for making pastry. Place the flour and butter in a food processor and, using the pulse button, process to cut the butter until the mixture resembles coarse breadcrumbs. Add egg yolk and water and process until a dough is just formed. Turn dough onto a lightly floured surface and knead until smooth. Wrap in plastic food wrap and refrigerate for 30 minutes before using. When making pastry in the food processor you may not require as much water as when making it by hand. Use sufficient water to bind the ingredients together.

TIPS FOR PERFECT PASTRY MAKING

Practice makes perfect pastry so they say. To some, the thought of making pastry can be intimidating. Pastry is in fact easy to make and handle if a few ground rules are followed.

❦ The best pastry is made using chilled butter and water. It also helps to have cool utensils, so in hot weather it is a good idea to place them in the refrigerator for 10-15 minutes before making your pastry.

❦ Handle pastry quickly and lightly, as overhandling will result in tough pastry that will be difficult to roll.

❦ The amount of liquid used to bind the ingredients together will vary depending on the quality of the flour. If the dough is too soft the pastry will shrink on cooking.

❦ Kneading the pastry should be done using the coolest part of your hands, the fingertips. After kneading, wrap the pastry in plastic food wrap and refrigerate for 30 minutes before rolling out.

❦ Always roll pastry out in light, short strokes, starting from the middle of the pastry, rolling away from you and lifting the rolling pin off the edge of the pastry. This ensures even thickness.

❦ Lift and turn the pastry on a floured surface as you roll.

❦ Line the pie dish, trim the edges and rest the pastry in the refrigerator for 10 minutes longer before baking.

BAKING BLIND

Baking blind means to precook the pastry case without a filling. This is done if the filling you are using requires little or no cooking. It is also used when a liquid filling, such as a quiche filling, is being put into the pastry case. The precooking prevents the pastry becoming soggy.

To bake blind, line the pastry case with nonstick baking paper, then cover the base with uncooked rice, pasta or dried beans. This keeps the base of the pastry case flat during cooking. Bake the pastry case at 200 °C/400°F/Gas 6 for 10 minutes or as directed in the recipe. Remove rice, pasta or beans and paper and bake for 7-10 minutes longer. Allow pastry case to cool before filling.

GLOSSARY

Al dente: Just firm to the bite, the correct texture for pasta and some vegetables.

Au gratin: A cheese and breadcrumb topping, browned under the grill or in the oven.

Baste: To moisten meat or vegetables during cooking.

Blending: Mixing a liquid such as water with a dry ingredient such as cornflour. The mixture should be smooth and well combined.

Bind: To hold dry ingredients together with egg or liquid.

Bouillon: Broth or uncleared stock.

Bouquet garni: A small bunch of herbs, usually parsley, thyme and bay leaf. A bouquet garni is added to stews, soups or stocks for flavouring. Commercially prepared sachets of dried herbs are also available from most supermarkets.

Buttermilk: This is a cultured dairy product that has the same food value as skim milk. It is a useful low-fat ingredient that is sometimes used in baked goods.

CHICKEN

To section a chicken:

1 Using a sharp knife, cut through the skin where the leg joins the body, then cut through the bone joint between the leg and the body. This section consists of the leg and thigh and is called a 'maryland'. Separate the thigh from the leg by cutting through the joint.

2 Cut a small amount of breast meat down through the wing section, bending the wing away from the body to reveal the joint. Cut through the joint bone.

3 Cut through the rib bones, along each side of the body between the breast and back to separate the two pieces. The back portion can be frozen and used at a later date for the stockpot.

4 Divide the breast section into two pieces by cutting through the centre of the breast bone. Trim all pieces of excess fat and skin.

Trussing a chicken: Trussing a chicken helps it maintain its shape during cooking. Insert a metal skewer widthwise, just below the thigh bone, right through the body of the chicken. The ends of the skewer should be exposed either side. Place the chicken, breast side down, on a work surface. Take a length of string and catch the wing tips, then pass the string under the ends of the skewer and cross over the back. Turn the chicken breast side up and tie in the legs and the parson's nose.

To test when a bird is cooked: Place a skewer into the thickest part of the thigh and when the skewer is removed the juices should run clear. If the juices are tinged pink, return the bird to the oven and cook for 15 minutes longer, then test again. On completion of cooking, allow whole birds to stand in a warm place for 10-20 minutes before carving. This tenderises the meat by allowing the juices to settle into the flesh.

CHOCOLATE

To melt chocolate: Place chocolate in a heatproof bowl and set aside. Partly fill a saucepan with water so that when the bowl is placed over it the water comes just below the bottom of the bowl. Bring water to the boil, then remove the pan from the heat and place the bowl with the chocolate in it over the saucepan. Stand off the heat, stirring occasionally until the chocolate melts and is of a smooth consistency. Use as required.

Melting chocolate in the microwave: Place 375 g/12 oz chocolate in a microwave-safe glass or ceramic dish and cook on HIGH (100%) for 2 minutes. When melting chocolate in the microwave you will find that it tends to hold its shape, so always stir it before additional heating. If the chocolate is not completely melted, cook for 30 seconds longer, then stir again.

Seized chocolate: Chocolate 'seizes' if it is overheated or if it comes in contact with water or steam. Seizing results in the chocolate tightening and becoming a thick mass that will not melt. To rescue seized chocolate stir in a little cream or vegetable oil until the chocolate becomes smooth again.

CHOCOLATE DECORATIONS

Chocolate caraques: Pour melted chocolate over a cool work surface such as marble, ceramic or granite. Spread the chocolate as smoothly as possible using a flexible metal spatula, in a layer about 1.5 mm/$\frac{1}{16}$ in thick; do not leave any holes. If the chocolate is too thick it will not roll. Allow the chocolate to set at room temperature. Holding a long sharp knife at a 45 ° angle, pull gently over the surface of the chocolate to form curls.

Chocolate curls or shavings: Chocolate curls are made from chocolate that is at room temperature. To make shavings, chill the chocolate first. Using a vegetable peeler, shave the sides of the chocolate. Curls or shavings will fall depending on the temperature of the chocolate.

Chocolate leaves: Use stiff, fresh, nonpoisonous leaves such as rose or lemon leaves, with as much stem as possible for holding on to. Wash and dry leaves, brush the shiny surface of the leaf with a thin layer of melted, cooled chocolate. Allow to set to room temperature then carefully peel away the leaf.

Piping chocolate: Chocolate can be piped into fancy shapes for decorating desserts or cakes. Trace a simple design on a thin piece of paper. Tape a sheet of baking paper to the work surface and slide the drawing under the baking paper. Pipe around the design outline with melted chocolate. Allow to set at room temperature, then remove carefully with a metal spatula.

Clarify: To remove milk particles and impurities from butter. It also means to clear stocks and jellies by filtering.

The process of clarifying butter separates it into three layers; a top layer of foam, a middle layer of pure butterfat and a bottom layer of milky-white solids. It is the middle layer that is used for sautéing; the other two layers contain water, milk proteins and carbohydrates.

To clarify butter, place it in a small saucepan and melt it over a low heat. Skim the foam from the surface of the butter, then slowly pour the butter into a bowl, leaving behind the milky-white solids. Ghee, which is used in Indian cooking, is a type of clarified butter.

Coconut milk: Coconut milk can be purchased canned, or as a long-life product in cartons, or as a powder to which you add water. These products have a short life once opened and should be used within a day or so.

You can make coconut milk using desiccated coconut and water: Place 500 g/1 lb desiccated coconut in a bowl and pour over 750 mL/1¼ pt boiling water. Leave to stand for 30 minutes, then strain, squeezing the coconut to extract as much liquid as possible. This will make a thick coconut milk. The coconut can be used again to make a weaker coconut milk.

EGGS

Separating eggs: To separate an egg, crack the shell by tapping with the back of a knife to break cleanly in half. Carefully pass the yolk from one half of the shell to the other, so that the white of the egg passes into a bowl. Then place the yolk in a separate bowl. If separating more than one egg, break into separate bowls to ensure freshness before adding to the other eggs. If the egg white is to be beaten to the soft- or stiff-peak stage, it is vital that not a speck of yolk goes into the white, as the white will not beat up.

Beating egg whites: To beat egg whites to 'soft peaks' or 'stiff peaks' requires a little care. Firstly, all utensils being used must be free of grease and very clean. The smallest amount of grease, or even the smallest amount of egg yolk, will spoil the end result. If the whites are overbeaten, they become difficult to fold through and the mixture could collapse during cooking. For the best volume have the egg whites at room temperature before beating.

Soft peaks: Round mounds form when beaters are lifted from the egg whites after beating for a short time at a high speed (if using an electric mixer).

Stiff peaks: Slightly dryer and more peaked in shape than soft peaks. Use beaten egg whites immediately; if left to stand they will collapse.

Leftover eggs: Keep leftover yolks and whites in airtight containers in the refrigerator. Place 1 tablespoon of water over yolks to prevent a skin forming. Yolks will keep for up to 3 days and whites for up to 10 days. You can freeze whites for up to a month.

Flake: To separate cooked or canned fish flesh into small pieces.

Folding in: To combine ingredients quickly and gently, without de-flating what is usually a light mixture. A large metal spoon or spatula is ideal for doing this. When folding egg whites into a mixture, first mix in 2-3 tablespoons of the egg whites to loosen the mixture. Then add the remaining egg whites and gently fold them in, using a metal spoon or spatula.

GARNISHES

Avocado fans: Using a small sharp knife and starting at the pointed end of the avocado, cut through the skin and flesh until you reach the seed. Run the knife around the avocado then, holding it in both hands, twist to separate the halves. Remove the seed and cut each half into two, lengthwise. Starting at the broad end, make 3-4 lengthwise cuts in each avocado quarter, leaving about a quarter of the avocado uncut at the narrow end. Peel away the skin, fan out slices and place on serving plate.

Celery curls: Cut the celery into even lengths, then split each piece of celery in half lengthwise. Using a small sharp knife, make thin parallel lengthwise cuts in celery, cutting almost to the end. Drop the celery pieces into a bowl of iced water and refrigerate for several hours or overnight, until the celery pieces curl and open out.

Chilli flowers: Choose small chillies or trim the ends from long

chillies, keeping the stem ends intact. Using a small pair of scissors cut around each chilli to form petals, taking care not to cut all the way to the stem. Remove the seeds, drop the chillies into a bowl of iced water and refrigerate until the 'flowers' open out.

Lemon and lime twists: Cut thin slices of lemon or lime, then cut each slice through to the centre. Twist the two bottom halves in opposite directions and place in position.

Omelette shreds: One of the classic Asian garnishes, omelette shreds are quick and easy to make when you know how. Use as a garnish for soups, fried rice and noodle dishes and in salads. To make, place 3 eggs, 1 tablespoon cold water, 1 tablespoon finely chopped fresh herbs and black pepper to taste in a bowl and whisk to combine. Heat a lightly greased frying pan. Add enough egg mixture to thinly coat the base of the pan and cook until the underside is set. Flip omelette and cook the second side for 10 seconds. Remove and set aside to cool. Use the remaining egg mixture to make more omelettes. To make shreds, place cold omelettes in a stack, roll up and cut into fine shreds. The omelettes can also be cut into 2.5 cm/1 in squares.

Spring onion whisks: Wash spring onions and trim off some of the green top. Trim the bulb end to where the white starts to turn green. Using a small pair of kitchen scissors, cut the onions from the top into fine strips, stopping about halfway down. Drop the onions into a bowl of cold water and leave until the strips curl. This takes only a few minutes at the most.

Hull: To remove green calyx from fruit such as strawberries.

Knead: This is usually done on a lightly floured surface. The hands or fingertips are used to turn the outside edge of a mixture into the centre. Do this to either shape a mixture into a ball (pastry) or alter the nature of the mixture by working it with your hands (bread dough).

Leeks: To clean and prepare, cut down lengthwise and dunk upside down in a bowl of cold water to remove dirt.

Lettuce: To wash and separate the lettuce leaves, remove the stem of the lettuce using a twisting motion with the hand until the stem comes free. For firmer, tighter stems, cut free from the lettuce using the point of a sharp knife. Place lettuce, stem side up, under cold running water. The weight of the continually running water will cause the leaves to separate. For crisp leaves, shake off excess water and place in a plastic food bag, tie and refrigerate for 30 minutes or until required.

Mangoes: Cutting a mango is easy once you know how. The waste from around the stone can be used to make mango ice cream, or cut into cubes, tossed in lime or lemon juice and served as a side dish to a main meal. Allow half a mango per person for dessert.

1 Place the mango on a chopping board and, cutting as close as possible to the stone, cut a large slice from either side.

2 Taking one slice, cut the flesh into cubes, being careful not to cut the skin. Repeat with the other side.

3 Turn the skin inside out. The flesh can now be easily removed.

MEAT

Boning a leg of lamb: Boning a leg of lamb is not nearly as daunting as you may think, as long as you remember that a sharp knife is essential and that the knife should always stay as close as possible to the bone.

1 Turn the leg of lamb so that the skin side is lying flat on your work surface and the thick end of the leg is facing you. Using a sharp knife, cut around the edges of the pelvic bone at the thick end (the pelvic bone is the one that you can see). This will loosen the bone.

2 Now cut deep around the pelvic bone, until you have freed it at the joint and through the tendons that connect it to the leg bone (the leg bone is the middle bone in the joint). Remember to keep your knife as close as possible to the bone so that you do not cut into

the meat.

3 The next step is to remove the shank bone. Hold on to this bone at the tip and cut close to the bone to free tendons and meat. Continue cutting down the bone until you reach the joint that connects it to the leg bone, cut through the tendons at this joint and remove the shank bone.

4 The leg bone is now removed in a tunnel fashion by gently loosening the meat at either end of the bone then cutting the meat from the bone and easing it out as you work. The leg of lamb is now boned and can be used as desired.

Butterflying a leg of lamb: First bone the leg of lamb as described above, then butterfly it by placing your knife horizontally in the cavity left by the leg bone and partially splitting the meat open. The flap is then turned outwards and the meat spread flat. Now make a similar horizontal cut into the thick muscle opposite so that it too can be opened out flat.

To roll and secure a loin: Place seasoning along the flap, roll loin up firmly and hold in position with skewers or poultry pins. Cut a long piece of string, place under the meat at one end, bringing the two ends – one long length, one short length – to the top of the meat. Twist the ends and knot. Then, working with the long length of string, extend out along the top of the meat 2.5 cm/1 in, hold in position with a finger at that point while passing the remaining length down the side, under and up the other side of meat. Loop under the finger position and pull long length to tighten. Continue in this manner along the loin, knotting at the other end.

Parboil: To boil for part of the cooking time before finishing by another method.

Paste: The secret to cooking pasta is to use lots of water and a large saucepan so the pasta does not stick together.

To cook pasta, bring a large saucepan of water to the boil. As a general rule allow 1 litre/1 $\frac{3}{4}$ pt water to 100 g/3 $\frac{1}{2}$ oz pasta. Stir in the pasta and salt to taste, bring back to the boil and begin timing.

The pasta is done when it is 'al dente' – that is, tender, but with resistance to the bite. Remove the pasta from the water by straining through a colander or lifting out of the saucepan with tongs or fork. Use the packet directions as a guide to the cooking time, but generally fresh pasta will take 3-5 minutes and dried pasta 12-15 minutes.

PASTRY DECORATIONS

Give a professional finish to your pies with simple pastry decorations.

Pastry leaves: Cut leftover pastry scraps into 2.5 cm/1 in strips then diagonally across to form diamond shapes. Mark with the back of a knife to resemble veins of leaves. Arrange decoratively in the centre of a glazed pie or overlap leaves and use as a decorative edging.

To make a lattice pattern for flans: Cut the pastry into 1 cm/$\frac{1}{2}$ in wide strips, long enough to cover the flan. Moisten the edges with water and lay half the strips over the filling, about 2.5 cm/1 in apart. Then lay remaining strips diagonally across these. Trim off excess and press edges together.

Poach: To cook by simmering very gently in liquid.

PORK

Butterfly pork steaks: These steaks are cut from the mid loin area, boned, cut almost in half and opened out flat. Try placing a fruit or savoury filling on one side of the steak, then folding it over and securing with toothpicks. You can then pan cook or bake these steaks.

Pork fillets: Pork fillets are lean pieces of meat taken from the loin ribs. Fillets are quick and easy to cook and they have no waste. You can roast or pan cook pork fillets, then serve, sliced, with a sauce.

Reduce: To concentrate or thicken a liquid by rapid boiling.

Refresh: To rinse freshly cooked food in cold water to stop the cooking process and set the colour, usually with green vegetables.

Rest: To allow the protein in flour (gluten) to contract after kneading and rolling pastry. To allow the starch cells in batter to expand, for example when making crêpes.

RICE

The time that rice takes to cook depends on the type of rice and the method you choose to use. The following are the most common methods used for cooking rice.

Rapid boil: Place 2 litres/3 $1/4$ pt water in a large saucepan and bring to the boil. Stir in 220 g/7 oz rice and return to the boil. Boil rapidly for 12-15 minutes for white rice or 30-40 minutes for brown rice or until rice is tender. Drain through a sieve or colander and serve.

Absorption method: An easy way to cook rice and the grains stay separate and fluffy. For white rice, place 375 mL/12 fl oz water in a large saucepan, stir in 220 g/7 oz rice, cover and simmer for 20-25 minutes or until the water is absorbed and the rice is tender. Uncover, toss with a fork and stand for a few minutes before serving. For brown rice, use 500 mL/16 fl oz of water and cook for 55 minutes.

Steaming: This is a popular Chinese method of cooking rice. Wash 220 g/7 oz rice, then drain and set aside to dry. Place the rice in a heavy-based saucepan and add enough water to cover the rice by 2.5 cm/1 in. Bring to the boil and boil rapidly until steam holes appear on the surface of the rice. Reduce heat to as low as possible, cover with a tight-fitting lid, or foil, and steam for 10 minutes for white rice or 25-30 minutes for brown rice. Remove lid, or foil, toss the rice with a fork and stand for 5 minutes before serving.

Microwave: Cooking rice in the microwave does not save time but it does guarantee a perfect result and there is no messy saucepan at the end of the cooking time. To cook white rice in the microwave, place 220 g/7 oz rice and 500 mL/16 fl oz water in a large microwave-safe container. Cook, uncovered, on HIGH (100%) for 12-15 minutes or until the liquid is absorbed. Toss the rice with a fork, cover and stand for 5 minutes

before serving. For brown rice use 750 mL/1 $1/4$ pt water and cook for 30-35 minutes.

Roux: A blend of melted butter and flour, cooked as a base for thickening sauces and soups.
Scald: To heat liquid, usually milk, to just below boiling point. To scald milk or cream, rinse a small heavy-based saucepan with cold water, add milk or cream and bring almost to the boil over a low heat, stirring occasionally. Scalding helps prevent curdling during cooking.
Sear: To brown meat quickly on a hot surface to retain juices.
Segment: To cut the peel and all the white pith from citrus fruit, then cut between membranes joining segments.
Skim: To remove scum or fat from the surface of liquid.
Spatchcocking: To spatchcock a bird means to split and flatten it. The easiest way to cut the bird is to use a pair of poultry shears. First cut off the wing tips then cut the bird along each side of the backbone to remove it. Now place the bird breast side up and using the heel of your hand push down sharply to flatten the bird and break the breastbone. To ensure that the bird hold its shape during cooking, thread two skewers through it. One skewer is threaded through the legs, avoiding the bones, and the other through the wings and breast.
Stock: Homemade gives best results (see the Basic Recipes chapter to make your own). For convenience, substitute 1 stock cube for every 500 mL/16 fl oz water.

TURKEY

Carving a turkey: A very sharp, pointed knife with a long flexible blade is best for carving turkey. Before you start carving, remove the string and skewers from the bird and place breast side up on a board or platter. Use a large carving fork to hold the bird steady.
1 Removing the first leg: Cut the skin between the thigh and the breast of the bird. Separate the leg from the body by bending the thigh outwards to locate the hip

joint. Slice down through the joint to remove the leg.
2 Separating the thigh from the drumstick: Hold a knife at an angle between the thigh and drumstick bones and cut firmly through the joint to separate the leg.
3 Slicing the drumstick: Cut a thick slice of meat and skin from each side of the drumstick, keeping the knife close to the bone, then cut these into smaller slices.
4 Slicing the thigh: Holding the thigh steady, cut into four or more pieces, depending on the size of the thigh. Repeat steps 1-4 for the other leg of the turkey.
5 Removing the wing: Slice down through the corner of the breast towards the wing. Push the wing out to show the joint and cut through the joint. Remove the wing with the piece of breast attached.
6 Carving the breast: Holding the breast steady, slice down through the meat. When you reach the incision above the wing joint, the slice will fall free.

Toasting coconut: Coconut can be toasted by spreading the required amount over a baking tray, then baking at 180 °C/350°F/Gas 4 for 5-10 minutes, or until the coconut is lightly and evenly browned. Toss back and forth occasionally with a spoon to ensure even browning. Coconut can also be toasted in the microwave. Place 90 g/3 oz coconut on a microwave-safe ceramic or glass plate or in an oven bag and cook on HIGH (100%), shaking or stirring every minute for 5-6 minutes or until the coconut is golden. The exact length of time can vary considerably depending on the moisture content of the coconut.
Toasting nuts: Nuts can be toasted in much the same way as coconut or placed on a baking tray and browned under a grill on a medium heat. Toss back and forth with a spoon until lightly and evenly browned.

INDEX